EARLY CHILDHOOD AND FAMILY EDUCATION

Analysis and Recommendations of
the Council of Chief State School Officers

HBJ **Harcourt Brace Jovanovich, Publishers**
Orlando • San Diego • Chicago • Dallas

This book examines issues related to the education of young children. Publication of this volume does not necessarily imply endorsement by the Publisher of specific recommendations for reform or of the views of individual contributors.

Copies of this publication can be ordered from:
Harcourt Brace Jovanovich, Inc.
Order Fulfillment Department
6277 Sea Harbor Drive, Orlando, Florida 32887

Toll Free: 1-800-CALL-HBJ (1-800-225-5425)
Fax: 407-352-3445

For permission to reprint from *Hunger of Memory* by Richard Rodriguez, copyright © 1982 by Richard Rodriguez, as it appears in "Now or Later? Issues Related to the Early Education of Minority Group Children," grateful acknowledgment is made to David R. Godine, Publisher, Inc.

For permission to reprint from "Psychological-developmental implications of current patterns of early child care" by E. Zigler and J. Freedman in *Psychosocial Issues in Day Care*, as it appears in "Child Care in America," grateful acknowledgment is made to American Psychiatric Press, Inc., Washington, D.C.

Support for preparation of portions of "Departments of Public Education and Leadership in the Collaborative Planning and Implementation of P.L. 99-457: Policy Challenges, Choices, and Changes" was provided by contract #300-87-0163 from the U.S. Department of Education.

Printed in the United States of America.

ISBN 0-15-306991-0

CONTENTS

ACKNOWLEDGMENTS

The Council of Chief State School Officers (CCSSO) has, for the past two years, focused its work on the assurance of educational success for at-risk students. In the second year of this effort, the Council, under the leadership of President Verne A. Duncan, has placed special emphasis on activities relating to the education of young children and their families. Current research examining the effect of such services on later educational success supports such a strategy for all children, but particularly for those children, and their families, considered at risk.

As a part of this strategy, the Council held a Summer Institute and produced three documents designed to call attention to the needs of and successful services for young children and their families, to identify services currently available from the states, and to provide guidance to states about the necessary next steps to expand these services.

The Council is especially grateful to the contributing authors of this volume for helping chief state school officers better understand the challenges for schools and state leaders to respond to the needs of young children and their families, especially those at risk.

At its annual meeting in November 1988, the Council unanimously adopted the documents "Early Childhood and Family Education: Foundations for Success" and "Guide for State Action: Early Childhood and Family Education." A third document, "State Profiles: Early Childhood and Parent Education and Related Services," was released for public use at the meeting.

Many persons have had a direct responsibility for the preparation of these documents in support of comprehensive services for young children and their families. One year ago, President Duncan appointed a Task Force on Early Childhood and Parent Education to oversee and direct all Council efforts in this area. The Task Force was chaired by Harold Raynolds, Jr., Massachusetts Commissioner of Education, and included seven other chief state school officers: H. Dean Evans (Indiana), Richard A. Boyd (Mississippi), Linda Creque (Virgin Islands), Bill Honig (California), Wayne G. Sanstead (North Dakota), Ruth Steele (Arkansas), and Gerald N. Tirozzi (Connecticut). Task Force members deserve special thanks for their leadership role throughout the past year.

The three Council documents were based, to a large degree, on information collected by the CCSSO Study Commission about educational and related services currently provided by the states to young children and their parents. This effort was skillfully directed by the Study Commission president, Robert R. Hill, South Carolina Deputy Superintendent of Education, and its Executive Board. Ronald D. Burge, Oregon Deputy Superintendent of Public Instruction, deserves special recognition for his direct oversight of the collection of state information.

The Task Force on Early Childhood and Parent Education was supported by CCSSO Executive Director Gordon M. Ambach and the staff of the Council's Resource Center on Educational Equity, directed by Cynthia G. Brown. Glenda Partee, Assistant Director of the Resource Center, was the primary author of the "Guide for State Action." Ann Samuel prepared the manuscript. Christopher Harris, also of the Resource Center, directed the collection and editing of the book of state profiles and wrote the Discussion and Summary chapter of this volume.

Recognition and appreciation are extended also to Anne Lewis, who served as a consultant to the Council, providing creative and thoughtful assistance in drafting the Council statement.

The Council thanks the Rockefeller Foundation and the Carnegie Corporation of New York for their generous support of our 1988 Summer Institute and early childhood and family education publications respectively. The opinions expressed in these publications do not necessarily reflect those of the Rockefeller Foundation or the Carnegie Corporation.

Finally, the Council wishes to thank Harcourt Brace Jovanovich, Inc.— specifically, the School Department of Harcourt Brace Jovanovich, Inc. and the School Division of Holt, Rinehart and Winston, as well as The Psychological Corporation—for their willingness to publish this volume because they believe it contains a message that requires dissemination.

OUR CONCERN IS CHILDREN
An Introduction

Verne A. Duncan
PRESIDENT
COUNCIL OF CHIEF STATE SCHOOL OFFICERS

Our concern is children—their health and nutrition, well-being, care, safety, housing, and, when these needs are met, their education. We know that children cannot gain from our schools the best that we offer unless other basic needs are met. Hence it is incumbent upon schools to consider and address child and family priorities and needs and to work with other agencies that provide child and family support services. This knowledge has prompted the nation's chief state school officers to affirm a commitment to young children and their families and to explore ways that schools can work to support the development of a strong family curriculum—the precursor and facilitator of the school curriculum.

This commitment was expressed in the Council of Chief State School Officers' (CCSSO) 1988 theme, "Early Childhood and Family Education: Foundations for Success." This theme flows from the Council's 1987 policy on assuring school success for students at risk and is a mechanism for furthering the underlying principle of that policy: "to provide education programs and to assure other necessary related services so that this nation enters the 21st Century with virtually all students graduating from high school."

In the summer of 1988, the nation's chief state school officers met at their annual in-service training institute to explore among themselves and with recognized experts in the field the pressing issues relating to the provision of early childhood and family education. These educators were soon to acknowledge the interrelationship of their education services with those of other service providers in addressing the needs of the total child undivorced from the family and other environmental and social influences.

Well documented are the:

- inability of children to benefit fully from the education resources available because of poor health or lack of family stability;
- loss in individual potential and the damage that occurs when early interventions are not available to children at crucial points in their development or to their families when experiencing distress and dysfunction;
- high cost to society of remediation, special education, welfare services, adjudication, and rehabilitation resulting from a lack of early interventions; and

3

• loss in productivity to the work force as a result of family members who cannot work or maintain employment because of the lack of proper child-care arrangements.

Another concern relates to equity and the quality of early childhood experiences available to children and their families.

Quality early childhood programs are needed by children and families at all income levels. Early childhood programs provide young children with experiences that promote intellectual, social, and physical development. They may also serve the child-care needs of families. The term *early childhood programs* encompasses programs found in preschools and nursery schools and day care for young children in homes and centers (Schweinhart and Koshel, 1986). Comprehensive early childhood programs provide necessary services in addition to those that are strictly developmental or academic.

Despite the wealth of data on the benefits of early childhood programs to low-income children, the accessibility of programs is strongly linked to family income and education levels. Children from low-income families are less than half as likely to attend preschool programs as are more advantaged children (*Child Care*, 1987). And assistance from one of the largest federal and state efforts to help families pay for child care, dependent-care tax credits, is of negligible benefit for low-income families.

According to Morgan (1988), policymakers, the media, and the public must consider a vision for the future which combines "the policy objectives of support for working parents on whom we rely for our national productivity and economic development, with education for young children, many of them living in poverty, who are the citizens and workers of tomorrow" (p. 1). This vision has prompted governments at local, state, and federal levels to formulate responses to the pressing concerns for child care and early education and to initiate new partnerships with families in support of the future welfare and productivity of all young children.

The Council of Chief State School Officers in its policy statement adopted November 1987, "Assuring School Success for Students At Risk," set forth a set of guarantees that state law should provide to address the special needs of at-risk children and youth. Among these guarantees are a "parent and early childhood development program beginning ideally for children by age three, but no later than age four," and "supporting health and social services to overcome conditions which put the student at risk of failing to graduate from high school" ("Assuring," 1987, p. 3).

In striving to provide these guarantees, states must address a variety of concerns and realities, and schools must develop new roles and seek new partnerships among health and service agencies, early childhood professionals and paraprofessionals, and parents.

Throughout 1988, the Council conducted a number of activities to make its theme "Early Childhood and Family Education: Foundations for Success" a reality for children at risk of school failure.

Foremost among those activities was the development of three interrelated documents: 1) "Early Childhood and Family Education: Foundations for Success," a statement on the nationwide importance of early childhood and family education; 2) "State Profiles: Early Childhood and Parent Education and Related Services," state-by-state profiles on state actions to meet the comprehensive needs of children ages zero through five and their parents; and 3) "A Guide for State Action," delineating steps for state involvement in early childhood and family education and related services. The statement and guide appear in Part 2 of this volume.

Although interrelated, the three documents are distinct publications and provide different levels of information. The statement provides a general overview of the issues and consequences to children and society if bold policies are not articulated and implemented to provide quality early childhood experiences and comprehensive family support mechanisms for those in need. It also sets forth the principles endorsed by the Council for state action in providing early childhood and family education and related services.

The state-by-state profiles comprise a resource document for use by state education agencies. The document provides information on a variety of state-level programs and special initiatives spanning health, social services, and education agencies supporting young at-risk children and their families. Descriptions and contact names are provided to encourage communication among and within states so that policymakers can avoid reinventing the wheel, better utilize existing efforts and services, and increase interagency collaboration.

The guide synthesizes many of the state and federal activities, detailed in the state profiles, that support at-risk children ages zero through five and their families. It is designed to assist states, as they move from their current status with regard to early childhood and family education policies and programs, by drawing upon the collective experience of other states. The expectation is that chief state school officers and state agencies could use such a guide in setting the direction and determining the next actions for implementation of programs in their respective states.

Information about state plans, programs, and actions in the profiles and guide comes primarily from the CCSSO Study Commission information collection instrument on early childhood education, child care, parental education, and health and social services programs for young children. This information was collected during the spring of 1988. Responses were received from 50 states, two territories, and the District of Columbia. Unless otherwise indicated, responses apply to FY 1988 activities. The quality of responses received varied greatly from state to state and among agencies responding within states. This variability accounts for the differences in the amount of information included in the profiles and for possible missing examples of state initiatives in the guide.

Nevertheless, this information provides the most comprehensive set of descriptions to date on state and agency actions to address the complex needs of young at-risk children and their families. The guide and related publications do not represent the end of a process of self-examination and assessment of services for these children and their families. Rather, these compilations represent the beginning of a process whereby states can build upon and better tailor service systems to meet the evolving needs of children and families in our society.

The Council of Chief State School Officers strongly believes there is much at stake and much to gain through improved early childhood and family services in the states and is committed to expanding the availability of these services.

REFERENCES

"Assuring School Success for Students At Risk." A Council policy statement, adopted November 1987. Washington, D.C.: Council of Chief State School Officers.

Child Care: The Time Is Now. Washington, D.C.: The Children's Defense Fund, 1987.

Morgan, G. "Two Visions, the Future of Day Care and Early Childhood Programs." Paper presented to the National Association of State Boards of Education Early Childhood Task Force, February 1–3, 1988.

Schweinhart, L. J., and J. J. Koshel. *Policy Options for Preschool Programs.* High/Scope Early Childhood Policy Papers, published in collaboration with the National Governors' Association. Ypsilanti, Michigan, 1986.

Part 1   **CCSSO 1988 SUMMER INSTITUTE**

Papers and Discussion

EN ROUTE TO
A JUST SYSTEM OF
EARLY CHILDHOOD AND
PARENTING EDUCATION

Sharon L. Kagan
YALE UNIVERSITY

By ordinary standards, implementing high-quality services for young children and their families should be comparatively easy. A growing body of research confirms that such programs are powerful tools for mitigating later academic, social, and health problems. Program models, developed and refined over decades, are readily available as helpful guides. Important commissions and the media have generated widespread public interest. Clearly the stage has been set for action. But in reality, things are not quite that simple. For many, early childhood education and parenting education, like the pot of gold at the end of the rainbow, remain a vision, pictorially clear but strangely elusive.

The purpose of this paper is to examine the dichotomy between what early childhood education and parenting education are and what they can and should be. In detailing what exists, it is suggested that current dialogue, while exuberantly supportive of children, families, and education, is clouded by mixed messages. The confusion is unraveled through a discussion of pedagogical, structural, and philosophical issues that have impeded implementation, and the paper concludes with a plea to consider the existing ecology of early childhood as new programs are crafted and implemented. To that end, short- and long-term strategies are offered.

THE CURRENT STATE OF
EARLY CHILDHOOD AND PARENTING EDUCATION

On the face of it, early childhood education (services for children ages 0–8) and parenting education (services enabling parents to be more effective in their parenting role) have never looked healthier. Since 1980, when 8 states had passed legislation and/or provided state revenues for state prekindergarten programs, the number has increased to 26 states (Marx and Seligson, 1988). For years, there was a paucity of federal legislation addressing the needs of children and families; currently there are many bills pending. Employers, becoming increasingly sensitive to the labor force participation of women, have instituted policies and programs to reduce the tension between work and family life (Galinsky, 1986). Head Start's budget continues to increase, and parenting education and family support programs, once barely understood, have become the sine qua non of quality in early childhood programs.

However, those close to the field see beneath the surface and realize that such accolades present an incomplete picture. For example, of the 6,000,000 employers in this nation, only 3,000 provide any child care help at all (Children's Defense Fund, 1988). That is one out of every 2,000. Of the many pieces of child-related legislation introduced during the second session of the 100th Congress, very few have passed both houses. In spite of program increases, Head Start continues to serve only an estimated 16 percent of eligible children (Children's Defense Fund, 1988). And fewer than 33 percent of four-year-olds whose families earn less than $10,000 were enrolled in preschool programs (U.S. Department of Education, 1985).

This dichotomy between euphoric expectations and hard-core realities is ubiquitous and difficult to reconcile. Throughout the land there is a common perception, with sound basis, that early intervention makes a difference. Who has not heard of the findings from research like the Perry Preschool Project (Berrueta-Clement et al., 1984), or the Consortium for Longitudinal Studies (Lazar and Darlington, 1978)? Who is not aware of the burgeoning number of women in the work force or the increase in the number of single parents? Who has not heard of the Committee for Economic Development's report, *Children in Need*, which sets forth a rationale and advanced strategies for tackling the problems of optimal child development and effective education? Who is not aware of the National Governors' Association report, *The First Sixty Months*, which extols the benefits of early intervention? And more powerfully, whose life remains untouched, directly or indirectly, by the reckless endangerment by drunk drivers or drug addicts, or by the diminished dreams of unemployed or unskilled workers? Regardless of where we live or what we earn, America has focused on PREVENTION as a tangible antidote to society's intractable problems. David Hamburg, in his Carnegie presidential essay (1987), stated it well when he dubbed the first few years of life a "great leverage point for the human future" (page 3).

This spirit of optimism that surrounds young children and their families is exciting: the time is ripe for action. Political ripeness—the first green light—emanates from politicians, be they conservative or liberal, local or national. Elected officials, who just two or three years ago would not have put their names to a piece of child-care legislation, are now fashioning their own. In the executive branch, former Secretary of Education Bennett pointed out in his recent publication, *American Education: Making It Work* (1988), that between 1981 and 1986, per-capita state spending on education increased 40 percent, and in all but two states, education is the largest single budget item. The importance of children and education was further confirmed at the National Association of State Budget Officers' annual meeting. Not only were children and education the conference themes, but chief budget officers from around the nation acknowledged that balancing resources—investments and children—was an important priority.

Beyond political ripeness, there is a new *professional* ripeness—a second green light. As never before, early childhood education has a sense of itself. For many decades, professionals in the field and in academia debated the elements of quality and what constituted appropriate early childhood pedagogy and practice. Guiding the field, researchers have studied and conceptualized quality according to structural, dynamic, and contextual features (Phillips, 1988). Practitioners agree that quality is intimately tied to three major variables: (1) the nature of the relationship between the adults and the children (Is it personalized? Is it motivating without being directive? Does it encourage verbal interaction? Is it stable?); (2) the nature of the instructional program and the environment (e.g., ratios, group size, quality of the materials); and (3) the nature of the relationship between parents and caregivers or teachers (Is it open, supportive, and characterized by mutual respect?).

The early childhood field is professionalizing itself. Professionals have codified quality into a volume that explicitly documents developmentally appropriate practice (Bredekamp, 1986). This unified vision suggests that quality exists in settings irrespective of auspices (Head Start; public, private, and for-profit child-care centers; or the public schools) and has helped to unify the field further. Professionals are working on position statements that will clarify early childhood as a distinct domain of education. Criteria for teacher education are being developed and reviewed nationally. And early childhood educators, sometimes considered an isolated group, are making concerted efforts to move beyond their own domain and work with major educational organizations: National Council for Accreditation of Teacher Education; National Association of State Boards of Education; Council on Exceptional Children; and Association for Supervision and Curriculum Development.

To the extent that parenting education can be considered a genre separate from early childhood, a similar ripeness characterizes it. Historically, parenting handbooks appeared as early as 1633, and Pestalozzi (1747–1827) argued in the eighteenth century that for children, "the teachings of their parents will always be the core." Spanning years and building on a middle-class core, parenting education rose to prominence during the 1960s when it was considered an instrument of social reform expected to overcome deficient home environments that were thought to contribute to lower skills and performance of "disadvantaged" children (Gallagher, Haskins, and Farran, 1979). Increasingly criticized over time, this deficit orientation has been replaced by a new vision of parenting education, one that acknowledges the universal challenges of raising children in an increasingly complex society. Current approaches underscore the skills that all parents can bring to their parenting responsibilities. Continuous support and intervention, as opposed to a single dose, has become desirable. Models have evolved, some even having been incorporated statewide. And—a sure sign of a field's maturity—evaluations are appearing (Wandersman, 1987), and workers in the field are charting new challenges: individualizing approaches, realigning the roles of staff and parents, and strengthening parents' social networks and community ties (Powell, 1988). So, professionally, a new vitality characterizes early childhood and parenting education.

And finally, a third green light—an *institutional* ripeness for change hallmarks the current *zeitgeist*. Altering traditional ways of doing business, many institutions are becoming more child- and family-oriented. Corporations, though not investing in child care to the extent some had hoped, are initiating benefits that provide parents with more time (flex-time, job sharing, parental leave) and more information (bag-lunch seminars, resource and referral centers) in addition to financial support. Foundations are launching pioneering work to help institutions collaborate in the delivery of human services. New family support services are emerging as appendages to hospitals, welfare offices, mental health clinics, and schools.

It is perhaps the schools that are drawing the most attention. With 40 percent of America's principals indicating they will leave their jobs within five years (Bennett, 1988) and with inadequate numbers of teachers coming into the field, education is realizing the seriousness of its plight. In an attempt to attract professionals into the field, new (and not always popular) recruitment methods are being advanced. For example, the New York City Commission on the Year 2000 (1987) called for expanding the pool from which principals are chosen to include managers from business, higher education, and government. Thirty-one states have instituted teacher recruitment programs designed to attract into the field those individuals who have expertise and experience but may lack formal education course credits (U.S. Department of Education, 1988). Education is looking beyond itself: partnerships are being crafted among schools, government, and businesses. Pushed ahead by the Carnegie Forum on Education and the Economy (1986) and by Futrell (National Education Association) and Shanker (American Federation of Teachers), schools also are considering new ways to diminish their autocratic formality and rigidity. New roles will bring teachers into the decision-making mainstream, thereby creating a more equitable and open school climate. This bodes well for early education. As schools and principals move toward more collaborative and shared roles, a new climate—one more conducive to parent and community involvement—will prevail.

This ripeness—be it political, professional, or institutional—has poised us for action. Yet those close to the field cite yellow lights, cautions, that need to be recognized before we dart ahead. The first yellow light is over-expectation. Widely publicized research findings were generated in very high-quality and very costly programs, with children from very low-income families. In a scurry to increase services, states are instituting programs often located in less than optimal settings, funded with fewer dollars per child, and with different populations than those specified in the research. While legislators and parents hope for comparable results, academics and early childhood specialists realize that the data have been overgeneralized and the programs have been under-funded—a recipe for disaster. A program funded at $2,750 per child will not yield the same results as one funded at $5,000 in 1981 dollars, the cost of the Perry Preschool Project (Berrueta-Clement et al., 1984). The first yellow light is the data must be used more diligently: despite the desire to establish programs, the same results can be anticipated only when inputs are comparable.

Yellow light two is the mismatching syndrome. Over and over, programs with little flexibility are established based on parents' *perceived* needs. Schedules (half-day, educational day, or full-day) and service levels (comprehensive to minimal) are predetermined. Often, if programs are half-day, an assumption is made that they are inadequate, that the real need is for full-day programs. While accurate in many cases, recent data affirm the need for half- *and* full-day programs. *Lives on Hold* (Porter, 1988), an analysis of programs in New York City, reports that many women whose children were enrolled in part-day programs did not need or want full-day services. Some had decided to put their "lives on hold" until their children grew up. Others held night or part-time jobs that enabled them to spend desired time with their youngsters. Others felt they benefited from the parenting education offered by the programs. Most of these women wanted job training/counseling so that they would be prepared to work when their youngsters entered full-day programs. Indeed, child care is a critical need in our county, and the nation needs more of it. But America's child-care policy must recognize that different families have different needs. The policy challenge is—and this is yellow light two—that rather than crafting a single program model, alternatives need to be designed so that families have both input and options.

The third, and perhaps most important, yellow light relates to our reason for expanding programs. In politicians' haste to engender constituent support, in parents' haste to find suitable alternatives for their youngsters, and with surplus budgets in some states, early childhood initiatives have been launched. In most cases, legislation is merely providing additional slots, on the premise that what worked for 20,000 children can work for 30,000. The problem that many policy makers do not see is that the existing nonsystem of child care and early education is somewhat dysfunctional. Adding on to it without considering structural alternatives promotes acrimonious situations.

For example, in most—if not all—communities, when preschool programs are located in public schools, the staff salaries are higher than those of community-based preschool programs. Benefits are usually better as well. When programs within the schools are expanded, staff from other community-based programs are naturally attracted. In some communities, this conversion is not problematic. In others, particularly large cities where there is apt to be a shortage of staff, the depletion of staff is devastating. Centers are forced to close, to move, or to staff with less-qualified personnel. All are undesirable alternatives that usually leave a residue of hostility for the schools. Because of a lack of salary comparability, adding on slots without addressing this structural issue can foster grave problems within the early care and education community. Of course, new programs should open, but they need to nest within the extant ecology of services, one that has evolved over time. The third yellow light indicates that the zealousness to serve children by increasing slots must be matched by a willingness to improve the infrastructure of early education.

In sum, then, early care and education are at a critical juncture. The social sentiment, the *zeitgeist,* of the time expects that the field must move ahead, in spite of uneasy hesitancies. In their theory of policy construction, Julius Richmond and Milton Kotelchuck (1984) help clarify why we are in this green light–yellow light dilemma. They suggest that three factors must come together before "we can really talk about the development and implementation of public policy." These are (1) an appropriate knowledge base; (2) political will; and (3) social strategy. I suggest that the field and the nation are meeting two of the three conditions. Both a solid knowledge base and political will have been amassed. The inhibiting element is the absence of an agreed-upon social strategy —the blueprint that will allow the application of this knowledge base and political will to program improvement.

PUTTING HIGH-QUALITY PROGRAMS IN PLACE: ISSUES IN OUR SOCIAL STRATEGY

Over-expectation, mismatched services, and a "slots only" approach, the yellow lights discussed above, are important signals because they threaten to thwart the expansion of early childhood services. But they are more important as symptoms of deeper issues—issues of pedagogy, of structure, and of philosophy. Before considering strategic alternatives, we need to consider and unravel deeper issues.

PEDAGOGICAL ISSUES

There has been much debate about what should be expected from early education and, consequently, about what young children should be learning. The debate relates to the first yellow light, the over-expectation syndrome. Are preschool programs preparing youngsters for kindergarten and the demands of later academia, or are they preparing children for later life, where motivation, curiosity, and creativity are important skills? Lillian Katz (1987), David Elkind (1987), and other child developmentalists express concern that children are being pushed down an academic track too early. Such pressure is manifest in direct instruction and didactic curriculum. Katz, Elkind, and others contend that such emphases prevent children from experiencing the joys of childhood and from developing the dispositions they will need in later life: independence and self-reliance. Professional organizations, including the National Association of Early Childhood Specialists in State Departments of Education (1987), have taken rather strong positions on this, as well as on testing, which many see as an inducer of more-regulated programs. On the other hand, some early childhood professionals do favor a more structured approach, suggesting that the sense of accomplishment children get from learning cannot be underestimated nor can valuable time and money be wasted.

Pedagogical debate extends beyond the content of the curriculum to the content of the program. Some contend that comprehensive services (health, parent involvement, nutrition, social and psychological services, and training) are integral components for early education programs; others feel that these are not necessary in all programs, particularly those that serve middle-class children. Debate revolves around how much parent involvement is really necessary. What is the role of nutrition and health services education in programs for young children?

Quite naturally, such debate on curriculum and program content generates questions about who should be working in such programs. Are certified teachers necessary? Why cannot upper-grade teachers work with young children? Is experience an adequate substitute for formal training in early childhood and parenting education programs? Why, when major national reports (the Holmes report, the Carnegie Forum on Education) stress the need for more liberal-arts training followed by a single year of graduate work in education, do early childhood people say that staff needs less general training, and in some cases indicate that experience will suffice?

STRUCTURAL ISSUES

Debate here focuses on *where* services should be delivered and on *who* should control them—issues of place and power. From one perspective, the major contenders are education and human services; from another, they are public and private services. Education advocates hold that schools are the ideal locus for early childhood and parenting services because schools are available, community-based, and accessible. Further, because schools have experience administering large budgets, they are more qualified and more stable than other alternatives. Shanker (1976) argues that schools have professional standing which would help the early childhood profession and that, because they have a vested interest in ensuring that children are well-prepared for kindergarten, schools should be the main deliverer of early services. Zigler (1987), though not advocating formal schooling for young children, suggests that schools are appropriate facilities where child care and family support services should be located.

Conversely, many observers suggest that schools have not done such a terrific job with older children. They question why our youngest and most vulnerable children should be "turned over" to the schools, arguing that schools already have an overloaded agenda. Some advocates for minority children express concern that schools, dominated primarily by white middle-class teachers, cannot reinforce the social and emotional development that begins in the minority home. The National Black Child Development Institute, particularly concerned about the well-being of black youngsters, has issued its excellent volume on "Safeguards" (1987)—ten safeguards to be met before very young children are placed in schools.

For-profit programs, which have a vested interest and serve an estimated 45 percent of the child-care industry, are legitimately concerned that enlarged public subsidies, coupled with more stringent regulation, will cut into both their markets and their profits. In general, they are vociferous opponents of public sector expansion and of regulation, and they take issue with the broad regulatory exemptions afforded many public schools and religious institutions. Churches, too, even though they charge minimal fees, are not delighted with the prospect of public sector expansion of preschool services.

Clearly money is an important factor in the debate, but so is control. Everyone realizes that the sponsor of additional subsidized services, be it human services or education, will not only get more dollars but will also exercise great control in shaping the destiny of the profession. If funds go into education, standards for certification are likely to be professionalized according to that system's requirements. Conversely, if funds are awarded to human services, credentialing will require less formal training and will acknowledge experience. Those favoring more formalized training side with the schools; those who favor experience and more competency-based credentialing systems side with human services.

PHILOSOPHICAL ISSUES

Although the above issues are difficult, philosophical issues are the most perplexing. What do we want early education to do for society? Must it be value-neutral, or should it be a socializer to democratize? How much equity should be ensured? Should all children have access? At whose expense? Is early education a public right, a private responsibility, or both? Basically, the philosophical issues are equity, access, and comparability.

In the current system of care and education, there is no equity, no comparability, and uneven access. Essentially, children from wealthy and middle-class homes—those who, many educators contend, need services least—can buy them, while low-income children are forced to battle for a limited number of subsidized slots. Further, because of the incomparability of program regulation and eligibility requirements, this nation has created a de facto system of segregated services at the preschool level, with the poor (and often minority) trotting off to subsidized centers, and the middle-income and rich to "pay-as-you-go programs." Via this system, the nation has sanctioned the segregation of children, a reality that reflects neither the law nor the spirit of the land. How has this malaise set in? Does this inequity perpetuate the pervasive class imbalances we see growing in this nation? Should the field consider universal services, as Ed Koch did in New York, and if so, what questions does this raise? For example, even with universal services, how is integration ensured, given our country's housing patterns? Does providing services for all mean that all will use them? Equally troubling is that equity does not exist even for adults working in early childhood services. The salaries, benefits, and working conditions for individuals in education are usually higher than those afforded adults in child care with, in some cases, the same training and education. The national turnover rate is 41 percent, so employers cannot even begin to fill current openings, much less fill the positions that accompany program expansion.

There is limited equity for children, limited equity for adults, and limited equity for programs. Often, within a single community, licensing and monitoring standards may be totally discrepant, with schools and churches often exempt. One must question why, in a single community, there are varying standards for safety or for preentry immunizations.

Finally, there are important issues of "who pays?" By governmental subsidization of services for all families, will parents be robbed of their right to raise their children? Are policies infringing on family privacy? If services are instituted at parental option and with sliding fees, as most plans suggest, is early education again fostering a two-tier system where those who are rich may opt for the service, while those of more limited means may regard it as "nice but not necessary"? From the institutional perspective, hard questions need to be answered as to which services should be provided at no cost and which should be paid by parents. Today districts and schools in this nation are comparing the relative importance of free after-school programs with free services for four-year-olds. How should finite resources be allocated to achieve the common good?

These issues form the bedrock of early education, the foundation upon which to build solutions. That the issues are complex and multifaceted raises important challenges; answers are not easy and vary with the perspective of the analyst. In responding to the issues, this analysis combines the intertwined perspectives of an academic and a practitioner.

PEDAGOGICAL ISSUES REVISITED

Of all the issues, these are the clearest because there is a core of early childhood pedagogy, rooted in child development principles, to which our programs should adhere. It is child-centered in orientation, allows maximum time for child choice, and encourages language development and creative expression. Recognizing individual differences, this orientation believes that teachers of four-year-olds probably have more in common with teachers of infants than with teachers of eight- and nine-year-olds, even though the number of years separating the children is the same. Irrespective of setting, the staffing pattern of quality preschool programs will *always* reflect the community in which the program exists, so that children's home culture and language is respected, and so that parents will always be welcome. Staff will be composed of both certified and noncertified personnel. Each noncertified person will have had experience or training, perhaps the Child Development Associate (CDA), and will have opportunities for advancement. High-quality programs do not require that every single staff member be a certified teacher. Rather, every staff member, certified or not, must be knowledgeable about child development and must have opportunities for professional support.

STRUCTURAL ISSUES REVISITED

Where should programs be housed? Programmatically it really does not matter: high-quality programs can be implemented anywhere. Data from the Center Accreditation Program confirm that (1) quality programs exist regardless of auspices and (2) they are achievable when funds come from the state, the city, the federal government, or parents.

Although there may be a few *programmatic* differences across funding streams, there are *start-up* differences. Because schools usually do not have to go through the lengthy licensing procedures required of nonschool facilities, it is easier to start programs in schools. Schools are also advantaged because they can attract staff more easily. On the other hand, schools have remarkably different orientations and constraints. Typically, they are more bureaucratic, less flexible, and harder to change. Interestingly, when 200 parents were asked about services they and their children received in the New York Giant Step program in Head Start, child-care centers, and the public schools, their reactions were similar. Most parents loved the program, irrespective of auspices. Of those who had children in Head Start or day care, some would not have enrolled their four-year-olds in a public-school-based program; others, voicing equally strong sentiments, wished only to have their youngsters in public-school-based programs. The point is that schools can be excellent homes for children's programs, but so can child-care centers and Head Start programs.

PHILOSOPHICAL ISSUES REVISITED

Very few of the nation's new early childhood initiatives systematically address the hard philosophical questions raised earlier. Expanding access by increasing slots has been the primary goal. But there are difficulties with this strategy that the Carnegie Foundation for the Advancement of Teaching (1988) has summed up well. They suggest that to expand access without improving quality "is simply to perpetuate discrimination in a more subtle form." Certainly this caution needs to be well heeded in the area of early care and education. In reality, program after program calls for targeting services to needy children. By increasing services without addressing the racial and economic integration of children, we are reinforcing a segregated system of early education. Why are innovative efforts and incentives that will help integrate programs not being seriously considered?

In terms of equity for adults, adding new slots without addressing the salary issue yields classes that are funded but unopened simply because there are limited numbers of qualified staff. Bureaucrats and program directors all over the country are confronted with the choice of either opening programs with less than optimal staff or denying services to waiting children and families. The field needs to push boldly for salary enhancements, as was recently done in New York State and New York City. Further, professionals and practitioners need to push for comparability of regulations within a state so that children are ensured equal quality.

STRATEGIES AND RECOMMENDATIONS

How can all this be accomplished? A two-pronged strategy is needed. One part requires a vision, a long-term approach, and the other, a more immediate approach.

A LONG-TERM APPROACH

It has been argued that social policy for children and families in our country is invoking a Darwinian metaphor: society is a jungle where only the fittest survive; those who are weak fall by the wayside. Theoretically on target for the animal kingdom, Darwinism is misapplied in the realm of social policy. Yet it is an accurate reflection of America's approach to children's services. Maybe this year there is an add-on here or a demonstration program there, but typically, policy makers do not think or act for all children—they tinker at the edges. In some states, usually those with fairly healthy economies and staunch advocates, there are high-quality services. But even those are a far cry from what they should be. Those concerned with the well-being of America's young children and their families need to stop the charade and realize that current policies are a camouflage for an inadequate system that is inadequately financed.

Ultimately, an ideal child-care system would resemble the public schools on one key dimension—universal availability. It would differ from the public schools in that participation would be voluntary and it would not be publicly financed for those who could afford to pay. Given its universality, voluntary nature, and shared financing, such a plan, though helpful in alleviating the inconsistencies and fragmentation discussed above, would be a challenge to implement. Consequently, to seed such a plan, two variables are critical. First, demonstration efforts are necessary to try out such a strategy. And second, alternative funding mechanisms need to be considered. Although strong on the former, the field is weak on the latter. Only a handful of scholars are considering the economics of enhancing services to young children and their families generally. To date, the provocative Children's Trust concept, being advanced by Jules Sugarman (1988) and others, is receiving widespread attention. Essentially, this plan creates a much-enlarged pool of revenues, financed by employer and employee contributions, similar to Old Age and Survivors Insurance. While there are some serious questions about the Children's Trust concept, it is generating rich dialogue that is helping refocus the field's attention on revenue generation.

Unfortunately, we are decades away from universal, publicly supported services for low-income families and their children. In the meantime, there is the political will to move ahead. What is a realistic interim strategy that will both build upon our current system and prepare us for the advent of a more comprehensive approach?

AN IMMEDIATE APPROACH

To capitalize on the current *zeitgeist,* the field needs to stress collaboration and involve local, state, and federal governments, as well as the private sector. At the community level, there are three steps. First, *each community needs to identify what it regards as desirable services for children and families.* An ideal list might include the following: prenatal care; parenting education and health education; parental leave; home visitors through the first years of life; resource and referrals; family day care bolstered by a family day-care provider support-and-training system; full-day, developmentally appropriate services for three- and four-year-olds; and after-school care for school-age children. Communities might not feel that all these services are necessary. The point is that *they* should decide.

Second, *communities need to identify sacrosanct principles upon which to base their programs.* Preserving choice for parents and ensuring that children of all economic strata have access to racially and economically integrated programs are only two examples. Other principles might stress programmatic variables: quality should be safeguarded so that all children, including language-minority and special-needs youngsters, are in environments that optimize, not overburden, their development. Communities need to codify their beliefs into principles that can guide action.

Third, *communities need to survey existing services and needs, determine priorities, and develop action plans.* Such plans should consider which are the most appropriate resources and facilities. How should services be funded? What are the local resources, and what is the role of the corporate sector? In some areas, sliding fees may be appropriate for some services while other services, like public libraries, may be made available as part of a community's retinue of services. In some locales, schools might be the best setting, and in others, a child-care or Head Start program might serve as the locus for coordinating services. The idea is simple and builds upon which individualized services and form of delivery works with children and families.

Because states control licensing, set standards, establish monitoring procedures, and have the ability to enjoin appropriate parties, they can and should be catalytic in fostering change in these ways: (1) Mirroring local efforts, states need to develop comprehensive cross-agency plans. (2) States need to look at the comparability of regulations across systems and to understand which services are exempt and which are not. The field needs to understand if and how the lack of regulatory comparability is affecting service delivery. (3) States need to seed staff. Via support for teacher-training institutions, incentives to potential teachers, or other mechanisms, states must build up the supply of trained personnel. (4) States need to look at the content of teacher-preparation programs, considering alternate viable staffing patterns for early childhood programs. (5) States need to guide municipalities as they look at assumptions about space availability in light of projected growth. Space limitations can be a very real deterrent to program expansion. (6) States need to encourage the creative use of funds. Regulations in existing state and federal programs may need to be loosened so that more effective use can be made of available monies. This sounds simple, but in the era of accountability, when many of these programs were launched, strict guidelines prevented the co-mingling of funds. Today, program administrators need to be freed to use funds creatively, though not indiscriminately.

Finally, in states where there is no office to coordinate these functions, consideration could be given to establishing one. To be successful, such an office would need to have sufficient funding and cross-agency authority to carry out program planning and development. One variation might be to establish an interagency office within an existing agency, but it must be perceived as neutral and must have resources and clout.

Although this strategy places a heavy burden on municipalities and states, there are also important roles for the federal government. First, the federal government should take on the role of uncovering new knowledge and disseminating information. Research that fortifies the knowledge base should be federally funded, as should distribution of information about how to evaluate programs. Information about programs that work should be collected and shared. Second, the federal government should set up demonstration programs that will try out new ideas, with the goal of incorporating into existing services the ideas that work. Such demonstrations should focus on structural alternatives to the current piecemeal delivery system. Third, the federal government should create inducements that will expand the supply of services and personnel. Fourth, the government should take swift leadership in helping to alleviate crises in the field, such as the insurance crisis. Finally, working with the states, the federal government should reexamine its policies and procedures, including regulations and program performance standards, to ensure that quality and collaboration are facilitated.

How real is such a strategy? Can it succeed? Success is quite likely, particularly since the nation already has several important efforts from which to learn. In the 1970s, many communities established child-care coordinating councils (Four C's). Some of these councils were highly successful in mapping long- and short-term goals and in building an infrastructure. Although not well funded, the Four C's concept took root in many communities. Head Start demonstration programs (e.g., Child and Family Resource Program, Developmental Continuity) are effective examples of collaboration; many such programs were community-based and reached out beyond Head Start.

Further, many communities already have early childhood councils or resource and referral groups that link services. In some communities, R & R's have already become the conduit for new funds and have been instrumental in coordinating a community's catalogue of services.

In some states, offices for children have been established to facilitate this coordination. In northern Virginia, the Office for Children not only provides direct services but also links providers. In New York City, the Mayor's Office of Early Childhood Education does the same. States are establishing such offices, and most of the new federal legislation, recognizing the need for collaboration, mandates the establishment of such councils or teams.

Collaboration is not easy in any field. It is indeed complex in the field of early childhood, given the intractable turf issues. Paradoxically, precisely because of the existing fragmentation, collaboration is a necessity. Further, in addition to yielding better "means," that is, better-coordinated services and better use of resources, collaboration yields effective ends—generating a united early childhood community and high-quality, universally available early childhood services.

For decades, wonderful early childhood legislation has fallen by the wayside because early childhood professionals could not reach a consensus. This is not surprising. Early childhood professionals had no advocacy training: they were taught to plant seeds with children, not to plant seeds of ferment in state houses or legislatures. Further, there were few mechanisms to solidify a community of early childhood practitioners. Separate funding streams, separate guidelines, and separate regulations led to differences. Today, though, early childhood people are being mobilized through efforts of NAEYC, the Children's Defense Fund, and the Child Care Action Campaign. Though still in their infancy, local and state advocacy groups can form a nucleus around which effective collaboration and effective advocacy for this long-term vision of universal, publicly supported services can coalesce.

In conclusion, the challenge is to capitalize on the current *zeitgeist* while recognizing its challenges. Policy makers must match the amassed knowledge base and political will with short- and long-term social strategies that fuse the "what is" and the "what should be." With perseverance, the field will reach its goal, one far more significant than the pot of gold at the end of the rainbow—one of a just and joyous system where all children will thrive.

REFERENCES

Bennett, W. J. *American Education: Making It Work*. Washington, D.C.: U.S. Government Printing Office, 1988.

Berrueta-Clement, J. R., L. J. Schweinhart, W. S. Barnett, A. S. Epstein, and D. P. Weikart. *Changed Lives: Effects of the Perry Preschool Program on Youths Through Age 19*. Monograph of the High/Scope Educational Research Foundation, 8. Ypsilanti, Mich.: High/Scope Press, 1984.

Bredekamp, S. *Developmentally Appropriate Practice in Early Childhood Programs Serving Children From Birth Through Age 8*. Washington, D.C.: National Association for the Education of Young Children, 1986.

Carnegie Forum on Education and the Economy, Task Force on Teaching as a Profession. *A Nation Prepared: Teachers for the 21st Century*. Washington, D.C., 1986.

Carnegie Foundation for the Advancement of Teaching. *An Imperiled Generation: Saving Urban Schools*. Lawrenceville, N.J.: Princeton University Press, 1988.

Children's Defense Fund. *A Call for Action to Make Our Nation Safe for Children: A Briefing Book on the Status of American Children in 1988*. Washington, D.C., 1988.

Elkind, D. "Early Childhood Education on Its Own Terms." In *Early Schooling: The National Debate*, edited by S. L. Kagan and E. Zigler. New Haven, Conn.: Yale University Press, 1987.

Galinsky, E. *Investing in Quality Child Care: A Report for AT&T*. Short Hills, N.J.: AT&T Human Resources Organization, 1986.

Gallagher, J. J., R. Haskins, and D. C. Farran. "Poverty and Public Policy for Children." In *The Family: Setting Priorities*, edited by T. B. Brazelton and V. C. Vaughn, III. New York: Science & Medicine, 1979.

Hamburg, D. A. *Fundamental Building Blocks of Early Life*. New York: Carnegie Corporation of New York, 1987.

Katz, L. "Early Education: What Should Young Children Be Doing?" In *Early Schooling: The National Debate*, edited by S. L. Kagan and E. Zigler. New Haven, Conn.: Yale University Press, 1987.

Lazar, I., and R. B. Darlington. *Lasting Effects After Preschool: A Report of the Consortium for Longitudinal Studies* (DHEW Publication No. [(OHDS)] 79-30178). Washington, D.C.: U.S. Government Printing Office, 1978.

Marx, F., and M. Seligson. *The Public School Early Childhood Study: The State Survey*. New York: Bank Street College of Education, 1988.

National Association of Early Childhood Specialists in State Departments of Education. *Unacceptable Trends in Kindergarten Entry and Placement: A Position Statement*. Chicago: National Association of Early Childhood Specialists in State Departments of Education, 1987.

National Black Child Development Institute, Inc. *Safeguards: Guidelines for Establishing Programs for Four-Year-Olds in the Public Schools*. Washington, D.C., 1987.

New York City Commission on the Year 2000. *New York Ascendant: The Commission on the Year 2000*. New York, 1987.

Pestalozzi, F. J. *The Education of Man*. New York: Philosophical Library, 1951.

Phillips, D. "Quality in Child Care: Definitions and Dilemmas." Paper presented at the A. L. Mailman Symposium. White Plains, N.Y., June 27, 1988.

Porter, T. *Lives on Hold*. New York: Child Care, Inc., 1988.

Powell, D. R. "Emerging Direction in Theory, Research and Practice." In *Parent Education As Early Childhood Intervention,* edited by D. R. Powell. Norwood, N.J.: Ablex Publishing, 1988.

Richmond, J., and M. Kotelchuck. "Commentary on Changed Lives." In *Changed Lives: Effects of the Perry Preschool Program on Youths Through Age 19,* edited by J. R. Berrueta-Clement, L. J. Schweinhart, W. S. Barnett, A. S. Epstein, and D. P. Weikart. Monographs of the High/Scope Educational Research Foundation, 8. Ypsilanti, Mich., 1984.

Shanker, A. "Public Schools and Preschool Programs: A Natural Connection." Testimony presented to a joint meeting of the House Select Subcommittee on Education and the Senate Subcommittee on Children and Youth. Item # 67. Washington, D.C.: American Federation of Teachers, June 5, 1976.

Sugarman, J. *Financing Children's Services: A Proposal to Create the Children's Trust.* Olympia, Wash.: Department of Social and Health Services, 1988.

U.S. Department of Education. *Common Core of Data Survey.* Washington, D.C.: U.S. Government Printing Office, 1985.

U.S. Department of Education. *Fifth Annual Wall Chart of State Education Statistics.* Washington, D.C., 1988.

Wandersman, L. P. "New Directions for Parent Education." In S. L. Kagan, D. R. Powell, B. Weissbourd, and E. Zigler (eds.), *America's Family Support Programs.* New Haven, Conn.: Yale University Press, 1987.

Zigler, E. F. "A Solution to the Nation's Child Care Crises: The School of the Twenty-First Century." Paper presented at the Yale University Bush Center in Child Development and Social Policy. New Haven, Conn., October 14, 1987.

EARLY INTERVENTION AND THE PUBLIC SCHOOLS

Barbara Bowman
ERIKSON INSTITUTE, CHICAGO

I. WHO IS AT RISK FOR SCHOOL FAILURE, AND WHY?

There are many changes in American life to which schools must respond. One of the most important is the requirement that they educate more children to higher levels of academic achievement than ever before. Children of the twenty-first century will face a new and dramatically different world, a world in which academic and cognitive skills will be critical to the well-being of the nation. The challenge for schools is to educate not just the brightest and the most privileged of the nation's children, but to educate all children for participation in the social, political, and economic world of the twenty-first century.

Some children have been more difficult than others for schools to educate and are likely candidates for failure—poor children, children with handicapping conditions, children who mature at slower or faster rates, black and Hispanic children, children who do not speak English, children who receive inadequate care, and children whose families are disrupted or irresponsible. These are the children who traditionally have fared poorly in public schools and who compose an increasingly large proportion of the school population.

At-risk children may be divided into two categories: those with established biological disabilities and those at statistical risk for problems in biological and psychological/social functioning. The biological-disabilities category includes children who have sensory deficits, such as deafness or blindness; children with chromosomal disorders, such as Down Syndrome; and children with malformations, such as spina bifida. The limitations of children in this category range from relatively minor handicaps to profound disabilities.

Other children are viewed as being at risk because of their membership in a group that has a greater incidence of school failure than the average. One group at statistical risk includes children who, because of environmental hazards, experience biological stress. In this group are children with low birth weight and/or short gestational age, children whose mothers used addictive drugs during pregnancy, and children who have been exposed to lead and other noxious materials. Children affected in these ways are more susceptible to developmental delays and to psychological and social difficulties.

The largest group of children at risk have no biological difficulties but, because of experiential disadvantages or differences, fail to develop and achieve in ways that lead to school success. Their difficulties may involve cognitive and

25

social functioning, and while some children may have developmental delays, most are simply unable to learn effectively in school.

One group of such children merits special attention since their school failure has been called the time bomb of the twenty-first century. The school failure of so many black and brown children is being seen as a social and economic disaster for the next generation. The evidence of their failure is well known. At every step on the educational ladder, these children of color do worse in school than the white majority. There are at least three reasons for their vulnerability. The first stems from poverty and affects all poor children. However, more minority children are reared in low-income families than are white children. Second, some black and brown minorities have cultural styles that conflict with the school culture, making school adjustment more difficult. Third, prejudice and discrimination alienate many of these children from teachers, administrations and classmates.

Poverty. There are a number of factors that account for why poverty predicts such dismal outcomes for children. Being poor sometimes causes biological stress, as when children are not adequately supplied with the basic requirements: food, shelter, and care. For most poor children in America, however, the danger lies in the psychosocial arena. Being poor is not just having too few of the basic necessities. In the consumer-driven American society a great deal is considered essential—not only food and shelter, but telephones and televisions and Easter outfits and occasional treats. Families that cannot provide themselves with what they think they need feel demoralized and disorganized, angry and depressed, and their ability to care for people and things is diminished. Communities where poor people live reflect this psychological impoverishment and become less desirable. As W. Wilson (1987) has pointed out, families that are "making it" move out, leaving poor children without role models for economic achievement or social stability in either home or community.

Many poor families are also disorganized because poverty exacerbates the stresses of daily life. Responsive and responsible parenting, so essential to healthy development, is often precluded by the exigencies of living in poverty. For instance, poor working mothers are usually forced to make inadequate arrangements for the care of their children. The strain of poverty may also lead to depression, anger, and violence in adults, and this compromises the child-rearing environment. Even if the family itself is functioning well, living in a disorganized and depressed community makes life dangerous and unpredictable, conditions that are stressful for children.

Children protect themselves as best they can. They learn to passively "accept" because there is little hope, or they burn with rage because of dashed hopes. They learn to be like adults who are powerless, or they imitate those who are aggressive—in either case, their behavior is not consistent with what schools expect. Schools want children who are responsive, not passive; they want children who attend to adults and try to please them, not children who ignore or fight with them. Schools want children who control their anger and are able to concentrate on abstractions far removed from the stresses of daily life. What is learned in many poor communities and families does not prepare children well for the world of school.

Cultural Style. Many minority children find success in school difficult to achieve because their cultural style is antithetical to that of the school. Cultural groups teach their children styles of relating and world views that affect how they perceive the world, how they understand the nature of the physical and interpersonal environment, and how they organize and categorize people and things. Hale (1982) and others have characterized the black style, for instance, as being more relational, more people-oriented, and more expressive than mainstream white culture. Cultural style is not a straitjacket for members of a community; rather, it is a pattern of thinking and relating found more often in one community than another. However, when people have different cultural styles, communication becomes more difficult and misunderstanding of each other's motives, beliefs, and meanings is more likely.

Cultural style does not compromise development or preclude other orientations, other ways of thinking and acting. But it does define the preferred ways of a particular group. Children can become bicultural, that is, use the cultural style of more than one group, but this is not easy. The encouragement and understanding of the family is essential if biculturalism is to be achieved at all. When applied to individuals, the concept of cultural style can be a form of stereotyping because it does not take into account individual and subgroup differences.

Prejudice and Discrimination. Bias against minorities also helps account for minority children's school failure. Prejudice and discrimination—and just as important, the expectations of them—encourage children and adults to avoid interaction with the majority group. It is within the circle of family and community that children feel loved and cherished, that they can relax and find acceptance and status. In order to belong to any community, children must act like and strive to be like other members of the group. For many minority children this means rejecting the behavior and values of school, because schools, as mainstream institutions, are different from and even hostile to the behavior and values of the children's relatives and friends. As long as children feel that school is alien to all they love, their motivation to work hard and be successful will be minimal.

Minority children and poor children are the largest groups of at-risk children in schools today. But it is almost impossible to foretell during early childhood which individuals in these groups will become school failures. The limits of individual development cannot be predicted in advance. Biological resiliency, family nurturing, and community institutions like school and church may buffer environmental stress so that some children escape relatively unscathed while others are severely affected (Werner, 1988).

It is often difficult in early childhood to diagnose a child's developmental lag or achievement difficulty. The range of normal development is broad, and symptoms may be nonspecific. In any case, treatment is similar despite different etiologies, for the younger children are, the more similar are their developmental requirements. For instance, all young children need to interact with a responsive caregiver across all domains of development whether they are physically handicapped, were born prematurely, or are being reared by an adolescent mother. That is why it is not wise to focus intervention for a young child solely on the treatment of a particular condition and to ignore the human needs he or she has in common with all children. During early childhood the essential ingredients for development are the same: consistent and emotionally attentive relationships with available adults, an opportunity to interact safely with people and things, caregivers who temper high hopes with respect for the uniqueness of each individual's style and patterns of growth, and opportunities both to express and to control feelings.

II. EARLY INTERVENTION

There is now a rich body of evidence that early intervention can prevent or ameliorate educational disadvantage for children at risk (R. Wilson, 1987; Province, 1987; Ramey and Ferran, 1983; Consortium for Longitudinal Studies, 1983; McKey et al., 1986). Early education programs can affect not only short-term school-related skills but also long-term social outcomes (Lazar, 1982). During the 1960s, one of the best-known programs (Berrueta-Clement et al., 1984), the Perry Preschool Project, enrolled three- and four-year-old black children from low-income families. The children were compared with a control group. The long-term data revealed that the children who attended the experimental preschool not only performed better during the preschool years, but stayed in school longer, were more often employed or in school during adolescence and early adulthood, were less often involved with the juvenile justice system, and had fewer teenage pregnancies than their peers.

The assessments of Head Start, Follow Through, Chapter 1, and special education projects have all pointed to the benefits of an early-intervention program for children's social and academic achievement. This has put early childhood education on the front line in the search for educational equity.

PUBLIC POLICY

The success of early intervention has led to its incorporation into public policy. This is not unusual. Prevention of developmental and educational failure has frequently been the subject of legislative action. Aid to Families With Dependent Children, laws prohibiting child labor, and Medicaid are examples. However, for a number of reasons it has not been easy to find sound preventive policies to address educational risks. Some policies have not had the intended effect. Desegregation of schools in some communities simply resulted in resegregation; public assistance sometimes encouraged dependent attitudes and behavior, which embedded poverty more deeply in families and communities. In other instances, policies proposed to eliminate risks conflicted with strongly held values. Adolescent mothering may increase a child's chance of academic failure (Broman, 1981), but public policies designed to prohibit adolescent sexual activity or to make abortion easily available and desirable for this population are unacceptable to large segments of our society. Entitlement programs, once considered the best approach to eliminating risk for different groups, have become less attractive because of their high cost.

Categorical early intervention programs are often recommended as attractive alternatives to entitlements and to unpredictable and socially divisive public policies. Some advocates claim that early childhood programs can be targeted to individuals and groups most in need of services, thus avoiding the expense of entitlements. Others contend that early intervention programs can educate children, families, and communities to deal more effectively with their disabilities or disadvantages without necessitating major changes in the social system.

EARLY INTERVENTION ALONE IS NOT ENOUGH

While early interventions have permitted a more precise targeting of resources, they have not fully offset the effects of detrimental social conditions. Poor children who receive a quality early childhood program achieve better than their peers who do not, but not as well as middle-class children. Low-birth-weight infants can recover without incurring intellectual insult, but not as well in homes characterized by low socioeconomic status (SES) variables (W. Wilson, 1987). Such ills as racism, sexism, lack of jobs, inadequate health resources, drugs, and poor schools are society's problems. There is no reason to believe that programs for young children can compensate for these social deficiencies and injustices.

On the other hand, early intervention programs can be effective adjuncts to public policies designed to address these issues. Much of the success of Head Start was probably due to its being linked with economic development, adult education, political education, and health, social, and nutritional services (Zigler, 1987a). Other programs and policies which have been effective combined include welfare reform, job training, and subsidized day care; Medicaid, pre/postnatal care, early screening and intervention for infants; and adult and child literacy initiatives.

COMPREHENSIVE SERVICES ARE NEEDED

Most children at risk have a cluster of risk factors in their lives. Minority children endure the effects of prejudice and discrimination and are also apt to be poor; live in substandard housing; receive poor health care; attend schools with low per-capita expenditures; experience greater family and community stress due to violence, drugs, and disease; and be at odds with mainstream values. Children with special needs more often come from families disrupted by divorce than children who do not have special needs; they are apt to experience less freedom and autonomy than their peers, and they have more expensive health care needs. Yet Marx and Seligson (1988) report from their study of early childhood programs in public schools that many schools limit their services for at-risk children to classroom programs and "pull-out" therapies.

In order to be effective, intervention programs must provide a match between the risks to which the child is exposed and the intensity and breadth of the intervention. Interventions that include only classroom educational programs are usually insufficient for children at risk. Poor children may need health, nutrition, and psychological services; young children with disabilities need a wide range of services as well as specific therapies. Parents of both groups of children need support and involvement. Single-purpose services are generally inadequate for high-risk populations.

INTERVENTIONS CAN BECOME NEW RISKS

While many early intervention programs have contributed immeasurably to children's achievement, some have become new risks, and themselves threaten children. Victims of such double jeopardy include normal but culturally different children who are misdiagnosed as handicapped and have their educational opportunities curtailed and children subject to special education placements in more constricted environments than necessary. Other problems include poor communication between preschool and kindergarten/primary programs, resulting in different expectations and standards, and poor communication between intervention programs and primary caregivers, resulting in cultural and interpersonal conflict. Early intervention programs must be constantly monitored and evaluated to assure their helpfulness.

III. WHY IS THERE NOT EQUAL ACCESS TO HIGH-QUALITY EARLY CHILDHOOD PROGRAMS IN PUBLIC SCHOOLS?

Despite the evidence that early childhood programs are effective in changing the lives of children at risk, they do not always achieve their objectives. The reasons for the failure are sometimes related to traditional service patterns of the sponsoring organizations. For instance, programs located in hospitals and social services agencies often approach children and families from a pathological model and fail to take advantage of the participants' potential for health.

Public schools also have traditions and patterns of service delivery that may limit the effectiveness of the early childhood programs they sponsor. Zigler (1987a) has pointed out that successful intervention programs differ from conventional schooling in a number of ways—particularly in their comprehensive character and in their emphasis on the family as opposed to the individual child. Although many exemplary programs are conducted by public schools (Campbell, 1987), it is necessary to consider some of the potential difficulties of the public school as a delivery system for quality early intervention programs. My comments are limited to difficulties in programs administered by public schools, but social services agencies and private schools and centers also have their own constraints and limitations in providing quality programs.

FUNDING

The competition for educational dollars is a severe deterrent to providing early intervention programs. Although the Committee for Economic Development's report (1987) makes it clear that the social costs for school failure must be paid now or later, schools' commitments to their present programs often preclude extending their mission to include young children. Another argument against the downward extension of public schools to include early childhood programs is equally cogent: if schools are currently failing to educate adequately all of the older children already in schools, should not the highest priority be to improve programs for these children?

Even when funds are available for high-risk children, the level of funding often precludes effective programs. The costs of the most successful intervention programs are inevitably high. The Perry Preschool Project cost approximately $5,000 per child in 1981 dollars (Weikart, 1988, page 68). Today, most federal- and state-funded programs spend far less and expect to achieve similar results. No studies show that programs can achieve the long-term results of the pilot projects at considerably lower funding levels. Early childhood programs are labor-intensive, and personnel accounts for 60 to 80 percent of program expenditures, making it difficult to reduce their costs.

Although schools themselves have less control over funding than legislators and voters, they often fail to lobby effectively for adequate funding. This may occur partly because few administrators in public schools are sufficiently familiar with developing programs for young children—particularly young children at risk—to be persuasive.

SCHOOL STAFFING, LEADERSHIP, AND STRUCTURE

The second reason at-risk children may be poorly served in public schools is that the program components believed by many to be critical to success are often inadequately planned and implemented. Early childhood programs differ from programs for school-age children in a number of ways and conflict with the customary practices of public schools. Among the most important differences are that they require: (1) greater commitment to parent and community involvement; (2) different curriculum content and methods; (3) different assessment and evaluation strategies; (4) staff trained in early childhood caregiving; and (5) coordination with day care. When schools do not meet these requirements, inadequate and ineffective programs result.

1. PARENT AND COMMUNITY INVOLVEMENT.

The component most often associated with effective early childhood programs is parent involvement. Affecting the way in which parents respond to and support their children is considered essential in all model intervention programs, and a number of programs have reported successful intervention aimed solely at parents. Children who have high-quality classroom programs may show improved knowledge and skills, but long-term effects seem to depend on parental support, guidance, and modeling (Clark, 1983).

Effective parent involvement has three components: parent education, which provides information on child development and parenting; parent support, which focuses on the parents as individuals and provides social networks and resources for them; and parent empowerment, which encourages parents to develop confidence and control in their lives, and hence in their interaction with their children. These last two components are quite different from those addressed by traditional Parent-Teacher Associations—where the central focus is on educating parents to fit into the school's agenda (Schlossman, 1976)—or of Parents as Teachers programs—which encourage parents to teach academic skills. Family support and empowerment assumes that children's school performance is affected by the dynamics of their family life as well as by their exposure to school-related knowledge and skills. Clark (1983) pointed out that family "powerlessness, mistrust, discord, confusion and anger" (page 210) predict poor school orientation. Helping families cope more effectively with the stresses in their lives is often essential if children are to achieve.

Public schools often have been unsuccessful in involving the parents of children at highest risk—poor children, minority children, children from multi-problem families. Recent testimony before the National Association of State Boards of Education brought out quite clearly the differences between the ways in which public schools and Head Start define parent involvement. Head Start parents and staff spoke of the commitment of the program to how parents lived their lives, not just to how they related to the center. Home visits, family support, networking, and resource referral were integral parts of their programs. On the other hand, public school personnel tended to report their involvement as newsletters, parent nights, and problem-oriented conferences. Observers attribute the differences between these two approaches as critical to the success of many Head Start programs and the failure of many public school programs. If this is so, public schools must change their approach if they are to attain the benefits customarily attributed to Head Start and other model intervention programs.

2. DEVELOPMENTALLY APPROPRIATE CURRICULUM AND METHODS.

In recent years there has been increasing pressure from parents and public figures, including legislators, to push academic achievement to earlier and earlier ages. This pressure has been fueled in part by new knowledge about the learning capacity of young children. *The competent infant, the active learner, natural curiosity, the young scientist* are all terms that reflect the new understanding that instead of being passive, ignorant, and unworthy students, young children are active learners with impressive abilities. Child development research over the past 30 years has documented the strategic ability of young children to develop rules that unravel the complexities of language, reading, writing, and logical mathematical knowledge in just a few short years. However, sometimes developmental research has been misunderstood to suggest that children should be taught the formal school skills of reading, writing, and arithmetic at an earlier age.

Unfortunately, pressure for academic achievement may conflict with the development of other important intellectual characteristics—high self-esteem, self-directed learning, and enjoyment of school.

Developmentally appropriate curriculum synchronizes teaching the knowledge and skills of the society with the developmental characteristics of the young child. Developmentally appropriate curriculum recognizes that the first six to eight years are a period in life when children develop the basic structures for learning. Academic content (information and skills) is often the raw material needed to form these structures, but its acquisition is not an end in itself. For instance, young children need to learn some letters and numbers in order to grasp the fact that these two symbol systems are different. They do not, however, need to learn the entire alphabet or all the numbers in order to grasp the fact that there is a difference between these two sets of symbols.

While there may be some disagreement about the precise subject matter appropriate for young children, there is essential agreement that the best preprimary curriculum should be perceptual, concrete, and context-bound, and that it should build upon the child's prior experience and cultural style, including his or her family language. At a recent meeting of the National Association of State Boards of Education Task Force on Early Education, Lilian Katz noted that developmentally appropriate instruction for young children should be largely informal. She says that developmental teaching should include (1) spontaneous play in which children use a variety of manipulatives, (2) project work in which children learn from their own efforts but with the guidance of the teacher, and (3) formal instruction which, over the primary years, moves gradually from one-to-one teaching to small-group instruction.

The learning style characteristic of young children makes informal teaching methods more effective. Informal teaching depends upon the child for pacing and direction and is difficult to preplan in great detail. Therefore, it is hard to describe in lesson plans. Early childhood classrooms are apt to be noisy—children are encouraged to talk with one another and with the adults, to move independently from one activity to another and from one social group to another, and to be physically active, selecting the equipment and materials that interest them. Rarely do all the children do the same thing at the same time, and when they do, the activity tends to be brief and fast-paced. More than one adult is required to teach in an early childhood classroom, which means that adults must collaborate and work as a team.

This is a quite different model of education from the one traditional in public schools, where the teacher alone preplans the curriculum and the children follow her plan, where children sit quietly at desks doing work with pencil and paper, where talking out of turn is discouraged or punished, and where other adults are in a helping role rather than acting as members of the teaching team.

A report by the California panel on school readiness (Howes, 1988) found that most California kindergarten and first-grade classes are characterized by a skill-specific formal instructional approach that the panel declared is inconsistent with the developmental and learning styles of children at the ages in those classes. California is not alone in failing to provide developmentally appropriate curricula or in failing to understand that young children are different from older children and that what they learn and how they learn is different.

Inappropriate curriculum is more serious the earlier it occurs. Early intervention programs that do not recognize developmental differences not only shortchange the young child but also may play a role in some children's negative attitudes about school. This is another instance in which the intervention itself increases the child's risk.

3. CHILD ASSESSMENT AND EVALUATION STRATEGIES.

Traditionally schools have relied on tests to evaluate children's learning. Tests sample a child's information and skills and assume that children who respond correctly to questions have mastered the knowledge appropriate to their developmental age and the instructional emphasis. Using tests in a similar way with young children is problematic because of the emotional and social ability of children of this age and because of the developmental characteristics of early childhood.

Achievement Tests

The major developmental task for young children is to build cognitive structures. It is difficult to assess these structures just by sampling a small amount of information and a limited number of skills; developmental change is not dependent on a specific body of information or set of skills. For instance, a young child may have grasped the notion of invariant order in counting, yet not use the correct counting tags (number words) to count. Therefore, one cannot assess whether a child has mastered the idea of invariant order on a single counting trial. In addition, culturally different children may be developmentally normal without knowing the same information and/or skills that are characteristic of middle-class white children.

Young children do not develop evenly over 8 years or over 12 months, and sampling their capabilities at any point in time is not necessarily predictive of their future developmental rates; thus it is seldom an advantage to the child to repeat a grade level. Shepard and Smith (1986, page 85) reported that in four out of five studies that assessed transition-year programs for young children, those children who had the extra year fared no better than their peers who did not. In fact, they cite a study by May and Welch that showed no difference in academic performance between children who were held back and those who had continued in grade. Shepard and Smith concluded that there seems to be no academic benefit to the extra year for maturation in helping children be successful in school.

Young children's emotional and attentional immaturity also makes their test results suspect. They may find the testing situation frightening or may simply choose not to respond to particular questions, thus making their answers inadequate guides to their skills and knowledge.

Screening Tests

Most programs attempt to identify at-risk youngsters through mass screening procedures. Screening instruments and procedures are not diagnostic and will incorrectly assess many children who are perfectly normal in development and achievement. The inclusion of such children in a high-quality early childhood program certainly should do them no harm. However, when teachers and parents believe that screening tests are diagnostic and treat children accordingly, their expectations can become self-fulfilling prophecies. Inappropriate intervention may be more harmful than no intervention.

Curriculum Evaluation

It is also poor practice to use standardized tests to select and evaluate curriculum. Test-driven curriculum constricts opportunities to learn, particularly for young children. When teacher competence is determined by children's test scores, the pressure to teach to the test becomes attractive to the most professional teacher, and the developmentally appropriate curriculum is distorted into mindless memorization and decontextualized experiences. Both Head Start and the National Association for the Education of Young Children recommend extensive procedures for evaluating early childhood classrooms, yet few school districts or state boards have adopted these standards. When early childhood programs are judged solely on the basis of the test scores of the children, programs are biased toward testable content rather than toward the developmental needs of the young child.

4. ADEQUATELY TRAINED STAFF.

One of the criteria most often associated with effective early childhood programs is teacher training. Early childhood teachers have different roles and responsibilities than teachers of older children. As already noted, the curriculum and methods are different, and the program includes responsibility for parent involvement. In addition, because of the age of the children, the early childhood teacher must be prepared to engage in more "maternal" types of behavior (i.e., meeting children's need for warmth, attachment, dependence) than teachers of older children.

While a few states have certification requirements for prekindergarten teachers that capture these differences, most states do not have separate certification standards for teachers of young children, and other states have minimal requirements. Illinois, for instance, requires only one course in child, family, and community relationships, one course in child development, and one course in preschool curriculum for teachers seeking early childhood certification. This means that few public schools have teachers trained well enough to implement early childhood programs. In order for public schools to expand their service to include preschool at-risk children, an extensive training program will be needed. Preservice certification requirements will need to be developed; but even more essential, ongoing in-service education will be needed if public schools are to provide quality early intervention programs.

Support personnel also have little training to work with preschool-age children. For instance, most speech pathologists have not been prepared to work with young children. Their typical pattern of pulling children out of the classroom for brief periods of individual work is not the most effective treatment for most young children with speech problems. Further, many speech behaviors that are problems in older children (such as unclear articulation) are normal in young children. Other support personnel also are frequently unprepared: curriculum consultants, library and resource teachers, and psychologists are usually unfamiliar with the development of preschool children.

School leaders have critical roles to play if early intervention programs are to be effective. They must understand the unique character of the prekindergarten-kindergarten primary program and support it. Klugman and Benn (1987) contend that the principal's role includes supporting professional development of teachers, approving curricular materials, scheduling parent and family events, providing access to specialists, setting policies which assure that parents are welcome in the school, and facilitating networks between early childhood and primary programs.

Yet, currently there are few administrators who understand the dimensions of an effective early intervention program and have the ability to implement and support such a program. Few principals or superintendents have themselves had experience working with young children or providing supportive services to families. Few can provide leadership or supervision for teachers in planning, implementing, or evaluating programs. It is understandable that many school leaders see the early childhood program as one that will require little of their time and effort. Young children are seldom so disruptive as to demand attention from the administration, particularly from an administration also responsible for pre-adolescents, who are apt to be considerably more disruptive.

Administrative separation of the preschool (and perhaps the primary grades) from programs for older children is an essential step to effective management of programs for young children and families.

5. INTEGRATION OF EDUCATION WITH DAY CARE.

More mothers work outside the home now than ever before in our history. More than 50 percent of the mothers of preschool-age children and upwards of 80 percent of mothers of school-age children are in the work force. Many parents are divorcing or never marrying. It is estimated that one-half of all children will spend some of their childhood in a single-parent family. Families are reorganizing; sex roles are changing as women are more independent and less willing to assume a minor role in the workplace. Families are having fewer children, and many parents are more concerned that each child reach his or her maximum potential.

At-risk children are not immune from these changes in family life; indeed, their families are often the ones coping least well with these changes. Poor families find it particularly difficult to arrange for adequate care for their children. Day-care services funded through Social Service block grants have huge waiting lists in inner city neighborhoods, and most parents are unable to afford care in for-profit centers or licensed homes. Housing deterioration in poor communities also makes licensed day care difficult to find even for families who can afford it. Children with handicapping conditions are difficult to place in day care because their need for extra attention induces higher costs. The children most at risk are also most likely to be in inadequate day care.

Public schools rarely do much to help with this problem. The vast majority of intervention programs in public schools operate half-day for 10 months, often leaving children inadequately supervised and cared for during the remainder of the day or year. Although some public schools are providing before- and after-school programs for school-age children, this arrangement is not always ideal for young children at risk. They require greater consistency and continuity in their lives than do older children if they are to learn and develop well. Makeshift arrangements, multiple caregivers, and frequent changes in care are more likely to have an adverse effect on vulnerable children. Half-day programs promote these stressful arrangements.

Most public schools are not accustomed to cooperative planning and integration of their programs with those of other delivery systems. In Illinois's program for at-risk children, for instance, in which school districts are permitted to contract for services with nonprofit organizations, only 10 percent have done so, and no district has made a cooperative agreement with a day-care facility.

Districts have preferred to use the format with which they are most familiar—half-day programs in self-contained classrooms.

New models need to be devised and publicized to encourage public schools to develop cooperative arrangements with other programs for at-risk children as well as with day care. Children at risk in Head Start, in private schools and centers, in family day-care homes, and in their own homes will be attending public schools when they are six years old. It is in the interest of the schools to work with these programs so that the children and their parents will receive the support they need. Schools can no longer draw sharp divisions between their responsibilities and those of the families and institutions that prepare children for school.

Only when and if schools can change their tradition of working alone will young children at risk be prepared for school success.

IV. THE PUBLIC SCHOOL RESPONSE

I have described the potential and limitations of early childhood programs for at-risk children. Given the difficulties enumerated, should public schools get involved? While it may be tempting to contend that the needs of young children are just too different for them to fit into schools, it might be more advantageous to welcome them and rearrange schools to accommodate them—for three reasons:

1. Preventing learning problems is easier than curing them later. The children who are helped in an early intervention program will become members of the school community at age six, whether or not they are ready.

2. Establishing an effective relationship with parents during the preschool years may make cooperation between parents and school more likely as the children get older. Obtaining the loyalty and support from parents that emerge from a good early childhood program can pay dividends to the school for as long as the child and family are there.

3. Many of the qualities characteristic of a good early childhood program, such as enthusiasm for learning and responsiveness to teachers, might spread to classes for older children. As noted by the California Task Force, the National Association for the Education of Young Children, the Association of State Early Childhood Specialists, and other organizations, the ideas and practices of quality preschool education are needed equally in programs for kindergarten and primary-grade children.

Chief state school officers have an important role to play in determining whether and how early childhood programs are integrated into school. Without their strong leadership in obtaining funds and assisting in developing quality programs, the benefits of an early childhood program are not going to be realized. They are needed to interpret both the promise and the needs of this new kind of program to lawmakers, policymakers, and laypersons.

It is even more important, however, that chief state school officers use their leadership position to invest the early childhood program with the significance it deserves. In view of its distinctiveness, early childhood education should be a component in the state offices comparable to elementary and high school programs—not just a downward extension of what is already there. The perception that early childhood intervention is no more than an "add-on" program is validated when there is only a single early childhood specialist in the state department of education, and he or she is well down on the administrative ladder.

Early childhood education is at a critical juncture in public schools. Schools can add their unique strengths to the mix of programs that serve young children and families. Or, they can remain on the sidelines and let other institutions and services be responsible for preparing young children for school. Schools can pay attention to what has already been learned about child development and about how to organize and structure programs for young children. Or, they can try to fit the children into the system the way it is, knowing that the status quo is unlikely to result in meaningful education. Schools can develop programs to enrich the lives of children and families and to protect the future of our society. Or, they can ignore what is known and can complain a generation from now that early childhood intervention was a failure.

REFERENCES

Berrueta-Clement, J. R., L. J. Schweinhart, W. S. Barnett, A. E. Epstein, and D. P. Weikart. *Changed Lives: The Effects of the Perry Preschool Program on Youths Through Age 19*. Ypsilanti, Mich.: High/Scope Press, 1984.

Broman, S. "Longterm Development of Children Born to Teenagers." In *Teenage Parents and Their Offspring, edited by K. Scott, T. Field, and E.G. Robertson*. New York: Grune & Stratton, 1981.

Campbell, B. "From National Debate to National Responsibility." In *Early Schooling: The National Debate,* edited by S. Kagar and E. Zigler. New Haven, Conn.: Yale University Press, 1987.

Clark, R. *Family Life and School Achievement*. Chicago: University of Chicago Press, 1983.

Committee for Economic Development. *Children in Need: Investment Strategies for the Educationally Disadvantaged*. New York: Committee for Economic Development, 1987.

Consortium for Longitudinal Studies. *As the Twig Is Bent*. Hillsdale, N.J.: Lawrence Erlbaum Associates, 1983.

Hale, J. *Black Children: Their Roots and Learning Styles*. Provo, Utah: Brigham Young University Press, 1982.

Howes, C. *Here They Come: Ready or Not!* Sacramento: California State Department of Education, 1988.

Klugman, E., and J. Benn. "The Elementary School Principal's Role in Integrating Early Childhood Perspectives." *SAANYS Journal* (Spring 1987): 5–18.

Lazar, I. "Lasting Effects of Early Education: A Report from the Consortium for

Longitudinal Studies." *Monographs of the Society for Research in Child Development* 45 (203, Serial No. 195), 1982.

McKey, R. H., L. Condelli, H. Ganson, B. Barrett, C. McConkey, and M. Plant. *The Impact of Head Start on Children, Families, and Communities.* Washington, D.C.: DHHS, 1986.

Marx, F., and M. Seligson. *The State Survey.* New York: Bank Street College (The Public School Early Childhood Study), 1988.

Province, S. "On the Efficacy of Early Intervention Programs." In *Annual Progress in Child Psychiatry and Child Development,* edited by S. Chess and A. Thomas. New York: Brunner/Mazel, 1987.

Ramey, C., and D. Farran. "Intervening with High-Risk Families via Infant Day Care," (ERIC 230–289). Washington, D.C.: Educational Resources Information Center, 1983.

Schlossman, S. "Before Home Start: Notes Toward a History of Parent Education in America, 1897–1929." *Harvard Educational Review* 46 (1976): 436–467.

Shepard, L., and M. Smith. "Synthesis of Research on School Readiness and Kindergarten Retention." *Educational Leadership* 44 (1986): 78–85.

Weikart, D. "Quality in Early Education." In *A Resource Guide to Public School Early Childhood Programs,* edited by C. Warger. Alexandria, Va.: Association for Supervision and Curriculum Development, 1988.

Werner, E. "Individual Differences, Universal Needs: A 30-Year Study of Resilient High-Risk Infants." *Zero to Three* 8:4 (1988): 1–5.

Wilson, R. "Risk and Resilience in Early Mental Development." In *Annual Progress in Child Psychiatry and Child Development,* edited by S. Chess and A. Thomas. New York: Brunner/Mazel, 1987.

Wilson, W. *The Truly Disadvantaged: The Inner City, the Underclass, and Public Policy.* Chicago: The University of Chicago Press, 1987.

Zigler, E. "Assessing Head Start at 20: An Invited Commentary." In *Annual Progress in Child Psychiatry and Child Development,* edited by S. Chess and A. Thomas. New York: Brunner/Mazel, 1987a.

Zigler, E. "Formal Schooling for Four-Year-Olds? No." In *Early Schooling,* edited by S. Kagan and E. Zigler. New Haven, Conn.: Yale University Press, 1987b.

WHAT NEW RESEARCH SAYS ABOUT THE DEVELOPMENTAL PATTERNS AND NEEDS OF YOUNG CHILDREN

Sheldon H. White and Diane E. Beals

HARVARD UNIVERSITY

Over the past 20 years, there has been a steady enlargement in Americans' use of preschool education. About 11 percent of three- and four-year-olds attended preschools in 1965; in 1985, 39 percent did so. Over 60 percent of all four-year-olds are now in preschool programs. The principal stimulant to this growth appears to be an increase in women working. In 1986, almost 60 percent of women with children between the ages of three and five were in the labor force (Grubb, 1987). This rising use of early care and education has been accompanied by demands for public support. As has been true in several historical cycles in the past, demand for publicly supported preschooling has been initiated by the well-to-do, but, when government finally acts, the programs go to the poor (S. Kagan, 1987; White and Buka, 1987). Significant new questions about children's needs and about appropriate means and ends of early education arise as early care and education becomes an instrument of public policy and is turned toward a new clientele.

In the 1980s, we are resuming a dialogue that began when some developmental psychologists became intensely involved with Head Start and early education in the 1960s. Head Start and early education are not quite synonymous. Gilbert Steiner (1976, pp. 28–29), in his excellent political history of the early years of Head Start, remarks, "Once in place, Project Head Start itself generated a further expansion of interest in and study of early childhood but it was neither invented as nor did it ever become an appropriate model for a universal preschool program."

Zigler and Valentine's history (1979) gives a sense of this breadth. A chapter by Richmond, Stipek, and Zigler in that volume discusses the series of legislative and administrative actions that established Head Start and the variety of services offered by Head Start. Non-preschool Head Start programs include: (a) Health Start, providing medical and dental services and health education; (b) Home Start, providing health and educational services to children in their own homes; and (c) the Child and Family Resource Program, which enabled some Head Start centers to make referrals to a variety of community services. Head Start was first implemented as a Community Action Program, and there were data to show that the presence of a Head Start center in a community was associated with widespread changes in community institutions, changes benefiting poor children and their families (Kirschner Associates, 1970).

Policymakers concerned with Head Start and other programs for children made efforts to use research on child development for guidance. The first thing that needs to be said about the discussion that resumes in the 1980s is that our scientific picture of the child is considerably richer and more three-dimensional than it was 20 years ago.

THE CHILD OF THE 1960s

Every single child is different, of course, but when we try to design large-scale programs and social arrangements for children, we often have to be guided by conceptions of the needs and abilities that are common to most children. A classic function of research has been to create a richer picture of the "average," "typical," or "normal" child to be addressed by school programs. As our research work progressively enlarges our view of children, not only may we see more details, but we may change our sense of the central dynamisms and tasks in child development. Just that has happened in the past 20 years. Let us consider two prototypical children, the child of the 1960s, whose development centered on the growth of reasoning, and the child of the 1990s, whose development centers on the growth of social competence.

Psychology's child of the 1960s was largely Jean Piaget's child, just crossing the water to the United States at that time and having enormous influence on the work and the thinking of American developmental psychologists. Piaget's child was a cognitive theorist. The child had a structure of thought and a logic, and whatever the child thought and did was governed by the quality of that logic. Piaget's child thought about basic things—space, time, number, geometry, causality, chance, morality—and as the child acquired more powerful logics, its thought became deeper and more powerful. There is a wondrous chemistry in physical growth. Whatever little Lester Smith eats—cookies, hot dogs, sodas, hamburgers, peanut butter and jelly and marshmallow-fluff sandwiches, pizzas—all goes to make more Lester Smith. Piaget said the mind had the same wondrous chemistry. Whatever little Lester Smith studies and thinks and learns about all goes to advance the preordained sequence of Piagetian stages.

It was common in the 1960s for people to talk about "cognitive development" as though it were synonymous with "child development." Theories about early education flowed from this simplified conception. The Grand Design of cognitive-developmental stages provided a blueprint of intellectual growth. Parents and teachers ought to understand the blueprint, to go along with it at least, and to help it if possible.

Some people felt early education might accelerate cognitive development. There were so many Americans who tried in one way and another to accelerate children's movement into the higher-level thought that Piaget in the latter years of his life came to speak of this as "the American Question." Some felt early education should follow cognitive development, not trying to accelerate it but enriching and enlarging the child's experience at each level. Most people nowadays would have trouble with the proposition that cognitive development *is* child development, but some interesting and powerful approaches to early education followed this strategy (DeVries and Kohlberg, 1987). David Weikart's Perry Preschool at Ypsilanti, one of the most effective and influential preschools of that era, was built upon a thoughtful and careful translation of Piaget's work into preschool curriculum (Hohmann, Banet, and Weikart, 1979).

We are talking only about developmental psychologists' conceptions of the possibilities of preschool education, of course. At the grass roots, in the Head Start centers, this cognitive theorizing was never very influential or powerful. Head Start headquarters in Washington never dictated curriculum to its centers. Surveys of the preferences of Head Start center directors generally revealed a two-thirds/one-third pattern. Two-thirds of Head Start center directors said they were working principally toward social goals: one-third espoused cognitive goals.

THE CHILD OF THE 1980s

Much research has led developmental psychologists toward a different conception of the early needs of children. The movement seems to be something more than a matter of changing trends and tastes. There has been a laborious, authentic research process in which some people, embracing Piagetian theory, have had to confront a rising tide of anomalies and contradictions; others, looking beyond the university experiments, have more and more found ways to study the child in the real world in which he or she lives.

Researchers in the 1980s are still concentrating on cognitive development, examining the ways in which thinking and reasoning change as children grow. The effort is to infer how the child makes sense of experience. Piaget's image lingers; the child "constructs reality," beginning with simple ideas of how things work, then as more and more powerful forms of thought emerge, recognizing and understanding more and more of the complexity of the world around him or her. The child of the 1980s remains a cognitive theorist, but the cognitive theorizing is embedded in the child's broader movement through a series of human societies.

THE PLURALIZATION OF COGNITIVE DEVELOPMENT

The Piagetian view that there is one Grand Design—changes sweeping across children's thought in stage after stage—is now contradicted by much research literature. Infants show limited abilities to infer, deduce, plan, count, explain, take the role of the other, use a morality of intentions, much earlier than the theory says they should. Older children, who ought to follow one stage and one kind of logic consistently, show a dismaying pattern of up-and-downness as they think about different kinds of things. They are uneven and they fluctuate. Shifts in emotions and moods, or minor changes in the way problems are presented and staged, shift their levels of thought. We have to recognize that there is something more than the growth of logic behind human intellectual performances.

From the very beginning of work on intelligence testing, some psychologists have resisted the notion that there is only one human intelligence, one "general intelligence" determining the level and the quality of every ability a person has. Recent studies of "microgenesis," day-by-day studies of a child learning, seem to turn Piagetian theory sideways: all the logics and stages—a sensorimotor intelligence, a logic of images, and a logic of propositions—seem to be at work at once, interacting with one another when a child addresses a problem. We need to find ways of dealing with the multiple intelligences of children.

COGNITIVE DEVELOPMENT IN THE REAL WORLD

The majority of Piaget's work deals with the child as a tabletop theorist. He or she watches physical events involving little cubes, pegs, watches, toy cows, glasses, etc. The adult "stages" the event for the child and asks questions about quantity, category, speed, extent, etc. But the complex reality a small child deals with from day to day cannot be modeled by a set of half-hour episodes on a tabletop (White, 1980).

There is a new movement toward "ecological validity, "an effort to study children in the everyday world in which they live. Thirty years ago, Roger Barker and his associates at the University of Kansas recognized the need to consider and map the human environment in which children live (Barker and Wright, 1954). Neither children nor adults live in the imaginary jungle posed by romantic evolutionists of the nineteenth century: "nature red in fang and claw." We live in a world of buildings, streets, automobiles, supermarkets, newspapers, ketchup bottles. Many of the objects we deal with are man-made, impregnated with human design, intentions, and intelligence. A child facing a short fat glass half full of water might ask some reasonably elegant question about physical quality. The child might be very inclined to ask other questions. "Where can you go to buy a glass like this?" "Who made this glass?" "Why is this strange adult sitting around here asking me funny questions about this glass?" Much of what the small child has to learn and think about is the human world, within which are the roles and purposes and rules and idiosyncrasies governing the transactions of human society.

CHILD DEVELOPMENT IN A SERIES OF HUMAN SOCIETIES

If there is a Grand Design governing children's development, it is formed by biology and society. Biology provides an orderly sequence of physical growth. Society builds upon that a social sequence, a set of social "stages." The newborn begins life in a family. The growing infant marches into a wider world—an extended family, peers, the school, the spaces and places of the larger community. The child builds skills and knowledge in several milieus, and the child experiences not one but several forms of social development in the early years. Children's needs are based upon that biologically and socially given pattern of movements.

HOME

Children need to form a reasonably secure attachment relationship with their parents, and this attachment seems to be a substrate for other social relationships. Children need love and warm, sensitive, and responsive parenting. In the post-Freudian era, we have dwelt on the emotional responsibilities of families, and we have given relatively little emphasis to the other responsibilities and capabilities families must have. In the early years of life, families manage and mediate a child's dealings with the larger society, and they work with the child as he or she makes a series of entrances and choices about peers, schooling, and the people and situations of the larger community.

STRESS, RISK, AND DISADVANTAGE IN EARLY CHILDHOOD

Childhood disadvantage takes on new meanings when one examines the child's participation in the larger society. Piaget's child lives in a world of brief, tidy, polite, somewhat superficial transactions with adults. This kind of transaction is not wholly ecologically invalid. Schools, businesses, and other bureaucracies depend upon formal human encounters limited to certain proper purposes and governed by rules. Purposeful human cooperation is built using such institutional forms of human interaction. But childhood *disadvantage* often reflects a difficulty in operating effectively within conventional social forms; to study it, we need to explore the limits of children's ability to engage in extended social activity. Developmental psychologists have more and more joined forces with clinical psychologists and child psychiatrists interested in early vulnerability. Together, they have explored stress, risk, coping, and resiliency as manifested in children's early social transactions.

Certain events and experiences in a child's life may limit or disorganize the child's ability to learn and to function in a positive way. Such happenings are often referred to as *stresses,* and recently there has been an effort to explore when and how stresses act on a child. Usage of the term *stress* has been characterized by "chaos, confusion, and controversy" (Rutter et al., 1983, p. 1); yet the word is old and its use persists, presumably because it seems to point to some meaningful property of a broad class of events. What kinds of events are stressful? In a well-known study of the life events that stress adults, Holmes and

Rahe (1967) put forth the position that degree of life change, whether positive or negative, pleasant or unpleasant, is associated with stress. However, this has been questioned, and there are some grounds for believing that negative rather than positive events, "exits" rather than "entrances," events out of the individual's control rather than controllable events, and events that imply a long-term threat, may be the most likely to produce stress effects on the individual. Reasonably strong evidence shows that, in the case of adults, stressful life events play a significant role in provoking the onset of suicide, depressive conditions, neurotic disorders, and schizophrenia. There is also evidence that stresses tend to precipitate and maintain physical illnesses (Rutter, et al. 1983).

Different kinds of environmental configurations are stressful for children and for adults. Children live in a different milieu than adults; they have different resources; they understand events differently (Garmezy, 1983). One of the broad sources of stress is maternal deprivation. Maternal deprivation has been shown to have a deleterious effect on child development (Rutter, 1981). There are a number of family configurations and situations that, to a degree, participate in this negative effect—family discord and disharmony, parental rejection and neglect, or an institutional upbringing.

STRESS VS. RISK

A number of events in a child's life are known to have a moderately disturbing character. They lead to emotional distress, behavior disturbances, and disruptions in the child's social behavior. But available evidence indicates that these disturbances tend to be relatively mild and transient (Rutter, et al. 1983).

Hospital Admission. Evidence shows that children show emotional disturbance associated with hospital admission (Rutter, 1981; Vernon, Foley, Sipowicz, and Schulman, 1965). The disturbance may be present for months after the child has returned home from the hospital, but one hospital stay of less than a week does not produce any significant long-term consequences (Douglas, 1975; Quinton and Rutter, 1976).

Birth of a Sibling. Moore (1975), studying a small sample of London children, found that about 15 percent developed difficulties—"problem behavior" or a disturbed mother-child relationship—following the birth of a sibling. Dunn and associates (Dunn and Kendrick, 1980a, 1980b; Dunn, Kendrick, and McNamee, 1981) found problems in a sample of two-to-three-year-old children they studied. More than half became more tearful; one-fourth developed sleeping difficulties; nearly half showed new toileting problems. But there is little evidence for substantial long-term effects of such difficulties; such effects would, in all likelihood, be entangled among other issues in problems of sibling rivalry.

Divorce. Available evidence suggests that the disturbance children experience in divorcing families may come more from the marital discord prior to the separation and less from the fact of the divorce itself (Rutter, 1971, 1982).

However, longitudinal studies by Hetherington and her associates (Hetherington, Cox, and Cox, 1978, 1979a, 1979b) and by Wallerstein and Kelly (1980) seem to show emotional disturbance in children immediately after a divorce.

COPING

One task of the 1980s has been to try to understand what happens to children in times of stress and transition. Another has been to examine what children *do* about the vicissitudes of life when they encounter them. Some young people are *resilient*. They maintain a reasonable level of functioning even though they have experienced a form of stress which in the population as a whole is known to carry a substantial risk of an adverse outcome. Children are, of course, not simply passive, reactive participants in the several social worlds in which they live. Faced with a problem in one of those social worlds—a move to a new neighborhood, trouble in school, loss of a friend, mother's illness—they try to correct and compensate much as adults might do. In order to *see* such efforts at coping and adjustment, psychologists have had to move beyond the traditional standardized, 30-minute, one-moment-in-time encounter with a child.

Figuratively speaking, we need to follow a child moving through the significant places and situations of his or her life. We need to see the child repeatedly encountering problematic situations and examine the devices the child uses to try to cope with it—attempts at repair, shifting social groups, withdrawal, asking for help, etc.

There has been a turn toward a greater and more complex consideration of ego development in children, of their motives to organize their world and to be effective in it, and of coping and mastery in childhood. Lois Barclay Murphy (1962), at the very beginning of the Head Start era, reported on a Coping Study at the Menninger Foundation in Topeka. She and her associates studied a sample of 32 children from the time they were 2 or 3 years of age until they were 11 or 12, working out relatively detailed accounts of the children's transactions with school, family, and friends.

We are beginning to harvest the great longitudinal studies early child development researchers initiated in the 1930s and 1940s, looking at long-term trends in people's lives. Only as we look at people across the long term, and as we are able to examine each individual's orchestration of activities and purposes across a number of behavior settings, can we begin to understand the larger influences of risk and coping strategies in determining the factors that lead toward childhood disadvantage.

During the 1960s, most evaluations of preschools looked for short-term, straightforward, logical benefits of program experiences for children. A program built around the conception that language skills are important for the intellectual development of children ought to produce measurable effects on children's language or IQ test performance. A preschool program seeking to give children the cognitive prerequisites for schooling ought to produce graduates who are measurably better on school achievement tests. There were experienced preschool teachers who said that this kind of if-then, production-oriented assessment was a poor way to look at what happens to a child as the result of a year in a preschool classroom. But evaluators were driven to look for short-term benefits. Limitations in research methods, together with an ethos of the era oriented toward management by objectives, brought forth a picture of curiously evanescent preschool effectiveness. Preschooling produced positive changes on IQ tests and school achievement tests and language tests—some preschools more, some less. But all such effects, great and small, tended to fade away by the fourth grade.

PROGRAMS THAT HAVE REDUCED RISK IN EARLY CHILDHOOD

Curiously, it is only through longer-term, wider-reaching studies that we have begun to understand the larger effects of preschooling on children. We have been, as it were, inadvertently studying the use of preschooling to reduce risks and to increase the coping skills of children and their families. One of the truly striking and interesting lessons of the 1960s was the way in which demonstration programs conceived in the cognitively oriented ideology of the time, oriented toward cognitive goals, served to increase children's life chances without measurably producing the long-term shifts in cognitive functioning which they addressed.

DAVID WEIKART'S PERRY PRESCHOOL STUDY

David Weikart's Perry Preschool Project has become a bellwether of early education in public discussions. Initiated in 1962, the study examined the effects of participation and nonparticipation of 123 disadvantaged black children who were at risk for school failure. The children have now been studied from ages 3–19 (Weikart, 1967).

The center was cognitively oriented and used a careful and elaborate translation of Piagetian theory into preschool curriculum; preschool teachers were actively involved in both making the translation and assessing the curricular impact in theoretical terms. Teachers also visited homes weekly for 90 minutes and involved parents and children in educational activities.

Weikart (1967), p. 171, summarizes the results of the program as follows:

> Nineteen-year-olds who had attended the program were better off in a variety of ways than a control group who did not participate in a preschool program. The program apparently *increased* the percentage of participants who were

- functionally literate, from 38 percent to 61 percent.
- enrolled in postsecondary education, from 21 percent to 38 percent.
- employed, from 32 percent to 50 percent.

The program apparently *reduced* the percentage of participants who were

- classified as mentally retarded during school years, from 35 percent to 15 percent.
- school dropouts, from 51 percent to 33 percent.
- pregnant teens, from 67 percent to 48 percent.
- on welfare, from 32 percent to 18 percent.
- arrested, from 51 percent to 31 percent.

Note how remarkably un-Piagetian these findings are. These changes in children, found as the result of their programmatic experience, fall outside of all the terms in genetic epistemology. One might say to Jean Piaget, "Your philosophy touches more things on heaven and earth than are revealed in your philosophy." Indeed, what is remarkable about the Weikart study is the extent to which the program succeeded without reaching its targeted cognitive objectives.

THE CONSORTIUM FOR LONGITUDINAL STUDIES

Pretty much the same thing, on a wider scale, is seen in the work of the Consortium for Longitudinal Studies. The Consortium was a group of investigators of early education who, in 1975, put their efforts together to explore the long-term consequences of early intervention projects. Every early intervention study that had a specific curriculum, focused on children of low-income families, was completed prior to 1969, and had an original sample in excess of 100 subjects was invited to join in the effort. The investigators of all but one of the 15 eligible studies accepted the invitation. In their review of the Consortium's findings, Royce, Darlington, and Murray (1983, p. 412) note that the Consortium effort included essentially the whole population of large-scale preschool intervention studies in existence at the time the work was begun.

This group began its work after a first wave of evaluation studies had shown discouraging effects of experimental preschools for poor children. Irving Lazar of Cornell University was the central coordinator of the Developmental Consortium's effort. Children who originally had been students in 11 projects were located and tested and their educational status ascertained. The findings of the Developmental Consortium's follow-up studies (Darlington, Royce, Snipper, Murray, and Lazar, 1980; Lazar and Darlington, 1982; Consortium for Developmental Studies, 1983) showed what appeared to be significant long-term effects on the programs. Consider briefly the intended directions of the 11 programs (Lazar and Darlington, 1982, Appendix A):

The Philadelphia Project, directed by E. Kuno Beller of Temple University, offered a nursery-school program to children three and one-half to four and one-half years of age, supplemented by efforts to work with the children's families.

The Institute for Developmental Studies at New York University, directed by Martin Deutsch and Cynthia P. Deutsch, was a prekindergarten program oriented toward "language development, concept formation, perceptual and overall cognitive development, and self-concept" (p. 68).

The Florida Parent Education Program, directed by Dr. Ira Gordon, provided home-visitor, parent-focused intervention to children from 3 months to 3 years old.

The Early Training Project, directed by Dr. Susan Gray at George Peabody College, gave children one or several summer preschool experiences with the program to enhance perceptual, cognitive, and language development and to teach attitudes favorable to schooling.

The Curriculum Comparison Study, directed by Dr. Merle Karnes at the University of Illinois, compared several programmatic approaches. Dr. Karnes's GOAL (Game-Oriented Activities for Learning) program was compared with four other approaches—a traditional preschool approach, the Bereiter-Engelmann DISTAR program, a Montessori program, and a "community-integrated" approach in which a small number of low-income children were integrated into middle-class preschools.

The Mother-Child Home Program was established by the Verbal Interaction Project, directed by Dr. Phyllis Levenstein. "Toy demonstrators" visited children 2 to 3 years of age and their mothers to demonstrate techniques designed to encourage more verbal interaction in the family.

Experimental Variation of Head Start Curricula was a program directed by Dr. Louise Miller in Louisville. Four programs were implemented: (a) traditional Head Start; (b) the Bereiter-Engelmann approach teaching school-relevant skills; (c) a Montessori approach; and (d) the program of Dr. Susan Gray at Peabody.

The Harlem Research Center, directed by Francis Palmer, taught 2- and 3-year-old children basic concepts ("in," "out," "big," "little") using one-on-one tutors.

The Perry Preschool Project was the David Weikart Perry Preschool Study described above.

The Micro-Social Learning System, directed by Myron Woolman, was a behavioral engineering program intended to improve skills and concepts necessary for first-grade performance. Children aged 3 1/2 to 6 were given exercises directed toward building language, reading, capacities for social interaction, and motivation toward long-term goals.

The New Haven Follow-Through Study dealt with a group of Head Start graduates who attended Follow-Through programs in New Haven and Hamden, Connecticut, for four years, from kindergarten through the third grade. The Follow-Through program they experienced followed the model of the Bank Street College of Education. Bank Street, it might be said, was not an invention of academic developmental psychologists but was in large part a crystallization of the wisdom of traditional preschool education. Though Bank Street did not exactly predict what the Developmental Consortium would find, certainly those findings are most easily reconciled within Bank Street's philosophy of preschool education.

The Consortium found and tested program graduates who were between 9 and 19 years old. Consortium programs had produced short-term increases in IQ scores. There was a median difference of 7.42 IQ points on post-tests immediately following the programs, diminishing to a median difference of about 3 IQ points three years after completion. By 1976, there were almost no differences between the program and the control children. Graduates of the programs had shown gains in school reading and mathematics achievement in the third grade. Some mathematics achievement gains were seen in fourth- and fifth-grade tests, but by the sixth grade, program graduates and control children were equal in both reading and mathematics. Rate of placement into special classes averaged 14.5 percent for program graduates and 34.9 percent for control children, a highly significant difference. The rate of retention in grade average was 19.8 percent for program graduates and 32.0 percent for the control children. Four programs had graduates old enough for program effects on high school graduation to be looked at. For the four programs, 64.8 percent of the graduates completed high school, vs. 52.5 percent of the control children, a statistically significant difference (Lazar and Darlington, 1982; Royce, Darlington, and Murray, 1983).

Certain special features of these programs seemed to augment their effects (Royce, Darlington, and Murray, 1983, p. 442):

1. Intervention begun as early as possible.

2. Services provided to the parents as well as to the children.

3. Frequent home visits.

4. Involvement of the parents in the instruction of the child.

5. As few children per teacher as possible.

The findings of the Developmental Consortium are of considerable potential importance, because they seem to show that under some conditions preschool interventions can produce lasting and practically important effects on children's lives. Some puzzles and uncertainties remain.

Why, after short-term effects seem to have washed out, does one find a later emergence of long-term effects of preschool intervention? Possibly there was a "sleeper effect"—some benefit to the child's self-concept or motivation that was created by the programs but that did not reveal itself in the early years, emerging only in times of pressure during the later years of schooling. The hypothesis that there was a sleeper effect—a positive effect that lay dormant for a few years and then came to life later—is controversial (Clarke and Clarke, 1981; Seitz, 1981). Possibly, the programs had immediate positive effects, but the tests much used for the evaluation studies were so narrow or misdirected that they missed what the preschools were accomplishing.

Why are the Developmental Consortium's graduates doing better at school and school-related activities even though formal school achievement tests do not register changes? Possibly, the attitudes of the children were changed. It may be remembered that James Coleman's (1966) massive study of the academic performances of black and white children reported that attitudes of the children had a major effect on their school achievement. Smith (1972, p. 231), in his reconsideration of the Coleman Report's major conclusions, points out that this is one finding that has not been challenged.

Were the changes found by the Developmental Consortium primarily due to the programs' effects on children, or were they due to changes in the families of the children? Some time ago, Urie Bronfenbrenner reviewed some of the early evaluation literature dealing with preschool effectiveness and concluded that preschools could instigate changes in children if and only if they worked with the children's families. It is conceivable that the 11 programs of the Developmental Consortium had their principal effects not on children but on the families, helping the families to understand what was expected of their children in school, to support and encourage their children, and to negotiate for their children's needs in the schools. Several direct and indirect considerations support this possibility:

- the fact that the graduates of the Developmental Consortium's programs showed little measurable improvement in school competence but did better with regard to educational decisions where families might plausibly have played a role.

- the fact that three of the five factors that seemed to augment the effects of the Consortium programs, the factors discussed above, reflected programs' effectiveness at reaching families and working with them.

- the fact that the Developmental Consortium found indications of program effects on familial aspirations for children. Lazar and Darlington (1982, p. 54) report:

    In brief, mothers whose children participated in early education programs were more satisfied with their children's school performance than were control mothers. For program children but not control children, mothers' aspirations for the children were higher than were the children's aspirations for themselves. Together with the trend for treatment mothers to have higher absolute aspirations for their children, this suggests that early education may have affected the familial context with respect to achievement-orientation.

- the fact that, over the course of the school years, families play an increasingly important role in facilitating children's academic achievement, at least until the 12th grade (Coleman, 1966; Smith, 1972).

THE NEW YORK STATE EXPERIMENTAL PREKINDERGARTEN PROGRAM

An on-line early intervention program based on a comprehensive philosophy has shown a similar pattern of short-term cognitive gains followed by broader effects in the later years. The New York State Experimental Prekindergarten Program was designed to serve children who, because of conditions in their homes or neighborhoods, might not be able to receive the maximum benefit from school. Participating schools had to provide (1) a developmentally oriented program designed to increase self-initiated and independent learning; (2) physical, mental, dental, and nutritional services; (3) referrals to social services; and (4) parent involvement through home visits, parent visits to the schools, parent training programs, participation in decision making, and employment (Irvine, Flint, Hick, Horan, and Kikuk, 1982; Campbell, 1987).

The year-by-year pattern of the New York findings shows trends that have by now become familiar: (1) relatively rapid gains on tests of problem solving and language; (2) relatively rapid subsequent loss of those gains; (3) some indications of benefit to the social skills and competence of the children—hard to interpret because of the weakness of tests in this area; and (4) indications of more practical benefits in the long term. By the third grade, fewer program graduates, as compared with waiting-list children, had repeated grades or been placed in special-education classes.

EARLY EDUCATION: THE POLICY QUESTIONS

We confront, in 1988, a rapidly developing set of political commitments to early care and education. *In principle,* support comes from several directions. The National Governors' Association (1986) has called for (1) kindergartening for all five-years-olds; (2) preschools made available to all at-risk four-year-olds, with additional places for as many three-year-olds as possible; (3) accreditation procedures for preschools; and (4) incentives to make preschools of high quality. Real, in-hand support is limited so far, and it must be borne in mind that preschooling in the United States has a long history of short-lived political victories (White and Buka, 1987).

In the short run, at least, what we are going to have are publicly sponsored preschools providing for some children at risk. Grubb (1987, Table 1) summarizes 18 recent state- or city-level initiatives in early education; almost all the programs he lists are targeted to disadvantaged children. He remarks (p. 14) that all of his listed initiatives are rather limited in scope and might well be regarded as pilot projects. Zigler (1987, p. 31) observes that almost all states that now provide school-sponsored programs for four-year-olds limit enrollment to low-income, handicapped, and, in some cases, non-English-speaking youngsters. He says, "There is a large body of evidence indicating that there is little if anything to be gained by exposing middle-class children to early education" (p. 32) and he concludes that "we can make the most effective use of limited funds by investing them in intervention programs that target three overlapping groups: (1) the economically disadvantaged child, (2) the handicapped child, and (3) the bilingual child" (pp. 32–33).

Nowadays, middle-class families are able to afford preschools for their children, while poorer families are not. Shanker (1987, p. 48) reviews evidence indicating that the preschool enrollment rate is 29 percent for families earning below $10,000 per year, 46 percent for families earning below $20,000, and 64 percent for families earning above $20,000. The enrollment rate for children of elementary school dropouts is 23 percent; for children of college graduates, 58 percent. Not all developmental psychologists would agree that preschooling is without effect for middle-class children (e.g., Fowler, 1986; Sigel and McGillicuddy-DeLisi, 1984; Sigel, 1987). William Fowler, a distinguished early educator, has long argued for preschooling for average and advantaged children. A comprehensive statement of his case is given in his recent two-volume *Potentials of Childhood* (Fowler, 1983). Fowler, who in his earlier writings was much interested in the early stimulation of intellectual potential, now argues that middle-class families need support in raising children. The traditional family practices that historically made the middle-class home a learning environment are weakening.

> Children must be guaranteed acquisition of the body of abstract and specialized knowledge and skills demanded by ever more complex technology, yet they cannot be assured of learning adequately without planning. The public school system, founded for just these reasons at an earlier historical phase of the rising technology, is testimony to this need. But children start school only at age 5 or 6, and their preschool years remain without any widely planned provisions for buttressing the outmoded, divergent, and collapsing folk traditions of socialization. It is not necessary to believe that a good early educational base is a panacea for the tangle of social and educational problems in contemporary industrial society to see its role in the developmental scheme of things. Nor need one advocate early formal schooling in order to stress that certain patterns of cognitive stimulation must be the right of every child during the early years as well as during the later years of development (Fowler, 1983, vol. 2, p. 1).

Let me, on the basis of these remarks, offer some comments about policy.

ABOUT COMPREHENSIVENESS OF INTERVENTION

Generally speaking, our contemporary data on child development, our vision of the child of the 1980s, leads us to think about early care and education in social terms and to see the school as one of many communities of socialization in which children live. If we are to reduce risks and help children to develop coping capacities, then we have to look beyond children's cognitive and social traits—to ask about children's relationship to families and peers, and about the family's ability to support the child's health and safety and development.

At first blush, schools are obvious, cost-effective places for a nationwide set of centers to provide early care and education for the child, together with support and training for the family. Sharon Kagan (1987) has pointed out the problems schools face when preschools within are used for nonacademic goals. Schools have a large, complicated, politically tricky agenda to begin with. Social tradition gives schools a stable and accepted place in the community; keeps the lines clear between education and other service institutions; and establishes a safe ground on which school people can operate with reasonable protection from groups with a variety of political axes to grind. Can schools, picking and choosing their way so carefully, tell people how to raise children?

We have substantial evidence showing that programs offering services to disadvantaged children have to reach beyond conventional professional boundaries if they are to be effective. Lisbeth Schorr's (1988) just-published book, *Within Our Reach,* identifies health-care, family-services, early-education, and public-school programs that have been effective with children at risk; a common feature of all Schorr's programs is that they cross boundary lines. Zigler (1987) notes that most of the existing reports of favorable preschool effects (a) show positive effects for disadvantaged children and (b) report programs that depart from conventional preschooling, since they deal with health, family, and social-services issues.

Can early childhood programs, situated in schools, deal with issues that go far beyond the schools' traditional turf—book learning, literacy and numeracy, the "basics"? Early educators have for some time sought to address "the whole child," and there is a long history of contention among early educators, school people, and parents about what the proper scope for early education programs should be (White and Buka, 1987). The fact that the struggle keeps coming up seems to show that it reflects some fundamental and recurrent dilemmas.

The dilemmas may not be acute. Perhaps we do not have to set about turning schools into mental health centers, settlement houses, or centers for family therapy. During the 1960s, by some process that we do not yet fully understand, we were able to use relatively narrow cognitive-developmental conceptions of children's needs to implement programs that were here and there successful but whose nature and effects transcended those conceptions. Perhaps it is possible to reconcile cognitively oriented programming with a comprehensive approach and processes of outreach and referral. Our data to date suggest that this is promising.

ABOUT RHETORIC VS. REALITY

Sooner or later, we are going to have to get our practices, our philosophies, and our politics together. If early education is to be made a matter of policy—to claim a share of tax dollars, to compete against other services for resources, to draw able people to commit their careers to it—then its methods and purposes will have to be discussed and defended in rational terms. Yet early education is not, and cannot be, an expert business to be articulated and planned for only by specialized scientific, technical, and political professionals.

We simply do not want to re-enter the theater of the 1960s, where public discussions for and against the possibility of IQ modification obscured the fact that no one concerned with the management of Head Start gave much credence to IQ modification as a desideratum or an issue. Other things being equal, if two-thirds of Head Start center directors were orienting their work toward social development, it might have been desirable if research and public discussion dealt with topics other than cognitive development.

We will have to find ways, in the 1990s, to mix the wisdom of practitioners with the wisdom that research on children's development and needs gives us and to find closer fits between the rhetoric and reality of programs for children.

ABOUT THE NEED TO EXPLORE PROCESS

To examine the effects of early care and education, we are going to have to look at children's social development and the development of children's conceptions of themselves. We will have to do studies along a longer time line, looking beyond short-term consequences and immediate outcomes. Rather than looking at preschools as places to build desirable cognitive and social traits in children, we are going to have to look at a child's transactions in school as something that initiates changing relationships among the child, family, friends, and the people of the school. New kinds of research programs, microdevelopmental studies rather than treatment-vs.-control group comparisons, will be needed to explore the subtle and complex consequences of program participation in children's lives.

ABOUT THE DIFFERENCES BETWEEN
PRESCHOOL AND SCHOOL-AGED CHILDREN

The 200-year-old history of early education shows a recurrent conflict between proponents of early education and professional educators. The conflict emerged during the development of Rogert Owens' infant schools in eighteenth-century England, the growth of the Froebelian kindergarten in the United States near the turn of this century, and (with a different set of political actors and issues) the growth of the kindergarten in late nineteenth-century England. A preschool movement gets started and grows. The public schools move toward preschooling, incorporating it, expanding its use, generally turning toward poorer and more disadvantaged children. The preschool movement withers. The life and sparkle go out of it, in part because schools make it more pedantic and didactic and in part because the schools are able to offer a lean implementation—teacher-pupil ratios that make it impossible to implement programs such as Owens' or Froebel's in any kind of adequate way. The preschooling movement levels off or withers away. The early education does not seem as attractive as it once did, or it seems "confused" (White and Buka, 1987).

Some of the conflict emerges from the fact that the political surge of the movement toward early education meets cost barriers. Some of it has to do with a basic issue: educators and preschool people deal with children at different levels, with different capacities and needs. They address children differently because they have to. If schools bring their conventional ways of doing business down to the preschool level, many of the small children will be poorly served. In part because they are aware of their history, in part because they sense the elements of the problem, early educators are wary of alliances with the public schools. Schools, feeling friendly toward early education and seeking to make a connection with it, tend to underestimate the issue. (Educators often do not regard preschool people as fully professional, and they have a tendency to take the warm, playlike atmosphere of preschools and the "whole child" philosophy of preschoolers as symptomatic of goodhearted amateurism.)

There is substantial evidence from developmental psychology indicating that the differences in philosophy between preschool people and school people reflect real differences in children. There are massive changes in children between five and seven years of age. Theorists in developmental psychology, disagreeing on what they regard as the essence of higher human mental process, nevertheless converge on the argument that whatever that essence is, it emerges or is significantly augmented in the five-to-seven age range. A wide variety of research material shows transitions and changes in this age range (White, 1965, 1970; White and Pillemer, 1979).

Western traditions of diverse kinds have placed age seven as an age of reason in child development. Catholic Canon Law says that children first know right from wrong at age seven. So children can have first communion and first confession at that age. The English Common Law traditionally has held that children first know right from wrong at age seven; under that code, children could be tried for a crime and be found guilty at that age.

The diverse changes in children at this time might reflect the fact that children begin schooling in Western society at age five or six. However, there is evidence that in non-Western, tribal societies, the practices of many cultures assign new roles and responsibilities to children at this time. Children are said to have "minds," to be able to learn and remember. They are regarded as sexual; there are new demands for modesty, and controls are sometimes placed on children's opportunity to see or engage in sexual behavior. Very often, societies begin serious training in the norms and rules of proper behavior at this time. Very often, there is a beginning of apprenticeship for serious adult work; boys go off to be with men who engage in herding, hunting, or farming, while girls go off to be with women and begin to learn their expected activities in the home and village (Rogoff, Sellars, Pirotta, Fox, and White, 1975).

We have evidence indicating that children need different training environments in the preschool and early school years, and the remarkably persistent tensions between preschool people and school people probably reflect that fact. It may be useful to say that the data show the difference in children is real. It is not an illusion of romantic, warmhearted preschoolers. Younger children will not respond well to simple downward extensions of good professional teaching practices in the first and second grades.

To help schools and early educators as they attempt to establish distinctive and appropriate environments for younger and older children, we need to explore and articulate the differences in learning environments best suited to preschoolers vs. schoolchildren. There is a wealth of research material suggesting what the differences might be; this can and should be fruitfully combined with the clinical wisdom of sophisticated teachers who have worked in the two settings.

REFERENCES

Barker, R.G., and H.F. Wright. *Midwest and Its Children: The Psychological Ecology of an American Town.* Evanston, Ill.: Row, Peterson, 1954.

Campbell, B.D. "From National Debate to National Responsibility." In *Early Schooling: The National Debate,* edited by S. L. Kagan and E. F. Zigler. New Haven: Yale University Press (1987): 65–82.

Clarke, A. D. B., and A. M. Clarke. " 'Sleeper Effects' in Development: Fact or Artifact?" *Developmental Review* 1 (1981): 344–360.

Coleman, J. *Equality of Educational Opportunity.* Washington, D.C.: U.S. Government Printing Office, 1966.

Consortium for Longitudinal Studies. *As the Twig Is Bent: Lasting Effects of Preschool Programs.* Hillsdale, N.J.: Lawrence Erlbaum Associates, 1983.

Darlington, R.B., J. M. Royce, A.S. Snipper, H. W. Murray, and I. Lazar. "Preschool Programs and Later School Competence of Children from Low-Income Families." *Science* 208 (1980): 202–204.

DeVries, R., with L. Kohlberg. *Programs of Early Education: The Constructivist View.* New York: Longman, 1987.

Douglas, J. W. B. "Early Hospital Admissions and Later Disturbances of Behavior and Learning." *Developmental Medicine and Child Neurology* 17 (1975): 456–480.

Dunn, J., and D. Kendrick. "Studying Temperament and Parent-Child Interaction: Comparison of Interview and Direct Observation." *Developmental Medicine and Child Neurology* 4 (1980a): 484–496.

Dunn, J., and D. Kendrick. "The Arrival of a Sibling: Changes in Patterns of Interaction Between Mother and First-Born Child." *Journal of Child Psychology and Psychiatry* 21 (1980b): 119–132.

Dunn, J., C. Kendrick, and R. McNamee. "The Reaction of First-Born Children to the Birth of a Sibling: Mothers' Reports." *Journal of Child Psychology and Psychiatry* 22 (1981): 1–18.

Fowler, W. *Potentials of Childhood.* Lexington, Mass.: Lexington Books, 1983.

Fowler, W. "Early Experiences of Great Men and Women Mathematicians." In *Early Experience and the Development of Competence* (New Directions for Child Development, No. 32), edited by W. Fowler, 87–109. San Francisco: Jossey-Bass, 1986.

Garmezy, N. "Stresses of Childhood." In *Stress, Coping, and Development in Childen,* 43–84. New York: McGraw-Hill, 1983.

Grubb, W. N. *Young Children Face the States: Issues and Options for Early Childhood Programs.* U.S. Department of Education: Center for Policy Research in Education, 1987.

Hetherington, E. M., M. Cox, and R. Cox. "The Aftermath of Divorce." In *Mother-Child Relations,* edited by J. H. Stevens, Jr., and M. Mathews. Washington, D.C.: National Association for the Education of Young Children, 1978.

Hetherington, E. M., M. Cox, and R. Cox. "Play and Social Interaction in Children Following Divorce." *Journal of Social Issues* 35 (1979a): 26–49.

Hetherington, E.M., M. Cox, and R. Cox. "Family Interaction and the Social, Emotional and Cognitive Development of Children Following Divorce." In *The Family: Setting Priorities,* edited by V. Vaughn and T. Brazelton. New York: Science and Medicine, 1979b.

Hohmann, M., B. Banet, and D. P. Weikart. *Young Children in Action: A Manual for Preschool Educators.* Ypsilanti, Mich.: The High/Scope Press, 1979.

Holmes, T. H., and R. H. Rahe. "The Social Readjustment Rating Scale." *Journal of Psychosomatic Research* 11 (1967): 213–218.

Humphrey, J. H. (ed.) *Stress in Childhood.* New York: AMS Press, 1984.

Irvine, D. J., D. L. Flint, T. L. Hick, M. D. Horan, and S. E. Kikuk. *Evaluation of the New York State Experimental Preschool Program: Final Report.* Albany: State Education Department, 1982.

Kagan, S. L. "Early Schooling: On What Grounds?" In *Early Schooling: The National Debate,* edited by S. L. Kagan and E. F. Zigler, 3–23. New Haven: Yale University Press, 1987.

Kirschner Associates. *A National Survey of the Impacts of Head Start Centers on Community Institutions.* Washington, D.C.: Office of Economic Opportunity (ED045195), 1970.

Lambert, W. E. "Effects of Bilingualism on the Individual." In *Bilingualism: Psychological, Social, and Educational Implications,* edited by P.A. Hornby, 15–28. New York: Academic Press, 1977.

Lazar, I., and R. Darlington. "Lasting Effects of Early Education: A Report from the Consortium for Longitudinal Studies." In *Monographs of the Society for Research in Child Development* 47, Serial No. 195 (1982).

Moore, T. "Stress in Normal Childhood." In *Society, Stress, and Disease: Childhood and Adolescence* (volume 2), edited by L. Levi. London: Oxford University Press, 1975.

Murphy, L. B. *The Widening World of Childhood: Paths Toward Mastery.* New York: Basic Books, 1962.

National Governors' Association. *Time for Results: The Governors' 1991 Report on Education.* Washington, D.C.: National Governors' Association, 1986.

Quinton, D., and M. Rutter. "Early Hospital Admissions and Later Disturbances of Behaviour: An Attempted Replication of Douglas' Findings." *Developmental Medicine and Child Neurology* 18 (1976): 447–459.

Richmond, J. B., D. J. Stipek, and E. Zigler. "A Decade of Head Start." In *Project Head Start: A Legacy of the War on Poverty,* edited by E. Zigler and J. Valentine, 135–151. New York: The Free Press, 1979.

Rogoff, B., M. Sellers, S. Pirotta, N. Fox, and S. H. White. "Age of Assignment of Roles and Responsibilities to Children: A Cross-Cultural Survey." *Human Development* 18 (1975): 353–369.

Royce, J. M., R. B. Darlington, and H. W. Murray. "Pooled Analyses: Findings Across Studies." In Consortium for Longitudinal Studies: *As the Twig Is Bent: Lasting Effects of Preschool Programs,* 411–459. Hillsdale, N.J.: Lawrence Erlbaum Associates, 1983.

Rutter, M. "Parent-Child Separation: Psychological Effects on the Children." *Journal of Child Psychology and Psychiatry* 12 (1971): 233–260.

Rutter, M. "Maternal Deprivation: New Findings, New Concepts, New Approaches." *Child Development* 50 (1979): 283–305.

Rutter, M. *Changing Youth in a Changing Society: Patterns of Adolescent Development and Disorder.* Cambridge, Mass.: Harvard University Press, 1980.

Rutter, M. *Maternal Deprivation Reassessed* (2d ed.). Harmondsworth: Penguin, 1981.

Rutter, M. "Epidemiological-Longitudinal Approaches to the Study of Development." In *The Concept of Development: Minnesota Symposia on Child Psychology* (vol. 15), edited by W. A. Collins. Hillsdale, N.J.: Lawrence Erlbaum Associates, 1982.

Rutter, M., O. Chadwick, D. Shaffer. "Head Injury." In *Developmental Neuropsychiatry,* edited by M. Rutter. New York: The Guilford Press, 1983.

Rutter, M., and H. Giller. *Juvenile Delinquency: Trends and Perspectives.* New York: Penguin, 1983.

Schorr, L. B., with D. Schorr. *Within Our Reach: Breaking the Cycle of Disadvantage.* New York: Doubleday, 1988.

Seitz, V. "Intervention and Sleeper Effects: A Reply to Clarke and Clarke." *Developmental Review* 1 (1981): 361–373.

Shanker, A. "The Case for Public School Sponsorship of Early Childhood Education Programs Revisited." In *Early Schooling: The National Debate,* edited by S. L. Kagan and E. F. Zigler, 45–64. New Haven: Yale University Press, 1987.

Sigel, I. E. "Early Childhood Education: Developmental Enhancement or Developmental Acceleration?" In *Early Schooling: The National Debate,* edited by S. L. Kagan and E. F. Zigler, 129–150. New Haven: Yale University Press, 1987.

Sigel, I. E,, and A. V. McGillicuddy-DeLisi. "Parents as Teachers of Their Children: A Distance Behavior Model." In *The Development of Oral and Written Language in Social Contexts,* edited by A. D. Pellegrini and T. D. Yawkey, 71–92. Norwood, N.J.: Ablex Publishing, 1984.

Smith, M. "Equality of Educational Opportunity: The Basic Findings Reconsidered." In *On Equality of Educational Opportunity: Papers Deriving from the Harvard University Faculty Seminar on the Coleman Report,* edited by F. Mosteller and D. P. Moynihan, 230–342. New York: Random House, 1972.

Steiner, G. Y. *The Children's Cause.* Washington, D.C.: The Brookings Institution, 1976.

Vernon, D. T. A., J. M. Foley, R. R. Sipowicz, and J. L. Schulman. *The Psychological Responses of Children to Hospitalization and Illness.* Springfield, Ill.: Charles C. Thomas, 1965.

Wallerstein, J. S. "Children of Divorce." In *Stress, Coping, and Development in Children,* edited by N. Garmezy and M. Rutter, 265–302. New York: McGraw-Hill, 1983.

Wallerstein, J., and J. B. Kelly. *Surviving Breakup: How Children and Parents Cope with Divorce.* New York: Basic Books, 1980.

Weikart, D. P. *Preschool Intervention: Preliminary Results of the Perry Preschool Project.* Ann Arbor, Mich.: Campus Publishers, 1967.

White, S. H. "Some General Outlines of the Matrix of Developmental Changes Between Five and Seven Years." *Bulletin of the Orton Society* 20 (1970): 41–57.

White, S. H. "Evidence for a Hierarchical Arrangement of Learning Processes." *Advances in Child Behavior and Development* 2 (1965): 187–220.

White, S. H. "Cognitive Competence and Performance in Everyday Environments." *Bulletin of the Orton Society* 30 (1980): 29–45.

White, S. H., and S. Buka. "Early Education: Programs, Traditions, and Policies." *Review of Research in Education* 14 (1987): 43–91.

White, S. H., M. C. Day, P. A. Freeman, S. A. Hantman, and K. P. Messenger. *Federal Programs for Young Children: Review and Recommendations.* Washington, D.C.: U.S. Government Printing Office, 1972.

White, S. H., and D. B. Pillemer. "Childhood Amnesia and the Development of a Socially Accessible Memory System." In *Functional Disorders of Memory,* edited by J. F. Kihlstrom and F. J. Evans, 29–73. Hillsdale, N.J.: Lawrence Erlbaum Associates, 1979.

White, S. H., and A. W. Siegel. "Cognitive Development in Time and Space." In *Everyday Cognition: Its Development in Social Context,* edited by B. Rogoff and J. Lave, 238–277. Cambridge, Mass.: Harvard University Press, 1984.

Zigler, E. "Formal Schooling for Four-Year-Olds? No." In *Early Schooling: The National Debate,* edited by S. L. Kagan and E. F. Zigler, 27–44. New Haven: Yale University Press, 1987.

Zigler, E., and J. Valentine (eds.). *Project Head Start: A Legacy of the War on Poverty.* New York: The Free Press, 1979.

NUTRITION

A Vital Ingredient in Child Development and Educational Success

Johanna Dwyer, D.Sc., R.D.

PROFESSOR OF MEDICINE,
TUFTS UNIVERSITY SCHOOL OF MEDICINE AND
DIRECTOR, FRANCES STERN NUTRITION CENTER,
NEW ENGLAND MEDICAL CENTER HOSPITAL, BOSTON

INTRODUCTION

Nutrition is a vital ingredient of educational success. This paper discusses the role of nutrition in the development of preschool and school-age children. It reviews definitions of malnutrition and of "at-risk" status and discusses their causes. It raises critical questions involving the associations between nutrition and educational success and provides responses. It discusses questions and challenges facing educators today, especially in the area of early childhood and parenting education, and it outlines steps to enhance the development of preschool children by nutritional and related educational means. Finally, it proposes practical recommendations for bettering school-based efforts.

DEFINITIONS

Several terms which are commonly used by educators and nutritionists deserve definition.

Malnutrition is an abnormal state caused by either the lack or excess of one or more essential nutrients which the body is unable to make and which must be obtained in food. Table 1 summarizes the major types of malnutrition. Several well-known types of malnutrition, often collectively referred to as poverty-related malnutrition, are common among people who do not get enough to eat because of poverty and food scarcity. These forms of malnutrition include *starvation,* or not getting enough of anything to eat, which is sometimes seen in children who are neglected and fail to thrive or in adolescents who suffer from anorexia nervosa; *undernutrition,* or simply not getting enough food energy or calories, which can be observed in someone on a weight-reducing diet; and *deficiencies* of vitamins and minerals such as iron, fluoride, or vitamin D. Poverty-related malnutrition has long been apparent to educators. In response to it, educators in the 1800s led the drive for school meals and for the use of government funds to assist in building up their pupils' nutritional status so that they would be in better shape to learn.

TABLE 1

Types of Malnutrition

Poverty and Disease-Related Malnutrition	*Malnutrition of Affluence*
Starvation	Overnutrition
Undernutrition	Imbalances and Excesses
Deficiencies of Vitamins and Minerals	Toxicities

Undernutrition, starvation, and deficiencies of vitamins and minerals are often associated with disease and handicapping conditions. In these instances malnutrition occurs as a result of the disease, not the diet, although dietary lacks may be secondarily involved because of reduced appetite. For example, a child afflicted with cerebral palsy, a chronic low-grade fever, a kidney infection, or one of the childhood cancers might suffer from disease-related malnutrition in spite of abundant food in his or her environment.

Other forms of malnutrition, sometimes referred to as the malnutritions of affluence, involve excesses rather than shortfalls of intake. They include *overnutrition,* which results when calorie intake exceeds energy needs; *imbalances* such as diets that have too much fat, saturated fat, cholesterol, sugar, and sodium or too little starch and fiber; and *toxicities,* or ingestions in such excessive amounts that poisoning results, as when an individual overindulges in alcohol, suffers from lead poisoning, or greatly overdoses on vitamins A and D.

Hunger, or not getting enough to eat of one's usual or desired diet, is immediately relieved by the provision of food. Sometimes hunger refers only to unpleasant physiological sensations caused by actual deprivation of foods, which can be relieved by providing any food. In other contexts hunger describes psychological preferences and a scarcity of desirable food. Hunger is sometimes confused with starvation, which is a chronic condition, evident in changes in bodily tissues, due to persistent undernutrition.

What is the difference between hunger and malnutrition? Hunger tends to be defined solely in psychological or economic terms, while malnutrition is defined in both physiological and clinical terms. This leads to confusion in discussions between those in various disciplines who are attempting to define and intervene in remediating the problems. People who are truly starving show outright clinical signs and symptoms of emaciation, while those who are hungry may not.

Most arguments among policymakers about the prevalence of malnutrition revolve around which definition to use, the number of people who are hungry, and what government should do about it (Citizens' Commission on Hunger in New England, 1984; President's Task Force on Food Assistance, 1984; Brown and Allen, 1988; Nersesian, 1988). There is more consensus among experts about the number of people who are clinically malnourished in the United States than there is about the number who are hungry, since national survey data are more readily available on malnutrition than on hunger, and since malnutrition is easier to measure objectively by height, weight, physical examinations, and blood tests (Dwyer, 1984; National Food Consumption Survey, 1985; Peterkin and Rizek, 1984; Swann, 1983). Because hunger is more elusive to define, the number of individuals subsisting below the poverty line (e.g., the maximum income permitted to qualify for a means-tested federal program) is often taken as an indicator of the number of people who are hungry. Whether in fact such individuals should be regarded as hungry and what percent regard themselves as hungry remains obscure.

CAUSES AND PREVALENCE OF MALNUTRITION

The causes of malnutrition are listed in Table 2. Some are related to the environment inside or outside the family, others to inappropriate or inadequate child care, and still others to temporary or more lasting genetic or acquired disease or disability. Some of the feeding, eating, and health problems that cause malnutrition can be relatively minor so that overt malnutrition may become apparent only after weeks or months.

Any or all of the various types of malnutrition can arise from any one or a combination of these causes, and the actual cause is not always immediately apparent. Thus, it is important to identify, root out, and eliminate or neutralize the specific causes of malnutrition in each individual case.

How common are the various types of malnutrition? Poverty-related malnutrition remains a problem among some children and their families today, although it is on the downswing compared to several decades ago. The causes of these dietary inadequacies are complex but usually include lack of money for food. Other problems often complicate the situation, such as problems in childrearing and home management, behavior, emotional and learning difficulties, lack of general health education, lack of information and age-specific anticipatory guidance, and the presence of disease.

Children at risk for poverty-related malnutrition today include the homeless living in hotels and shelters and children in families whose incomes are below the poverty line, especially racial and ethnic-minority-group children with physical, emotional, or mental health problems. Children whose parents are mentally retarded or who lack education, who have emotional problems, or who reside in states or areas with very poor welfare benefits are also at high risk.

The face of malnutrition has changed among these children in poverty. In addition to the problems of dietary inadequacy, they often suffer from problems of affluence, including obesity, dietary imbalances, and toxicities, including lead poisoning. Thus, the poor living in affluent societies are afflicted not only with the ills associated with dietary inadequacy but also with diseases of dietary excess.

The malnutritions of affluence are also on the rise in the large economically

TABLE 2

Causes of Nutrition-Related Problems of Preschool Children

Environmental: Inadequate physical, cultural, or community environment owing to lack of resources or poor use of resources at home, school, preschool, or other places in which child spends a significant part of his or her time.

Childrearing and Home Management: Poor parental management of food, money, clothing, or household goods and schedules, or inadequate provision for child care.

Behavioral, Emotional, and Learning Problems: Behavioral and emotional problems associated with food, mental retardation, or other factors altering food intake or practices; presence of parent with alcohol or drug problems which affect child emotionally and influence his or her eating behavior.

Lack of General Health Information or Education: No source of referral for health or nutrition information, lack of age-specific anticipatory guidance in nutrition and other areas for parents, lack of parental and child motivation for carrying out preventive and health-promotion measures.

Disordered or Inadequate Growth and Development: No anticipatory guidance and supportive counseling appropriate to age, or disregard of such advice if offered.

Temporary Deviations in Growth and Development: Inadequate or poor psychological development, inappropriate or inadequate food intake, short-term transient illnesses or conditions such as acute illness, surgery, or disruption of home and foodways due to family disruption.

Long-Term Illnesses with Special Developmental and Health Problems: Potential handicapping problems due to neurologic, neurosensory, muscular or orthopedic difficulties; or mental retardation; chronic illnesses of the gastrointestinal tract, kidney, heart, immune system; and other conditions, such as inborn errors of metabolism, allergies, dental caries, anemias, obesity.

Multiple and Involved Problems Involving One or More of Above
Source: Adapted from U.S. Department of Health, Education, and Welfare: *Nutrition Problem Classification for Children and Youth.* Public Health Service, Health Services Administration, Bureau of Community Health Services, Rockville, MD. DHEW Publication No. (HSA) 77-5201, 1977.

comfortable middle class, even in preschool and school-age children. Children of all social classes suffer from a rising prevalence of overnutrition and obesity (Dietz and Gortmaker, 1985), dietary imbalances, and excesses which increase the risks of chronic degenerative diseases (Strong and Dennison, 1988; Dwyer, 1986). All social classes are also afflicted with an unsettlingly high prevalence of alcohol abuse in adolescence.

Disease-related malnutrition in children is on the decline due to better health education, increased emphasis on anticipatory guidance, earlier recognition, prevention, and better medical means of treating many disorders. Knowledge of age-appropriate anticipatory guidance in nutrition and health is also improving so that temporary deviations in growth and development are recognized and dealt with sooner. Nutritional difficulties involving long-term illnesses, handi-capping conditions, and multiple interrelated problems are probably on the rise, however. More children with such difficulties are surviving today because of these same medical advances. In a sense, we pay a price for our medical triumphs when nutritional problems arise from our success in keeping alive some children who formerly died prematurely from birth defects, handicapping conditions, or chronic degenerative and other diseases in childhood such as Down Syndrome, cystic fibrosis, cerebral palsy, spina bifida, respiratory depen-dence, and AIDS. Among those with such special long-term developmental and health needs, disease-related nutrition problems and special dietary needs are still common. As more and more of these handicapped children are main-streamed and enrolled in regular rather than special schools, educators must increasingly deal with their needs.

Like the educator who regards children who are unlikely to graduate from high school as being educationally at risk (Council of Chief State School Officers, 1987), the nutritionist considers children to be nutritionally at risk when they already suffer from or have a high probability of developing one or more of the types of malnutrition or feeding problems mentioned previously. The "at-risk" concept is useful in nutrition as well as in education since it allows us to intervene before nutritional and health status is seriously affected.

NUTRITIONAL NEEDS OF PRESCHOOL CHILDREN

Schools are increasingly required to deal with all the various forms of malnutrition in children, and the children are at younger and younger ages. No single institution in society, including parents, can do this alone. In order to meet the nutritional needs of preschool children, all people who are responsible for children must work together to:

- provide adequate food, thus avoiding poverty-related malnutrition, includ-ing starvation, undernutrition, and nutrient deficiencies;
- ensure that parents and other caretakers use appropriate nutrition infor-mation and education so that children are fed and will choose to eat diets that promote health and avoid caloric overnutrition, nutrient imbalances, and toxicities;
- cope with the special nutritional needs of children who have handicapping conditions and other special developmental or long-term health needs to the extent that is possible in the educational setting; and
- ensure that the physical, sociocultural, and emotional aspects of the

feeding environment foster good nutrition. Table 3 presents some ways to enhance the nutrition of preschool children.

TABLE 3
Steps to Enhance
the Nutrition of Preschool Children

1. Ensure that levels of physical activity and rest are sufficient to maintain normal growth and development and a good appetite.
2. Provide nutritious foods in the home and other settings in which the child eats.
3. Teach the child to choose and eat a nutritious diet by emphasizing nutrition in meal planning.
4. Help the child to distinguish between promotional messages and reliable sources of guidance on food choices.
5. Foster appropriate eating behaviors by providing suitable role models and eating experiences.
6. Handle struggles over food to avoid the development of feeding problems.
7. Feed and hydrate children appropriately during illness.
8. Teach the child to avoid the mouthing or eating of nonfood substances (lead paint, pills, dirt, lotions, and chemical solutions, etc.).

CRITICAL QUESTIONS ABOUT FOOD, NUTRITION, AND LEARNING

Nutritionally and educationally at-risk children are often, but not always, one and the same individuals.

Doubly high-risk children include those from poor and otherwise socioeconomically disadvantaged families, especially when this risk occurs along with ethnic or racial minority status and discrimination, poor parental mental or physical health, or severe family pathology. Also, children who have special long-term developmental and health needs due to disease or handicaps are often educationally as well as nutritionally at risk. Such children include those who were born extremely premature, or small for full-term babies; those who suffer from serious hereditary or acquired disease; and the children of drug addicts, alcoholics, the mentally ill, the mentally retarded, and others who are unable or unwilling to nourish or nurture their children properly.

The overlap between nutritional and educational high risk, though not necessarily causal, must be dealt with if learning is to be optimized.

THE EFFECTS OF NUTRITION ON LEARNING AND SCHOOL PERFORMANCE

Many factors contribute to a suitable environment for satisfactory learning and school performance. Among these are genetics, social factors such as family and school stimulation, and other environmental influences, including the state of nutrition and health (Lazar, 1982). A child's nutritional status can affect physical growth and maturation. Lack of proper food can result in deprivation and altered social behavior, including decreased motivation and performance, even when the individual has the capacity to complete the task.

School performance depends not only on cognitive abilities such as memory and the ability to learn categories, to process and structure information, to solve problems, to acquire and use language, to think abstractly, and to learn and react to social and environmental cues (Klein, Habicht, and Yarbrough, 1973), but also on motivation to actually accomplish tasks (Pollitt, 1982). Even if intellectual ability is present, such factors as passivity, apathy, shortened attention span, poor short-term memory, failure to learn repetitive tasks quickly, and lags in the development of the ability to integrate information available from the different senses can still lead to poor achievement. Thus, if a child's state of nutrition and other health-related factors affect either his primary learning ability or those processes associated with cognitive function, school performance may be affected.

The effects of poor nutrition on learning and performance are difficult to demonstrate for several reasons. First, undernutrition and malnutrition usually exist in combination with poverty and other social, environmental, or genetic conditions which are less than ideal, especially in affluent countries such as the United States. When several factors which adversely affect health are present together, their effects may be synergistic and greater than they would be if each were present alone. The presence of multiple factors which may affect school performance in the same individual makes it difficult to make cause-and-effect statements about the influence of any one factor, such as nutrition. Of course, ethical considerations make it impossible to perform deprivation studies in children (Klein, Habicht, and Yarbrough, 1973).

Second, we know that the effects of malnutrition, and especially the effects of undernutrition, are powerfully related to non-nutritional experiences and events. Malnutrition changes children's reactions to others, their priorities for attention, and the like. In a child who is already suffering from multiple disadvantages, this may be enough to tip the balance away from learning.

Third, the effect of nutritional problems on learning and school performance depends partly on the severity of the problems. The scientific literature is abundant on the effects of acute and severe malnutrition and on infantile malnutrition. Much less is available, however, on preschool or school-age children who are afflicted with mild or moderate forms of malnutrition.

It is well known that when undernutrition is severe, behavior worsens. Severely undernourished or starved infants and children usually do poorly on achievement and other psychological tests during their illnesses compared to well-nourished children. Children who have experienced long and severe episodes of undernutrition, particularly if these episodes occurred before the age of two, exhibit reduced levels of intellectual development and school performance several years later (Pollitt and Thomson, 1977).

Such children differ from better-nourished children not only in their previous nutrition but also in their greater likelihood to have experienced other adverse social and environmental problems which also affect mental development. That is, undernutrition is only one of the many factors which contribute to their poor school performance (Pollitt and Thomson, 1977: Richardson, Birch, Grabie, and Yoder, 1972).

In contrast to the extensive study of the clear, dramatic effects of acute, severe undernutrition on performance, little work has been done on mild or moderate forms of undernutrition of the type more commonly observed in this country. Because mild and moderate malnutrition are extremely prevalent in developing countries and are also present among some of the poor in highly industrialized countries, the largest studies on malnutrition and intellectual development have been done in those settings. This research suggests that mild and moderate malnutrition do not permanently impair basic intellectual capacity and the ability to learn. When effects of mild to moderate malnutrition are observed, they involve temporary impairments such as altered responsiveness, motivation, and emotionality, giving rise to performance problems such as apathy, reduced curiosity, inability to attend to and use complex inputs, and lack of persistence. All of these factors, although not necessarily cognitive, are likely to influence school performance. Moreover, reversibility and remediation of the deficits is possible if nutrition and other factors in the child's environment can be altered to foster learning.

Children in this country who suffer from mild to moderate malnutrition often live in social and physical environments with other limitations that are also associated with poor school performance. The result is a combined negative effect which is more detrimental to intellectual function than the sum of the individual effects. Improvements in a child's diet alone, without enriching the child's psychological and social environment at the same time, are likely to lead to only small changes in behavior or school performance. When dietary and intellectual enrichment occur together, larger improvements are evident. The earlier these interventions start, the longer they continue; and the broader the range of factors which are included in the interventions, the larger are their impacts.

A fourth reason the association among nutritional status, learning, and school performance is so difficult to demonstrate is that the types of tests employed to study behavior may be inappropriate. Studies of malnutrition and learning have concentrated excessively on cognitive performance, to the detriment of the exploration of noncognitive variables. Intelligence tests measure only a relatively narrow range of cognitive skills such as verbal, quantitative, and abstract reasoning abilities. Expert opinion at present is that the effects of malnutrition are most evident in noncognitive rather than in cognitive areas. Thus, characteristics that are difficult to measure, such as determination, motivation, ability to pay attention, social awareness, intuition, and creativity, may be equally important but are rarely assessed. Even within the cognitive domain, most exploration has used rather crude measures. Health, including nutritional status, mood, and attitudes, may affect learning and scores on such cognitive tests.

Fifth, good nutrition contributes in a special way to physical health, and its lack may have other effects, such as more illnesses and more school absences, which are not yet well documented. Whether nutrition is especially critical and unique among the other factors involved in poor achievement is more controversial. Current opinion is that intellectual achievement depends on having enough positive factors in the environment to outweigh negative factors (Dobbing, 1984). Thus, any one disadvantage, such as undernutrition, can be compensated for by an overwhelming number of advantages (Dobbing, 1984). Indeed, there is good evidence that infants who survive very severe malnutrition during the vulnerable period in early infancy, but who are otherwise subjected to a highly advantaged and enriched environment, do well on intelligence tests and in school performance (Lloyd, Still, 1976; Winick, Meyer, and Harris, 1975; Mylian, Mayer, and Winick, 1977). Nevertheless, owing to the clustering of adverse circumstances, such cases are the exception rather than the rule in day-to-day life.

In summary, food is an important part of a suitable environment for learning and is an absolute prerequisite for learning. Without such an environment, even the most intellectually able child whose learning processes are not impeded by any malnutrition-related dysfunctions will fail to learn. At the same time, food is insufficient by itself to overcome cognitive deficits in children who have histories of malnutrition. Curriculum and teaching methods are likely to be as important as nutritional effects (Ketcham, 1968), but the sources of funding are different and not likely to be transferable. Therefore, advocacy efforts should be activated to ensure that all the requisites as well as food are present.

MAGNITUDE OF THE EFFECTS OF MALNUTRITION ON EDUCATIONAL AT-RISK STATUS

The effects of malnutrition vary depending on how severe the undernutrition or malnutrition is, how long it was present, how long ago it occurred, and how unfavorable the larger social and physical environments are. The effects on performance are most severe when not only malnutrition but poor social and physical environmental circumstances are all present together. Severity of the effects of malnutrition and other deficits varies from one situation to another. For example, among low-income Colombian children, poor present nutritional status accounted for nearly one-third of the differences in performance found between malnourished and better-nourished preschool children, while social factors explained only about one-fifth of the differences (Weaber et al., 1981). In contrast, among Jamaican primary-school children, who had suffered from severe bouts of undernutrition in infancy, only five percent of the performance differences between them and children who had not been malnourished were due to poor nutritional status at present, while nearly one-third of the differences were explained by social factors (Richardson, Birch, Grabie, and Yoder, 1972). Among Korean children who were adopted into American homes with highly favorable social and physical environments, intelligence and school achievement were satisfactory even among those who had suffered severe malnutrition in later infancy (Winick, Meyer, and Harris, 1975; Mylian, Mayer, and Winick, 1977). From a practical standpoint, improvements in school performance are likely to be large enough to be meaningful only when dietary change is accompanied by enrichment of the child's psychological and social environment as well.

EFFECTS OF ABSENCE OF
SCHOOL MEALS ON BEHAVIOR

Studies of the effects of the absence of school meals on behavior are usually conducted in primary or secondary schools, but some studies of younger children exist (Keister, 1950). They support the commonly held opinion that the absence of school meals produces negative effects on behavior and school performance.

From the scientific standpoint, most of the studies are plagued with serious problems (Rapoport and Kruesi, 1983). Few are blind, so that both teachers and examiners know who ate and who did not eat the meals, which introduces bias. The very fact that a study is being done often influences behavior for the better. Effects of some meals, such as breakfast, are longer lasting than the effects of other meals. And effects seem to be largest in children whose habitual dietary intake patterns are disrupted. Thus, occasional omission of breakfast may have more deleterious effects than habitual omissions in an otherwise adequate diet, since it disrupts the child's usual routine and creates an unaccustomed nutritional stress.

The tests used to measure effects also influence outcomes. Some measures of performance, such as accuracy of responses in problem solving, decline sometimes, but not always. Other abilities, such as short-term memory, improve sometimes (Pollitt, Leibel, and Greenfield, 1981; Conners, et al., 1982; Dickie and Bender, 1982). Another shortcoming of the existing studies is that combinations of missing more than one meal each day, such as both breakfast and lunch, have rarely been studied. It is reasonable to conclude that when two of three meals daily are missed, the effects on performance may be profound (Pollitt, Gersovitz, and Gargiulo, 1978). Therefore, while the data are rather weak, the effects of the absence of school meals appear to be negative not only on immediate performance but also over the longer term.

The effects of the absence of school meals are generally negative on dietary intakes since school meals are rich in the protective vitamins, minerals, and proteins which are vital in high-quality diets. Children do not necessarily make up for missed meals by increasing their intakes at other times of day. Neither do the foods they bring to school contribute to intakes of vitamins and minerals as much as the equivalent school meals would (Parkin, 1982; Nelson and Paul, 1983). Also, the nutrients that are provided by school meals are not only those already in abundance in children's diets but also those problem nutrients for which intakes are low.

EFFECTS OF IRON-DEFICIENCY ANEMIA ON SCHOOL PERFORMANCE

Small and rather subtle differences in behavior and learning ability do appear to be present in most of the studies of iron deficiency. However, there are no convincing data to suggest permanent neurological damage resulting from iron deficiency, nor are the effects on intelligence sizable, from giving iron, as measured by standard IQ tests. Nevertheless, selected behaviors such as attentiveness, irritability, and persistence are decreased, and the extent of these effects depends on the degree of deficiency (Read, 1975).

Iron-deficient infants and children are usually described by physicians and parents as being irritable and lacking interest in their surroundings (Oski and McMillan, 1982). Treatment of very severe iron-deficiency anemia reverses irritability, anorexia, and vomiting even before hemoglobin levels have returned to normal (Oski and Honig, 1978). These observations have stimulated research to determine whether such relationships between iron intakes and performance are causal (Pollitt, Haas, and Levitsky, 1989).

Fortunately, few infants and children in this country suffer from severe iron-deficiency anemia (Dallman, 1986). Thus the most relevant research question for Americans is whether mild iron-deficiency anemia has effects on behavior which alter learning and school performance (Pollitt, 1982). Several investigators have suggested that iron deficiency decreases the child's capacity to pay attention to information in the immediate environment and that this leads to a failure to pay attention to cues that are helpful in problem-solving situations (Lee, 1978; Pollitt and Liebel, 1976; Pollitt, Haas, and Levitsky, 1989).

Some evidence supports the notion that iron deficiency affects mental performance, especially among infants and to a lesser extent in older children (Lozoff, Brittenham, Viteri, et al., 1982a, 1982b; Walter, Kovalskys, and Stekel, 1983; Oski, Honig, Hebu, and Horowitz, 1981; Oski, Honig, Hebu, and Horowitz, 1983; Dernard, Gilbert, Dodds, and Egeland, 1981; Avramadis, 1983). These studies have methodological shortcomings, including the inability to demonstrate that groups were similar before iron depletion in other ways which might affect performance, and lack of control for the effects of improved caretaking vis-à-vis the effects of iron treatment. Some studies note some positive effects in less than a week, both among infants who have mild iron-deficiency anemia and among nonanemic children with biochemical signs of iron deficiency (Oski, et al., 1981; Oski, et al., 1983; Walter, Kovalskys, and

Stekel, 1983). A recent, carefully controlled study of iron-deficiency anemia and iron deficiency found that iron-deficient infants scored lower than controls did on tests of mental development and that their scores improved 7–10 days after iron therapy began (Pollitt, et al., 1986). However, in other studies no such effects were apparent (Dernard, Gilbert, Dodds, and Egeland, 1981; Lozoff, Brittenham, Viteri, et al., 1982). Children who suffer from sickle cell disease who are anemic have also been studied, but no significant relationship has been found between the degree of anemia due to sickle cell disease and IQ, suggesting that anemia by itself may not be the cause of the problem (Logethetis, Lowenson, Augostaki, et al., 1972; Chodorkoff and Whitten, 1963). For example, the associations between anemia and iron deficiency may be due to an increased susceptibility to infection among deficient children. This greater vulnerability to infection might affect attendance at school and thus school performance. At present, evidence on the effects of iron deficiency on infection is only suggestive (Dallman, Beutler, and Finch, 1978).

Maternal variables may also be involved. The mothers of children who are iron deficient may differ from their peers whose children have normal blood values in ways that affect children's performance on tests. In one study, mothers of anemic infants were younger, had more children, and were less well-educated than those whose children were normal (Kallen, Haddy, Narins, et al., 1972). In another study the mothers of iron-deficient infants were poorer, more depressed, and more apathetic than those of nondeficient infants (Werkman, Shifman, and Shelly, 1954). Since mother-infant interactions are known to have powerful effects on mental development, these factors might also account for some of the problems of children with iron deficiency.

The highest prevalence of iron-deficiency anemia is in early life, from age six months to three years. By six months of age, fetal iron stores are depleted; dietary iron intakes often decrease; and growth rates remain fairly high, with risk of anemia rising as a result. As growth slows down in the preschool years, risks decline somewhat, but children whose diets are very low in iron or who have difficulty absorbing iron run special risks. Such children include those whose diets contain very large amounts of cereals that are not fortified with iron or made of whole grains; those who have low intakes of fruits or of the highly available sources of iron in animal foods; and those who consume very high amounts of milk, which is very low in iron and high in the minerals calcium and phosphorus, which form insoluble complexes with iron. Children who are infested with pinworms or hookworms lose blood; and if their diets are also low in iron, they are especially likely to become anemic. Chronically ill children also have an anemia, but it is not usually due to dietary iron lack. Fortunately, the prevalence of iron deficiency has decreased among infants and preschool children over the last decade or two (Vazquez, Seone, Windom, and Pearson, 1985; U.S. General Accounting Office, 1984). Nevertheless, some children are still at risk and should be treated on nutritional grounds alone.

NEW CHALLENGES FACING EDUCATORS
IN RISK MANAGEMENT

CHANGES IN AMERICAN FAMILIES
ALTER NUTRITIONAL RISKS

More than half of all families in the 1950s consisted of an employed father, a mother who was a homemaker and who did not work outside the home, and two or three children. Today, that is true of only slightly more than a quarter of all households. The divorce rate is nearly 50 percent; there are more single parents than ever before; and nearly 50 percent of all mothers work. Dual-earner couples now make up more than 40 percent of all married couples in the childbearing years. These trends are especially apparent among the parents of very young infants and children. These changes in household structures have altered the amount of time parents, especially the mothers of preschool children, have available for child and family food-related functions and have greatly expanded the need for custodial care of very young infants and children.

Over the past decade, the number of families with children in which both parents are working has increased. Tables 4 and 5 summarize these changes. The working mother is no longer a novelty but the national norm: more than half of all mothers in the United States today return to work or are actively seeking employment within a year of giving birth. In 1986, labor-force participation for new mothers was 50 percent; in 1987, it was 51 percent, up from 31 percent in 1976. In 1985, 12 million American children under age six had mothers who worked, and about two million of these were poor. When we consider all mothers, about 65 percent work today, whereas only 22 percent did so in 1950.

The share of families with children that were headed by women also swelled, from 10 percent in 1970 to 19 percent in 1985. In 1987, 52 percent of mothers whose youngest children were under two years of age were in the labor force, and at least 60 percent of these mothers worked full-time. Those mothers most likely to be working are the widowed, divorced, and separated.

Americans today can expect to spend nearly two decades as parents to dependent children and another two decades as the children of elderly and, probably, dependent parents. Job and home responsibilities must be juggled or helpers must be found to perform these caretaking tasks. Regardless how families manage these responsibilities, strains are involved both in working and in caring for children and aging parents. Because most Americans choose not to give up their jobs and incomes to do these caretaking tasks, they must hire others to do so, and the price is quite high. Day-care costs run about $2,000 to $3,000 per year; and costs of care for the elderly are even higher, often up to $22,000 or more per year for nursing homes. Attempts to economize lead to worries about the questionable quality of more affordable care. Splurging on nothing but the best can increase money worries. Those who try to cope with both job and home responsibilities by themselves may give short shrift to one or

TABLE 4

Working Parents

Year	1976	1986
Both Spouses Employed		
1+ Children	32.8	45.7
Childless	12.0	14.1
Husband Only Employed		
1+ Children	43.2	27.5
Childless	4.8	2.9
Other Couples	7.2	9.8

Source: U.S. Bureau of the Census, Report on Fertility of American Women, Washington, D.C., 1988

TABLE 5

Working Mothers

Year	1950	1960	1970	1980	1987
With Children under age 18	21.6	30.4	42.4	56.6	64.7
With Children age 6–17	32.8	42.5	51.6	64.3	72.0
With Children under age 6	13.6	20.2	32.2	46.8	56.7

Source: U.S. Bureau of the Census (Kosterlitz, 1988)

the other—or to themselves—and live in a state of constant stress. The increasing tendency within the health system to avoid institutionalization for any but the most seriously handicapped and ill children has also increased the burdens of special care, including nutritional care, on families of which such children are members. How can the government and the schools help parents to make sure that food and nutrition-related responsibilities are covered satisfactorily?

THE ROLE OF GOVERNMENT IN PRESCHOOL CHILD CARE AND EDUCATION

Controversy is great on what role, if any, government should play in preschool child care and education. Public opinion is still divided on the appropriate role of the federal government in the nurturance and protection of the very young, especially infants and preschool children both under and over three years of age (Bennett, 1987). Nevertheless, as those on welfare are increasingly pressured to find work and as mothers of younger and still younger children are seeking employment, government is being asked to take over many caretaking responsibilities formerly handled by parents. Evidence from focus groups conducted by the Public Agenda Foundation in 1987 reveals that expanding early childhood education for disadvantaged children, in combination with early childhood nutrition education programs, is popular and that taxpayers are willing to pay an extra $25 per year in taxes to fund such programs (Kosterlitz, 1988).

Implementing these public wishes is difficult, however. Faced with a huge deficit, the federal government is reluctant to take on these additional obligations. Many citizens do not want to see taxes rise, and businesses are trying to keep salary and benefit costs in line. Though most politicians are looking for ways to share or subsidize costs between businesses and individuals, a few advocate that government pay for the whole cost of the program. Consumers seem to favor government requirements on business to bear the costs, although businesses would inevitably pass these costs on to consumers. Some of the costs of these proposals may yield future dividends or offset other costs, but that remains to be seen. Tax incentives are also under consideration, but these, too, have budgetary implications since they result in foregone revenues in the future.

REDUCING THE NUTRITIONAL RISK OF PRESCHOOL CHILDREN

Nutrition is an essential part of health care. Thus, all preschool programs, not just those for poor children, need a well-planned health and nutrition component (Schloesser, 1986). Because children today are attending preschool from earlier in life and for more time per day than ever before, the food and nutrition components of these programs need to be examined. Nutrition plays an important supportive role in preschool education regardless of whether the child is handicapped, economically disadvantaged, or at lower risk. Good nutrition helps to foster a positive attitude toward school and schooling, which may result in multiplier effects from the standpoint of education. Preschools can build good nutrition into children's lives and help them become nutritionally self-directed. They should support, but not supplant, parental efforts and responsibility for child feeding and health promotion.

The question of whether preschool programs decrease educational and nutritional risk is best examined by reviewing what is known about poverty-group children, handicapped children, and other children at risk for poor educational or nutritional outcomes. Lower-risk children should be considered separately, since the effects from preschool programs are likely to differ among them.

POVERTY-GROUP CHILDREN AT NUTRITIONAL AND EDUCATIONAL RISK

Numerous studies of Head Start and other educational programs directed toward socially disadvantaged two- to four-year-old children have demonstrated gains in cognitive competence, school readiness, and school achievement, lasting at least three years after graduation from Head Start (Harrell, 1983; Woodhead, 1988). In addition, health status and socio-emotional development are improved (McKey, et al., 1985; Fosburg, 1984). Health was studied extensively in a large-scale longitudinal Head Start Health Evaluation. The health status of children prior to their entry into Head Start included many remediable health problems that required the attention of health care professionals. The diets of children joining Head Start were also marginal in calcium and iron, and, in some program sites, in other minerals and vitamins. In the Head Start program, many children received several mandated health services, including medical and dental exams, blood tests, immunizations, developmental assessments, speech and language evaluation, and hearing screenings. Only about half of all Head Start children received nutritional assessments, however, indicating that more needed to be done to identify all those needing help. Lesser numbers of children received follow-up services, and gaps in services were common. With respect to nutrition services, the Head Start children received meals and snacks that made up as much as 40 percent of their total intakes. In addition, the program placed many families in need of food assistance into other food programs. Finally, the family meals of Head Start children were superior in nutritional quality for several nutrients to those of non–Head Start families (Fosburg, 1984).

In summary, Head Start Health Services had a favorable impact upon the health status of children enrolled in the program when the health services were provided. Positive effects included identification and treatment of speech, language, vision, hearing, and other health and dental problems, improved dietary intakes, expanded participation by the families in other food programs, improved hematological indices, and better scores on developmental tests (Fosburg, 1984).

When the effects of Head Start and other early intervention programs were first studied, researchers thought that their long-term effects resulted from making children "smarter." Now it seems more likely that preschool makes children better prepared to cope with the demands of schooling and thus less likely to be referred to special education classes or to be retained in grade (Woodhead, 1988). Recent evidence suggests that many other "real-life" behavioral and psychological measures have also been positively influenced by Head Start over the long term. These findings and other considerations led to Head Start's being included as one of the Reagan Administration's safety net programs, and over the past decade funding for it has continued to increase.

Another large and well-conducted series of studies also shows that well-planned preschool programs have long-term impacts on the life chances of socially disadvantaged children, especially those who are black, and that the impacts often carry over into adult life (Consortium for Developmental Continuity, 1977; Consortium for Longitudinal Studies, 1978, 1983; Darlington, Royce, Snipper, Murray, and Lazar, 1980; Lazar, Darlington, Murray, and Snipper, 1982; Gray, Ramsey, and Klaus, 1982). These and other evaluations of even more intensive programs (Garber and Heber, 1983; Ramsey, Yeates, and Short, 1984) have strengthened the case for preschool programs for disadvantaged children and for amendments to P. L. 99–457, which requires public education for handicapped infants and preschoolers (Bryant and Ramey, 1985; Guralnick and Bennet, 1987; White, 1986). They have also been cited in the growing debate about extending public education downward to four-year-olds.

Taken together, these studies suggest that comprehensive services for the support of families with young, disadvantaged children have positive effects on the children both during participation in the program and in subsequent years. Evidence on how well or how poorly the services achieve other social objectives, such as assisting women in joining the labor force, fostering social egalitarianism in school, and increasing productivity, is less conclusive (Crittenden, 1984).

HANDICAPPED CHILDREN AND THOSE WITH OTHER SPECIAL NEEDS

During the late 1960s and 1970s, children with physical and mental handicaps received increased attention. This group includes youngsters who are visually impaired or blind, hearing impaired or deaf, mentally retarded, learning disabled, and those with other physical disabilities and emotional problems. Educational opportunities were enhanced by the passage of the Education for All Handicapped Children Act of 1975, which required that children who were identified as handicapped must receive education in the least restrictive environment possible. Instead of putting such children into special classes, they were to be mainstreamed into regular classrooms or programs whenever possible (Abeson and Zettel, 1977). The legislation also required the provision of individualized instruction designed to meet these children's special needs and of related supportive services (such as school health, speech, physical and occupational therapy, psychological services, and medical services) needed for the children to benefit from individualized instructional programs. Moreover, the law insisted that the "individualized educational plan" or instructional program be developed jointly by parents, teachers, and other appropriate individuals.

Implementation of this legislation has been slow but steady. A great deal of effort has been devoted to dealing more adequately with the problems of the handicapped in all spheres (Office of Technology Assessment Technology, 1987; Shelton, Jeppson, and Johnson, 1987; Gephart, Egan, and Hutchins, 1984; Newburger, Melnicoe, and Newburger, 1986). Guides for dealing with these special problems in preschool settings are available (Granato and Krone, 1972). Head Start now mainstreams handicapped children, reserving 10 percent of its slots for children with special needs. It has developed excellent materials that can be used in other preschool programs.

But these gains have been marked by setbacks. In recent years, programs for the handicapped have come under increasing fire, especially those for children in the preschool years. Some parents have complained that regular education programs are being cannibalized to serve children with special needs. Whether such a contention is true or not, it is clear that the definition of "special needs" is changing. For example, in Massachusetts, because the definition of special-needs children changed, the number of "special needs" children increased from 11,000 to 135,000 in spite of a decline in the number of school-aged children. In order to control costs and satisfy the demands of angry parents who feel that their "normal" children are being slighted, some school systems are now limiting provision of special-needs services to those who are not doing well in classes and who have special needs. Under legislation passed in Congress in 1988, such policies will no longer be allowed. Also, school districts are moving away from providing expensive private services and toward mainstreaming as many children as possible without placing children with special needs into inadequate programs.

IMPACTS OF PRESCHOOL PROGRAMS ON LOWER-RISK CHILDREN

Both parental demands for more adequate day care and parental concerns about the inadequacies of secondary schools are leading to requests by middle class parents for early intervention programs for their children. The effects of early intervention programs such as Head Start are indeed dramatic on poor children. But it is dangerous to generalize from studies of intervention efforts in socially disadvantaged preschool children to the likely effects of preschool intervention programs for all children under age five (Woodhead, 1988; Zigler, 1984). Because it is unlikely that the social context of preschool or school kindergarten programs for all children is similar to that of socially disadvantaged children in the early 1960s, it is doubtful that the effects of early intervention would be similar over either the short term or the long term. Children's, teachers', and parents' expectations would probably also differ. Indeed, one eminent educational researcher claims that the long-term results of the Head Start experience are not germane in current arguments for extending public education to four-year-olds or to even younger children (Zigler, 1984). Head Start was a very different type of program with a different target group.

One problem is that effective program design and intensity of intervention of these early intervention programs vary greatly with the population in question (Woodhead, 1988). It is not clear whether preschool experience can "jump-start" middle-class children academically, giving them an educational advantage that will allow them to compete more successfully with their peers. The effect of parental pressure and emphasis on early performance is also unclear. Preschools can lead to elitism and separation of children in grouping by income, workplace, or the like. In his book *Miseducation: Preschoolers At Risk,* David Elkind claims that parents often use preschools as status symbols of their own economic affluence.

High-quality day care and preschool facilities are scarce and expensive, and the demand far exceeds the supply. The *Washington Post* recently reported that private preschools in Washington, D.C., start at $3,000 and go up to more than $6,500 per year.

PROGRAMS FOR INFANTS AND CHILDREN UNDER THREE

Appropriate day care for the very young is developmentally geared. The vital components are that it:

a. *Serves as an extension of the family.* It extends and supplements parental care in ways that are consistent with the values and goals of the child's family and culture so as to strengthen the child's attachment to his or her parents and to sustain the parents as the major force in the child's personal development. Parents must be involved in day care so as not to subject children to conflicting rules, values, and expectations.

b. *Includes attention to health and nutrition* (Schloesser, 1986).

c. *Aids child development and mastery of certain tasks.*

d. *Helps the child to develop other skills.*

e. *Permits society to intervene constructively when families and children need help.* Appropriate day care for the very young is especially important for three groups of children: vulnerable children whose development is at risk; children from families living in poverty; and handicapped or disabled children suffering from severe mental retardation, physical handicaps, or childhood emotional disorders.

f. *Has trained staff.* Training those who will provide care to infants under three years of age whose parents are in the work force is a formidable challenge. Aside from issues related to instructing caretakers in the proper feeding and health of infants in day care, there are also issues to be faced such as the appropriate balance to be struck between developmental and custodial care, the implications of multiple mothering, and methods of keeping parents involved. Educators have a great deal to add in assuring that the new programs incorporate a developmental focus and integrate well with preschool programs.

WHAT SCHOOLS CAN DO TO HELP

In the next few years, pressures will increase for the establishing of publicly funded preschool programs and day care. At the same time, educators will be asked to increase students' educational performance and successful completion of secondary school by a substantially larger proportion than the 75 percent of students who do so today. All involved in the educational system face formidable challenges to satisfy these requests (Council of Chief State School Officers, 1987a, 1987b).

Whether the new responsibilities and authority for preschool and day care will devolve to state education departments or to a mix of other branches of state government remains to be seen. In many states, primary responsibility for children from ages three to five lies within the department of education, while responsibility for day care of infants and children below age three lies with the department of public health. State-level interagency cooperative agreements are needed among the various education, food, health, and social welfare agencies which provide services to preschool children. School-based collaborative agreements with health and social services providers can also be helpful in sharing expertise among institutions. Among the many relevant personnel are those working in Head Start, the Maternal and Child Health Block grant, program planners, and those involved in outreach and food programs, including child nutrition and food stamps.

TARGET COMPREHENSIVE PRESCHOOL PROGRAMS
FOR HIGHEST-RISK CHILDREN

Planning and policy efforts should target the children at greatest risk, including those whose families are living in poverty; those who are socially disadvantaged, especially those from minority or non-English-speaking households; and those who lack family or community support. Children who are physically or mentally handicapped (especially those who are poor, minority, or learning disabled) are also at high risk. Finally, there are other children who lack family and community support for a variety of reasons. For example, some children from single-parent households with other stresses upon their families may be at risk in some instances.

In addition to collaboration among traditional government agencies, outreach to new groups and programs in the community are vital, especially for at-risk children. Staff persons from the Head Start programs or child food services, as well as consultants on handicapping, nutrition, health, and special education, may be helpful. This collaboration must involve both state and local levels.

Close collaboration with parents is imperative. Involvement between preschool staff and parents in planning and implementing developmentally based food and nutrition education programs and food services is important, especially for children at high nutritional risk. If educational programs are to succeed, at-risk children need supportive, comprehensive, and developmentally based nutrition, health, social welfare, and other human services programs as well as the usual educational and custodial care. So do low-risk children. Because such a comprehensive kind of care cuts across many departments of government and involves the public, private, and voluntary sectors, it requires a greater degree of collaboration than has ever been necessary before. It also involves new forms of training of staff and parents.

The focus of the Council of Chief State School Officers on early childhood and parenting education provides an opportunity for leaders in education to ensure that education is considered in current efforts to reform welfare legislation. Participation in education, training, and employment programs is likely to be required for mothers who need child-care subsidies. States are likely to be required to offer comprehensive education, training, and employment programs for such welfare recipients. Many of these same individuals are those who have high-risk children. Educators must therefore be involved in shaping the new regulations to ensure that they include an educational focus as well as a custodial focus in implementing the child-care and work provisions of the bills now being considered, perhaps through the CCSSO Study Commission. The State Education Assessment Center of CCSSO may be able to assist in forecasting and focusing on solutions to problems of preschool children of welfare parents covered by this legislation.

Nutritional guidelines and standards for all preschool programs should ensure that programs contain a sound nutritional foundation for successful developmentally based preschool education in language, communications, and social skills. In the absence of other criteria the Head Start Nutrition Standards (ACYF, 1987) are helpful.

Finally, preschool curricula must be integrated with the curricula of later schooling. In most settings, the state education agency is best equipped for joint planning of curricula for at-risk children of preschool age. When schools become involved in preschools or day care, there is a better likelihood of integration between the two. Also, cross training of teachers as well as students for work in preschools and primary schools may be more easily accomplished when all are under the same aegis.

When dealing with nutritionally at-risk children, especially those who are economically disadvantaged and handicapped, educational planners must keep in mind the developmental as well as the skill-learning focus of preschool programs. The goal is to foster and maximize whatever skills the children are developmentally capable of, not simply to make them read at an earlier age. Individualized educational plans are helpful for maximizing their potential.

The goals of Head Start and the new law P. L. 99–457, Education of the Handicapped Amendments of 1986, are different from those of many other preschool endeavors in that they aim toward more comprehensive and global development rather than simply education alone. The goal of P. L. 99–457 is to improve the function of at-risk children and their families not only educationally but physically, socially, and educationally. No single institution can do this by itself.

Integration of the preschool curriculum with later schooling is necessary, but it is not sufficient to achieve this comprehensive and coordinated aim. The health, nutritional, and other social-services needs of all children at risk must be identified and integrated into an individual teaching and learning plan. This will ensure that learning will not be inhibited by failure to address physical, mental, and nutritional problems which slow learning. Schools cannot do this alone. The other nutrition-related components such as screening and assessment of nutritional risk, food service, liaison and integration with dental, health, welfare, and food assistance resources require outreach to other institutions and expertise within the larger community.

HOW EDUCATORS CAN DEVELOP BETTER PRESCHOOL NUTRITION PROGRAMS

COMPONENTS OF A WELL-DESIGNED NUTRITION PROGRAM

Designing the components of a preschool nutrition program is relatively straightforward. One useful model has been especially well-tested. Performance standards, operations manuals, and a nutrition curriculum are available (Head Start Bureau, 1979).

The operational components of the nutrition aspects of a successful preschool program are several. Staff must be trained to have basic competence in nutrition and feeding of young children, in sanitation and safety, and in management. Technical competence in menu planning, food purchasing, food receiving and storage, and quantity food protection are also necessary for those who operate preschool programs for large groups of children. All of these skills are in addition to competence and interest in education, in the overall health of the child, and in identifying those at risk.

The objectives of the nutrition component in Head Start programs are listed in Table 6 (page 84). Table 7 provides means for accomplishing these objectives in preschool programs for nutritionally at-risk children. Many points are also relevant in carrying out programs for lower-risk children.

In the Head Start program for disadvantaged children, screening for undernutrition and malnutrition and treating for disease and dental problems are often done through the program itself since children are unlikely to obtain such services elsewhere. Handicapped children sometimes have special nutritional or feeding needs, and ways to meet these needs during preschool meals need to be worked out in conjunction with parents and the children's physicians as well as Head Start staff. For children with lower nutritional, educational, and health risks, information on nutritional needs and status may already be available from other sources; or simple measurements such as height and weight may reveal that growth and nutrition are satisfactory. At the very least, menus need to be planned, with the usual Recommended Dietary Allowances for young children kept in mind. Several excellent references are now available for doing this (Pipes, 1986).

(Text contd. p. 86)

TABLE 6

Head Start Performance Standards in Nutrition

Objectives:

Provide food which will help meet the child's daily nutritional needs, either in the child's home or in another clean and pleasant environment, recognizing individual differences and cultural patterns, and thereby promote sound physical, social, and emotional growth and development.

Provide an environment for nutritional services which will support and promote the use of the feeding situation as an opportunity for learning.

Help staff, child, and family to understand the relationship of nutrition to health; factors which influence food practices; variety of ways to provide for nutritional needs and to apply this knowledge in the development of sound food habits after leaving the Head Start program.

Demonstrate the interrelationship of nutrition to other activities of the Head Start program and its contribution to overall child development goals.

Involve all staff, parents and other community agencies as appropriate in meeting the child's nutritional needs so that nutritional care provided by Head Start complements and supplements that of the home and community.

TABLE 7

Implementing Nutrition Components in Preschool Programs for At-Risk Children

Provide Nutrition Services to Identify Needs and Problems by Obtaining:

Nutrition assessment data (height, weight, hemoglobin, hematocrit) obtained for all children.

Information about family eating habits and special dietary needs and feeding problems especially of handicapped children.

Information about major community nutrition problems.

Use a Nutritional Plan to Assist in Meeting Children's Daily Nutrition Needs, Including:

Food in meals (preferably hot) and snacks which provide at least 1/3 of the daily nutritional needs in a part-day program or, if in a full-day program snacks, lunch, and other meals as appropriate to provide 1/2 to 2/3 of daily nutritional needs, depending on the length of the program, with consideration for meeting any special needs of children, including children with handicapping conditions.

A nourishing breakfast for all children in morning programs who have not received breakfast.

Meal patterns conform to Child Care Food Program standards and amounts to those required in Head Start.

(Table 7 contd.)

Meals and snacks scheduled appropriately to meet children's needs and posted along with menus for patrons to see.

Provide Nutrition Services to Help in Children's Development and Socialization:

Serve a variety of foods which broaden children's food experience in considering cultural and ethnic preferences.

Avoid use of food as punishment or reward.

Encourage but do not force children to taste or eat.

Consider individual children's needs in size and number of servings of food.

Allow sufficient time for children to eat.

Make chairs, tables, and eating utensils suitable for size and developmental level of the child with special consideration for meeting the needs of children with handicapping conditions.

Have children and staff, including volunteers, eat together sharing the same menu and a socializing experience in a relaxed atmosphere.

Provide opportunity for the involvement of children in family style service or other activities related to meal service.

Consider needs of handicapped children and accommodate them.

Establish a Nutrition Education Program for Staff, Parents, and Children:

Plan meals and use food as an integral part of the total education program.

Plan learning activities to effect the selection and enjoyment of a wide variety of nutritious foods.

Provide education on the selection and preparation of foods to meet family needs, guidance in home and money management, and help in consumer education so that parents can fulfill their major role and responsibility for the nutritional health of the family.

Train staff in principles of nutrition and their application to child development and family health, so that they can create a good physical, social, and emotional environment which supports and promotes development of sound food habits and helps children and families achieve adequate nutrition.

Involve Parents and Appropriate Community Agencies in Planning, Implementing, and Evaluating Nutrition Services:

Set up a Policy Council or Health Services Advisory Committee.

Discuss the nutritional status of each child with his or her parents.

Share menus and information on nutrition activities with parents.

Inform parents of the benefits of food assistance programs.

Enlist community agencies in assisting eligible families in participating in food assistance programs.

Comply with sanitary codes for food services and see that vendors do also.

Involve Nutritionists:

Employ full-time staff nutritionist or periodic, regularly scheduled supervision by a qualified nutritionist.

Provide preservice and in-service training to all nutrition services staff in menu planning, food purchasing, food preparation and storage, and sanitation and personal hygiene.

Keep appropriate records.

Once needs have been assessed, preschool programs must supplement home food intakes with healthful, enjoyable food, provided in a safe, sanitary manner, to help meet children's daily nutritional needs. For eligible programs, this can be accomplished through food programs, including the Child Care Food Program. Federal reimbursement for food served in some day-care centers enrolling poor or otherwise disadvantaged children has been available for two decades. The need for new government food programs directed to preschool children first became evident in the 1960s as more and more poverty-group mothers of small children entered the work force, and the prevalence of malnutrition and undernutrition among the poor became evident. The 1967 amendments to the Social Security Act established the Work Incentive Program, a training program for welfare recipients which also provided federal support for the care of poor children. Even earlier, in 1964, Head Start, under the auspices of the Office of Economic Opportunity in the Executive Office of the President, had begun preschool training for disadvantaged children under the Economic Opportunity Act. In 1968, the Special Food Service Program for children, which provided for the feeding of children in places other than schools, became a part of the National School Lunch Act. It extended food assistance both to year-round child-care programs such as day-care centers, settlement houses, and programs for handicapped children, as well as to summer programs for preschool and school-age children. Eligible institutions include family day-care homes and larger institutional programs. Priority is given to child-care institutions that serve children from areas in which poor economic conditions exist and in which there are high concentrations of working mothers.

Federal monies can provide eligible centers with reimbursement for free meals; with additional funding, in some cases, to supplement operating costs; with donated commodities such as surplus foods; and with nonfood assistance for equipment to prepare food. Any agency which wishes to apply for funds must have a nonprofit sponsor, such as a church or poverty program, and must also provide information on the economic status of local residents, the target population, the size and quality of the program, proof of nonprofit tax-exempt status, and evidence of proper licensing. The reimbursement level depends on the number of poor children and the needs of the center (e.g., if all or nearly all of the children need free meals but the service institution cannot meet these needs).

In preschools or day-care centers with sufficient numbers of disadvantaged children who qualify for the federal Child Care Food Program, the cost of meals is partially covered. Meeting certain meal patterns is required to ensure that the children's nutritional needs are met.

A sound menu-planning guide can help programs to provide an adequate, varied, balanced, moderate, and nutritious menu and to promote sound physical, emotional, and social growth, while recognizing individual, cultural, and ethnic differences in food preferences and practices. The easiest way to balance menus is to use a meal planning guide that incorporates these principles. Often, a cycle menu that repeats on a monthly or bi-weekly basis is used to provide variety while minimizing the cost and expense of menu planning.

The most obvious problem of balance is the danger of getting too many calories but too few of the non-energy-providing nutrients needed each day. Growing children need diets that are rich in protein, vitamins, and minerals as well as calories. One way to fulfill this need is to insist that menus meet or exceed each meal's fair share of the protective nutrients, protein, vitamins, and minerals needed each day.

Menu planning in Head Start programs follows the meal patterns specified by the Child Care Food Program, in which Head Start programs are required to participate. The food guide specifies that portions be about half the size of adult portions. Part-time programs are required to provide one-third of children's daily needs; and full-day programs provide from one-half to two-thirds of daily needs.

Finally, it is important that the menu be varied, balanced, and moderate so that children do not get too much of food constituents that are often present in excess in American diets. While no strict numerical guidelines apply, balance and moderation must be emphasized, especially for fat, saturated fat, cholesterol, sugar, and salt intakes. Some helpful suggestions are provided in a recent publication (Dwyer, 1986).

The amount and number of meals to be provided depends on the length of time children attend the preschool and on their home nutrition environment. As noted above, a common rule of thumb is that children in half-day programs should receive at least one-third of the Recommended Dietary Allowances for calories and protein, along with several vitamins and minerals each day. Children present for longer periods should have greater proportions of their needs met in day care—often from 50 to 60 percent or even more under special circumstances. For children at high nutritional risk it may be necessary for the preschool nutrition program not only to substitute for the meal which otherwise would have been served at home but also to improve upon it and provide more nutrition than it might have. This is especially true if children are from poor or otherwise disadvantaged families which are likely to have suboptimal nutrition.

Also, children who arrive at preschool without having eaten breakfast should be given breakfast. Within this basic pattern there is room for individual experimentation and variation for different cultural groups and for meeting the needs of handicapped children. Cycle menus which repeat after several weeks may be used. Cultural acceptability and food education are maximized by including parents and teachers in the menu-planning process. Colorful, simple foods that can be easily identified and eaten are emphasized. Snacks and desserts should be nutritious. Menus should be planned to make food handling and eating easy. Foods that can be eaten by hand, such as bite-sized pieces of fruit, egg, cheese, and meat, are acceptable. Finger foods are also good foods for blind children.

Handicapped children often require special types of food, assistance with feeding, or additional time for eating. Obviously, accommodations to special diets will vary from one setting to another, but whenever possible, children should be mainstreamed—that is, included in usual activities involving food and feeding.

The preschool nutritional environment should be safe, bright, clean, pleasant, and well-ventilated. Meal time should be used as a learning opportunity. Ample time should be allowed for eating. Permitting children and adults to sit together and serving food family style facilitate socialization and the development of appropriate meal-time behavior. Getting the children involved in clean-up can help to foster habits of cleanliness. Nutrition performance standards must also ensure high-quality food service and minimize the risks of food-borne illness.

Meticulous observation of sanitation and food-safety principles is vital. Kitchens are potential sources for the spread of food-borne illnesses and are also the places where food-related accidents, including cuts, burns, and poisoning, occur. Thus, both the kitchen environment itself and work practices used in the kitchen must be safe. Sanitary practices and first-aid procedures must be taught to all personnel. Kitchen safety is especially important when young children are permitted to observe or participate. The principles of sanitation include keeping food clean and wholesome, handling food properly, keeping equipment clean, having healthy workers, and conforming to local and state sanitary codes. If food vendors or caterers are used, they must be monitored with a spot-checking system. Food poisoning and other food illnesses compromise children's health and also parents' trust in the program.

Another objective of the preschool nutrition program is to encourage children to practice healthful food consumption practices by consuming and enjoying meals at preschool. The actual practice of sampling and eating new foods and menus has a considerable cumulative effect on food habits. For example, in the period immediately following World War II, schools in occupied Japan served the American-type school lunch, and observers have suggested that this was a potent influence on the development of Western food consumption practices among the post-war generation (Osio and Dwyer, 1981). The importance of teaching children healthful food consumption practices through modeling cannot be emphasized enough. Parents and teachers are powerful role models in these respects, but so are the meals themselves.

Food-service direction is a complicated business that involves menu planning, food purchasing, food preparation and storage, sanitation and personal hygiene for workers in the food service, and other management skills. Because these skills are specialized and because inefficiencies in food purchasing and preparation are extremely expensive, it is often worthwhile to engage the services of a qualified professional nutritionist to assist in setting systems into place as the program is established and to re-evaluate periodically. Also, since public monies may be involved, careful record keeping and accounting are important.

NUTRITION EDUCATION FOR
STAFF, CHILDREN, AND PARENTS

Nutrition education is essential, both for preschool staff and children. All staff need to know the basic principles of nutrition for preschool children, as well as how best to promote food education to children by offering meals that follow a food guide and by providing additional instruction. It is normal for preschoolers' intakes to vary considerably from day to day—much more so than do adults' intakes. Selectivity, emotionality, and appetites of children are also more variable from day to day than those of adults (Tuckermanty and Gallager-Allred, 1980). Only when these fluctuations are extreme are they likely to be detrimental to children's health (Dwyer, Dwyer, and Mayer, 1970). Caretakers and parents need to become aware of the differences between normal fluctuations and abnormal behaviors, and of whom to refer to for help if abnormal behaviors are observed. Excessive anxiety on the parent's or caretaker's part will only make matters worse, and so it is important to seek assistance early.

Although it should not need to be said, bribery, forcing children to eat, and withholding food or drink as a form of punishment have no place in preschool programs. It is important to emphasize this in training staff and to set up monitoring systems to make sure that misguided individuals who might use such techniques are dissuaded from doing so. These and other forms of child abuse and neglect are problems which must be faced and monitored in all settings in which preschool children participate (Russell and Clifford, 1987; Melton and Davidson, 1987).

Staff need instruction on what to do if a child chokes, swallows a poison or other toxic substance, becomes nauseous and vomits, or experiences other accidents.

The Handbook for Local Head Start Nutrition Specialists is an excellent training manual that is adaptable to any preschool setting in which nutrition services and education are provided (U.S. Department of Health and Human Services, 1984). The newly developed Head Start Nutrition Education Curriculum emphasizes parent involvement and preschool programs that integrate food and nutrition services and nutrition education for younger and older children (U.S. Department of Health and Human Services, 1988).

If we are to reach the highest-risk children, our traditional training programs need to be changed. In our undergraduate and graduate schools as well as in job training, more crossover and conjoint training is needed to involve all the people who are key to solving the problems of nutritionally and educationally at-risk children. For example, more common training among those who will become special education coordinators, teachers, nutritionists, community resource specialists, school food-service workers, and health personnel is essential for dealing with physically and emotionally handicapped children. Educating staff members about food programs such as WIC and the Child Care Food Program component of Head Start will better equip them to serve as resource and referral sources for high-risk families. Encouraging them to serve as liaisons between the preschool programs and these other services will also help to ensure that referrals are made. Finally, consideration must be given to innovative approaches for dealing with high-risk groups, such as pregnant teenagers and teenage parents and their children. Former members of at-risk groups provide good role models as preschool staff, and their use needs to be considered. The use of teachers in categorical programs as coaches in regular classrooms rather than in special classes will further the mainstreaming process for handicapped and other at-risk children.

Nutrition education for children is one of the factors that distinguish preschool programs from custodial day care. The major topics that need to be included in teaching preschool children about food are summarized in a recent publication that includes helpful learning activities (Goodwin and Pollen, 1980). Table 8 summarizes these topics. It is important to ensure that the food-education curriculum in the preschool is not totally left up to the teacher, who may have idiosyncratic or unsound views. The curriculum should also include attention to safety issues, since several studies show that children who are taught safety behaviors are more likely to practice them than are children who are not taught them (Parcel, Bruhn, and Cerreto, 1986).

It is also important to demonstrate the relationship of nutrition to other aspects of day care and child development and to integrate into the program activities that make nutrition principles come alive. Materials that are designed to help parents and teachers become involved with their children through television, play, and science can often be adapted and integrated with food education activities (U.S. Department of Health and Human Services, 1983).

Getting parents involved will help ensure that they are aware of and approve of what is being done in the preschool with respect to food and eating. The more actively involved they are, the better. It is especially important for parents to understand how critical their role is: they and they alone are legally responsible for their children's nutritional well-being, regardless of where the child is fed. Competence and interest on the part of parents, teachers, and food preparers are desirable so they can participate actively in all parts of the program.

The preschool should also encourage parents to participate in other federal and state programs if food assistance is needed. Head Start has been particularly effective in notifying parents in its program about their eligibility for other programs that enhance nutrition, overall health, and quality of life.

SERVING HANDICAPPED CHILDREN

As more and more children with handicaps enter regular community schools and preschools, educators are challenged to find ways to provide for their nutritional needs without stigmatizing them or singling them out as being especially privileged.

(Text contd. p. 92)

TABLE 8

Objectives for Food Education in Preschool Settings as Formulated Creative Food Experiences for Children
(Goodwin and Pollen, 1980) (Adapted)

Emphasize the Vital Role of Food for the Child Himself

Enhance self-image of developing knowledge and skills to:

- make wise decisions about food choices;
- select and shop for quality foods; and
- prepare simple, nutritious meals on one's own.

Stimulate appreciation for the role of food in health by:

- learning that food promotes growth and development;
- teaching how to reduce risk for diet-related illnesses and accidents (choking, poisoning accidents, pica); and
- practicing health and safety behaviors involving food.

Encourage enjoyment of sensory experiences involving food by:

- becoming aware of the sights, smells, sounds, textures, and tastes of good foods;
- including food experiences to provide subtle sensory refinement; and
- using sensory experiences and pleasures to help develop good food habits.

Appreciate ethnicity by:

- illustrating unique food behaviors and customs and sharing these with others.

Develop self-expression by:

- experimenting with different colors, shapes, textures, smells, and combinations of foods; and
- developing and eating imaginative dishes and meals.

Promote Interactions Between the Child and the Community

Provide socialization experiences by:

- obtaining, preparing, and serving food with others;
- sharing of food and increasing social participation;
- rituals, feasts, and celebrations around food.

Pass food skills from one generation to another.

Encourage regional awareness by stimulating awareness of and experiences with regional foods.

Encourage respect for the land and seasons.

Promote sound ecology in use of land, conservation, and decreased pollution and food waste.

Develop social responsibility through:

- prudent and non-wasteful eating patterns; and
- concern for others and for conservation as well as cooperation and charity.

Much research is now being carried out on the advantages and disadvantages of mainstreaming versus holding special classes for children with various handicaps (Heller, 1982). In addition to classrooms and teaching techniques, other school features, including eating facilities and school meals, may also need adaptation. Nutritionists and educators need to devote more attention to solving learning and other problems these children face in school situations.

The physical and mental capacities of some handicapped children make special diets and feeding techniques necessary (American Dietetic Association, 1981). In some cases, either at home or at school, these needs have not been met. When needs are not met, growth failure and other problems may decrease classroom performance.

Both physical and developmental retardation must be considered. Physically handicapping conditions include motor handicaps, inborn errors of metabolism, and the like. Children who suffer from developmental lags are unable to perform what is usually expected of typical children of the same age. Causes of developmental lags include sensory problems, mental retardation, environmental deprivation, and many other problems. Diet is not the cause of these problems, nor is diet their solution. Nevertheless, these children's nutrition needs may require attention so that poor nutrition does not become a secondary problem resulting in both behavioral and physiological consequences.

Federally funded health- and education-related programs have as part of their mandates training and technical assistance especially for handicapped children who are at high nutritional and educational risk. These programs include the University Affiliated Facilities (UAF) programs for children with long-term developmental and health needs; schools of public health; and various other specialized programs offered for handicapped children by state departments of health. Those who are socially disadvantaged may receive help from the child nutrition programs of the U.S. Department of Agriculture; from corresponding state programs; from the Extension Service's Expanded Food and Nutrition Education Program (EFNEP); from Special Supplemental Food Program for Women, Infants, and Children (WIC), from Food Stamps; and from state Nutrition Education and Training programs (NETs).

In developing and implementing individualized educational plans for handicapped children at high risk, it is often useful to build activities into an existing case management system. A person in charge of the educational aspects of a child's case can serve as a liaison between health experts and others who are involved in other aspects of planning for the child. This person can also help to handle any problems relating to food, eating, and nutrition which cannot be dealt with in the preschool or which need outside attention.

Certain nutritional and health benefits have gaps in coverage. Those that do have gaps need expansion and extension to a broader group of children at nutritional risk than those children who are currently eligible for WIC and Medicaid. Also, better coordination is needed among providers in programs funded by Maternal and Child-Health Block Grant monies, WIC, Medicaid, the

Education for All Handicapped Children Act, and the Community Mental Health Centers and Services legislation, so that all children are served (Kotch, 1987).

EFFECTS OF EXCESS SUGAR, ADDITIVES, AND OTHER SUBSTANCES ON SCHOOL PERFORMANCE

The constellation of behaviors commonly described as hyperactivity includes cognitive dysfunction, impulsivity, excessively high activity levels, distractibility, and deficits in attention (Tsong, et al., 1980). The disorder has many causes and in the vast majority of cases, diet does not appear to be either a causative or a curative agent. The negative effects of excess sugar and additives on learning have received much attention, but claims are exaggerated (Caballero, 1985; Dwyer, 1986; Lieberman, 1985).

The claim of Dr. Benjamin Feingold that a diet which eliminated certain food colorings and flavorings ameliorated the disorder has not been demonstrated in several well-conducted experiments in recent years. Nevertheless, a few hyperkinetic children do react adversely to very large doses of single food colorings given under experimental conditions (National Institutes of Health Consensus Development Conference, 1980).

Theories that hyperactivity or other forms of negative behavior are caused by excessive sugar intake or by hypoglycemia have also been critically examined and found deficient. Neither do hyperkinetic children obtain relief from evening primrose oil (Aman, Mitchell, and Turbott, 1987), tryptophan (Nemzer, et al., 1986), or other food substances. Pharmacological agents are not totally satisfactory in the treatment of hyperactivity (Rosenberg, 1986), but little is gained by putting children on special diets to remediate school performance or to control the disorder. Combinations of drugs, psychotherapy, and educational remediation appear to offer the greatest promise.

CONCLUSIONS

Good nutritional status is an adjunct to, but not a substitute for, education to improve the status of educationally at-risk children. Nutritional status affects learning and school performance. But nutritionally at-risk children are also often educationally at risk or at risk of ill health. These different factors are difficult to sort out for their relative impact on school performance. Demographics and changes in parental life-styles and work styles (particulary the rise in single-parent families and families in which both parents are working from early on in the child's life) are likely to increase rather than decrease nutritional stresses experienced by preschool children. Although negative effects of excess sugar and additives on learning and attention have received much notice, they are exaggerated. We know that the nutritional status of preschool children can be enhanced by the adoption of health promotion behaviors on the part of parents and school officials. These are listed in Table 3, on page 67.

Comprehensive and holistic preschool programs are effective in decreasing probabilities of poor educational performance later in life. Such programs need to include a feeding component and also a nutrition education component. Schools can make a major contribution in this effort and in teaching children to preserve and maintain their nutritional health.

REFERENCES

Abeson, A., and J. Zettel. "The End of a Quiet Revolution: The U.S. Education for All Handicapped Children Act." *Exceptional Children* 44 (1977): 115–128.

Aman, M. G., E. A. Mitchell, and S. H. Turbott. "The Effects of Essential Fatty Acid Supplementation by Efmol (Evening Primrose Oil) in Hyperactive Children." *Journal of Abnormal Child Psychology* 15 (1987): 75–90.

American Dietetic Association. "Infant and Child Nutrition: Concerns Regarding the Developmentally Disabled." *Journal of American Dietetic Association* 78 (1981): 443–452.

Avramidis, L. "Developmental Deficits in Iron-Deficient Infants." *Journal of Pediatrics* 101 (1983): 339–340.

Bennett, W. J. "The Role of the Family in the Nurture and Protection of the Young." *American Psychologist* 42 (1987): 246–250.

Berrueta-Clement, J. R., L. J. Schweinhart, W. S. Barnett, A. S. Epstein, and D. P. Weikart. *Changed Lives: The Effects of the Perry Preschool Program on Youths Through Age 19 (Monograph 8).* Ypsilanti, Mich.: High/Scope Press, 1984.

Birch, H. G. "Malnutrition, Learning, and Intelligence." *American Journal of Public Health* 62 (1972): 773–784.

Brown, J. L., and D. Allen. "Hunger in America." *Annual Review of Public Health* 9 (1988): 503–526.

Bryant, D. M., and C. T. Ramey. "Prevention-Oriented Infant Education Programs." *Children in Contemporary Society* 17 (1) (1985): 17–35.

Caballero, B. "Food Additives in the Pediatric Diet." *Clinical Nutrition* 4 (1985): 200–206.

Children's Defense Fund. *Maternal and Child Health Data Book.* Washington, D.C.: Children's Defense Fund, 1986.

Chodorkoff, J., and C. F. Whitten. "Intellectual Status of Children with Sickle Cell Anemia." *Journal of Pediatrics* 63 (1963): 29.

Citizens' Commission on Hunger in New England. *American Hunger Crisis: Poverty and Health in New England.* Boston: Harvard School of Public Health, 1984.

Conners, C. K., et al. "The Effect of Breakfast on the Cardiac Response and Behavior of Children." Abstract for the Society for Psychophysiological Research. Minneapolis, 1982.

Consortium for Developmental Continuity. *The Persistence of Preschool Effects.* Washington, D.C., U.S. Department of Health, Education, and Welfare, 1977.

Consortium for Longitudinal Studies. *As the Twig Is Bent: Lasting Effects of Preschool Programs.* Hillsdale, N.J.: Lawrence Erlbaum Associates, 1983.

Council of Chief State School Officers. *Children at Risk: The Work of the States.* Washington, D.C.: Council of Chief State School Officers, 1987. (a)

Council of Chief State School Officers. *Disabled Students Beyond School: A*

Review of the Issues. Position Paper and Recommendations for Achievement. Washington, D.C.: Council of Chief State School Officers, 1986.

Council of Chief State School Officers. *Elements of a Model State Statute to Provide Educational Entitlements for At-Risk Students.* Washington, D.C.: Council of Chief State School Officers, 1986.

Council of Chief State School Officers. *School Success for Students at Risk: A Policy Statement.* Washington, D.C.: Council of Chief State School Officers, 1987. (b)

Council on Foods and Nutrition, Malnutrition, and Hunger in the United States. *Journal of the American Medical Association* 213 (1970): 272–275.

Cox, J. H., and C. R. Gallagher-Allred. "Normal Diet: Age of Dependency." In *Nutrition in Primary Care,* Department of Family Medicine, Ohio State University, Columbus, Ohio, 1980.

Crittenden, A. "Head Start Pays Off in the End." *Wall Street Journal,* November 29, 1984.

Dallman, P. R. "Iron Deficiency in Weaning: A Nutritional Problem on the Way to Resolution." *Acta Paediatrica Scandanavica* 323 (1986): 59–67 (supplement).

Dallman, P. R., E. Beutler, and C. A. Finch. "Effects of Iron Deficiency Exclusive of Anemia." *British Journal of Hematology* 40 (1978): 179.

Darlington, R. D., J. M. Royce, A. S. Snipper, H. W. Murray, and I. Lazar. "Preschool Programs and Later School Competence of Children from Low-Income Families." *Science* 208 (1980): 202–207.

Dernard, A., A. Gilbert, M. Dodds, and B. Egeland. "Iron Deficiency and Behavioral Deficits." *Pediatrics* 63 (1981): 828.

Dernard, A. S. "Childhood Iron Deficiency and Impaired Attention Development or Scholastic Performance: Is the Evidence Sufficient to Establish Causality?" *Journal of Pediatrics* (1976): 162–163.

Dickie, N. H., and A. E. Bender. "Breakfast and Performance in School Children." *British Journal of Nutrition* 48 (1982): 483–496.

Dietz, W. H., and S. Gortmaker. "Do We Fatten Our Children at the TV Set? Television Viewing and Obesity in Children and Adolescents." *Pediatrics* 75 (1985): 807–812.

Dobbing, J. "Infant Nutrition and Later Achievement." *Nutrition Reviews* 42 (1984): 1–7.

Dwyer, J. "Are There Potential Effects of Nutrition on Learning and School Performance in Massachusetts?" Unpublished manuscript, Boston, 1984.

Dwyer, J. "Nutrition Perspectives: Monitoring and Surveillance." In *Monitoring Child Health in the United States: Selected Issues and Policies,* edited by D. K. Walker and J. B. Richmond, 131–142. Cambridge, Mass.: Harvard University Press, 1985.

Dwyer, J. "Promoting Good Nutrition for Today and the Year 2000." *Pediatric Clinics of North America* 33 (1986): 799–821.

Dwyer, J. T., F. M. Dwyer, and J. Mayer. "Feeding the Preschool Child." *Postgraduate Medicine* 48 (1) [1970]: 208–211.

Dwyer, J., and M. C. Egan, eds. *The Right to Grow: Putting Nutrition Services for Children With Special Long-Term Developmental and Health Needs into Action.* Boston: Tufts University School of Medicine, 1985.

Dwyer, J. T., and J. Freedland. "Nutrition Services." In *Maternal and Child Health Practices,* edited by H. Wallace, G. Ryan, and A. Ogelsby. 261–285. Oakland: Third Party Publishing Company, 1988.

Dwyer, J. T., and T. Oiso. "Changing Food Patterns." In Proceedings of the XIIth International Congress of Nutrition. New York, 1981.

Elwood, P. C., and D. Hughes. "Clinical Trial of Iron Therapy on Psychomotor Function in Anemic Women." *British Medical Journal* 3 (1970): 254–255.

Folkhand, S., T. H. Monk, R. Bradburg, and J. Rosenthal. "Time-of-Day Effects on School Children's Immediate and Delayed Recall of Meaningful Material." *British Journal of Psychology* 68 (1977): 45–50.

Food Research and Action Coalition. *Out to Lunch: A Study of the USDA's Day Care and Summer Feeding Programs.* Yonkers, New York. Gazette Press, 1974.

Garber, H., and R. Heber. "Modification of Predicted Cognitive Development in High-Risk Children Through Early Intervention." In *How Much Can Intelligance Be Increased?* edited by M. K. Detterman and R. J. Sternberg, 121–137. Norwood, N.J.: Ablex Publishing, 1983.

Gephart, J., M. C. Egan, and V. L. Hutchins. "Perspectives on Health of School-Age Children: Expectations for the Future." *Journal of School Health* 54 (1984): 11–17.

Goodwin, M. T., and G. Pollen. *Creative Food Experiences for Children.* Revised Edition. Washington, D.C.: Center for Science in the Public Interest, 1980.

Graham, G. G. "Searching for Hunger in America." *Public Interest* 78 (1985): 3–17.

Grantham-McGregor, S. "Chronic Undernutrition and Cognitive Abilities." *Human Nutrition–Clinical Nutrition*, 38C (1983): 83–94.

Gray, S. W., B. K. Ramsey, and A. Klaus. "From 3 to 20: The Early Training Project." Baltimore: University Park Press, 1982.

Guralnick, M. J., and F. C. Bennet. *The Effectiveness of Early Intervention for At-Risk and Handicapped Children.* New York: Academic Press, 1987.

Harrell, R. *The Effects of the Head Start Program on Children's Cognitive Development: Preliminary Report of the Head Start Evaluation Synthesis and Utilization Project.* Washington, D.C.: Department of Health and Human Services, 1983.

Head Start Bureau. *Training Guide for Food Service Personnel in Program for Young Children: A Manual for Nutritionists, Dietitians, and Food Service Specialists Who Are Developing and Conducting Training Programs.* Washington, D.C.: U.S. Department of Health, Education, and Welfare, Office of Human Development Services, Administration for Children, Youth and Families, Head Start Bureau, 1979.

Head Start Performance Standards. Washington, D.C.: U.S. Department of Health, Education, and Welfare, Office of Human Development Services, Administration for Children, Youth and Families, 1979.

Heller, K. A. "Effects of Special Education Placement in Educable Mentally Retarded Children." In *Placing Children in Special Education: A Strategy for Equity,* edited by K. A. Heller, W. H. Holzman, and S. Mesnick, 262–299. Washington, D.C.: National Academy Press, 1982.

Honig, A. S., D. B. Sponseller, J. David, B. L. Levadi, and C. S. Von Hippel. *Your Child's Attitudes Towards Learning.* Office of Health and Developmental Services, Administration for Children, Youth, and Families. Head Start Bureau, U.S. Department of Health and Human Services, Publication No. (OHDS) 83–31150, Washington, D.C.: U.S. Government Printing Office, 1983.

Hubbell, R. *A Review of Head Start Since 1970.* Washington, D.C.: U.S. Department of Health and Human Services, 1970.

Human Nutrition Information Service, U.S. Department of Agriculture.

National Food Consumption Survey, Continuing Survey of Food Intakes by Individuals. Report No. 85–5: Low-Income Women 19–50 Years and Their Children 1–5 Years, 4 Days, 1985. Hyattsville, Md.: U.S. Department of Agriculture, Human Nutrition Information Service, Nutrition Monitoring Division, 1985.

Huntington, D. S., S. Provence, and R. K. Packer. *Child Development: Day Care Serving Infants.* U.S. Department of Health, Education, and Welfare, DHEW Publication No. (OCD) 73–14, Washington, D.C.: U.S. Government Printing Office, 1973.

Kallen, D. J., T. B. Haddy, D. Narins, et al. *Maternal Correlates of Iron Deficiency Anemia in Infants.* Abstract IX, International Congress of Nutrition, Mexico City, 1972.

Keister, M. "Relation of Mid-Morning Feeding to Behavior of Nursery School Children." *Journal of American Dietetic Association* 26 (1950): 25–29.

Ketcham, W. A. "Problems of Measuring School Performance." In *Malnutrition, Learning, and Behavior,* edited by N. E. Scrimshaw and J. E. Gordon. Cambridge, Mass.: MIT Press, 1968.

Kitchen, W. H., A. L. Rickards, M. M. Ryan, G. W. Ford, J. V. Lissenden, and L. W. Boyle. "Improved Outcome to Two Years of Very Low Birth Weight Infants: Fact or Artifact?" *Developmental Medicine and Child Neurology* 28 (1986): 579–588.

Klein, R. E., J. P. Habicht, and C. Yarbrough. "Some Methodological Problems in Field Studies of Nutrition and Intelligence." In *Nutrition, Development, and Social Behavior,* edited by D. J. Kallen. Washington, D.C.: U.S. Public Health Service, DHEW Publication No. (NIH) 73–242, 1973.

Kosterlitz, J. "Family Crises." *National Journal,* April 16, 1988: 994.

Kosterlitz, J. "Reexamining Welfare." *National Journal,* December 6, 1986: 2926.

Kotch, J. "The Future of Maternal and Child Health Services." In *The Role of MCH and WIC in the Delivery of Local Health Services. Report of the First Ross Roundtable on Current Issues in Public Health.* Columbus, Ohio: Ross Laboratories, 1987.

Kotelchuck, M., and J. B. Richmond. "Head Start: Evolution of a Successful Comprehensive Child Development Program." *Pediatrics* 70 (3) (1987): 441–445.

Lazar, D. R. *Lasting Effects on Early Education: A Report of the Consortium for Longitudinal Studies.* Monographs of the Society for Research in Child Development, series 195, 1982.

Lazar, I., and R. B. Darlington. *Lasting Effects After Preschool: A Report of the Consortium for Longitudinal Studies* (DHEW Publication No. [OHDS] 79–30178). Washington, D.C.: U.S. Government Printing Office, 1978.

Lazar, I., R. B. Darlington, H. W. Murray, and A. S. Snipper. *Lasting Effects of Early Education: A Report from the Constorium for Longitudinal Studies.* Monographs of the Society for Research in Child Development 47: 195 Serial No. 2–3, 1982.

Lee, C. J. "Nutritional Studies of Selected Teenagers in Kentucky." *American Journal of Clinical Nutrition* 31 (1978): 1453–1464.

Levine, M. D., and C. B. Linden. "Food for Inefficient Thought." *Pediatrics* 48 (1976): 145.

Levine, S., and S. Viener. "A Critical Analysis of Data on Malnutrition and Behavioral Deficits." *Advances in Pediatrics* 22 (1976): 113–136.

Levinger, B. "School Feeding Programs in Less Developed Countries: An Analysis of Actual and Potential Impact."

Unpublished manuscript. New York: Horace Mann–Lincoln Institute, Teachers' College, Columbia University, 1983.

Lieberman, H. R. "Sugars and Behavior." *Clinical Nutrition* 4 (1985): 195–199.

Lloyd, Still, J. D., ed. *Malnutrition and Intellectual Development.* Lancaster, Pennsylvania: MTP Press, 1976.

Logethetis, J., R. B. Lowenson, O. Augostaki, et al. "Body Growth in Cooley's Anemia with a Correlative Study as to Other Aspects of the Illness in 138 Cases." *Pediatrics* 50 (1972): 92.

Lozoff, B., G. M. Brittenham, F. E. Viteri, et al. "Behavioral Abnormalities in Infants with Iron Deficiency Anemia." In *Iron Deficiency: Brain Biochemistry and Behavior,* edited by E. Pollitt and R. L. Leibel, 183–194. New York: Raven Press, 1982a.

Lozoff, B., G. M. Brittenham, F. E. Viteri, et al. "The Effects of Short-Term Oral Iron Therapy on Developmental Deficits in Iron-Deficient Anemic Infants." *Journal of Pediatrics* 100 (1982b): 351–357.

Lozoff, B., and A. Wolf. "Does Abnormal Behavior Account for Low Bayley Scores in Iron-Deficient Infants?" *Pediatric Research* 17 (1983): 100A.

McKey, R. H., L. Condelli, H. Garson, B. Barrett, J. C. McConkey, and M. Plantz. *The Impact of Head Start on Children, Families, and Communities.* Washington, D.C.: CSR, Inc., 1985.

Melton, G. B., and H. A. Davidson. "Child Protection and Society: When Should the State Intervene?" *American Psychologist* 42 (1987): 172–175.

Mylian, N., K. K. Mayer, and M. Winick. "Early Malnutrition and 'Late' Adoption: A Study of the Effects on Development of Korean Orphans Adopted into American Families." *American Journal of Clinical Nutrition* 30 (1977): 1734–1739.

National Institutes of Health. *Defined Diets and Childhood Hyperactivity: NIH Consensus Development Conference,* Vol. 4, No. 3, 1980.

Nelson, P. E., and A. Paul. "The Nutritive Contribution of School Dinners and Other Midday Meals to the Diets of School Children." *Human Nutrition: Applied Nutrition* 37A (1983): 128–135.

Nemzer, E. D., L. E. Arnad, N. A. Votolato, and H. McConnell. "Amino Acid Supplementation as Therapy for Attention Deficit Disorder." *Journal of American Academic Child Psychiatry* 25 (1986): 509–513.

Nersesian, W. S. "Infant Mortality in Socially Vulnerable Populations." *Annual Review Public Health* 9 (1988): 361–377.

Newburger, C. M., L. H. Melnicoe, and E. H. Newburger. "The American Family in Crisis: Implications for Children." *Current Problems in Pediatrics* 16 (1986): No. 12, December.

Nutrition and Feeding of Infants and Children Under Three in Group Day Care. Washington, D.C.: U.S. Department of Health, Education, and Welfare Publication No. (HSM) 72–5606, 1977.

Office of Technology Assessment. *Technology. Dependent Children: Hospital vs. Homecare.* Congress of the United States Office of Technology, Assessment OTA TMH 38. Washington, D.C.: U.S. Government Printing Office, 1987.

Oski, F. A., and A. S. Honig. "The Effects of Therapy on the Developmental Scores of Iron-Deficient Infants." *Journal of Pediatrics* 92 (1978): 21–25.

Oski, F. A., A. S. Honig, B. M. Hebu, and P. H. Horowitz. "Effect of Iron Deficiency Without Anemia on Infant Behavior." *Pediatric Research* 15 (1981): 483.

Oski, F. A., A. S. Honig, B. M. Hebu, and P. H. Horowitz. "Effect of Iron Therapy on Behavior Performance in Nonanemic Iron Deficient Infants." *Journal of Pediatrics* 71 (1983): 877–880.

Oski, F. A., and J. A. McMillan. "Iron in Infant Nutrition." In *Textbook of Pediatric Nutrition*, edited by R. M. Suskind, 63–77. New York: Raven Press, 1982.

Oski, F. A., and P. I. Nieburg. "Reply." *Journal of Pediatrics* January 1976: 163–164.

Parcel, G. S., J. G. Bruhn, and M. C. Cerreto. "Longitudinal Analysis of Health and Safety Behaviors Among Preschool Children." *Psychology Report* 59 (1986): 265–266.

Parkin, J. M. "Free Milk for Children." *Archives of Disabled Children* 47 (1982): 89–91.

Parkinson, C. E., R. Scrivener, L. Graves, J. Bunton, and D. Harvey. "Behavioral Differences of School-Age Children Who Were Small-for-Dates Babies." *Developmental Medicine and Child Neurology* 28 (1986): 498–505.

Peterkin, B. B., and R. L. Rizek. "National Nutrition Monitoring System." *Family Economic Review* No. 4 (1984): 15–19.

Pipes, P. *Nutrition in Infancy and Childhood.* Third Edition. St. Louis: Mosby Times–Mirror, 1986.

Pollitt, E., ed. *Research Strategies for Assessing the Behavioral Effects of Foods and Nutrients.* Cambridge, Mass.: MIT Press, 1982.

Pollitt, E., et al. "Iron Deficiency and Behavioral Development in Infants and Preschool Children." *American Journal of Clinical Nutrition* 43 (1986): 222–565.

Pollitt, E., M. Gersovitz, and M. Gargiulo. "Educational Benefits for the United States School Feeding Program: A Critical Review of the Literature." *American Journal of Public Health* 68 (1978): 477–481.

Pollitt, E., D. Greenfield, and R. Leibel. "Significance of Bayley Scale Score Changes Following Iron Therapy" (editorial). *Journal of Pediatrics* 92 (1978): 177–178.

Pollitt, E., J. Haas, and D. A. Levitsky, eds. "International Conference on Iron Deficiency and Behavioral Development." *American Journal of Clinical Nutrition* 50 (1989): 565–705.

Pollitt, E., and R. L. Leibel. "Iron Deficiency and Behavior." *Journal of Pediatrics* 1976: 372–381.

Pollitt, E., and R. L. Leibel, eds. *Iron Deficiency: Brain Biochemistry and Behavior.* New York: Raven Press, 1982.

Pollitt, E., R. L. Leibel, and D. Greenfield. "Brief Fasting, Stress, and Cognition in Children." *American Journal of Clinical Nutrition* 34 (1981): 1526–1533.

Pollitt, E., "Iron Deficiency and Cognitive Test Performance in Preschool Children." *Nutrition and Behavior* 1 (1983): 137–146.

Pollitt, E., and W. Mueller. "The Relation of Growth to Cognition in a Well Nourished Preschool Population." *Child Development* 53 (1978): 1157–1163.

Pollitt, E., and C. Thomson. "Protein Calorie Malnutrition and Behavior: A View from Psychology." In *Nutrition and the Brain*, Vol 2, edited by R. J. Wurtman and J. J. Wurtman. New York: Raven Press, 1977.

Pollitt, E., F., Viteri, Saco, Pollit, et al. "Behavioral Effects of Iron Deficiency Anemia in Children." In *Iron Deficiency: Brain Biochemistry and Behavior*, edited by E. Pollitt and F. Leibel, 195–208. New York: Raven Press, 1982.

Powell, G. F., J. F. Low, and M. A. Speers. "Behavior as a Diagnostic Aid in Failure to Thrive." *Journal of Developmental and Behavioral Pediatrics*, Supplement (1987): 18–24.

President's Task Force on Food Assistance. "Report of the President's Task Force on Food Assistance." Washington, D.C.: Executive Office of the President, 1984.

Ramsey, C. T., K. O. Yeates, and E. T. Short. "The Plasticity of Intellectual Development: Insights from Prevention Intervention." *Child Development* 55 (1984): 1913–1925.

Rapoport, J. L., and M. J. P. Kruesi. "Behavior and Nutrition: A Mini Review." *Contemporary Nutrition* 8 (10) [1983]: 1–2.

Read, M. S. "Anemia and Behavior." *Modern Problems in Pediatrics* 14 (1975): 189–202.

Ricciuti, H. N. "Adverse Environmental and Nutritional Influences on Mental Development: A Perspective." *Journal of the American Dietetic Association* 79 (1981): 115–120.

Richardson, S. A., H. G. Birch, E. Grabie, and E. Yoder. "The Behavior of Children in School Who Were Severely Malnourished in the First Two Years of Life." *Journal of Health and Social Behavior* 13 (1972): 276–284.

Rivlin, L. G., and M. Wolfe. *Institutional Settings in Children's Lives.* New York: John Wiley, 1985.

Rosenberg, M. S. "Psychopharmacological Interventions with Young Hyperactive Children." *Topics in Early Childhood and Special Education* 6 (1986): 62–74.

Russell, S. D., and R. M. Clifford. "Child Abuse and Neglect in North Carolina Day Care Programs." *Child Welfare* 66 (1987): 149–163.

Schloesser, P. T. *Health of Children in Day Care: Public Health Profiles.* Kansas City, Kan.: Kansas Department of Health and Environment, December 1986.

Shelton, T. L., E. S. Jeppson, and B. H. Johnson. *Family Centered Care for Children with Special Health Care Needs.* 2nd ed. Washington, D.C.: Association for Care of Children's Health, 1987.

Singer, D. G., J. L. Singer, J. David, B. L. Levadi, and C. Saaz Von Hippel. *Getting Involved: Your Child and TV.* Office of Health and Developmental Services, Administration of Children, Youth, and Families. Head Start Bureau, U.S. Department of Health and Human Services, Publication No. (OHDS) 83–31149, Washington, D.C.: U.S. Government Printing Office, 1983.

Singer, L. "Long-Term Hospitalization of Failure-to-Thrive Infants: Developmental Outcomes at Three Years." *Child Abuse and Neglect* 10 (1986): 479–486.

Singer, L. "Long-Term Hospitalization of Nonorganic Failure-to-Thrive Infants: Patient Characteristics and Hospital Course." *Journal of Developmental Behavioral Pediatrics* 8 (1986): 25–31.

Slaughter, D. T. *Early Intervention and Its Effects on Maternal Behavior and Child Development.* Child Development Monographs, Serial No. 203. Chicago: University of Chicago, 1983.

Sponsiller, D. B., J. David, B. L. Levadi, and C. Saaz Von Hippel. *Your Child and Play.* Office of Health and Developmental Services, Administration for Children, Youth, and Families. Head Start Bureau, U.S. Department of Health and Human Services, Publication No. (OHDS) 83–31151, Washington, D.C.: U.S. Government Printing Office, 1983.

Strong, W., and B. Dennison. "Pediatric Preventive Cardiology: Atherosclerosis and Coronary Heart Disease." *Pediatrics in Review* 9 (1988): 303–314.

Stull, G. A., and H. M. Eckert, eds. "Effect of Physical Activity on Children: A Special Tribute to Mabel Lee." American Academy of Physical Education Papers No. 119, Human Kinetics Press, 1986.

Swann, P. S. "Food Consumption by Individuals in the United States: Two Major Surveys." *Annual Review of Nutrition* 3 (1983): 413–432.

Swanson, J. M. "Iron Rebuttal." *American Journal of Diseases of Children* 134 (1980): 1124.

Tsong, R. Y. L., J. Mellon, and K. Bammer. *The Relationship Between Nutrition,*

Student Achievement, Behavior and Health: A Review of the Literature. Sacramento, Calif: California Department of Education, 1980.

Tuckermanty, E., and C. R. Gallagher-Allred. *Normal Diet: Age of Parental Control. Nutrition in Primary Care.* Columbus, Ohio: Department of Family Medicine, Ohio State University, 1980.

U.S. Department of Agriculture. *A Planning Guide for Food Service in Child Care Centers.* Alexandria, Va.: Food and Nutrition Service, U.S. Department of Agriculture, undated.

U.S. Department of Health and Human Services. *Handbook for Local Head Start Nutrition Specialists.* U.S. Department of Health and Human Services, Office of Human Development Services, Administration for Children, Youth, and Families, Head Start Bureau DHHS Publication No. (OHDS) 84–31189, Washington, D.C.: U.S. Department of Health and Human Services, 1983.

U.S. Department of Health and Human Services. *Head Start Program Performance Standards.* Office of Human Development Services, Administration for Children, Youth, and Families, Head Start Bureau, U.S. Department of Health and Human Services, DHHS Publication No. (OHDS) 84–31131, Washington, D.C.: U.S. Department of Health and Human Services, 1984.

U.S. Department of Health and Human Services. *Parent Nutrition Kit: Head Start Nutrition Education Curriculum.* Office of Human Development Services, Administration for Children, Youth, and Families, Head Start Bureau, Washington, D.C.: U.S. Government Printing Office, 1988.

U.S. Department of Health, Education, and Welfare, Office of Human Development Services, Administration for Children, Youth, and Families. *Nutrition Training Guide for Classroom Personnel in Head Start Programs.* Washington D.C.: U.S. Department of Health, Education, and Welfare, 1976.

U.S. General Accounting Office. "WIC Evaluations Provide Some Favorable But No Conclusive Evidence on the Effect Expected for the Special Supplemental Program for Women, Infants, and Children." Report to the Committee on Agriculture, Nutrition, and Forestry. Washington, D.C.: U.S. Senate, Washington General Accounting Office, January 30, 1984.

Vazquez, Seone, P., R. Windom, and H. A. Pearson. "Disappearance of Iron Deficiency Anemia in a High-Risk Infant Population Given Supplemental Iron." *New England Journal of Medicine* 313 (1985): 1239–1240.

Viteri, F. E. "Physical Fitness and Anemia." Proc. International Symposium on Malnutrition and Function of Blood Cells, Kyoto 1972, 559–583. Tokyo: National Institute of Nutrition, 1973.

Walter, T., J. Kovalskys, and A. Stekel. "Effect of Mild Iron Deficiency on Infant Mental Development Scores." *Journal of Pediatrics* 102 (1983): 519–522.

Weaber, D. P., L. Vuori, N. Ortiz, J. R. Clement, N. E. Cristianson, J. O. Mora, R. B. Reed, and M. G. Herrera. "Nutritional Supplementation, Maternal Education, and Cognitive Development of Children at Risk of Malnutrition." *American Journal of Clinical Nutrition* 34 (1981): 807–813.

Weiss, B. "In Rebuttal." *American Journal of Disabled Children,* 134 (1980): 1126.

Wender, E. M. "New Evidence on Food Additives and Hyperkinesis: A Critical Analysis." *American Journal of Disabled Children* 134 (1980): 1122.

Werkman, S., L. Shifman, and T. Shelly. "Psychosocial Correlates of Iron Deficiency in Early Childhood." *Psychosomatic Medicine,* 26 (1964): 125.

White, K. R. "Efficacy of Early Intervention." *Journal of Special Education* 19(4) [1986]: 401–416.

Winick, M., K. K. Meyer, and R. C. Harris. "Malnutrition and Environmental Enrichment by Early Adoption." *Science* 190 (1975): 1173–1175.

Woodhead, M. "When Psychology Informs Public Policy: The Case of Early Childhood Intervention." *American Psychologist* 43 (1988): 443–454.

Yperman, A. M., and J. A. Vermeersch. "Factors Associated with Children's Food Habits." *Journal of Nutrition Education* 11 (1979): 72.

Zigler, E. "Formal Schooling for Four-Year-Olds." *American Psychologist* 390 (1984): 916–917.

EARLY FAMILY INTERACTIONS OF YOUNG CHILDREN

Critical Stages and Different Contexts

Gloria G. Rodriguez
EXECUTIVE DIRECTOR
AVANCE FAMILY SUPPORT
AND EDUCATION PROGRAMS

AVANCE FAMILY SUPPORT AND EDUCATION PROGRAMS

At the 1988 Summer Institute of the Council of Chief State School Officers (CCSSO), I distributed a program brochure and showed a videotape divided into two segments: a special on Avance that had appeared on ABC World News Tonight earlier in the year, and a video presentation on the services offered by Avance.

The first segment of the video featured Eva, who—because of Avance—has learned to become a better mother to her children. Unfortunately, she learned those skills only after one of her children died. I have heard of several other cases in which children living in the high-risk area that we serve have died of dehydration, severe physical punishment, accidental injury, or diarrhea. Unfortunately, these deaths could have been prevented had the parents received information and support. Unlike handicapped children, the children Avance serves were born healthy and did not have physical problems with eating as you saw in the previous film. They were just victims of an environment in which their parents did not know how to care for them adequately or one in which the parents did not receive adequate support to nurture and care for their children in turn.

However, Eva's other children now have a better opportunity to survive and to do well in school and in life. Eva has structured one of her bedrooms in the housing project in which she lives into a learning center for her children. She not only knows how to better care for her children's physical needs but also understands the important role she must play as a teacher of her children. In fact, during the ABC filming, her five-year-old daughter was reading to the cameraman, indicating that Eva was applying what she had learned through Avance.

The word *avance* is derived from a Spanish verb that means "to advance, to progress." We want to provide parents and children with an opportunity to advance educationally, socially, and economically; to improve their quality of life; and to become productive, contributing members of society.

Avance was first conceptualized at Cornell University when two of Dr. Urie Bronfenbrenner's doctoral students submitted a grant to the Zale Corporation to

103

implement the Avance program in Dallas, Texas, in 1972. One year later, Avance San Antonio, Inc., was implemented, under my directorship, as a grass-roots organization located in a federally subsidized San Antonio housing project with the purpose of helping low-income mothers become "effective teachers" of their young children. Today, Avance has evolved into a comprehensive community-based family support and education center that works at stabilizing the home environment. It is concerned with the development of the individual as a whole person so that he or she can reach his or her fullest potential and become part of the American mainstream.

We have five centers in San Antonio and one in Houston. We receive funding from the city of San Antonio, United Way, the state and federal governments, the Carnegie Corporation, and the private business sector (including a grant from the General Foods Fund to open the center in Houston and from Hasbro Corporation to begin the Fatherhood Project).

Even though we now offer numerous programs to families, our core program is the Avance Parent/Child Education Program, through which we provide comprehensive education and support services to low-income families and their children under three years of age. We begin by providing support and information to the mother and her preschool children. The mother attends the center-based program once a week for three hours, for nine months of the year. The first hour is devoted to making educational toys and the second hour to lectures and class discussions relating to child growth and development. The third hour is used to familiarize parents with the various social services available in the community.

While the mothers attend the parenting classes, their preschool children participate in Avance's Developmental Day Care Center. The day-care center's services are divided into those for infants, crawlers, and toddlers. The parents work as volunteers in the day-care center on non-class days and are under the supervision of Avance caregivers. We administer the Denver Developmental Exam on the children, have nurses volunteer at the Avance's Day Care, and take many of the clients (both mothers and children) to clinics for health-related problems. In addition, the parents and children are taken on field trips to the zoo, the circus, Sea World, the rodeo, a grocery store, and the Ice Capades. Each mother obtains a library card, and the mothers and their children are taken to the library on a monthly basis.

Avance's curriculum consists of lessons on the child's physical, social, emotional, and cognitive stages of development; effective discipline practices; personal coping techniques; and decision-making/problem-solving skills. The parents learn about first aid, nutrition, childhood illnesses, safety and supervision, hygiene and cleanliness, and the importance of demonstrating love and giving their children attention. Many parents who are new to the program believe that it is foolish to talk or to read to very young infants because the parents feel that children do not comprehend at very early ages. They believe that their primary role as parents is to care for their children's physical needs but do not realize the importance of language, environmental stimulation, and stimulating the children's thinking. In response, Avance emphasizes the importance of education and urges the parents to stimulate the children's environment—to talk, to listen, and to read to their children and to build those important concepts that are essential for academic success.

The parents make approximately 30 toys (books, puzzles, dolls, puppets, etc.) that are used to teach educational concepts and skills that will prepare their children for school and for life. With each toy, the parent is given a possibility sheet that describes activities children can do with the toy, exercises the parent can use to enhance language development, and activities to stimulate the child's senses. Avance helps parents acquire the skill of "teaching" that can be generalized in different settings. Parents learn to teach things that they may have taken for granted—to label objects; to name colors, shapes, textures, and numbers; to stimulate thinking; to ask questions; and to help the child to be perceptive, inquisitive, and attentive to his or her environment. Parents then show a greater interest in what their children are doing, and they realize the importance of praising their children's efforts, demonstrating love, and having patience.

Avance brings existing under-utilized social, educational, economic, and mental health services to the families in the form of weekly guest speakers. Among them are nurses who provide information on childhood illnesses, cardiopulmonary resuscitation, and first aid; nutritionists from the U.S. Department of Agriculture who discuss the preparation of nutritious meals; Planned Parenthood workers who address family planning; and fire department officials who speak about fire safety. Parents learn to utilize these community resources to enhance their quality of life, to cope with crises, to strengthen relationships, and to develop a broader support system.

In addition to the center-based component, the Avance staff visits each parent at home twice a month to record and to videotape him or her and the child at play with a toy that was made at the center. The videotape is viewed during the third hour of class, and the parent receives continuous and constructive feedback from both the staff and other participants.

By meeting weekly for nine months and sharing common concerns and joyous moments, the mothers form close friendships that continue to grow beyond the program. This important support system creates a sense of community, in which neighbor helps neighbor caring for children, protecting each other's homes, or just being there whenever someone else is in need. After nine months, the mothers and children participate in graduation ceremonies at a local university during which each mother receives a parenting certificate and each child, dressed in cap and gown, receives a reading book.

It is very likely, had the parents not received Avance's support and education, that the children would have been less stimulated and enriched verbally and environmentally and may have felt less loved and secure. Without Avance, the schools would have received less-prepared children and the parents would likely be less committed to education and less involved in the educational process. The children would probably have had parents who were isolated, who lacked support, and who experienced stress and depression over their chronic economic and social conditions—factors that affect parents' energy levels and thus affect how they relate to and interact with their children. They might have eventually vented their frustrations on their children, and the children might have spent their time and energy in school worrying about their problems at home.

Through their involvement in the nine-month Avance program, the parents have made a big investment of time and energy establishing the child's foundation for learning. They know that they now have an important role in ensuring that their children will succeed academically. Upon completing the Avance Program, parents are also encouraged to place their children in Head Start or a day-care center so that learning can continue. Parents realize that they must continue as partners in the educational process by becoming involved and being a vital part of the school system. The parents also have higher expectations, goals, and dreams for their children, such as finishing high school and getting a good job, or going on to college.

Avance has been able to rekindle many parents' sense of hope and motivation. They aspire to have a better quality of life for their children, themselves, their family, and eventually for their community.

The Avance Educational Program for Parents and Children from birth to three is the hub of our intervention model for hard-to-reach families. Avance is a one-stop resource center for the family. Parents come in and out of it when they need it and as they need it. It is a comprehensive, community-based program that is an advocate for the family and makes the systems and resources that are available in the community work for them.

The chart outlines our intervention model for hard-to-reach families. We knew that to prevent educational problems among low-income Hispanic children and other high-risk children that intervention must (1) begin in the home; (2) be in the children's community; (3) begin when children are very young (birth to age three); and (4) reach the children through their parents (first the mother, then the father). One cannot separate children from their families or from their environment. If the family is weak, is not functioning well, or is in disarray, children's development and academic performance are adversely affected. Therefore, Avance begins by supporting and assisting parents so that they, in turn, can do a better job in rearing their children. We initiate contact with families by working first with the mother of the newborn to two-year-old child. If we begin to educate the mother, we will eventually reach all family members, and the best way to reach a mother is through her children. Once a mother receives information, guidance, and support, then each family member will be in a better position to develop.

From the hub of the chart, the child's growth is illustrated in the upper half of the circle; in the lower half is illustrated the growth of parents. When most

FAMILY INTERVENTION MODEL
FOR HARD-TO-REACH FAMILIES

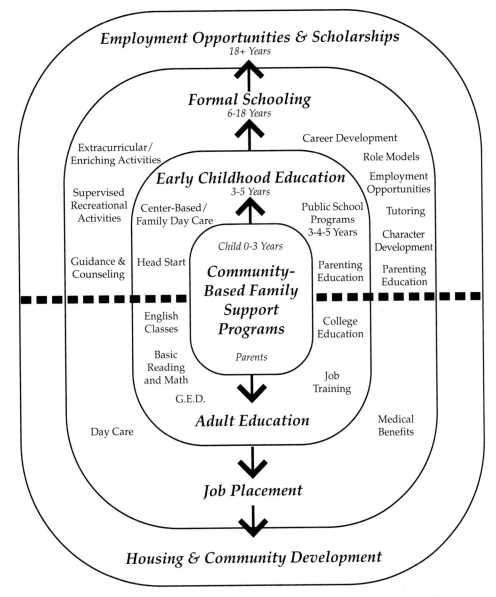

Employment Opportunities & Scholarships
18+ Years

Formal Schooling
6-18 Years

Extracurricular/
Enriching Activities

Career Development

Role Models

Early Childhood Education
3-5 Years

Supervised
Recreational
Activities

Employment
Opportunities

Center-Based/
Family Day Care

Public School
Programs
3-4-5 Years

Tutoring

Guidance &
Counseling

Head Start

Child 0-3 Years

*Community-
Based Family
Support
Programs*

Parenting
Education

Character
Development

Parenting
Education

English
Classes

College
Education

Basic
Reading
and Math

Parents

G.E.D.

Job
Training

Adult Education

Day Care

Medical
Benefits

Job Placement

Housing & Community Development

INTERVENTION MUST:

1. Begin in the Home
2. Be Community Based
3. Be Comprehensive in Scope
4. Be Preventive in Nature
5. Have Child (0 to 3) as the Entry Point
6. Provide Sequential Services to Child and Parents

parents enter Avance, they lack knowledge about child growth and development. Eighty percent of the parents have dropped out of school, and their mean educational level is eighth grade. They are under a great deal of stress; between 44 percent and 60 percent of our participants have been found to display depressive symptoms. They lack marketable job skills and support systems that could help them cope with their everyday problems. Many were abused as children; they were isolated, felt overwhelmed, lacked energy, and had lost most of the hope of improving their state in life. Avance responds to their needs by offering them information, love, guidance, and support. Through this intervention, a parent's self-esteem, energy, and motivation improve, thus affecting his or her attitudes and behaviors. The Carnegie Corporation's evaluation of Avance's program will enable us to test this hypothesis scientifically.

Avance has parents graduating from the parenting program who want to continue to grow personally and educationally beyond being effective parents. Now they want better lives not only for their children but also for themselves and for their families.

Many mothers begin to set goals: some want to return to school; some want to obtain employment; many begin to realize that buying a car and a house can become a reality. Avance provides an opportunity for those parents interested in pursuing a better education by offering classes. Teachers from Region 20 and the local community colleges come to the Avance centers and teach English, basic skills, GED, and college classes. Transportation and child care are provided by Avance. Hundreds of adults have enrolled in the classes; many have received their GEDs, and have taken college classes! One participant has become a schoolteacher, and a number have obtained associate's degrees.

For sixteen years Avance targeted the mothers. As hundreds of women each year attended Avance's educational classes, many who were married or who had partners were outgrowing their husbands or partners. Most of these men had had childhood experiences similar to those that the women had: many were abused as children, and they, too, lacked parenting and job skills and had dropped out of school. Therefore, Avance responded by initiating a fatherhood project in which the fathers learn to be effective parents and are encouraged to further their own education. Fathers participate in the program through their involvement with their children. This involvement includes making kites, initiating a Boy Scout troop, going on numerous family field trips, and attending parenting education classes.

As parents leave the welfare system and pursue a life of self-sufficiency, it is essential that day care and medical benefits be provided. Once the parents are employed, they may then be able to buy cars for transportation and to obtain affordable housing.

Parents' psychological states should improve somewhat as a result of the birth-to-three parenting program; but a significant improvement would result if parents obtained jobs and owned their own homes. Their sense of pride would be reflected in better upkeep of their yards and neighborhoods. Therefore, the last phase of intervention for parents should be Housing and Community

Development. There should be a sense of community, of families working and playing together, and of neighbor helping neighbor. Avance's motto is that the strength of the community lies in the strength of the families. Indeed, society's strength lies in the strength of its communities.

Avance's goals are to enable all family members to reach their fullest potential and to strengthen enough families in the neighborhood so that eventually the community will be strong and experience a sense of pride.

Since Avance began in 1973, I have seen Avance's children grow up in very-high-risk communities. Even though they had had sound early childhood foundations and more-stable families, the children still had to overcome a great many environmental obstacles. Intervention must begin at an early age, and it must be continuous in order to enable children to overcome adverse environmental conditions. We can leave neither the child nor the parents to chance. After the children graduate from Avance, we encourage the parents to enroll their children in Head Start or day care. The schools could begin to offer early childhood classes to children as young as three years of age. This would be the transition from the home to the school, with school-based community workers who would serve as liaison between the community-based family support and education programs. The schools could also contract with non-profit community-based organizations to provide continued services in the schools.

As the child grows, the parent needs to gain new skills and information to better help the child. Avance responds to this need by having mini-workshops at the schools, in which the parent learns how to better help the child make a transition from home to formal schooling. The mini-workshops also help parents become involved in the school system. School personnel have stated that Avance has the experience and skill to reach families and has a very sound and interesting curriculum.

The preadolescent and adolescent stages are another critical period for intervention. Avance has classes for parents of preteens and teenagers on the subjects of communication, sex education, and career development. These classes are offered in the schools and in the communities. Avance is trying to obtain funds to have positive alternative activities for the Avance preadolescents and adolescents within their communities and/or within the schools. If the youth in high-risk communities do not have something positive to do to occupy their free time, they can easily fall victim to peer pressure and be susceptible to the problems of drugs, alcoholism, and teen pregnancy. The school districts can easily provide existing under-utilized school facilities for this purpose.

Schools should provide proper role models, extracurricular activities, enriching activities, supervised recreational activities, and character-development activities. All children also need support, guidance, and counseling from the home and the school. If low-income, high-risk minority children participate in the above activities and receive a strong formal education, then they will have a better likelihood of finishing high school and developing to their fullest potential. These youths would be better prepared to enter the labor force immediately and become productive, contributing members of society, or they could become eligible for scholarships to pursue higher education. As a result, the pool of potential minority students entering college and going into science, technical, and engineering careers would be broadened.

One cannot use the Boston Compact Model, or Educational Partnership Program as it is called in San Antonio, as an incentive to keep children in school. Most children who take advantage of scholarships or special enriching programs are doing well in school and come from homes that are stable and that have provided them with a strong foundation for learning. Most children who physically drop out of the educational system do so cognitively and emotionally long before they reach the fourth grade—many when they enter formal schooling. We must begin in the home, through the parents, if we want to help alleviate the high dropout rate and the potential dropout rate.

Many social problems, including educational problems, teen pregnancy, delinquency, drug abuse, and poverty can be prevented by supporting the family. If a child begins life within a strong family, has a good foundation for learning, and continues to receive support, then he or she will have a better chance of staying on the right path and becoming a responsible and thriving member of society.

I have been asked whether, in my judgment, community-based programs are more effective at reaching high-risk families than attempts to reach them through the schools. I strongly believe that intervention must begin in the home and community. It must be comprehensive in scope, preventive in nature, and sequential in development. However, I realize that there is a school in every community and that the schools have the mechanisms in place to provide many of the services offered by Avance.

But the schools are too bureaucratic, and many high-risk families will not come initially to the schools; we must first go to the homes. Community-based programs like Avance can serve as the missing link between the homes, the schools, and other delivery systems. They can also serve as a buffer and a mediator so that parents can feel comfortable coming to schools and being part of the educational process.

Once rapport and trust have been established, schools can then offer vital services to the family—day care, adult education, before- and after-school care, and youth activities. The community-based family support program serves as the hub for further helping both high-risk children and parents to reach a higher educational level and a higher quality of life.

EARLY FAMILY INTERACTIONS OF YOUNG CHILDREN: CRITICAL STAGES AND DIFFERENT CONTEXTS

I have dedicated the past nineteen years of my life to designing and developing alternative methodologies and intervention programs that enable children and parents living in high-risk communities to share in the American dream of a good education and an opportunity for a better quality of life. Before

I was Executive Director of Avance, I was a first-grade teacher and had just received my mid-management certificate to become a principal.

In this paper, I have set down my thoughts, which are based on my past experiences as a former schoolteacher of high-risk children. I also drew upon my involvement in the development of Avance, the comprehensive community-based parent education program located in several high-risk communities in San Antonio and Houston, Texas, which were described earlier. On a personal note, I included reflections from my childhood experiences growing up in a low-income high-risk community.

Even though my family was economically poor while I was growing up in the San Antonio barrio, my life was enriched by many positive family interactions. When I was two years old, my father, a victim of the violence and crime in the neighborhood, was fatally injured, leaving my mother a widow with five children. However, we were able to overcome this tragedy and other negative conditions because there was great stability in the home and because my mother possessed substantial inner spiritual strength. The spirit of hope gave her the determination, resourcefulness, and motivation that enabled her and her children to make it out of poverty. My sisters and I felt we were loved and wanted; we felt important in the eyes of our extended and nuclear family, and we knew that we could turn to one another for support.

The majority of families in my neighborhood were stable, and we felt a great sense of community. The values of respect, the work ethic, education, and religion were stressed. We knew we had a purpose in life and that through hard work and with support from others, we were going to succeed. It was inculcated from youth that we should be sensitive to the needs of others—especially to those of our immediate and extended family, to our neighbors, and to those less fortunate.

These same family interactions were found in my husband's family, who lived in a barrio that was a haven for drugs and crime. My husband and I come from similar communities. There were eight children in his family, and both sets of our parents had only a third-grade education. In spite of this, their children were able to obtain good educations and much higher economic standards of living than those of our parents. In my family, I am a Ph.D. candidate, one of my sisters has a master's degree, one has a bachelor's degree, one has some college hours, and another is a successful entrepreneur. In my husband's family there are a medical doctor, three electrical engineers, a college professor, and a counselor with a master's degree.

I have spent many years struggling to understand why some Hispanics living in high-risk communities throughout the nation have been able to overcome adverse environmental conditions and to succeed socially and economically, while a disproportionate number have not been as fortunate. I have concluded that the success of my husband's family and that of my family is due largely to those strong early family interactions that both of us experienced that gave us feelings of security and positive self-concepts. In addition, there still existed a sense of community in which neighbors helped neighbors survive and overcome the effects of crime, drugs, prostitution, and discrimination. Finally, we were very fortunate to have had opportunities to obtain scholarships, grants, and loans toward higher education.

Throughout the nation, many families are suffering, in pain, and in need of support and assistance. When the majority of the families living in a concentrated area cease to function well, then the community in which they live slowly begins to decay. Negative forces around them become stronger and can overpower and crush many families. Children living in these neighborhoods helplessly fall prey to those forces that they cannot possibly control. Parents eventually lose whatever energy and hope they had of being able to guide and prepare their children for school and for life. This is the beginning of a vicious cycle for parents who are unable to bring up a new generation of youngsters with the skills necessary to survive and to overcome the obstacles they encounter so that they can become productive, contributing members of society. What kind of role models are these parents going to be for their children? If parents do not feel good about themselves and have lost control over their lives, how can they adequately care for their children? Such parents are concerned with basic survival on a daily basis. Consequently, their children have needs that are not being met.

Society has allowed families and communities to fall apart gradually, and the symptoms are reflected in many of today's social problems, such as child abuse and neglect, crime and delinquency, illiteracy and the high-school dropout rate, severe health and mental disorders, unemployment, and poverty. Drugs and alcohol are used as an escape from everyday reality.

These social problems can be symptoms of parents who experience continuous stress; who lack the knowledge and skills necessary to effectively nurture and supervise their children; who lack support in their parental role; and who feel overwhelmed and incompetent as parents and as individuals. During a critical period in their children's lives, these parents are in dire need of support and information to help them nurture and better guide their young children—yet many do not receive the support they need. These unmet needs can lead to problems that later may become deeply rooted, become learned behavior, and remain a way of life from one generation to another.

Many researchers have demonstrated that physical illness or emotional disorders can be linked to poverty, social estrangement, unemployment, low social status, and powerlessness. Individuals living in a marginal status in society have been deprived of meaningful social contact. Other researchers reporting a relationship between stress and physical and mental disorders have advocated the benefits of strong support systems. They imply that physical and mental disease can be prevented through stress reduction, increased self-esteem, mutual support groups, and community organization.

Life would be very different for me today if my mother had not received the support she needed when my father died, when our house burned down, and when she needed child-care assistance in order to work or to run errands. It was this support that alleviated the stress and enabled the positive family interactions to occur. Ultimately, it was these positive family interactions that helped my sisters and me to blossom.

Life would be very different for my husband had his mother not worked as a domestic helper in the home of a woman with young children. There, for the first time, she saw a different way of life—the family working and playing together, the mother talking and reading to her children. There were books, games, and writing materials in the house, and the value of education was stressed. All that my mother-in-law learned about child-rearing she applied to her own children, for she then knew what she needed to do. Thereafter, she became a role model to her married brothers and sisters, and their children benefited. Several of my mother-in-law's low-income nephews and nieces have attended college—one became an accountant, and another is studying to become a medical examiner.

All parents need support and information to help them help their children grow and develop to their fullest potential. If the parents do not receive the support and information they need, then their children will come to school unprepared and unable to learn, and their teachers will experience great frustration. I can attest to the frustration of a dedicated teacher attempting to work with children who are not adequately prepared.

Upon graduating from college in December, I became a schoolteacher of 35 first-graders who had been taken from four classrooms and whose teachers had already given up on them. They had been labeled as "slow learners" and "vegetables," and it had been decided they were going to be retained.

I considered the job a challenge. However, it was not long before I felt frustration. Even though the children were not "vegetables" and could indeed learn, they were nevertheless unprepared to meet the academic demands of school. Initially, I thought their shortcoming was just a language problem—Spanish-speaking children not understanding the English language. I soon realized, however, that the children were proficient neither in English nor in Spanish. I saw a six-year-old child hold a pencil like a dagger; children not being able to construct a circle; children who were inadequately clothed in the winter; hungry children; bruised children; children with lice. I immediately managed to change a school policy that kept children with lice from coming to school. The children were being denied an education because of a health problem.

These children had everything going against them. They were doomed to fail in the first grade because of the conflict between the home and the school. School is not designed to work with children who are below the expected level of development. School cannot adequately compensate for what should have been accomplished early in life or assume the role of parent after the child enters school. Ironically, the school assumes that all parents have done their part in preparing their children prior to entering school. Unfortunately, in many homes of high-risk children, this is not true.

Children entered my class with limited language proficiency in both English and Spanish. They lacked the mastery of many basic prereadiness skills, and they exhibited behaviors which indicated that physical punishment was the prevalent form of discipline in the home. For example, some of the children would shrink back as I approached them, as though I were going to hit them. I was overwhelmed as a teacher when I was given a set of books on handwriting, reading, and math that were inappropriate for the children's stage of development.

School is designed for children who come from stable families in which there are a lot of resources as well as positive verbal and environmental stimulation. There are many children who come to school with too few relevant experiences to be able to succeed academically. They may also come from families that are not functioning well due to lack of support and education. One cannot assume that all parents know what is expected of them; nor can one assume that parents are stable and in control of their own lives and those of their children.

I administered an informal attitudinal survey to the parents of children I had taught for a year and a half. The results indicated that all the parents wanted better lives for their children than they themselves had had and that they knew education was important. However, when asked to indicate when children start learning in life and who a child's first and most important teacher was, the mothers responded that "children start learning in school, and the first-grade teacher is the first teacher." When asked the question "What do you consider your role as a mother to be?" they responded that their role was to take care of the children's basic physical needs. They also stated they did not know whether their children would graduate from high school—they felt their children would complete at least the seventh or eighth grade. They definitely knew their children would not be going on to college. Paradoxically, while the school assumes that the mother did her part in preparing her child for school, the mother believes that she has no part in the education process—and the child is the victim.

Schools have responded by putting children such as these into special remedial classes such as (1) oral language development classes; (2) speech classes; (3) remedial reading and math classes; (4) LEP classes; and (5) ESL classes. Schools have migrant and bilingual programs that are essential in trying to address specific needs to help these children make the transition to a regular classroom. There are also extremely dedicated teachers who go beyond the call of duty to help these children.

Although one can always find exceptions, in the majority of cases these classes and programs are of no avail if the family is not stable and if the child does not feel loved and secure. Much of a child's time and energy is devoted to the problems at home.

Even when a child does feel loved and secure at home, the lack of an early stimulating and enriching environment will allow remedial classes to help a child advance to only a certain level. The gains made may be lost if the subsequent teacher does not pick up where the previous teacher left off. These children will most likely fall behind, be retained several times, be over-age for their grade, and finally drop out of school.

For a year and a half, I worked many long hours trying to enhance students' language skills that should have been acquired early in life. They eventually reached a point at which they were all reading and slowly progressing. Unfortunately, I later realized that their subsequent teachers did not continue where I left off and that the students would never be able to catch up to those children who came to school prepared. Of the 35 students I taught, 30 moved on to the third grade, and five stayed in the second.

The following year I had a group of children with characteristics similar to my first group. I could not see myself going through another year of frustration. I realized that the school, as it was structured, could not adequately meet the needs of so many high-risk children. So I decided to search for a better solution.

My training in early childhood education and my own family upbringing led me to believe that intervention needs to begin in the home during the child's early formative years, before the child is three years old. It is during this period that language development is so critical, when basic values are formed, when character and personality development are built, and when the foundation for learning is established. In addition, it is a period when children can develop a positive self-concept and learn to love not only themselves but also their family and all people. It is also a time when children learn from the early interactions they have had with their parents to trust and respect others. These are the qualities that are the foundation for becoming successful students and responsible citizens. Programs such as Head Start, which works with children at ages three and four, can be remedial for high-risk children, but prevention needs to begin at birth—and preferably before birth.

In order to help children during this vital period of development, one must help parents understand the important role they play in the educational process and also provide the needed support to overcome the obstacles that impede effective parenting. I decided to become a teacher of parents to help them learn the skill and art of parenting and to facilitate positive parent-child interactions, rather than to be a teacher of young children directly. I wanted to help parents manage their homes rather than to utilize my principal's certificate in managing a school. Lastly, I wanted to empower parents with the feeling that they could have control over their lives, their children's futures, and their own communities.

Being an effective parent does not come naturally—one has to learn the skill and have the opportunity to observe proper role models. Parents must feel good about themselves so that they can, in turn, help their children feel good about themselves.

Avance has become an alternative to the current school system, which has not worked for a high-risk population. It has become a community school, addressing the needs of all the members of the family in their community. Education can truly be defined as a lifelong process—from the cradle to the job. Avance has been concerned with development of the whole person—not just with intellectual development. It attempts to eliminate obstacles that prevent children and adults from learning and growing side by side. It has helped many individuals become productive, contributing members of society. It is also attempting to strengthen enough families in the neighborhood to rebuild communities that have been slowly decaying.

Today's schools are isolated from homes. They have grown so large and so bureaucratic that both parents and children feel anonymous, lost, and overwhelmed by the system. Schools are still designed for children who have parents waiting for them at home. Today, approximately 70 percent of mothers with school-age children work outside the home either full- or part-time, as do over half of mothers with preschool children.

Increased mobility and the breakdown of the extended family have greatly affected the stability of families and the way they rear their children. Many families live in neighborhoods, subdivisions, condominiums, and apartment complexes in which they hardly know their neighbors. Many lack appropriate role models to adequately guide and nurture their children. One out of every two marriages ends in divorce. Families have changed in the past two decades, but society, the schools, and the workplace have not effectively responded to the changes.

Nearly one in four children is poor, and there are eight million more poor Americans today than there were a decade ago. Half of the children who live in poverty live in single-parent families, and half of the single-parent families' incomes fall below the poverty line. The conditions are worse for minorities—43 percent of black children and 38 percent of Hispanic children are poor. Nearly 50 percent of the poor are paying half of their income for rent and utilities; nearly a million more units of low-income housing disappear every year. Welfare benefits have lost a third of their value over the last 15 years because the benefits have not kept up with inflation.

If low-income parents do not receive the support and assistance that they need to help them nurture and guide their children, then the children will not be able to learn and to develop as well as they should. More children will suffer insecurity, anxiety, and distractibility because their complete needs are not being adequately met by strong, caring, and responsive adults.

Problems become worse for schools in which the majority of children come from homes that are not functioning well. Can the schools continue to say, "We are here to educate the young and not to take care of society's social problems"? How can these two elements be separated? The problems that families experience in the home affect whether a child is receptive to education. How can children learn when they are hungry or concerned that their mothers will be beaten up that evening? Instead of concentrating on what they are being taught, their energy is spent in figuring out how to survive or wondering what they can do to get the love and attention that they so desperately need from their parents.

Traditional schools are unable to address the complex set of problems that children bring to school. Schools need to change in order to address the needs of the changing family and the needs of the rising high-risk minority population living in poverty.

Today, 40 percent of Hispanic students drop out of school; of those that graduate, 25 percent are still illiterate. The problem will only worsen, since the Hispanic population will double in size by the year 2005, and will become the largest minority. In states in which there is a concentration of Hispanics, such as New York, California, and Texas, minority children today already are the majority. By the year 2000, ten states will have the minority population as their majority. What will be the conditions of these states when these minority children who were reared in poverty and illiteracy become adults? We all know that the only way out of poverty for these children is to obtain a good education. A good education begins in the home because the parent is the first and most important teacher.

One way to modify schools to address the needs of high-risk minorities is to begin to work with hard-to-reach parents of children from birth to three, through community-based family support programs. Parenting classes for all parents with children under the age of six should be offered several times during the week to accommodate diverse schedules. As the child grows older, parents need new knowledge and skills to better relate to the child, to provide developmentally appropriate support, and to learn how to complement the school.

Parenting education classes should also be offered to all students in middle school and high school so they can begin to understand the responsibilities of being parents and to acquire the knowledge and skills needed to prepare for effective parenting.

Parents need to be welcomed in the schools and encouraged to get involved in the educational process through schools having an "open door" policy for parents. Schools could open their doors earlier and close them later, as many private schools now do in order to accommodate the working parent and to prevent latchkey children from wandering the neighborhood unsupervised. Opening the schools to parents for day-care services, for educational or job-skills classes, or for support groups will make parents feel more comfortable in coming into the schools to participate in their children's education.

Schools should also open their doors year-round to allow taxpayers to better utilize empty facilities. Supervised recreational and enriching activities could be offered before and after school and during the summer. Children from middle-income families have more opportunities to participate in summer camps, arts-and-crafts programs, computer classes, and recreation programs. What do children of low-income families do all summer? They are the same children who have more obstacles to overcome. If we want youth to say no to drugs, early sex, delinquent behavior, and so on, then we must provide alternative activities to which they can say yes.

They could say yes to computer training, sports, field trips, Boy Scouts, Girl Scouts, dancing classes, gymnastics, piano lessons. They could serve as volunteers or be paid to do community work and serve as tutors for young children. We could use our creative minds and come up with a variety of challenges and stimulating activities for youth. If we *do not,* they may easily become another statistic—by dropping out of school or by becoming pregnant. (One teen in five becomes a parent—and we can change those statistics.)

The Avance concept could easily be expanded to reach pregnant teenagers by offering parenting education and the school's regular curriculum in the youths' communities—for example, in housing projects. The school district could provide the teachers to teach regular classes in the community. In addition to regular classroom instruction, students would also learn to care for a young child. The concept of working with delinquent students in storefront schools is being implemented successfully in San Diego. There is an opportunity to work with the "whole person" and to establish recreational and educational programs within the community. The programs offered can become sequential. A student takes a basic skills class, gets her GED, and then takes her first two semesters of college at the community-based program. Then she is individually counseled and guided to pursue a job-training program or a college education on campus. There is also an opportunity to work with the youth's parents in an environment that is not threatening to them, so that they in turn can better support the youth.

One of the most important reasons minority children stay in school is because of extracurricular activities that help them improve their self-esteem and make them feel part of the school. Unfortunately, those children who need these activities the most are often denied the opportunity due to poor academic performance. Schools need to be concerned with the development of the whole child, not solely with the cognitive domain. Children need to be part of sports and other extracurricular activities that will help them develop social and leadership skills. For many minorities in high-risk communities, being involved in extracurricular activities is a great motivator for staying in school and later pursuing a college education.

Minorities need role models whom they can emulate. Numbers of minority teachers are declining, and every effort should be made to recruit and train minorities from poor communities to become schoolteachers.

All teachers also need to be trained in the cultural and learning styles of minority children. They should visit homes to communicate with families and to encourage parents to support their children's educational growth.

Assuming that all teachers are dedicated and nurturing, I also recommend that classroom teachers instruct the same group of children for a minimum of two or three years. My experience teaching the same group of children for a year and a half was very productive and beneficial for the children. I was able to establish rapport with the children and their families, as well as to spend a longer time working with each child at his or her developmental level and rate of learning. However, I wish that the subsequent teachers and I could have continued with the children for even longer. A competent and caring teacher can make the difference in the lives of children, as we saw in the movie *Stand and Deliver*. Teachers like Mr. Escalante need more than one year to establish rapport and to move each student along the learning continuum. Teachers need to have more control over the classroom, and they need to feel they have a real stake in the future of the children.

The complex problems that families are experiencing do not have simple solutions. It is not solely up to the educational system to provide the solutions to society's problems. Nor is it solely up to the families, the social services, the legal systems, or the judicial systems. All the systems need to work together on behalf of our children. National, state, and local governments, the United Way, philanthropic organizations, non-profit organizations, and the private business sector need to come together to find ways to support the family and to rebuild communities. The following are some basic family needs that all concerned should strive to meet.

1. Every parent needs knowledge and support in the rearing of children—especially during the critical formative years from before birth to age three. Children need to start life in good health, and what a mother eats and does to her body will affect the development and health of the child both in the uterus and throughout life. Children need stimulating, enriched environments in which they establish foundations for learning. During this critical stage, children need to learn positive moral and social values which will enable them to be a productive part of society. Most importantly, every child needs to feel loved and wanted.

2. Both mothers and fathers need to be literate and to have at least a high-school education. They need to have opportunities to develop saleable job skills or to pursue a professional education. Supportive services such as day care and transportation are essential if we want individuals to become self-sufficient.

3. Every family needs to have affordable housing and comprehensive health care.

4. Every child needs to have a good education with a loving and responsive teacher and a challenging and stimulating environment.

5. The home, school, and community need to know how to respond to preadolescents and adolescents and to provide them with activities that will help them develop into responsible, competent, special, and unique adults.

National policies need to be established that will strengthen families and keep them together. This country must have a strong national policy in support of the family. Of all the industrialized countries of the world, only the United States and South Africa do not have national policies in support of the family. Other nations see the family as playing a vital role in the development of the nation's human resources. These nations support the family so that children will develop well and become productive and responsible members of society. They do not see children as personal property of their parents, nor is children's development left to chance. The other nations realize that each child can have a positive or negative impact on others and on the country, depending on how he or she is reared. They see an investment in families and children as critical to the political and democratic strength of the country; to the national defense; to the economic development of the country; and to the stability and quality of life of each community. They see that putting money up front in preventive programs is less costly and more effective than in treating problems after they develop. By investing in the basic unit of society—the family—they strive to build a stronger society and a more perfect union.

It is less costly and more effective to fund family support programs, employment training, and community development than to pay the high cost of lifelong support of prisons, residential and institutional centers, foster care, and welfare benefits. It makes more sense to help parents become effective teachers of their children and to enable them to prepare their children for school rather than to pay for remedial education later. Remedial education may not be effective if the family is not involved in the educational process and if it is not stable. It is beyond the question of cost when across this country we cannot build enough jails to address the crime and drug problems.

We have many individuals in high-risk communities who have been forced into situations in which they have not been able to adequately care for themselves and for their children's basic needs. Consequently, the children have grown up in families in which they felt they were not loved, respected, or cared for. As adults, they in turn may find it difficult to love, respect, and care for others. To make matters worse, many of these children have grown up in environments in which there is domestic violence, violence in the community, and violence on television. If they are not watching television, they may be playing with guns, swords, Rambo knives, and G.I. Joe characters.

Our nation as a democracy may be in danger as these children growing up in such hostile environments begin to realize they have been alienated, mistreated, and kept from what they feel they so rightfully deserve.

We may have another social uprising as the gap between the haves and the have-nots continues to widen. The anger that has been inflicted inward with drugs, alcohol, and inhalants can easily become unleashed outwardly against institutions and the privileged few. We are beginning to see signs of this outward hostility in Los Angeles and in New York state in the form of gangs; and across the country we are seeing serious disrespect for police officers and the law. We, as a nation, have created this because we have failed to support the family when children were young and growing up and because we have failed to modify the school system to address the needs of high-risk youth and the changing family.

Why must we wait to respond to an uncontrollable national crisis? The crisis of the poor, the homeless, the delinquent, the uneducated, the institutionalized can be alleviated and prevented by investing now in families and children and in their communities in a comprehensive manner.

Let history not repeat itself, for some have said that the fall of the Roman Empire was due to the dissolution of the family—when parents ceased to care for their children, and the children grew up caring for no one but themselves and their pleasures. There was no love or respect for their fellow citizens or for law and order. The 1970s and the 1980s have been periods of the "me" generation and the materialistic "yuppie" generation. What we do now and into the 1990s will determine whether we can continue to preserve this great nation and its democracy into the next century. At a time when society is becoming more complex technologically, when we are more vulnerable to serious communicable health diseases, and when we are faced with possible instant annihilation, it is imperative that we invest in our young children today.

Every young child counts—we cannot afford to lose even one to poverty and lack of education. We all have a vested interest in our children. Chief state education officers of this nation can adopt policies and practices that can assure education success for all children—especially for the children at risk. I want to commend you and thank you for placing early childhood education and parenting education programs at the top of the nation's education agenda. We are exploring a new frontier. Together we can make a difference in the lives of our children and in the preservation of our democratic society.

REFERENCES

Cassel, J. "The Contribution of the Social Environment to Host Resistance." *American Journal of Epidemiology* 104 (1976): 107–123.

Committee for Economic Development. *Children in Need: Investment Strategies for the Educationally Disadvantaged.* New York, 1987.

Edleman, P. B. *America's Discarded Children: How Can We Put Them on the Political Map?* A summary of discussion and conclusions from the Strategy Meeting on Children in State Care, funded by The Rockefeller Foundation. New York, May 22–23, 1987.

William T. Grant Foundation Commission on Work, Family, and Citizenship. *The Forgotten Half: Non-college Youth in America.* An interim report in the School-to-Work Transition. Washington, D.C., 1988.

Hamburg, D. A. *Fundamental Building Blocks of Early Life.* New York: Carnegie Corporation, 1988.

Hispanic Policy Development Project. *Closing the Gap for U.S. Hispanic Youth.* Report from the 1988 Aspen Institute Conference on Hispanic Americans and the Business Community. Washington, D.C., 1988.

Kessler, M., and G. Albee. "Primary Prevention." *Annual Review of Psychology* 26 (1975): 557–591.

Perry, N. J. "Saving the Schools: How Business Can Help." *Fortune* 118 (November 7, 1988): 42–56.

Rodriguez, G. G. "The Right to an Adequate Education: Implications for Family Support Programs and Educational Reform." *Family Resource Coalition Report* 6 (1987): 8.

Rodriguez, G. G. "Family Support Programs Are Critical Investments." *San Antonio Light*, B5, January 13, 1988.

Rodriguez, G. G. "Family Support in the Home: Programs, Policy, and Social Change." A paper prepared for the Family Support in the Home Conference. Honolulu, February 6–10, 1988.

Rodriguez, G. G. "The Importance of Early Childhood Education and Family Support." A paper presented at the Rockefeller Brothers Fund Education Meeting. Pocantico Hills, N.Y., 1988.

NOW OR LATER?

Issues Related to the Early Education of Minority-Group Children

Lily Wong Fillmore
UNIVERSITY OF CALIFORNIA, BERKELEY

INTRODUCTION

In this paper I discuss issues related to the early education of children from cultural and linguistic minority backgrounds. Some of these children may come from circumstances that are disadvantageous to their intellectual, social, and physical development. Most of them do not. Their caregivers—whatever their economic and social circumstances—provide them with nurturance and a loving start for life, just as they should. The beliefs and practices that guide the socialization of these children may be quite different from those followed in mainstream American homes, however, since their families come from many different cultures. Some of them are newcomers to the society—they are immigrants and refugees of diverse origins. Others have been in the United States for several generations, or were here when the first European immigrants arrived. This paper deals with the adjustments the society expects the children of these families to make in order to gain an education and to take their places in the society at large eventually. These adjustments are necessary—but they can be hard on children and disruptive of their relationships with their families and primary groups. Specifically, I address the following issues:

1. Parents prepare their children for living and learning through the socialization process that takes place in the home. This preparation may differ substantially from the preparation the school assumes children have had. What are the consequences of early education experiences that attempt to resocialize children by teaching them the ways of learning that the school expects?

2. It is often assumed that children who come from non-mainstream backgrounds are deficient in foundational skills for academic learning and that early education programs must compensate for the deficiencies in their preparation for school. How appropriate are programs that stress compensatory skill development, and should preschool programs for children from minority backgrounds be different from those designed for mainstream children?

3. When the language of primary communication in the home is not English, how do early education programs that promote the exclusive use of English in school affect communication between parents and children?

This paper is divided into three sections. In the first, I discuss sources of learning-style differences in children, drawing from observational research of several different cultural groups. In the second section, the issues raised in this paper are discussed in relation to those observations. In the third section, I offer recommendations on how early education programs can help minority-group children adjust to school without damage to their family relationships.

I. PREPARING CHILDREN FOR LEARNING—SOME CULTURAL DIFFERENCES

To researchers who study the educational adjustment of language-minority children, the great disparity found across groups in academic performance is an especially vexing problem. Language differences are not the only barriers to school performance—if they were, all non–English speakers would be similarly affected. The phenomenal success of students from Asian backgrounds, despite initial problems with the language of the school, suggest that language is—at least for this group—just a temporary problem. Their success makes it difficult to attribute the continued lack of educational success of other groups—Hispanic, American Indian, and even Black American—exclusively to linguistic differences.

In recent years, there has been a growing awareness among educational researchers of the many ways in which cultural background can influence school participation. Shirley Brice Heath's ethnographic research on the socialization practices of working-class blacks and whites and of mainstream families in a rural Appalachian community revealed how greatly groups can differ in their beliefs about how children learn, the roles their parents play in their education, and how to prepare children for literacy (Heath, 1983). Although her work deals with English-speaking families rather than with linguistic minorities, Heath's work on child socialization is important here because it offers us a basis for examining the practices and beliefs of other groups.

In the mainstream families she studied, Heath found the child-rearing patterns that are often taken as the "norm": The child is regarded as a "separate, knowing individual" even before birth—thoughts, emotions, and even words are attributed to the child while still in the womb. Heath describes a pattern of interacting with infants that is familiar to us all: Parents speak to infants as if they were able to respond, and they respond for them. They talk to their babies about the objects and people in the home, and they assume that the babies are responsive to their communicative efforts.

Heath notes that from the earliest period, "there is a consistent emphasis on the baby as an individual, a separate person with whom the preferred means of communicating is talk." The members of the family see this communication as the means for teaching children what they need to know about the world—they envelop their babies in a web of words and very early introduce them to the world of books. Mother shows the baby a picture book. She teaches him or her the names of the objects depicted on its pages and asks questions she knows the baby cannot answer. These question routines are carried out solely by the mother at first, according to Heath, but they train the child to act as a conversational partner and information giver. Later, when the child is able to speak, he or she is encouraged to ask questions, and is praised for initiating talk about books, and for inventing tales or engaging in make-believe about materials that have been drawn from books.

By the time the children from Heath's mainstream community enter school, they are ready for it. They have had five years of preparation for literacy. They are familiar with the verbal routines that form the basis of instructional discourse. In fact, school, while new for these children, is nonetheless familiar to them. There is a seamless splice between home and school, and they enter that new world without missing a beat.

Heath found quite different socialization patterns in the black and white working-class communities in the region. The white working-class families also talked to their babies, and they asked questions of them. These were not the same kinds of exchanges she found in mainstream families, however. The working-class parents saw what they were doing as "instructing" their children rather than as conversing with them. They saw their role as teachers of the children rather than as conversational partners:

> They believe that if adults teach children to "pay attention, listen, and behave," children not only learn how to talk, but also how to learn. (Heath, 1983: 127)

In this community, parents believed that there was a "correct way to talk," and as they interacted with their children, they instructed them in what to say, in how to say it, and in what was worth talking and learning about. They insisted on their children's learning the correct names for objects and people. There were few acceptable alternatives. In this way, the parents taught their children what they should know and think. Much of this was carried out in question routines in which the questioner had in mind a specific answer: "What's this?" "What do you call this?" They frequently asked questions that were not questions at all, but were directives instead: "What did I tell you to do?" In this community the children were prepared for school by learning that there was a limit on what they should seek to understand and question. They learned that there were rigid constraints on communication and on learning. According to Heath, they were not encouraged to seek or to recognize alternatives, either in what to learn or how to learn.

When these children begin school, they do not find the adjustment as easy to make as do mainstream children. They have been socialized to be passive as learners. They are unprepared to be the source of information or to be independent learners, as they must eventually be. They do well enough in school until they have to take an active role in learning. At that point, they begin to lose ground.

In sharp contrast to both the mainstream and white working-class patterns, Heath found that black working-class families tended not to talk to babies. They surrounded their infants with human contact—and indeed human communication—but they rarely spoke directly to them. The adults in this community did not regard babies as ready for verbal communication. Babies were lovingly cared for and constantly in the presence of adults, but the main mode of interacting with them was non-verbal. The adults believed that children learned when they were ready. It was neither desirable nor productive to try to hurry them in any way. Children were encouraged to imitate and to follow the example of adults in their non-verbal behavior, however. Children learned by "picking things up"—and they did it in their own good time. Heath cites this comment by a mother of a two-year-old:

> Ain't no use me tellin' 'im: learn this, learn that, what's this, what's that? He just gotta learn, gotta know; he see one thing one place one time, he know how it go, see sump'n like it again, maybe it be the same, maybe it won't. (Heath, 1983: 67)

According to this view, children set the pace for their own development and parents do not assume the role of teachers to their children. Their role is to create a social context in which children are able to make observations, and to draw on their ability to connect events, objects, and meanings. Adults reward the child's emerging verbal behavior with expressions of delight, or they may comment on the child's efforts, but they do not engage him or her in direct discourse since these early attempts are seen not as true verbal behavior but as precursors to talk. The child meanwhile is busy at work learning the language of home and developing the ability to find connections between events and meanings.

According to Heath, children in this community acquire language by practicing overheard bits and pieces of adult speech. They imitate parts of conversation they hear, together with gestures and intonational patterns they observe adults using as they speak. The adults engage in storytelling and in the recounting of events that take the form of stories. Children learn to tell stories as early as two to four years of age, although the adults may or may not see these early efforts as more than play. When their efforts are recognized as true talk by family members, the children are ready to join in the family discourse as full participants. In order to gain access to the adult-dominated talk, children must be assertive. They learn that they can enter a conversation by relating what they have to say to the ongoing discourse, and once in, they can say their piece. At that point, adults may ask questions of them, but these are seldom the instructional or collaborative questions of the mainstream or working-class white families. Adults tend not to ask children for explanations or to be specific about their characterizations of events or objects. What they value is verbal virtuosity in the recreation of events—the creative spin that an imaginative person can add to the recounting of an event that makes for an interesting tale.

Heath reports that when the children of this community go to school, the adjustment is not an easy one. They have difficulty dealing with questions they are asked in school, especially when the questions take the form of requests for explanations or for specific details. Furthermore, the skills the children have developed for getting into conversations put them at odds with their teachers, who expect them to adhere to the turn-taking rules that govern classroom discourse. Their inclination to speak out in class whenever they find an opening is seen by their teachers as aggressive, undisciplined, or disrespectful behavior. They have difficulty adapting to the restrained behavior required of children in classrooms. It is no surprise that they also have difficulty dealing with the desk-bound activities that are so important in school.

The children in Heath's research are English-speakers. Their families have deep roots in the United States. There have been other studies, however, of child-rearing practices in recent immigrant families. In discussing the cultural patterns of some of these families, I will draw on research that has been done in Chinese and Mexican American homes, especially my own continuing study of child socialization in these two cultures. A caveat first, however: In looking at cultural patterns in groups as heterogeneous as Mexican or Chinese people, one can at best make rough generalizations. The pictures presented here come from many sources and are based on observations of many families. They are composite images that match no family exactly, but are nonetheless representative of most.

Christina Cheung (1988) has been studying child-rearing practices in Chinese immigrant families who come primarily from Hong Kong and Vietnam and who now live near San Francisco. Her findings tell us much about the role Chinese parents play in preparing their children for school. From the perspective of the Chinese culture, parents have full responsibility for their children's mental, physical, social, and emotional development. Infants have potential, but that potential is realized only if parents shape and guide their child's development. Parents train their children to conform to adult expectations from birth. Infants are expected to sleep through the night by the time they are six weeks old—and they do, through gradual adjustments of their feeding schedules. Although babies are doted on and pampered, their parents are constantly mindful that they must teach and guide their offspring.

One mother put it this way: "Children come into the world knowing nothing—they are like untrained animals at first. They don't know thick from thin, right from wrong. It is the parent's job to civilize them—to turn them into people who can live in human society." The content of this instruction has been described by Cheung as "ga-gau"—the civilizing influence of the family and home. It includes moral rectitude, good manners, decorum, respect for elders, a sense of responsibility, humility, and skill and alacrity in the discharge of one's duties. The shaping of these characteristics begins early, since parents believe it takes a lifetime to develop them fully. Parents judge themselves, and are judged by others, on how well they impart these values and qualities to their children.

A mother of a child who was reportedly misbehaving in school said, "I have failed as a mother—I am so ashamed that I cannot face the teacher. He is eight already, and he has not been taught proper behavior." This woman wept as she talked to the researcher about her failure as a mother. The failure was hers, not her son's, nor the teacher's for making a faulty assessment of her son's behavior. Our observations of the child in his classroom indicated that he was as well-behaved as anyone had a right to expect a lively eight-year-old to be. He was polite, agreeable, and almost as obedient as anyone else in class. The teacher, however, was "on his case." She believed he was not working at full capacity. He was unusually capable—he could get by on minimal effort, and he did. The teacher's request for a conference to discuss her concerns with the child's mother was what precipitated the mother's self recrimination.

And so the job of training children begins early in Chinese homes. The lessons of life begin with learning one's place in the social hierarchy of the family. Well before they can speak, babies are taught to address family members by proper kinship terms that specify relationship and rank of each individual— "gugu" for elder brother, "didi" for elder sister, "sam-dai-gu" for father's third elder sister, and so forth. With their parents speaking for them, they are taught politeness terms and are gently exhorted to use them with anyone who is older than they are: for a toddler, that includes just about everyone. They are taught from babyhood to be especially respectful of elders and to turn to adults for guidance in all things.

There is a heavy emphasis on training children to do things well. Children as young as two or three are given little tasks to perform. The first ones are quite specific and simple: a toddler is asked to pick up a toy and put it away, to bring Mother a diaper, or to wipe up a drop of spilled milk. In each case the person making the request hovers over the child, guiding and correcting the performance to ensure that it is done as well as the child can manage. Adults may praise the child's performance if he or she is still quite young—say, age three or younger. The tasks children are given after that age increase in complexity, but they continue to be quite specific.

After age three, however, there is rarely any direct praise for the child's efforts. Successful performance is noticed, but not commented on. A less-than-successful performance calls for more instruction, usually by demonstration rather than by explanation, and gentle—or not-so-gentle—exhortations to do a better job. Gradually, children are "jaw-boned" into a level of performance that is acceptable to the adults. The level of performance adults find acceptable is nothing less than what they themselves strive for. This might seem unreasonable since we are, after all, talking about children. The tasks that children are asked to perform, however, are small and specific and, as noted earlier, are within their capacities. But they have to stretch in order to meet their parents' expectations, and this is where learning takes place.

Parents closely supervise the work of young children. They do not allow them to do anything that is risky or beyond their means. They remind children that the tasks they have been given are not difficult; if they find them so, they must not be trying hard enough—or they are lazy! In this way, children develop both their skills and their capacity to plug away at perfecting their performance in whatever they do. The skills, whether of producing Chinese characters that represent their names or of stringing beans for Mother to cook, are acquired as discrete and somewhat isolated tasks that have been reduced to a manageable size from the larger activities they figure in.

There are correct ways to perform each task. The strokes in a written character must be produced in a particular order, and in specific directions. Horizontal strokes go from left to right; vertical ones, from top to bottom. When strokes cross, the horizontal ones are produced first, and then the vertical ones are drawn in. Beans have strings on front and back seams—both must be removed. Snap the stem and pull the string from the back spine, and then snap the other end and pull the string from the inner one. These instructions, as noted above, are given through demonstration rather than verbal means, e.g., "Do it this way. No, not like that, like this. Watch now—see?" Children are advised to listen, watch, and learn before attempting new tasks. Questions are not actively discouraged, but neither are they encouraged. The advice that is constantly reinforced is that adults know best, and that children should listen to them, watch how they do things, and learn from them.

While most Chinese parents are literate to one degree or another, they do not ordinarily read to their children or otherwise make use of written materials in interacting with them (Cheung, in progress). The idea of reading books or stories to children is a foreign one, and while more modern or westernized parents read to their children occasionally, it is not an activity these parents engage in naturally.

Chinese parents nonetheless have firm opinions about the sorts of reading materials that are suitable for their children once they have learned to read (Beh-Bennett, 1984). They prefer materials for their children that are factual or educational. They regard fantasy or fictional works as "a waste of time" and not useful in their children's preparation for life. These parents, in fact, draw a distinction between assigned and self-selected reading materials (Cheung, in progress). They view their children's reading of assigned materials as "studying," an activity that takes precedence over the children's household chores and other responsibilities. The reading of self-selected materials is just "reading"—it serves no useful purpose. If there is nothing else to do, children may do such reading. Reading strictly for pleasure is regarded as a frivolous activity; it is not something that serious people engage in much.

When the children from this community enter school, they are well prepared for it—but not in the way most people think they are. They have had few experiences with books; they have not been read to; they have not been encouraged to explore the world much or to ask questions about it. What they have, however, is a set of work habits and skills that is truly astounding. These habits and skills do not work for everything the children encounter in school, but they work well enough to allow them to get along.

For a look at socialization patterns in Mexican background families, we turn to work in progress by Guadalupe Valdés, who has been studying early literacy development in homes of recent immigrants in the Southwest; we also turn to studies of language socialization by Charles Briggs (1984) and Ann Eisenberg (1982) and to Robert Coles' (1977) study of Chicano children. Valdés' work was conducted in the homes of 10 families residing in a southwestern community near the Mexican border. The purposes of her research were to examine the function of literacy in the daily lives of recent immigrant families and to study the way these families help their children adjust to school. She found that, for the most part, literacy played only a minor role in their everyday activities. Some of the parents read, but they did not read to their children.

Children, because they are part of the family and a source of joy for its members, are treasured, but the family does not revolve around them. The family unit, according to Valdés, takes precedence over all else in Mexican culture, and the socialization of children is seen as preparing them to become contributing members of the family. It is believed that children are born with quite distinct characteristics or natures and that these will, to a degree, determine what the individual children will be like as they mature. Parents believe that children develop in their own ways, according to the dictates of their personalities, and that it is not appropriate or feasible to change them substantially. A child's characteristics can lead to a nickname—"el flojo," the lazy one, or "la sentida," the sensitive or touchy one.

Valdés (1986) observes that such nicknames are not meant to denigrate the child—they merely acknowledge his or her salient characteristics. These characteristics are not regarded as personal failings, but as simple facts about individuals. Family members accept these facts, and make allowances for one another accordingly. The words used by the mothers of the Chicano children Robert Coles studied (Coles, 1977) while talking about their children's futures have a fatalistic tone. Three-year old Carlos' mother believed that he would die by violence someday:

> They will beat him up. They will drive him to the county line and dump him on one side of the road. We won't even see him—the body will be thrown away, and we won't know where. (Coles, 1977: 309–310)

She had been sure of her son's terrible fate at the time of his birth:

> Carlos is Carlos; I had him inside me for many months, and when my sister took him out of me, I looked at him, and I heard his cry, and I told her: He will be a handful of trouble, I know it. My sister thought I was delirious, but I wasn't. I have a child now in me, just beginning to grow, and I think it will be a quiet one. The last one, my little daughter—she is quiet too. In life there are periods of quiet, or suddenly there is much noise. So with children: quiet ones and noisy ones. A mother cannot

> expect that each child be the same. I look at some of my children, and
> I wonder how it can be that each of them has the same parents. But that
> is what the priest would call "a mystery of God's." (Coles, 1977: 310)

This is not to suggest that such fatalistic beliefs prevent Mexican parents from taking an active role in shaping their children's characters. Parents regard helping their children become respectable and honorable members of the family and community as their top priority. That is the family's responsibility to the community. They monitor the development of their children carefully, but they tend not to push them toward those goals. Instead, they serve as role models, demonstrating the behaviors and values that lead to respect and honor. Parents worry about their children, and they are tough disciplinarians. They do not attempt to control them; they guide them, but in the end they accept their children's right to be what they are. Coles illustrates this perspective by presenting the views of a Chicano mother:

> (The girl) is given to solitary walks; they worry her parents. Why should
> someone ten years old want to leave her family and her friends for the
> sake of paths that lead to wide, cultivated fields? The mother will not
> talk with the girl about this habit of hers. Even a child of ten is entitled
> to her own preferences, her willfulness; even a girl: "My husband
> worries. Let the girl be like everyone else. She is, of course—most of the
> time. Occasionally she wants to go off, be alone. Is that so bad, such a
> terrible wish? . . . " (Coles, 1977: 238)

Charles Briggs (1984) refers to the epistemology of the Mexican family in describing their child-rearing practices. An agricultural metaphor is used, he notes, to explain how a person acquires skills or knowledge. In order to grow plants, one must have seeds. These seeds are talents, God-given aptitudes for learning particular subjects or skills. But talent does not develop in isolation. It must be exposed to a growth medium. Seeds must be scattered in good soil to grow. Briggs says Mexican parents believe that children learn both through observing people who have the skill or knowledge that is being learned and through practice. Children must want to learn and must be able to concentrate in order to profit from their observations and practices. It takes time to learn, and this takes patience. Skills and knowledge are not absorbed immediately, and anyone who thinks he or she can be an expert overnight will not become competent. According to Briggs, precocious behavior is viewed as a sign of disrespect to those who have earned their expertise the hard way. "*Respeto*," Briggs says, is "a central cultural value," and it requires that novices defer to older and more skilled individuals who have a greater command of the skills to be learned.

Children observe the members of the family as they go about their tasks. When they are ready, they join in. Children's activities that contribute to the well-being and functioning of the family unit are especially valued, according to Valdés, and anything that detracts from the family is not. A child who takes an interest in cooking or in repairing cars is developing skills that benefit the entire family; he or she will be encouraged to pursue that interest. The child who wants to study piano is interested in something that requires the investment of the family resources and benefits the individual but not the family. If the family has money to spare, it might invest some of it to develop an individual child's interest or talent, but if money is tight, the family is unlikely to spend any of it for such a purpose, no matter how great the child's interest.

Children take on tasks around the home gradually. When they do, family members may provide guidance, but like Chinese parents, they rarely give explanations or verbal instructions. The tasks that children take up vary in size, but they are often adult-size jobs: for example, making tortillas for the entire family, assuming responsibility for a younger sibling, or attempting to repair the family car. Parents comment favorably on the child's efforts, even when it is clear that the child is not yet capable of handling the job. "He is such a good worker—a real little man!" they say to one another. (According to Valdés, the Mexican parents she studied rarely praise a child directly, but they sometimes expressed their approval to other family members while the child was present.) Parents do not expect a child to do these jobs as well as an adult might. They recognize that it takes time and practice to develop competence, so they are tolerant of a child's immature or imperfect performance. The tortillas the child makes at age 8 may have the texture and heft of plasterboard, and the car may spew noxious fumes into the air after the child has tinkered with it, but the family appreciates the effort.

In the area of language learning, both Briggs and Ann Eisenberg (1982) report that Mexican-American parents actively teach their children appropriate forms of speech when they approach the age of two. Proper speech behavior is important to families like the ones she studied. Using the "dile" (tell him/her) expression, parents model the forms and patterns of Spanish for their children. "Tell him, 'Give it back to me'"; or "Tell her, 'Thank you very much,'" they coach their two-year-olds.

A part of this instruction is devoted to preparing children to defend themselves verbally, according to Eisenberg. She describes the use of teasing to help children develop the social maturity and skills that are valued by the families she studied. Briggs also reports observations of this practice in the families he studied in New Mexico. From a relatively early age, children are teased by older siblings or by aunts and uncles. They are gently insulted—"You have ugly braids—what ugly braids." When the child begins to cry, the mother or some other non-teasing relative, like a grandparent, instructs the child to stop crying and to defend herself—the child is told, "Dile, 'Leave me alone!'" In this way, children are taught not only to defend themselves against verbal abuse but to avoid showing signs of immaturity, like crying.

By age five, these children are ready for school. They are respectful of adults, and they know the virtue and value of work. They know who they are, and they are aware of their capabilities and limitations. Among the qualities this culture promotes in its children are respect, cooperation, patience, responsibility, and interdependence. And yet they do not prosper in school. They do well enough during the first few years of school, but over time, many fall by the wayside. National statistics indicate that over half of these students drop out before completing high school (Steinberg, Blinde, and Chan, 1982).

I have briefly characterized the way several groups prepare their children for school. The qualities and skills these groups promote are important ones; veracity, seriousness, a concern with facts, respect for authority, and obedience can also be added to the qualities listed for Mexican Americans. Despite their strengths, only two of the five groups discussed in this paper succeed in American schools. The other three are notably unsuccessful. Individuals within those groups can and do prosper in school, but on the whole, the groups do not. The groups that prevail are middle-class in orientation, if not in economic circumstances; the ones that have not done as well tend to be from working-class backgrounds. Is educational success simply a matter of social class, economics, and tradition? Which is cause and which is effect? And if it is a matter of socioeconomic advantage, how can other groups acquire it?

The position I argue in this paper is that even more important than socioeconomic advantage is a compatibility between the values and models of learning promoted in the home and school. The children from each of the cultures discussed here have been carefully prepared for school according to a different model of learning. In the case of the mainstream children, there is a perfect match between home values and models and those of school. The mainstream mothers Heath studied were, in fact, schoolteachers. They provided their own children with the skills and values they believed all children need, and they expected other parents to prepare their children for school by providing similar skills and values. For children from that background and culture, school is a real extension of the home. Instructional activities in school are generally literacy-based and literacy-dependent. These are activities for which mainstream parents have prepared their children. Mainstream children are familiar with books and other printed materials. They are aware that books can represent real experiences as well as imagined ones. Well before they learn to read and write, these children know the value of literacy; they are aware that it figures in many aspects of adult life. When they enter school, they are ready to tackle the next step—the acquisition of the literate behaviors they associate with their parents.

The Chinese children come from homes that operate with quite a different— but not incompatible—model of learning and set of values from those of mainstream homes. In fact, one explanation for the unprecedented success of Chinese, and indeed, of most Asian children in American schools is that the work habits, values, skills, and inclinations promoted in Asian cultures go beyond those required in school.

In addition to their literacy bias, instructional activities in school are also adult-structured, organized around step-by-step development of specific skills, dependent on drill and practice, and disconnected and decontextualized. These are characteristics of instructional practices that educators generally regard as antiquated and wrong-headed, but that are nonetheless standard procedure in schools throughout the country (Goodlad, 1984).

As noted earlier, Chinese children have not had much experience with literacy in their homes, but they have had many experiences with tasks that are structured much like the ones described above. By the time they enter school at age five, they have had almost five years of practice in tasks that develop just the skills and abilities needed to handle the drudgery and tedium of workbook exercises, "Skil-Pak" pages, ditto sheets, and the like. They have the conviction that they can handle just about any task assigned to them. Their culture has given them a "can-do" attitude and provided them with skills that are suited to the type of work they are given in school. Their culture does not require them to understand the purpose of such assignments. They can apply themselves to the work their teachers give them, even when they do not understand its purpose or meaning. Furthermore, their culture does not make allowances for individual differences in ability. Their parents have told these children, "There is no such thing as can't—anyone can learn to do anything. The difference between can and can't is effort. If you fail, it is your fault—you have not tried hard enough."

By paying close attention to what the teacher and peers do and say, even limited-English-speakers can get along for a time in school (Wong Fillmore, 1976, 1979, 1982, 1983, 1985). In that way, they eventually learn the language of school. Asian children are no quicker or better at learning English than any other group of non–English speaking children (Wong Fillmore et al., 1985). Some are good language learners; others are not. They do have an advantage over other groups, however. Because of their ability to function in school even when they do not understand much, they do not have much difficulty catching up with their classmates when they finally do learn enough English to understand what their teachers are saying. While they are learning English, they plug along, doing what their classmates do, and keeping pace with them.

Their early experiences have not given them the learner attributes that are the most prized by their teachers: their imaginations tend to be poorly developed; they are not especially independent; they lack curiosity and rarely question things; they do not like to take risks; and they are not especially talkative. There are exceptions, of course, but on the whole, Chinese children are less verbal, imaginative, and independent than are the other groups discussed in this paper. These shortcomings, however, are not as influential as their strengths, at least in dealing with the demands of the American school system. The academic performance of Asian-American students has been so remarkable that in the past several years there have been numerous stories about it in the media—including several cover stories in national magazines. As educators, we might well ask why poorly developed imaginations, low levels of curiosity, and an unquestioning acceptance of adult authority are not more serious drawbacks in school.

And what about the groups that do not do as well? Children who have been prepared by their cultures to learn through observation, whose cultures have encouraged them to trust their own developmental calendars, and whose parents have emphasized social development óver the development of literate behaviors will not have an easy time adjusting to their teachers' expectations. They will have an especially difficult time adjusting to school if they do not speak English. To what extent do their educational problems stem from the way they are taught at school rather than from the way they have been reared at home? Schools, as presently structured, are prepared to deal with children from just a few backgrounds. They make few allowances for children who have been prepared differently from the mainstream norm.

II. DISCUSSION OF EARLY EDUCATION ISSUES

Keeping in mind the foregoing discussion of cross-cultural child-rearing practices, let us return to the issues raised at the beginning of this paper.

To put it bluntly, one of the beliefs on which early education programs for minority-background children are based is that their parents are not doing an adequate job preparing them for school. The assumption is that these children cannot succeed in school or later in life unless they become more like mainstream children. They need early education programs that give them the mainstream experiences and training they lack, it is argued. In other words, these children need to be "better socialized."

More harm than good can come from programs that are founded on such beliefs. While children from low-achieving groups can benefit from opportunities to acquire some of the experiences, strategies, and outlooks that are expected in school, they gain little if these programs cause their parents to lose confidence in their child-rearing abilities. Consider the message they convey to parents: *You are inadequate; you are doing a poor job preparing your children for school; there is something wrong with your culture.* Such messages cannot be good for parents—or for their children.

And what happens if programs succeed in resocializing children? They may create social problems with quite serious consequences for the children. The socialization process is the means by which a group turns out individuals who can fit comfortably into the life of the community. A person who thinks and behaves in ways that are in conflict with the behavioral or social norms of the group will have problems relating to its members. When children learn new ways at school, and they invariably do, they acquire behavioral patterns and expectations that may conflict sharply with the ways of the home. They find themselves in cultural clashes with parents and family members.

Minority-background children must make cultural adjustments to the world of school eventually, and they will experience some difficulty when they do. If they come into contact with the world of school early in childhood, they face these adjustments at a time when they may be too immature to handle them well. The more securely they are anchored in their primary culture when they come into contact with a new one, the better the chances are for coming through the experience psychologically intact. There is evidence (albeit largely in the form of anecdotal reports by teachers) that Mexican children who received some of their schooling in Mexico perform markedly better in American schools than do ones who have received all of their education here (Baral, 1979). In planning early education programs for children from minority backgrounds, we must be aware that these programs can create as well as solve problems.

The second issue raised in this paper concerns the focus of early education programs intended for language-minority and cultural-minority children. The emphasis on basic skill development found in many early childhood programs is an obsession in programs for minority-background children. The rationale for such an emphasis is that these children need a running start on the elementary school curriculum if they are to keep pace with their classmates even during the first few years of school. It is thought that they will not be ready for kindergarten or first grade without a year or two of preschool phonics and number facts. That seems to be the justification for giving these children a compensatory preschool experience.

Such practices, however, are counter-productive. Minority-group children are children, first and foremost. Irrespective of background and experience, children have the same need to develop their curiosity, to explore their physical and social environments, to ponder the mysteries of life, and to develop social relationships. What they do not need is to be turned off about school before kindergarten. Minority-background children need the same enriched preschool experiences that mainstream children do.

And now let us consider the third issue—the one that is the closest to my research interests. There is a troubling proposal that surfaces from time to time among policy makers as an easy solution to the "bilingual education problem." The proposal is this: *Set up preschool programs in which children from limited-English-speaking homes can be immersed in English, because the younger they are, the faster they can pick it up as a second language. At age three or four, children are linguistic sponges—they can learn a new language in a year or less. They will not need bilingual education when they enter kindergarten or first grade, because they will be English-speakers by then.*

For the policy maker, this is a quick and easy fix for a big problem. The foregoing, while just a proposal, is de facto policy in many places. In countless preschool programs, non-English-speaking children are taught exclusively in English. This is true even in many programs that are described as "bilingual."

Limited-English-proficient (LEP) children are taught in English as soon as they enter school, whether it is preschool, or kindergarten, or first grade. This creates enormous problems for preschool children—not because they have difficulty learning English, but because they do it so easily. Children between the ages of two and four are in their prime period for language learning. All children are biologically predisposed to learn the language of their caretakers. The predisposition to learn language is nature's way of ensuring that children will acquire a system for communicating with, and learning from, their primary group, namely, their parents and other family members. During that period, children learn whatever language is spoken to them, whether it is a grammatically complex language like Russian or Spanish, or a relatively simple one like English or Chinese. They can, in fact, learn more than one language, as long as the social environment supports those languages. In the preschool period, children need no "instructional assistance" from teachers to learn a new language. They can do it on their own in just a year or so, just by being around people who speak it, provided these speakers are willing to interact with them in the new language. In fact, they can become fluent almost effortlessly.

The problem confronting these children is to maintain their primary language while they learn English. Countless children from non-English-speaking families have lost their mother tongues as they learned English in school. They do not become bilingual by learning English. Instead, English replaces the language of the home, sometimes even before English has been fully mastered. One might wonder how children can lose their primary language so easily, especially when parents speak nothing but that language at home. It is easy, when the new language enjoys a status advantage over the home language.

Young children are keenly aware of status differences. They can sense the position of their family or group in relation to the larger community. For many minority-background families, that position is one of low status. When children are exposed to English in school, they come to associate it with their teachers and their higher-status English-speaking playmates. English represents the social world of school and of the larger community; it is the means by which the children may enter that world. There are no external forces that can equal the internal pressures that motivate children to learn English in this society: the need to belong and the desire not to be different. For many, if not most, LEP children, the home language comes to symbolize the social and cultural barriers to easy participation in the social world outside of the home. As they learn English, they put aside the language of the home. Some children simply stop using their first language once they have learned enough English to get by.

A well-documented case of a child doing just that was reported by Ruth Berman (1979). Berman found her four-year-old daughter, Shelli, rejecting the use of Hebrew after just a few months in an English-speaking environment. Shelli accompanied her parents, an Israeli couple, on a year-long sabbatical visit to the United States. After just 6 weeks in an American nursery school, Shelli refused to speak Hebrew any longer with her parents. When she had picked up just enough English to interact with playmates and to communicate with her parents, she switched to speaking in English only. After a short time, she had learned enough English that her ability in her new language was roughly equal to the English proficiency of her three-and-a-half-year-old American playmates. Her rapid second-language learning was not without cost, however. Over the course of the year, Shelli lost her ability to speak or understand her mother tongue. Berman reports that Shelli appeared genuinely not to understand her parents when they spoke to her in Hebrew, and would not tolerate anyone else's speaking to her in that language.

How is that possible? It appears that a first language may not be firmly anchored, as it were, until children are 7 or 8 years of age. It is subject to loss, as we have found repeatedly in studies of immigrant children learning English. Berman's daughter Shelli was more fortunate. After a year in the United States, the family returned to Israel, and Shelli eventually relearned Hebrew. Once most LEP children who live in the United States lose their first language, it is gone.

How big a loss is this? Should we, as educators, be concerned about minority children's losing their first languages? The school's responsibility is to help language-minority students learn the language of the society. Whose responsibility is it to help children preserve the minority language? Is it even desirable for them to do so? A preschool teacher recently commented, "Look, these kids need English before they go to school. So what if they lose their first language? In this world, you gotta give something to get something! They lose their mother tongue, but they gain English, and with it, access to what they can learn in school. That's not such a big price," she argued.

But what about the lessons to be learned in the home? Will children have access to what parents can teach them if they no longer understand their parents? This is not much of a problem for children whose parents or other primary caregivers speak adequate English. In such cases, it is unfortunate when the familial language is lost to the children, but it is not tragic. Communication in the home switches to English, and the parents continue socializing their children and teaching them the lessons of life that are important to the family and community.

The problem occurs when the parents do not know English well enough to communicate easily in it. Such is the case in a great many immigrant families; parents and children are unable to communicate because they no longer share a common language. The loss is not immediate, since children seldom give up a language as dramatically as Berman's daughter Shelli did. For a year or two, most children continue to understand the parental language even if they no longer use it productively. The parents speak in their language, the children in English. Comprehension gradually erodes until the children no longer understand what the parents are saying. Talk becomes strained and limited—too limited to convey the lessons that parents should teach their children as they mature. What is lost is more than the language; family unity and closeness are also endangered. Richard Rodriguez (1982) describes the effects of that loss on his family in the *Hunger of Memory*:

> Matching the silence I started hearing in public was a new quiet at home. The family's quiet was partly due to the fact that, as we children learned more and more English, we shared fewer and fewer words with our parents. Sentences needed to be spoken slowly when a child

addressed his mother or father. (Often the parent wouldn't understand.) The child would need to repeat himself. (Still the parent misunderstood.) The young voice, frustrated, would end up saying, "Never mind"—the subject was closed. Dinner would be noisy with the clinking of knives and forks against dishes. My mother would smile softly between her remarks; my father at the other end of the table would chew and chew at his food, while he stared over the heads of his children . . . (Rodriguez, 1982: 23)

It is interesting that Rodriguez argues against bilingual education on the grounds that children cannot and should not expect to hold onto the intimacy afforded by the family language if they are to enjoy the public identity that English offers. "Bilingual enthusiasts sin against intimacy," he avers, by suggesting that the language itself is the "source of family ties." Nonetheless, there is pathos in his account of the changes that took place in his family as the language of his home shifted from Spanish to English:

My mother and father, for their part, responded differently as their children spoke to them less. She grew restless, seemed troubled and anxious at the scarcity of words exchanged in the house. It was she who would question me about my day when I came home from school. She smiled at small talk. She pried at the edges of my sentences to get me to say something more. (What?) She'd join conversations she overheard, but her intrusions often stopped her children's talking. By contrast, my father seemed reconciled to the new quiet life. Though his English improved somewhat, he retired into silence. At dinner he spoke very little. One night his children and even his wife helplessly giggled at his garbled English pronunciation of the Catholic grace before meals. Thereafter he made his wife recite the prayer at the start of each meal, even on formal occasions, when there were guests in the house. Hers became the public voice in the family. On official business it was she, not my father, one would usually hear on the phone or in stores, talking to strangers. His children grew so accustomed to his silence that years later, they would speak routinely of his shyness . . ." (Rodriguez, 1982: 24–25)

Is this loss of familial closeness in immigrant families an inevitable part of the assimilation process? How is the school responsible for that loss? In Rodriguez's case, the school's role was quite clear. He describes a visit from the nuns who were teachers at the parochial school he attended as a boy. They asked his parents:

"Is it possible for you and your husband to encourage your children to practice their English when they are at home?" Of course, my parents complied. What would they not do for their children's well-being? And how could they have questioned the Church's authority, which those women represented? In an instant they agreed to give up the language that had revealed and accentuated our family's closeness. The moment after the visitors left, the change was observed. "Ahora, speak to us en inglés," my father and mother united to tell us. (Rodriguez, 1982: 21)

Is the school responsible for what happens to the family? The school cannot and should not function in a way that diminishes the capacity and role that the family plays in the education of its children. The family, after all, has the primary responsibility for preparing its children for life. Unless the school and society are willing to accept the responsibility for doing so, it is crucial that they do nothing to weaken the family's ability to meet that obligation.

III. RECOMMENDATIONS

Let us consider what we as educators and children's advocates can do about the issues raised in this paper. What early education policies are needed in view of the special needs presented by young language- and cultural-minority children? How can schools meet the diverse needs of the groups that make up the society? The school plays a major role in socializing children in the common culture of society they live in. But how is this to be achieved when the cultures of the home are at odds with the one at school? Do we encourage families to modify the way they prepare their children so there is a better match between the experiences of the home and school? Or do we change the school? And what about the children? Do we try to change them, or do we change teachers so the two are more compatible? The answer to all of these questions is indeed that there must be change: change in educational policies, change in pedagogy, change in teachers, but also change in families and children.

Minority-background families need to know what teachers regard as necessary preparation and experiences for school. That knowledge would perhaps allow them to prepare their children differently for school. However, we must consider carefully what we can ask families to do and what we cannot ask of them. For example, it would be thoughtless to tell an illiterate parent that she must read to her children. Such advice might spur her to learn to read, but it is more likely to make her feel inadequate. It would be downright cruel to tell non-English-speaking parents that they should not speak Spanish to their children because it is hurting them in school, as Rodriguez's teachers did. Non-English-speaking parents should not be discouraged from talking with their children. Instead, they should be advised about ways they can help their children become more proficient speakers in their native language—for example, by encouraging questions and by asking them to talk about their school experiences.

At the same time, however, it is necessary to consider ways in which the school can and should change to accommodate the needs of different groups of children. This is hardly a new proposal. Over the past 20 years, there have been many efforts to make such accommodations. Most of these efforts—although well-meant—have been misguided. For example, in many schools, minority-group children are offered a watered-down instructional program in the mistaken belief that the regular program would be inappropriate or irrelevant for them. Whereas other children are encouraged to interpret the texts they read and to explore the subjects they are studying, minority-group children get little more than training on the mechanical aspects of reading or a set of facts to memorize. Few teachers expect them to get much more out of school or believe that they are capable of handling more demanding or more substantive materials. Sometimes, minority-group children are given just those experiences or activities that are the easiest or most comfortable for them, culturally speaking. For example, Chinese children can participate verbally in class, but they do not find it easy to do so. For that reason, they generally prefer written exercises over oral assignments. In many classes, they are given a steady diet of written exercises, and are seldom required to say more than a word or two because they are "not very verbal." Written exercises are useful, but Chinese children, like all children, need to be challenged to develop skills that do not come easily to them.

The point is that these are misguided attempts to change the school for the sake of minority-background students. What must change are not necessarily the goals or content of school, although both should be reassessed. What can and should be adjusted to accommodate the cultural patterns of students are the ways instruction is organized and presented, the models of teaching that are used, the structure of the learning and social environment in the classroom, and the roles and relations of teachers and students. Such efforts must be based on careful considerations of the cultural patterns of the groups the school serves. An example of a highly successful effort to make the school a more congenial place for students, based on their cultural characteristics, can be found in a program founded by Ronald Gallimore and Roland Tharp in Hawaii.

The Kamehameha Early Education Program, or KEEP, was based on over a decade of interdisciplinary study of Hawaiian cultural patterns (Tharp and Gallimore, 1989). The aims of that program were to improve school performance and increase literacy rates among native Hawaiian children, who ranked among the lowest-achieving students in the country. Gallimore, Tharp, and their associates had agreed that they would not adjust the curricular objectives of school for the sake of the students, since the students had to learn whatever the society had decided children needed to learn. Instead, they would find more culturally appropriate ways to deliver that curriculum to Hawaiian children.

Over a decade and a half, the KEEP researchers and educators modified the structure of the classroom setting, the way classroom discourse was managed, the way reading was taught, and the management of the instructional setting as they discovered what was needed. They gave the children a role in managing their own learning activities and the classroom environment, for example. An open-door policy was adopted, allowing the children to come to school before class (as early as 6:30 A.M.) to do the chores associated with setting up the classroom for instruction and with its upkeep.

This practice was instituted when it was learned that native Hawaiian children have a need, because of the way they have been reared, to organize and structure their own physical and social environment. In the Hawaiian culture, parents and other adults coordinate and oversee the day-to-day affairs of the family, but the actual work of child-rearing and of maintaining the household is carried out by children of all ages. Older children look after younger ones; they teach them to talk and to participate in the work of the family. The children, who were largely responsible for maintaining the physical environment in their own homes, had been made to feel incompetent and useless in school because their teachers insisted on structuring and controlling the classroom environment and all activities conducted in it. (Many of the teachers in the school serving these children were Asians.) This change, among others, made an enormous difference to the Hawaiian children in school. The open door made them feel wanted and useful in the classroom, and that, in turn, freed them to learn.

Programmatic solutions to the problems discussed in this paper must be based on careful study of the early experiences of children of other language and cultural background families. There are many practical problems to be addressed in considering their early education needs. In order to have culturally and linguistically appropriate programs, there must be teachers who are knowledgeable about the groups to be served by these programs. How can this be achieved, given the shortage of well-prepared early education teachers of any sort? Do we know enough about the diverse groups in this country to develop appropriate instructional strategies for working with them? How are teachers to be prepared?

These may seem like insurmountable problems, but they are not. There are both stopgap and long-term solutions to be found. A long-defunct early education program I developed in the late 1960s exemplifies one approach to preparing teachers to work with children from groups for which there is a shortage of trained teachers.

The "Spanish Dame Project" was a bilingual preschool program which was conducted in the homes of Mexican-American families in San José, California. There were few Spanish-bilingual teachers at any grade level when the program was established in 1968. The project undertook to recruit and train as preschool teachers women from the community it was serving. Mothers of families who were knowledgeable about their own culture and skilled in working with children were hired and put through an intensive teacher education program that continued for the life of the project (five years). The Dame-teachers (or Dames) received a bit of theory about child development, language acquisition, or early education each day—just enough to support the instructional activities they would conduct in their classes the next day. The training and supervision of the Dames was provided by three professionals—two early education specialists (Toni Micotti and Marion Gonzales-Licano) and a language development specialist (myself). During their daily three-hour "training" session, the Dames prepared materials for their classes, planned and rehearsed their instructional strategies, and learned about child development, preschool education, and language acquisition. There were eight Dames the first year, and four were added each year until we reached a total of twenty Dames. Most of them had had some high-school education. Several had completed high school, and one had a year of junior college. All of them were bright, enthusiastic, and competent individuals who enjoyed working with children.

Each Dame worked with a total of five families (for a total of 40 during the first year of the project); each family had at least one child who was between 3 years, 9 months of age and 4 years, 9 months of age. These children were the "official students." There were countless unofficial students in addition to the official ones—siblings and cousins who attended class more or less regularly. Class was held in the homes of a given Dame's five official students on a rotational basis, each home serving as class one day each week. The children's mothers served as assistant teachers when class was held in their homes. The Dame-teacher would arrive an hour before class to set up materials for the day's activities. After setting up, she would share with the hostess the bit of theory she had learned the day before during the training session. The hostess and Dame would then consider the activities for the day, and discuss the purpose of each activity in light of that bit of supportive theory for those activities. Most of the activities were conducted in the language of the home, Spanish. At least one activity each day was designed to help the children acquire some English.

Class was held when the other children arrived—usually with several of the mothers in attendance. After the two-and-one-half- to three-hour session, the Dame-teacher and mother would evaluate the session: "Did you notice how many good questions Jesús asked today?" or, "Maritza is still pretty quiet. How can we draw her out more?" In this way, the Dame helped the mother see how the early education activities conducted in the home supported the social and intellectual development of young children.

It should be noted that some of the activities were the kind we find in any rich preschool program; others were more homely ones that made use of everyday materials that were readily available to low-income families. An October activity, for example, might be planned around a pumpkin. During class, the pumpkin would be cut open, and the children invited to inspect the fibers and seeds inside. Together, the children and adults would examine, touch, taste, smell, and describe the pumpkin's surfaces and contents. The seeds would then be removed—some to be roasted and eaten, others to be dried and planted in the spring. The pumpkin would then be transformed into a jack-o'-lantern. The children would be asked what shape they wanted for its eyes: "Squares, circles, or triangles—which shall it be?" In the end, the pumpkin would be left for the hostess—along with a recipe for pumpkin empanadas (turnovers).

The recipe gave instructions like these: "Ask your child to measure out two cups of flour. Help her count as she is getting it: one, two. Let your child smell the *canela* (cinnamon). Teach her to say *canela*. You can also teach her the English name for it—cinnamon." Some of the mothers were undoubtedly better bakers than we were, but we were trying to show them how to transform an everyday task into an instructional event. In this way, we hoped to demystify schooling for these parents and to show parents how much they contribute to the education of their children just by talking to them and showing them how to do things in the home.

The Dame Project was—by all measures—an unqualified success. It ended when the federal funds (ESEA, Title VII) were gone, but the model is still used in a few places. It demonstrates one way to get families involved in the educational process, to tailor programs relatively easily for diverse groups, to build (rather than diminish) the capacity of families to educate their children, to promote the development of English without taking away the family's means of communicating with its children, and also to train teachers—all in one package.

CONCLUSION

I have argued that in establishing an early childhood education program for children from minority families, the society must carefully examine its assumptions about these children and their families and consider the possible consequences of programs that do not recognize the validity of their primary cultures and experiences. While educators generally acknowledge the need to respect the language and culture of minority-background children, they nevertheless tend to regard their parents and homes as handicapping conditions that can be overcome only by educational intervention applied at the earliest possible time. The early experiences of such children are judged against mainstream norms and are found wanting. An examination of several cross-cultural ethnographic studies of child socialization, however, has revealed the care with which these groups prepare their children for learning, and the belief system and logic behind different patterns of child-rearing. Nonetheless, the children of such groups often fail to thrive in school. I have tried to show that the problem lies not in a lack of preparation for learning but instead in the mismatch between the preparation provided by the home and that which is expected by the school. What is needed are programs that build on the children's home experiences while providing some of the experiences needed for school. Two examples of programs that attempted to do just that were described to show that solutions can be found to help minority-group children adjust to the American school, provided we are clear about what needs to be adjusted.

REFERENCES

Baral, D. P. "Academic Achievement of Recent Immigrants from Mexico." *NABE Journal* 3:3 (1979): 1–13.

Beh-Bennett, S. T. "Chinese Children's Response to Literature in the School Environment." A pilot study presented to the Language and Literacy Faculty of the Graduate School of Education, University of California, Berkeley, 1984.

Berman, R. A. "The Re-emergence of a Bilingual: A Case Study of a Hebrew-English Speaking Child." *Working Papers on Bilingualism* 19 (1979): 157–179.

Boggs, S. T., K. Watson-Gegeo, and G. McMillan. *Speaking, Relating and Learning: A Study of Hawaiian Children at Home and at School.* Norwood, New Jersey: Ablex Publishing, 1985.

Briggs, C. L. "Learning How to Ask." *Language in Society* 13 (1984): 1–28.

Cheung, C. "The Socialization of Chinese-American Children." A presentation at the 1988 AERA Mini-Conference, Berkeley, Cal., 1988.

Cheung, C. *The Tao of Learning: Socialization Practices in Chinese-American Homes.* (In progress).

Coles, R. *Children of Crisis, Vol. IV: Eskimos, Chicanos, Indians.* Boston: Little, Brown, 1977.

Eisenberg, A. R. *Language Acquisition in Cultural Perspective: Talk in Three Mexicano Homes.* Doctoral dissertation, University of California, Berkeley, 1982.

Goodlad, J. *A Place Called School: Promise for the Future.* New York: McGraw-Hill, 1984.

Heath, S. B. "Sociocultural Contexts of Language Development." In *Beyond Language: Social and Cultural Factors in Schooling Language Minority Students.*

Los Angeles: Evaluation, Dissemination and Assessment Center, California State University, 1986.

Heath, S. B. *Ways with Words: Language, Life, and Work in Communities and Classrooms.* Cambridge, Mass.: Cambridge University Press, 1983.

Heath, S. B. "What No Bedtime Story Means: Narrative Skills at Home and at School." *Language in Society* 11 (1982): 49–76.

Rodriguez, R. *Hunger of Memory: The Education of Richard Rodriguez.* New York: Bantam Books, 1982.

Steinberg, L., P. L. Blinde, and K. S. Chan. *Dropping Out Among Language Minority Youths: A Review of the Literature.* NCBR Working Paper No. 81–3W. Los Alamitos, Cal.: National Center for Bilingual Research, 1982.

Tharp, R., and R. Gallimore. *Rousing Minds to Life: Teaching, Learning and Schooling in Social Context.* Cambridge, Mass.: Cambridge University Press, 1989.

Valdés, G. "Brothers and Sisters: A Closer Look at the Development of 'Cooperative' Social Orientations in Mexican-American Children." Paper presented at the 37th annual convention of the California Association of School Psychologists, 1986.

Valdés, G. *Socialization Practices in Mexican-American Homes.* (In progress)

Wong Fillmore, L. "Individual Differences in Second-Language Acquisition." In *Individual Differences in Language Ability and Language Behavior,* edited by C. J. Fillmore, W. S. Y. Wang, and D. K. Kempler. New York: Academic Press, 1979.

Wong Fillmore, L. "Instructional Language as Linguistic Input: Second-Language Learning in Classrooms." In

Communicating in the Classroom, edited by L. C. Wilkinson. New York: Academic Press, 1982.

Wong Fillmore, L. "The Language Learner as an Individual." In *On TESOL '82: Pacific Perspectives on Language Learning and Teaching,* edited by M. Clarke and J. Handscombe. Washington, D.C.: Teachers of English to Speakers of Other Languages, 1983.

Wong Fillmore, L. *The Second Time Around: Cognitive and Social Strategies in Second Language Acquisition.* Ph. D. Dissertation, Stanford University, 1976.

Wong Fillmore, L., in collaboration with C. Valdez. "Teaching Bilingual Learners." In *Handbook of Research on Teaching,* edited by M. Wittrock. New York: Macmillan, 1985.

Wong Fillmore, L., B. McLaughlin, P. Ammon, and M. S. Ammon. "Learning English Through Bilingual Education." Final Report submitted to the National Institute of Education. Berkeley, Cal.: University of California, 1985.

CHILD CARE IN AMERICA

Edward Zigler and Pamela Ennis
YALE UNIVERSITY

Two decades ago, the 1970 White House Conference on Children deemed a lack of affordable, good-quality child care to be the most serious problem facing our nation's children and families. The following year, Congress delivered to President Nixon the Child Development Act, which called for an expansion of day-care facilities, increased federal day-care subsidies to welfare recipients, and augmented tax deductions to families using day care. However, due to political pressure from opponents of day care, President Nixon vetoed the bill. Since then, the United States has come no closer to instituting major reforms in regard to child care, and the situation has grown still more serious.

THE MAGNITUDE OF THE DAY CARE PROBLEM

Almost two-thirds of all school-age children and more than half of all preschoolers have mothers in the out-of-home work force (Kahn and Kamerman, 1987). Still more startling, approximately 50 percent of all mothers with infants under one year were in the work force in 1984 (Select Committee on Children, Youth, and Families, 1984). It is anticipated that by 1990, fully half the labor force will consist of women, and 80 percent of those women will be of child-bearing age. Ninety-three percent will become pregnant at some point during their work lives (Freidman, 1984). As a result, there will continue to be a large and growing need for child care.

Some conservative individuals claim the solution to the child care problem is to send mothers home. It is not. The driving force behind the massive entrance of women, especially mothers, into the labor force is economic. A recent U. S. Bureau of Labor Statistics report states that "women seem driven more than ever before into the marketplace to provide or supplement family income" (Schroeder, 1988). This is a response to two major changes: (1) the radical alteration of the American family as a consequence of recent increases in divorced and never-married parents and (2) the decline in median family income.

In 1940, there was one divorce for every six marriages; in 1980, that ratio had reached one for every two. Almost 25 percent of all families and more than half of all black families are headed by single mothers. Roughly 90 percent of single-parent families are headed by women. In 1986, approximately one-fifth of all single mothers had incomes below half the adjusted poverty line (below $3,974 for a family of three). Approximately 40 percent of these families had incomes below the adjusted poverty line (Select Committee on Children, Youth, and Families, 1988).

146

Prospects were only marginally better for married women. According to the most current data, 40 percent of married working women have husbands who earn less than $15,000 annually (Schroeder, 1988). The median income for American families, adjusted for inflation, has fallen by an average of $300 per year over the past 11 years. This means the average American family has $3,300 less today than in 1975 for basic living expenses such as housing, education, food, and clothing. The report of the Joint Economic Committee (1986) indicates that, though the median family income in America fell 3.1 percent between 1973 and 1984, if mothers had not joined the work force to support their families, the drop in median income would instead have been 9.5 percent. It is clear that such a drastic decline in family income would have had immediate, concrete, and devastating effects on children and families. Instead, in the words of Wisconsin Congressman David Obey, working wives and mothers have assumed a role that "carries with it both the anguish of worrying about children left in others' care and the fatigue and frustration of working longer hours, usually at lower pay than [that] given working men" (Joint Economic Committee, 1986). These women must work, and their children need care while they do so.

THE PROBLEM DEFINED

The social scene today is replete with books and media presentations with titles such as *The Child Care Crisis* (Maynard, 1985) and *The Day-Care Dilemma* (Blum, 1983). This level of concern is appropriate, for some of the main determinants in parents' choice of child care are often more expedient than developmentally sound. These factors include considerations of cost and of proximity to home. High-quality child care can be prohibitively expensive, even for families with two wage-earning adults. On the private market, high-quality day care for infants and toddlers can cost from $200 per child per week (Hewlett, 1986). Costs for older children are generally lower; however, even these fees are taxing for low- to moderate-income families. In consequence, high-quality care can become a privilege of the wealthy. Less fortunate parents may be forced to place their children in such care as they can afford or resort to a patchwork of informal arrangements involving friends and relatives. Many of these arrangements are less than optimal for the child's development, and almost all of them induce stress and anxiety for parents (Kahn and Kamerman, 1987).

A second factor that can lead busy parents to place a child in care that may be less than desirable is simple proximity to home (Endsley and Broadbard, 1981; McCartney, Scarr, Phillips, Grajek, and Schwarz, 1982). In their attempt to accommodate inflexible schedules and demanding job requirements, some parents must place a child in a home that is convenient, rather than in one that is carefully selected to meet the child's needs. It is not that these parents do not love the child. Many do not know what characterizes good care (Endsley and Broadbard, 1981). Others fail to recognize that the day care they are purchasing is not simply a convenience that frees them to work but the child's daily environment for months and even years, an environment that will affect the child's development.

These "methods" of choosing day care are a sign of a deeper issue. For too long, child care has been regarded as a private problem, one to be resolved by individual families as best they can. Government and corporate policies have too often continued to reflect past rather than present realities and to function as if every mother were a housewife. This is no longer the case: (1) less than 10 percent of all families have a mother at home full-time while the father supports the family (Schroeder, 1988); (2) the number of "traditional" (wife at home, husband at work) and single-parent families being formed is now roughly equal (Moynihan, 1987); and (3) even in two-parent families, only one-fourth can survive comfortably without two wage earners (Hayes, 1982). Yet parents receive little expert guidance and still less practical support in their efforts to provide their children with appropriate care. As a result, the problem of child care in America has now reached such vast proportions that it strikes many as insoluble.

It is not. The problem must be separated into its constituent units, and each aspect of the problem must be addressed individually, including parent education, availability of high-quality care, development of more child care settings, and cost. Recognizing the problem is an important first step; when the Child Development Act was vetoed almost two decades ago, the nation saw the dangers of the "sovietization" (Nelson, 1982) of the American family as more serious than the problem of out-of-home care. Today, the depth of the need for day care is evident to everyone. This is an important step forward, since no nation tries to solve a problem before there is a deep sense that the problem exists.

Some progress has recently been made in addressing this issue. Following the termination of the White House Conferences on Children and the downgrading of the Children's Bureau (Zigler and Muenchow, 1985), for many years there was no national podium to discuss family issues. Today, there is the bipartisan House Select Committee on Children, Youth, and Families chaired by George Miller (D-7th-CA) and the Senate Subcommittee on Children, Families, Drugs, and Alcoholism chaired by Senator Dodd (D-CT) in the Senate. Unfortunately, however, there is a dearth of leadership in the executive branch of government. Other than maintaining Head Start, which provides care for less than 20 percent of the eligible families (Zigler, 1985), the Reagan Administration failed to implement a single positive program in dealing with the child care problem. However, while no programs have been implemented, the problem has received some attention; Secretary of Labor Ann McLaughlin has recently published a lengthy summary of the child care situation in this country (U. S. Department of Labor, 1988). This initiative is a positive first step; however, even here, a sanguine attitude is evident—the problem does not receive the regard it deserves. Considering the proportions of the problem, this is a serious failure of leadership.

DAY CARE—A DEVELOPMENTAL APPROACH

The most important aspect of this problem, however, is the impact that child care is having on the development of our nation's children. Recent research has focused on differences within the population of children enrolled in day care settings and the quality of the care provided (Howes, 1986; McCartney, Scarr, Phillips and Grajek, 1985; Steinberg, 1986). Specifically, researchers have found that the needs of children vary across ages; the needs of infants and toddlers are very different from those of preschoolers, and these in turn are different from those of the school-age child. Any viable child care system, therefore, must be developmentally appropriate; it must answer the needs of children at each stage of development.

It is useful to distinguish among three developmental stages; babies from birth to about two-and-a-half years; preschoolers up to age five; and school-age children. Quality care is always essential, but the particulars that distinguish quality will differ for these three age groups, as determined by children's developmental needs.

INFANT DAY CARE

Infant care is an area of special concern, since it is a relatively new social form—so new that there is little research carried out on children 10 or more years after they were enrolled in infant day care. It is clear, however, that some crucial developmental landmarks occur during infancy (Kolata, 1984; Lampl and Emde, 1983). Some of the most important new work on infancy, and arguably the most relevant to issues of day care, has been in the area of attachment. The work of Stern (1985) and others (e.g., Brazelton, 1986) demonstrates the need for parents and infants to spend sufficient time with each other to grow "attuned" to each other. Family systems theory suggests that the birth of a new baby necessitates the adjustment of all family members to the presence of the new infant and to consequent changes in family roles and family functioning (Belsky, 1985; Goldberg and Easterbrooks, 1984; Minuchin, 1985). In a recent controversial review of day care placement of children under one year, Jay Belsky (1985) found a cause for concern in a possible relationship between insecurity of attachment, aggression, noncompliance, and social withdrawal in the preschool and early school years. A number of researchers have taken issue with this finding, asserting that Belsky's review of the research was selective, and that children who have attended high-quality developmentally appropriate part-time day care are no different from children reared at home on measures of socio-emotional adjustment (Chess, 1987; Phillips, McCartney, Scarr, and Howes, 1987).

The crucial socio-emotional developmental task of infants during this period is the formation of secure attachments, and numerous studies have linked secure attachment in infancy with increased competence in preschool (Pastor, 1981; Waters, Wippman, and Stroufe, 1979). Although infants do form multiple attachments and more than one caregiver can play a significant role in an infant's development, continuity of care is essential (Bretherton, 1985; Parke, 1981), and it is unfortunate that the 60 percent of mothers in the work force who are allowed virtually no maternal leave from work are unable to spend time with their infants if they so choose (Ad Hoc Day Care Coalition, 1985). (A more complete discussion of infant-care leave will appear later in this paper.) In addition, some concern has been expressed over the developmental prepared-ness of toddlers to engage in peer relations (Rutter, 1982).

PRESCHOOL DAY CARE

Numerous studies have demonstrated that there is less cause for concern in the case of preschoolers. High-quality care seems not to result in adverse effects; on the contrary, it can benefit children intellectually and socially, particularly children from low-income families (Howes, 1983, 1985, 1986; McCartney, Scarr, Phillips, and Grajek, 1985; Select Committee on Children, Youth, and Families, 1984).

At this age, according to Michael Rutter: "Children gain much from their peers and there is less exclusive reliance on adults for meeting their needs" (1982). Researchers have shown that the opportunity to interact with children of the same age is not only desirable but necessary for normal social development. Children who do not play with age-mates miss important social learning experiences and are at risk of becoming uncertain of themselves in interpersonal situations. Whereas children learn from their parents how to get along in one sort of social hierarchy, that of the family, it is from their interactions with peers that they learn how to interact with equals in a wide range of social situations (Hartup, 1978; Mueller and Vandell, 1979). Given the trend toward later marriage and reduced family size (Select Committee on Children, Youth, and Families, 1984), high-quality preschool may be a very valuable arena for peer socialization among preschoolers. In addition, excellent remedial programs for the disadvan-taged have succeeded in spurring the developmental and cognitive growth of three- and four-year-old children from low-income families (Ambach, 1986; Berrueta-Clement, Schweinhart, Barnett, Epstein, and Weikart, 1984; Deutsch, Deutsch, Jordan, and Grallo, 1983; Lazar and Darlington, 1982; Pierson, Tivnan, and Walker, 1984).

SCHOOL-AGE DAY CARE

Although the fact receives little attention either from academic journals or the popular press, more than half the children needing day care are over six years of age (Zigler and Muenchow, 1985). In 1982, two to four million children returned to empty homes each day after school (School-Age Child Care Project, 1982). This largely unmet need for school-age day care has contributed to the growing number of "latchkey" or "self-care" children, i.e., children who are not under adult supervision after school hours. Researchers are at odds concerning the consequences of self-care. Some researchers have found no difference between self- and adult-care children on a variety of measures regarding locus of control, self-esteem, and social and interpersonal competence (Leischman, 1980; Rodman and Pratto, 1980; Rodman, Pratto, and Nelson, 1985). At least one worker has gone on record as believing that self-care contributes to independent functioning (Korchin, cited in Langway, Abramson, and Foote, 1981).

In contrast, other researchers report that children in self-care tend to be more fearful (Long and Long, 1982). Some researchers have warned of safety hazards to unattended children, and links have been found between self-care and juvenile delinquency (Zigler and Hall, 1988). In testimony before Congress in 1984, a number of latchkey children spoke of being afraid of not knowing what to do in emergencies and even of being afraid of being sexually abused (Select Committee on Children, Youth, and Families, 1984). Recent work by Laurence Steinberg (1986) and Melanie Ginter (1981), among others, has helped explain some of these contradicting findings. As they cogently point out, not all self-care situations are alike, nor are all children alike. A 14-year-old who returns home promptly after school, telephones an adult, and arranges to engage in appropriate activities until an adult returns is unlike a 7-year-old youngster from a ghetto who is either left alone in a small apartment or spends afternoons on street corners. These researchers stress that it is essential to identify the salient characteristics of each child's situation, the child's developmental needs, and the ways in which variations within the latchkey population affect relevant outcome-measurers, e.g., children's fears, the dangers to which children may be exposed, and the likelihood that they will engage in undesirable behavior they would not engage in if adults were nearby. What remains clear, however, is that many children in need of supervision are not receiving it, and that measures should be taken so that those children who presently need care will be adequately supervised.

QUALITY OF CARE

Despite these findings concerning the developmental needs of children, most assessments of day care continue to rest on the implicit assumption that the term *day care* describes a single experience consistent as to quality and kind for all children. Numerous researchers have demonstrated that this characterization is invalid (Clarke-Stewart and Fein, 1983; Etaugh, 1980; Rutter, 1982; Scarr, 1984; Zigler and Gordon, 1982). In reality, day care is highly variable as to quality. Presently, the environments available for parents to choose from may be placed on a continuum of quality from excellent to horrible. All the evidence indicates that children develop better when they receive care of higher quality and that if the quality of care falls below a certain minimum on the continuum of quality, the optimal development of the child will be compromised. Unfortunately, however, just as there is no coherent set of national public policies about child care, there is no great concern with child care regulations. Instead, available child care services constitute an uncoordinated patchwork of programs, funded from a host of different sources, that serve fragments of the population in need of child care. Quality varies tremendously within every type of child care setting.

Regulation of child care programs, for the most part, provides a mechanism for establishing a floor of quality below which children's safety is jeopardized (Morgan, 1980). Licensing is the primary means of regulation currently operating; it is controlled by the states. Licensing offers a means of monitoring programs for compliance with health and fire codes as well as with additional guidelines established and enforced by state agencies responsible for child care. The states' guidelines are typically framed in terms of *minimum* standards that reflect a philosophy of preventing harm to children in child care rather than one of providing high-quality, developmentally sound programming (Kendall and Walker, 1974).

The need for regulations that protect children's safety in child care is widely accepted. Even critics of a strong government role in child care have asserted that children's health and safety should be safeguarded by some public regulator body (Phillips and Zigler, 1987). There is no controversy as to what minimum standards define this boundary; in fact the degree of consensus is surprising in a field usually fraught with conflict. Experts concur that staff-child ratios, group size, and staff training affect children's development. The consensus dissipates, however, as discussions turn to whether the federal government should assume responsibility for this protective function.

The federal government has been struggling with the problem of standards for almost two decades. When the original Federal Interagency Day Care Regulations (FIDCR) were established in 1965, they were largely impracticable (Nelson, 1982). Subsequently, in 1971, the Office of Child Development, under the direction of the author, was responsible for the day care component of President Nixon's proposed Family Assistance Plan (FAP), and the standards were made more concrete and enforceable (Nelson, 1982). Even then, however, decision makers within Health, Education, and Welfare (HEW) conflicted over the federal government's role in promulgating standards. This conflict was resolved by Elliott Richardson, then Secretary of HEW, who argued that we owed children in day care no less protection than that which is provided the aged in nursing homes. Those standards became moot, however, with the collapse of FAP. The 1971 standards were slightly revised in 1980 in an effort led by the Children's Defense Fund. The revised standards were endorsed by Secretary Patricia Harris of the Carter Administration after a lengthy analysis within Health and Human Services (HHS), and sent to Congress for their consideration. Congress took no action pending further cost studies, and the standards quietly vanished without a trace. The most recent effort to produce standards, which took place in 1985, was precipitated by Congress's urging of HHS.

The result can be described only as a travesty. Instead of simply updating the thoroughly researched, developmentally sound standards of 1980, Congress largely ignored the problem of child care quality. Instead, the focus was on sexual abuse, which is exceptionally rare in child care settings. The real problem is less the rare occurrence of sexual abuse in centers than the unregulated care so many children are receiving, or the care that is regulated at so low a level as to compromise the children's development. In consequence, it is safe to say that the quality of care children are receiving can best be described as heterogeneous. Moreover, while increasing numbers of three- to five-year-olds are now attending preschool programs, there seems to be a growing divergence in child care patterns by family income and parents' educational levels (Ambach, 1986; Select Committee on Children, Youth, and Families, 1984). There is a very real danger that this may mark the emergence of a dual system of child care in which children of affluent and well-educated parents attend high-quality child care programs while children of low-income families are placed at even greater risk of poor developmental outcomes by being forced into very poor child care settings. The long-range implications of such a situation are ominous. As these children become adults, the consequences of their different pathways to development will remain. One group will have received environmental nutrients that will enhance optimal development. The other group, except for the rare invulnerable child, will have experienced the negative effects that result from poor care.

PRINCIPLES OF CHILD CARE

After a review of both the reality of the day care situation in America today and the developmental needs of children, it is clear that certain guidelines or "principles" must be adhered to in the creation of any viable child care system.

The first such principle is that child care services in this country must be made reliable and stable in the quality of service, in the assurance of financial support, and in their ultimate incorporation into a known major societal institution. In short, this issue must be made a priority; accessible child care must become a very real part of the structure of our society.

A second major principle is that every child must have equal access to child care, and all ethnic and socioeconomic groups should be integrated as fully as possible. Child care, like education, is not mentioned in the Constitution, and therefore, like education, child care must be primarily a state-based system. However, there is still an important federal role. The federal government must fund research efforts aimed at defining exactly what "adequate child care" is, and it should subsidize care for the most needy and the handicapped (as it currently does with Chapter 1 in the Elementary and Secondary Act and Public Law 94–142).

As a third and central principle, child care must be committed to the optimal development of the child across the entire range of human development. This principle encompasses two domains. First, parents and policymakers must be made cognizant of the fact that a child care environment does not just represent a babysitting service that allows parents to work; instead, it represents an environment that will invariably affect the early and later development of a large proportion of this nation's children. Therefore, the care offered in the child care system must be of good quality as defined by those Federal Interagency Day Care standards in 1980. Second, the child care system must be committed to the optimal development of the child across the entire range of human development. The child care system must be concerned with the development of the "whole child"—with children's social, emotional, and physical development as well as with their intellectual development.

A fourth principle is that the child care system must be predicated on a true partnership between parents and the children's caretakers. This is a lesson learned from the nation's Head Start program. The planners of Head Start realized that any attempt to reach the "whole child" must include the family, for the family, not the school, is the major source of a child's values and behavior. From its inception, parents of children in Head Start were asked to take an active role in the program. The extent to which this intervention has proven successful may be measured by the fact that approximately 95 percent of parents who utilize Head Start believe that it is an important and successful program (Abt Associates, 1978).

Another principle is that the crucial role of the caretakers must be recognized. A quality child care system is impossible without quality caretakers, individuals who have been trained to understand the developmental needs of children. The adults who take care of the children of working parents must be supported to receive proper training, an upgrade in pay, and an increase in status. In 1984, 90 percent of private-household child care workers and 58 percent of all other child care workers earned less than the poverty level wage (Children's Defense Fund, 1987). This arrangement is unacceptable. While every attempt must be made to make the child care system as cost-effective as possible, this cannot be done at the expense of good quality care.

Finally, as a last principle, the great heterogeneity of children must be recognized and appreciated. While all children will share a common system, the system must be designed so as to be sensitive to variations and varying needs of children and their families. A family should not be forced to fit itself to the characteristics of the system; rather, the system should be able to adapt to the varying needs of the families and children it serves.

UNREALISTIC SOLUTIONS

Although researchers and policymakers have the knowledge to provide good-quality child care to all children in this country, until recently, few initiatives existed to meet the growing needs of American families. Moreover, the proposed solutions that do exist are largely unrealistic and unworkable. For example, the Reagan Administration suggested that employers should provide or underwrite the cost of employee child care. While this suggestion is intriguing, the very nature of our private enterprise system guarantees the failure of this approach as a real solution.

A case in point: of the millions of employers in the United States, only 3,000 assist with child care, and often this assistance is in the form of information and referral services (Freidman, 1986). Perhaps rightly so, employers assert that we do not expect business to pay for education and ask why we should expect business to pay for child care.

Others have suggested that the task of child care be assigned to a conglomeration of caring individuals representing churches, YMCA's, and other non-profit agencies. While the people who run these organizations are not lacking will or dedication, most lack the funds needed to produce quality child care and the expertise required to ensure the appropriate growth and development of our nation's children.

A third solution that has been posed suggests that the 1971 Child Development Bill be resurrected and implemented into a national network of child care settings. Given, however, the federal government's current precarious financial condition, this solution too is unrealistic. Finally, certain government officials have touted the Head Start program as the vehicle for providing day care services. Unfortunately, Head Start is not the answer either. This program is not broad enough in regard to the ages that must be served, nor is it widespread enough. Head Start is currently serving only 15 percent of the children who are eligible for it (Zigler, 1985).

There are a few recent efforts which hold some promise. A number of bills addressing the child care needs of this country have recently been introduced before Congress. The majority of these bills propose that funds be funneled into existing day care systems around the country, with many specifically targeting children of low- to moderate-income families. However, while the amounts being requested seem significant, in reality they would not begin to have an impact on the magnitude of the current child care problem. In addition, even if these monies were made available, the lack of a coherent child care system into which they could be placed would prevent the optimal expenditure of even these modest funds.

Despite these concerns, there is a positive side to these bills. First, all of the bills have provisions for licensing and standards, and all require parental involvement. More importantly, these bills illuminate and underscore the pressing need for federal action on the day care front. However, these bills are not the final answer to this problem. Ultimately a comprehensive child care system will have to be created that, like education, will be affordable and equally available to all of our nation's children. Child care was once a "family problem," but this is no longer true. Presently well over half of our children need child care; this is now a national problem and, as such, demands a cohesive national solution.

CONCLUSION—A REALISTIC SOLUTION

As has been suggested, any viable solution must address the question of quality: what kinds of care are appropriate for what children at what developmental stage?

Infants

If this fine-grained question is posed with regard to infants, the early work of a number of researchers represents a broad range of opinion. At one end of the spectrum is the view held by Clarke-Stewart and her colleagues, who believe that "in terms of cognitive gains or achievement of social competence, age of starting day care does not seem to matter" (Clarke-Stewart, 1982). At the opposite end of the spectrum is child psychoanalyst Selma Fraiberg, who warns against the dangers to children of changing caregivers, regimented day care homes, and inadequately staffed and equipped centers. She urges mothers to stay with their children to provide them with proper care and a stable human relationship (Fraiberg, 1977).

There is a range of views between these two extremes. Through a recent review of the research on attachment and infant care (Gamble and Zigler, 1986), this author reached a number of tentative conclusions, including:

> (1) In families facing significant life stresses, substitute care during the first year increases the likelihood of insecure parent-child attachments. (2) An insecure attachment makes the child more vulnerable to stress encountered later on. (3) The best predictor of later pathology is a cumulative frequency of stressful life events coupled with an insecure attachment in infancy. (p. 35)

Finally, it was suggested that:

> . . . alternatives to infant day care should be made available to those working couples who would prefer to be with their infants during the first months of life. . . . The most attractive alternative to infant day care is a policy of paid infant care leaves during the first few months of [the] baby's life. (p. 40)

This opinion is far from unique. A committee of experts recently convened by the Yale Bush Center in Child Development and Social Policy reached the conclusion that parents should receive a minimum of six months' leave of absence to care for a newborn or newly adopted infant, and that the leave should include partial income replacement (75 percent of salary) for three months, up to a realistic maximum benefit. In fact, more than two-thirds of the nations of the world, including almost all industrialized nations, have some provisions for parents of infants to take paid, job-protected leaves of absence from the workplace for physical recovery from labor and birth and to care for their newborn infants.

Preschoolers and School-age Children

For three- to five-year-olds and for school-age children, we propose a solution to the problem which makes use of an already existing institution—the neighborhood school. We need a school that provides care for every child in need of care. By making use of the neighborhood school, we can create a system that could meet the needs of working parents, offer play and educational opportunities for children, strengthen community and family ties, and solve the child care crisis.

The most cost-effective way to provide universally available—however, not compulsory—care would be to work from the school; to create the School of the Twenty-first Century. We are advocating a return to the concept of the community school as a local center for all the social services required by the surrounding neighborhood. An arrangement of this sort would benefit both the community and the school system. Through tax dollars, citizens of this nation have already invested at least two trillion dollars in the public school system, and they deserve more of a return than they are currently receiving. By instituting child care into existing, centrally located school buildings, we will afford parents the care they are seeking—child care that is equitable, affordable, and geographically accessible. In addition, in an era when fears of sexual abuse occurring in privately owned day care centers are not uncommon, parents want secure options. The trusted neighborhood school offers just such an option.

This plan will benefit the school system as well. A recent report released by the National Black Child Development Institute (NBCDI, 1985) indicated that 40 percent of minority youth are functionally illiterate; black children are twice as likely as whites to be suspended from school or to suffer corporal punishment; and black children are three times as likely as whites to be placed in classes for the educable mentally retarded. Public schools are obviously not sufficiently meeting the needs of minority groups, and a great deal of animosity has arisen between these minority groups and the public schools as a result. A return to the concept of the community school could help rebuild a vital, positive parent-school relationship. For example, were schools to reach out and assist parents from the time of birth (e.g., Parents as Teachers [PAT] program), or were the schools able to offer information as to where families in the neighborhood could find good, accessible day care for their infants and toddlers, the school would then become a supportive and good place in the eyes of the parents. All educators must realize how important this relationship is; effective education simply cannot occur in a vacuum within the school walls.

Such a program offers schools financial benefits as well. Within the past decade, public schools have witnessed a sharp decline in the enrollment of middle-class working families. Because of their desperate need for child care, these families are opting more and more often to send their children to private schools that offer the child care services they need. However, public schools lose some of their funding for every child that leaves the system. It is reasonable to assume that if parents were able to secure their child care needs within the public school, their children would return to attend their neighborhood school. The enrollment in some public schools has declined so much recently that this program might ultimately be viewed as the salvation of many schools (Moore, 1987).

The school building, then, could be used for two purposes: formal education for six- to twelve-year-olds; and, in a second system, full-day high-quality child care for three- to five-year-olds, early-morning and after-school care for six- to twelve-year-olds, and full-time care for all children during vacations.

For two reasons, this program, although operating on school grounds, should not be staffed solely by teachers. First, teachers are already overburdened with the task of educating our children; it would be unfair to ask them to take sole responsibility for on-site care as well. In addition, many elementary school teachers are not trained to work with very young children and their families. When we speak of on-site child care, we are not advocating early formal education. What we envision is a quality child care system that will be structured to meet the developmental needs of preschoolers, a place where they would go primarily for recreation and socialization—the real business of preschoolers. We propose, therefore, that teachers should have the option to participate in the before- and after-school program. The school-based child care programs for three- and four-year-olds, on the other hand, should be headed by an early education specialist who will be assisted by Child Development Associates (CDAs), certified child care givers currently being used in our nation's Head Start program.

On a larger scale, many aspects of the funding issue will have to be addressed. Currently, there are 13 Twenty-first Century schools operating within two school districts in Missouri. Administrators of these school districts have found that because this system makes use of an already existing resource (the neighborhood school building), the cost of implementing their programs has been kept to a minimum. This initial funding may come from one of three sources: charitable foundations, state governments, or the federal government. In Missouri, start-up funds were obtained from the Kansas City Association of Charitable Trusts and Foundations. The state of Connecticut has pursued a different course. That state has recently passed a bill that authorizes $500,000 for start-up funds and eventual evaluations of demonstration schools to be placed in rural, urban, and suburban areas throughout Connecticut. Finally, at the federal level, a bill calling for $120 million for the funding of a minimum of 60 demonstration Twenty-first Century schools (at least one per state) has been introduced before Congress by Senator Christopher Dodd of Connecticut and Representative Dale Kildee of Michigan. Beyond the initial funding, parents will be expected to pay for the maintenance of the program on a sliding fee scale.

This family-oriented, multiservice community school could meet the many different needs of children and their families by offering a variety of programs from which families could select. Three such outreach programs would include a family support system for parents of newborns, such as the Parents as

Teachers program currently operating in Missouri (Vento and Winter, 1986; Meyerhoff and White, 1986); support for family day care homes within the neighborhood; and information and referral services. In this way, the school can act as a provider of day care, but it will also be a training and referral agency for other day care workers in the area. The importance of such flexibility and variety in our changing society is obvious. The time has come to operationalize a high-quality day care system that will be available and affordable to all who need it. The future of our nation depends on this.

REFERENCES

Abt Associates, Inc. *A National Survey of Head Start Graduates and Their Peers.* Cambridge, Mass. (Contract No. HEW 105-76-1103) (ED 152 422), March 1978.

Ad Hoc Day Care Coalition. *The Crisis in Infant and Toddler Child Care.* Washington, D.C.: Ad Hoc Day Care Coalition, 1985.

Ambach, G. "Should 4- and 5-Year-Olds Be in School? Yes, Optional Public Preschool Is Essential." *The Christian Science Monitor* (March 28, 1986): B7–B9.

Belsky, J. "Experimenting with the Family in the Newborn Period." Child Development 56 (1985): 407–414.

Berrueta-Clement, J.R., L. J. Schweinhart, W. S. Barnett, A. S. Epstein, and D. P. Weikart. *Changed Lives: The Effects of the Perry Preschool Program on Youths Through Age 19.* Ypsilanti, Mich.: High/Scope Press, 1984.

Blum, P. M. *The Day-Care Dilemma: Women and Children First.* Lexington, Mass.: Lexington Books, 1983.

Brazelton, T. B. "Issues for Working Parents." *American Journal of Orthopsychiatry* 56 (1986): 14–25.

Bretherton, I. "Attachment Theory: Retrospect and Prospect." *Monographs of the Society for Research in Child Development* 50 (1985): 3–35.

Chess, S. "Comments: Infant Day Care–A Cause for Concern." *Zero to Three* 7 (1987): 24–25.

Children's Defense Fund. *A Children's Defense Budget.* Washington, D.C., 1987.

Clarke-Stewart, A. *Day Care.* Cambridge, Mass.: Harvard University Press, 1982.

Clarke-Stewart, A., and G. Fein. "Early Childhood Programs." In *Handbook of Child Psychology* (4th ed.): Vol. II, *Infancy and Developmental Psychobiology,* edited by P. H. Mussen. (917–1000). New York: Wiley, 1983.

Deutsch, M., C. Deutsch, T. Jordan, and R. Grallo. "The IDS Program: An Experiment in Early and Sustained Enrichment in Consortium for Longitudinal Studies." In *As the Twig Is Bent* (377–411). Hillsdale, N.J.: Erlbaum, 1983.

Endsley, R., and M. Broadbard. *Quality Day Care: A Handbook of Choices for Parents and Caregivers.* Englewood Cliffs, N.J.: Spectrum, 1981.

Etaugh, C. "Effects of Maternal Care on Children: Research Evidence and Popular Views." *American Psychologist* 35:4 (1980): 309–319.

Fraiberg, S. *Every Child's Birthright: In Defense of Mothering.* New York: Basic Books, 1977.

Freidman, D. Cited in "Select Committee

on Children, Youth, and Families—
Families and Child Care: Improving the
Options." Washington, D.C.: U.S.
Government Printing Office, 39-146-0,
1984.

Freidman, D. "Child Care for Employees'
Kids." *Harvard Business Review* 64
(1986): 28–32.

Gamble, T. J., and E. Zigler. "Effects of
Infant Day Care: Another Look at the
Evidence." *American Journal of Orthopsy-
chiatry* 56 (1986): 26–42.

Ginter, M. "An Exploratory Study of the
'Latchkey Child': Children Who Care
for Themselves." Unpublished predis-
sertation project. Yale University, New
Haven, 1981.

Goldberg, W. A., and M. A. Easter-
brooks. "Role of Marital Quality in
Toddler Development." *Developmental
Psychology* 20 (1984): 504–514.

Hartup, W. W. "Perspectives on Child
and Family Interaction: Past, Present
and Future." In *Child Influences on Marital and Family Interactions: A Life-Span
Perspective,* edited by R. M. Lerner and
G. B. Spanier. New York: Academic
Press, 1978.

Hayes, C. D. *Making Policies for Children:
A Study of the Federal Process.* Washington, D.C.: National Academy Press,
1982.

Hewlett, S. *A Lesser Life: The Myth of
Women's Liberation in America.* New
York: Morrow, 1986.

Howes, C. "Care Giver Behavior in Center and Family Day Care." *Journal of
Applied Developmental Psychology* 4
(1983): 99–107.

Howes, C. Current Research on Early
Day Care—A Review. Paper presented
at the San Francisco Psychoanalytic
Institute Seminar on "Infant and Toddler Care—Meeting the Needs of Parents and Children in a Changing Society," September 20–21, 1986.

Howes, C. "Sharing Fantasy: Social Pre-
tend Play in Toddlers." *Child Development* 56 (1985): 1253–1258.

Joint Economic Committee of the U.S.
Congress. Press release: "Obey
releases report on working mothers."
May 10, 1986.

Kahn, A., and D. Kamerman. *Child Care:
Facing the Hard Choices.* Dover, Mass.:
Auburn House, 1987.

Kendall, E. D., and L. H. Walker. "Day
Care Licensing: The Eroding Regulations." *Child Care Quarterly* 13:4 (1974):
278–290.

Kolata, G. "Studying Learning in the
Womb." *Science* 225 (July 20, 1984):
302–303.

Lampl, M., and R. Emde. "Episodic
Growth Spurts in Infancy: A Preliminary Report on Length, Head Circum-
ference and Behavior." In *Levels and
Transactions in Children's Development,*
edited by K. Fischer. San Francisco:
Jossey-Bass, 1983.

Langway, L., P. Abramson, and D. Foote.
"The Latchkey Children." *Newsweek,*
(February 16, 1981): 96–97.

Lazar, I., and R. Darlington. "Lasting
Effects of Early Education: A Report
from the Consortium for Longitudinal
Studies." *Monographs of the Society for
Research in Child Development* 47 (1982):
2–3, Serial No. 195.

Leischman, K. "When Kids Are Home
Alone: How Mothers Make Sure
They're Safe." *Working Mothers* 3 (1980):
21–25.

Long, L., and T. Long. *Latchkey Children.*
National Institute of Education Contract No. 400-76-0008, 1982.

Maynard, F. *The Child Care Crisis.*
Markham, Ontario: Viking, 1985.

McCartney, K., S. Scarr, D. Phillips, and
S. C. Grajek. "Day Care as Intervention: Comparisons of Varying Quality

Programs." *Journal of Applied Developmental Psychology* 6 (1985): 247–260.

McCartney, K., S. Scarr, D. Phillips, S. C. Grajek, and J. C. Schwarz. "Environmental Differences Among Day Care Centers and Their Effects on Children's Development." In *Day Care: Scientific and Social Policy Issues,* edited by E. Zigler and E. Gordon, 126–152. Boston, Mass.: Auburn House, 1982.

Meyerhoff, M. K., and B. L. White. "New Parents as Teachers." *Educational Leadership* (1986): 42–46.

Minuchin, S. "Families and Individual Development: Provocations from the Field of Family Therapy." *Child Development* 56 (1985): 289–302.

Moore, E. K. "Child Care in the Public Schools: Public Accountability and the Black Child." In *Early Schooling: The National Debate,* edited by S. L. Kagan and E. F. Zigler. New Haven: Yale University Press, 1987.

Morgan, G. "Federal Day Care Requirements: One More Round." *Day Care and Early Education* 8:2 (1980): 26-30.

Moynihan, D. P. C. "The Family Security Act of 1987." *Letter to New York,* United States Senate, Washington, D.C., May 26, 1987.

Mueller, E., and D. Vandall. "Infant-Infant Interaction." In *Handbook of Infant Development,* edited by J.D. Osafsky. New York: Wiley, 1979.

National Black Child Development Institute. *Excellence and Equity, Quality and Inequality: A Report on Civil Rights, Education, and Black Children.* Washington, D.C., 1985.

Nelson, C. "The Politics of Federal Day Care Regulation." In *Day Care: Scientific and Social Policy Issues,* edited by E. Zigler and E. Gordon, 267–306, 1982.

Parke, R. *Fathers.* Cambridge, Mass.: Harvard University Press, 1981.

Pastor, D. C. "The Quality of Mother-Infant Attachment and its Relationship to Toddlers' Initial Sociability with Peers." *Developmental Psychology* 17 (1981): 326–335.

Phillips, D., L. McCartney, S. Scarr, and C. Howes. "Selective Review of Infant Day Care Research: A Cause for Concern." *Zero to Three* (February 1987): 18–24.

Phillips, D., and E. Zigler. "The Checkered History of Federal Day Care Regulation." In *Review of Research in Education, Vol. 14,* edited by E. Rothkopf. Washington, D.C.: American Educational Research Association, 1987.

Pierson, D., D. Tivnan, and T. Walker. "A School-Based Program from Infancy to Kindergarten for Children and Their Parents." *Personal and Guidance Journal* 4 (1984): 448–455.

Rodman, H., and D. Pratto. "How Children Take Care of Themselves: Preliminary Statement on Magazine Survey." Report submitted to the Ford Foundation, 1980.

Rodman, H., D. J. Pratto, and R. S. Nelson. "Child Care Arrangements and Children's Functioning: A Comparison of Self-Care and Adult-Care Children." *Developmental Psychology* 21 (1985): 413–418.

Rutter, M. "Socio-Emotional Consequences of Day Care for Preschool Children." In *Day Care: Scientific and Social Policy Issues,* edited by E. Zigler and E. Gordon, 3–33. Boston: Auburn House, 1982.

Scarr, S. *Mother Care/Other Care.* New York: Basic Books, 1984.

School-Age Child Care Project. "School-Age Child Care." In *Day Care: Scientific and Social Policy Issues,* edited by E. Zigler and E. Gordon, 457–475. Boston: Auburn House, 1982.

Schroeder, P. "Parental Leave: The Need for a Federal Policy." In *Infant Care Leave: Toward A National Policy,* edited by E. Zigler and M. Frank. New Haven: Yale University Press, 1988.

Select Committee on Children, Youth, and Families. *Children and Families in Poverty: The Struggle to Survive.* Washington, D.C.: U.S. Government Printing Office, 1988.

Select Committee on Children, Youth, and Families. *Families and Child Care: Improving the Options.* Washington, D.C.: U.S. Government Printing Office, No. 39-146-0, September 1984.

Steinberg, L. "Latchkey Children and Susceptibility to Peer Pressure: An Ecological Analysis." *Developmental Psychology* 22 (1986): 433–439.

Stern, D. *The Interpersonal World of the Infant: A View from Psychoanalysis and Developmental Psychology.* New York: Basic Books, 1985.

U.S. Department of Labor. *Child Care: A Work Force Issue.* Report of the Secretary's Task Force. Washington, D.C.: U.S. Government Printing Office, No. 1988-212-248:80384, 1988.

Vento, V. A., and M. Winter. "Beginning at the Beginning: Missouri's Parents as First Teachers Program." *Community Education Journal* 14 (1986): 6–8.

Waters, E., J. Wippman, and L. A. Sroufe. "Attachment, Positive Effect and Competence in the Peer Group." Two studies in construct validation. *Child Development* 50:3 (1979): 821–829.

Zigler, E. "Assessing Head Start at 20: An Invited Commentary." *American Journal of Orthopsychiatry* 55 (1985): 603–609.

Zigler, E., and E. Gordon (eds.). *Day Care: Scientific and Social Policy Issues.* Boston: Auburn House, 1982.

Zigler, E. and N. Hall. "Day Care and Its Effects on Children: An Overview for Pediatric Health Professionals." *Journal of Developmental and Behavioral Pediatrics* 9 (1988): 38–46.

Zigler, E., and S. Muenchow. "A Room of Their Own: A Proposal to Renovate the Children's Bureau." *American Psychologist* 40 (1985): 953–959.

HOW POLICYMAKERS CAN HELP DELIVER HIGH-QUALITY EARLY CHILDHOOD PROGRAMS*

Lawrence J. Schweinhart

One of today's major domestic political issues is whether and how we will assume public responsibility for providing uniformly *high-quality* early childhood programs for the nation's children, especially those who live in the families that can least afford such programs.

The issue is not merely the provision of early childhood programs. Today, as shown in Table 1, our best estimate is that 30 percent of the nation's children under age five—5 million out of 16 million youngsters—receive some type of out-of-home care and education from nonrelatives. Of the 3.9 million children under age five receiving such care while their mothers are at work, about 1.9 million are in caregivers' homes, and about two million are in such organized facilities as centers, nursery schools, and public schools. In addition, about one million three- and four-year-olds whose mothers are *not* employed attend nursery schools and kindergartens. In percentages, more than twice as many three- and four-year-olds receive such care and education as do younger children (45 percent vs. 21 percent), and more than four times as many receive care and education in organized facilities (35 percent vs. 8 percent). Excluding tax breaks, all public early childhood program funds subsidize in whole or in part about 1.7 million young children; about one-third of these receive out-of-home care and education from nonrelatives (Schweinhart, 1984, pp. 16, 34). Publicly funded programs must be closely studied if we are to assume greater public responsibility for early childhood programs.

Longitudinal research consistently shows that high-quality early childhood programs help children in poverty improve their intellectual and social development and experience less school failure (McKey et al., 1985; Lazar, Darlington, Murray, Royce, and Snipper, 1982). The High/Scope Foundation's Perry Preschool study and a few other studies show that such programs can lead children in poverty to greater socioeconomic success and social responsibility as adults,

* This paper was prepared (1) for the Early Childhood Task Force of the National Association of State Boards of Education, with funding from the U. S. Administration for Children, Youth, and Families and from the Exxon Foundation, and (2) for the 1988 Summer Institute of the Council of Chief State School Officers, with funding from the Rockefeller Foundation. High/Scope received additional funding for such work from the Carnegie Corporation of New York. These organizations do not necessarily endorse the opinions herein expressed.

thereby producing large economic returns to taxpayers (Berrueta-Clement, Schweinhart, Barnett, Epstein, and Weikart, 1984). Although most such research has been conducted on children living in poverty, it bears witness to the importance of good early childhood experiences for all children, at home and in programs. Poverty is not a fixed and permanent characteristic of a person but rather a set of experiences, just as preschool programs are sets of experiences. Thus custodial care and excessively academic programs that do not provide good

TABLE 1

U. S. EARLY CHILDHOOD CARE AND EDUCATION IN 1988

(in thousands)

Population Category	*Ages*		
	0–2	*3–4*	*0–4*
Children [a]	9,629	6,454	16,083
	100%	100%	100%
A. *With mothers in labor force* [a]	4,921	3,497	8,418
	51%	54%	52%
1. Parental care during work [b]	1,226	783	2,009
	12%	12%	12%
2. Relative and in-home care [b]	1,628	908	2,536
	17%	14%	16%
3. Nonrelative care in other homes [b]	1,265	621	1,886
	13%	10%	12%
4. Centers and schools [b]	802	1,186	1,988
	8%	18%	12%
B. *With mothers not in labor force* [a]	4,708	2,957	7,665
	49%	46%	48%
1. Parental care only	4,708	1,940	6,648
	49%	30%	41%
2. Centers and schools [c]	0	1,017	1,017
		16%	6%
C. *All extrafamilial, out-of-home*	2,067	2,824	4,891
care and education	21%	45%	30%

[a]U. S. Bureau of Labor Statistics, unpublished data, November 30, 1988.

[b]From U. S. Bureau of the Census, *Who's Minding the Kids? Child Care Arrangements: Winter 1984–85*, Series P-70, No. 9 (Washington, D.C.: U. S. Government Printing Office), 5. Given figures multiplied by 1.058 for ages 0–2 and .995 for ages 3–4 to match 1988 totals.

[c]From National Center for Education Statistics, *The Condition of Education—1986 Edition* (Washington, D.C.: U. S. Government Printing Office, 1986), 5, 13. The specific source of estimates is that 34.4 percent of 3- and 4-year-olds with mothers not in the labor force were enrolled in centers and schools in 1984.

early childhood experiences for young children do not contribute to their development and may even harm it.

WHAT IS QUALITY?

Research on early childhood programs confirms what experience and common sense suggest: their *quality* is the key to their success. Research has largely laid to rest an earlier generation's fears that young children might suffer permanent psychological damage from the extended separation from their mothers that accompanies maternal employment (Ainslie, 1984). The common belief today is that if a child care program has harmful effects, it is because it provides children with bad experiences. David Elkind (1986, 1987) has lately articulated the problem of the *miseducation* of young children, of low-quality programs which, although their intended purpose may be to reduce risks to young children's development, actually increase such risks.

Building on both research findings and the collective experience of the past two decades, we have developed a seven-point definition of quality in early childhood programs (Schweinhart, 1988; Phillips, 1987; Epstein et al., 1985).

- A child-development-curriculum approach
- Low enrollment limits
- Staff who are trained in early childhood development
- Supervisory support and in-service training
- Parents as partners with teaching staff
- Sensitivity to children's and parents' needs
- Developmentally appropriate evaluation procedures

1. *A child-development-curriculum approach*, the most important component of quality, promotes sound intellectual, social, and physical development by providing a supportive environment in which children choose their own learning activities and take responsibility for completing them. They learn by exploring their environment with all their senses both actively and reflectively. Rather than having to sit at desks, they are free to move around the room and use a variety of toys and everyday materials. The National Association for the Education of Young Children (NAEYC, 1986a, 1986b) endorses this curriculum approach, which serves as the basis for many curriculum models, including High/Scope's (Hohmann, Banet, and Weikart, 1979).

2. *Low enrollment limits* and low staff-child ratios are hallmarks of good early childhood programs. According to the National Day Care study (Ruopp, Travers, Glantz, and Coelen, 1979, pp. 93–95, 158–160), a program expected to enhance the intellectual and social development of three- to five-year-olds should enroll no more than 16 children, with two trained adults in the classroom. An enrollment limit of more than 20 three- to five-year-olds could

result in below-average growth in their knowledge and skills. Because children under three years old need even more individual attention, groups that include such children should have a trained adult for every four children and enroll no more than 12 children, and no more than eight if children under two years old are included.

3. *Staff who are trained in early childhood development* probably provide better programs. The National Day Care study confirmed that adults are better at providing early childhood care and education when they have early childhood training. Such training can lead to college degrees in early childhood education or the early childhood field's competency-based Child Development Associate credential, now widely used in Head Start (Ruopp et al., 1979, pp. 98–102).

4. *Supervisory support and in-service training.* Administrators at all levels need to understand and actively support the goals and operation of early childhood programs and their child-development-curriculum approach. In public schools, these administrative leaders include school board members, super-intendents, curriculum and evaluation directors, and building principals. They should provide the programs with the needed equipment and resources; ensure that staff, children, and programs themselves are evaluated with developmentally appropriate measures and standards; and be able to explain and defend the curriculum approach to parents and others. They are especially responsible for early childhood staff development, including meetings at least monthly that deal with the issues of day-to-day operation of a child-development-curriculum approach.

5. *Parents as partners with teaching staff.* The staff of good early childhood programs seek to be partners with parents and recognize the central importance of parents in children's development. Being partners means staff are neither too authoritarian, claiming to know what's best for children regardless of parental perceptions, nor too accommodating, succumbing to parental pressure to place inappropriate academic expectations on young children. Staff are the recognized experts on child development principles and are treated as such by parents. But parents are recognized as the ultimate experts on their children's behavior, traits, and family background.

6. *Sensitivity to children's and parents' physical and social needs.* Since half the nation's young children have mothers who are employed, if one early childhood program arrangement does not fully meet a family's child-care needs, another one must. The various program providers should get to know each other, since they are partners in caring for the child when parents are unavailable. Further, many prekindergarten programs are directed at children living in poverty, who in 1986 included 22 percent of the nation's children under age six and 44 percent of all black and Hispanic children under age six (U. S. Bureau of the Census, 1987, p. 30). Children living in poverty may well

need publicly provided meals and preventive health care. Families living in poverty are often under stress and may need help in finding agencies that address their needs. Although program staff cannot be all things to all people, they can be counselors and friends to children and their families who need help and can refer them to the agencies and services that can help them.

7. *Developmentally appropriate evaluation procedures.* Valid, reliable, and developmentally appropriate observation procedures, ratings, and tests help early childhood teachers make decisions about a program's quality and how well it enhances children's development. Observers assess program quality by viewing programs from the perspective of standards of quality such as those listed here. They assess children's development in knowledge, thinking, and social skills, and in their dispositions to learning, in order to provide guidance to staff and assurance to all that children and staff are accomplishing what they are expected to accomplish (National Association for the Education of Young Children, 1988; National Association of Early Childhood Specialists in State Departments of Education, 1988).

A good early childhood program can take place in any setting that has adequate financial and physical resources and an adequate number of qualified staff—a private home, center, nursery school, public school, or Head Start program. The basic definition of early-childhood-program quality applies to *all* these programs. Indeed, it applies in principle to child-rearing by parents themselves—especially the idea that parents understand and apply information about child development in their child-rearing practices.

It is still possible to strive for a good program when obstacles prohibit the full realization of certain components. For example, a teacher without formal early childhood training can team up with a teacher trained in early childhood; a kindergarten classroom with 25 children can nevertheless maintain a child-development-curriculum approach. However, these are *emergency, temporary solutions* and are not legitimate excuses for administrators or staff to become complacent and stop striving for all aspects of high quality.

NO PROGRAM SETTING IS PERFECT

Parents are unquestionably the primary providers of early childhood care and education. It is in society's best interest for parents to have supportive social networks of family and friends, access to parenting education, and adequate levels of income to be able to carry out their essential job of raising the next generation. Since many parents delegate a part of this job to early childhood teachers and caregivers, it is likewise important for these people to have supportive social networks, early childhood training, and adequate levels of income.

Although exemplary early childhood programs can and do exist in homes, centers, nursery schools, Head Start settings, and public schools, each of these program settings now needs fundamental improvements in order to provide consistently good early childhood education. Each has its strengths and weaknesses; none of them is inherently bad or good. Advocates for one program setting or another do the early childhood field a disservice when they focus only on the weaknesses of other program settings and the strengths of their own. So let's take a hard look at each of these program settings.

Far from being an organized system, the nation's child care supply beyond children's homes and families is a rich mixture of caregivers' homes, nursery schools, and centers that are church-based, nonprofit and for-profit, funded and unfunded. With an adequate level of public subsidy, decently paid caregivers may be able to provide affordable, high-quality early childhood care and education throughout the country. As it is, paid home caregivers and center staff receive appallingly low salaries, averaging $9,204 annually, and very few employment benefits. Such dismal compensation leads to an annual turnover rate of 36 percent, almost double that of other occupations (U. S. Bureau of Labor Statistics, 1986). Too many trained caregivers are leaving the field. It is no wonder that the existing child-care work force cannot consistently provide good child care. Indeed, it is a tribute to the field that good care exists despite such working conditions.

Head Start, dubbed the "Crown Jewel of the Great Society" by William Safire of the *New York Times*, has become a relatively stable institution with a multiple-services design that includes not only early childhood education but also parenting education, child nutrition, preventive health care for children, and family access to social services. Two-thirds of Head Start teachers now have either a bachelor's degree in early childhood education or a Child Development Associate credential. The national Head Start effort has been somewhat successful in resisting the pressure to reduce its per-child funding level in order to serve more children although it serves only about one-fifth of three- and four-year-olds living in poverty in the U.S. (Among the 1,629,000 three- and four-year-olds living in poverty in the U.S. in 1987 were 345,767 Head Start children.) Nevertheless, the average annual salary of Head Start teachers is only $8,460 (Head Start Bureau, 1988, personal communication).

The potential strengths and weaknesses of early childhood programs in *public schools* are almost the reverse of child care and Head Start. The strengths of the public schools are professionalism, accountability, and universality. Although public school teachers may not be paid as much as they deserve, their average annual salary, now $28,031 (National Education Association, 1988), is three times the average salary for Head Start teachers and caregivers. Along with higher salaries, they have a higher degree of organizational support and a more secure status in the community. School boards, usually elected, govern public schools, and local, state, and federal levels of government provide them with annual funding.

The weaknesses of the public schools come from some of their traditions. Sizes of classes, including kindergartens, are typically 25 to 30 with one teacher, much larger than desirable for early childhood programs. Typical public school classrooms, including many kindergartens, provide teacher-directed instruction rather than the child-initiated learning that is the basis of a child-development-curriculum approach. Focused on education, public schools typically give low priority to providing for child health and nutrition needs, child-care needs, and needs of some families for social services. Too often, public schools perpetuate a narrow middle-class orientation that unnecessarily alienates low-income families and ethnic minority groups.

THE ROLE OF REGULATIONS IN PROMOTING QUALITY

It should be an urgent national priority to maintain and improve as necessary the quality of all early childhood programs in home and center child care, Head Start, and the public schools. To achieve this end in any of these program settings, policy makers should use regulations judiciously and seek to promote the professionalism that incorporates and goes beyond regulations and fosters the pursuit of excellence (McDonnell and Elmore, 1987; Timar and Kirp, 1987).

The approach to regulations described here has developed as a reaction to the educational reforms of the past few years that were mandated from state capitals. There is a growing recognition that while educational change can be stimulated by policymakers outside the community, it must be enthusiastically embraced and "owned" by teachers and local administrators. Another relevant national debate concerns child-care standards, most recently stimulated by the introduction before Congress of the Act for Better Child Care Services. Unaware of the research cited herein, which shows how central child care quality is to children's development, some have challenged not just specific standards or uniform standards, but the need for any standards at all. However, given the need for standards, there remains the question of how standards are best put into practice.

Just as authority styles that employees experience at work have been found to influence their parenting styles (Hoffman, 1984), so may teachers' relationships with administrators be expected to influence their teaching styles. The *professional* administrator-teacher relationship is like the teacher-child relationship in the child-development-curriculum approach: The administrator uses regulations to create a framework in which the teacher has responsibility and can take initiative. In contrast, an *autocratic*, exclusively regulatory administrator-teacher relationship can resemble teacher-directed instruction, with the administrator enforcing rules upon a teacher.

In either case, *regulations* rely on strong central authority, derived from political consensus, to compel minimal program quality by prescribing program inputs and procedures. When applied by an autocratic administrator, regulations may encourage a "just enough to get by" attitude that leads to low personal investment of energy. Nonresident monitors are essential to enforcing regulations, although it seems that most states have too few such monitors to do an adequate job. Increased funding not only enables nonresident monitors to carry out their regulatory responsibility but also typically permits them to provide the kind of training that leads to professionalism and makes nonresident monitoring less essential.

The proper role of regulations is to compel conformity to such static, easily measured criteria as enrollment limits and staff-child ratios, staff possession of degrees or certification, and hours of in-service training. Regulations may also broadly require the existence of a child-development-curriculum approach, developmentally appropriate assessment, and parent involvement; but the proper implementation of these components goes well beyond an effective regulatory approach. An innovative and potentially valuable use of regulation would be for a large early-childhood-program system to specify the trainer-staff ratio at, say, one trainer for every 20 teachers. Lack of such a practice can strangle in-service training and, ironically, undermine the development of professionalism.

Professionalism relies on strong staff responsibility, personal autonomy, and high personal investment of energy. It achieves high program quality by focusing on program outputs and accomplishments. It works best with high staff qualifications and salaries, although high salaries do not guarantee professionalism. A professional approach requires that staff have both the desire and the capacity to operate good programs (Berman, 1987). If they have the desire but not the capacity, training and resources are the answer. If they do not have the desire, enforced regulations may be the only alternative. In Gwen Morgan's words (1987), "Regulation is a blunt instrument for achieving quality, but it is of great importance in creating a safety net under the field of practice" (p. 14–1).

Regulations are not a good way to achieve dynamic, subtle, hard-to-measure goals. Regulations are inadequate for ensuring implementation of a child-development-curriculum approach, good preservice or in-service early childhood training, supervisory support, parent involvement, and staff sensitivity to the physical and social needs of children and parents. For example, implementation of a child-development-curriculum approach calls for teachers to encourage children to solve problems by turning everyday occurrences into problem-solving situations. A careful observer can document and review such opportunities with a teacher, but the process is much too subtle for regulatory monitoring.

ADDITIONAL POLICY INSTRUMENTS
FOR PROMOTING QUALITY

Various policy instruments besides basic regulations can foster professionalism by offering staff incentives to achieve objectives using broadly defined procedures. Such policy instruments include financial grants, flexible program accreditation criteria, resident monitoring of program quality, and various types of staff development activities.

Grants provide financial incentives to accomplish outcomes rather than to follow procedures. Grants are typically obtained by an agency that solicits proposals and then selects those that best meet identified criteria. The proposal process is sometimes criticized for favoring agencies or districts that have effective proposal-writing capacities. Ideally, proposal-writing capacity should be closely related to planning capacity, so it is actually relevant to the selection process. However, the proposal process can be easily altered to match desired selection criteria even more fully—for example, by requiring that proposed personnel with early childhood degrees or credentials write actual program work plans.

Program accreditation takes place through national associations such as the NAEYC and Head Start or through state departments of social services and education. The prevalent approach to program licensing by state social services agencies requires conformity to minimal regulations to reduce risk of harm to children. Such an approach is necessary but must be combined with a more ambitious approach, such as that used by Head Start and the NAEYC, of defining the *ideal* early childhood program and proposing levels of quality beyond the minimum which may not be fully attained, but which are worth striving for nonetheless—for example, full and enthusiastic involvement of all parents. In a good early childhood program, staff strive to improve and develop the program rather than merely to meet minimal regulations. Indeed, one pernicious effect of the minimal-standards approach can be the public misperception that it guarantees program quality.

Resident program monitoring is carried out either by staff themselves or by their day-to-day supervisors—directors or principals. The nonresident program monitoring approach, in which regulators visit program sites a few times a year, is at best a supplement to day-to-day monitoring. However, the day-to-day supervisor must have a clear vision of good early childhood education. This can pose a problem in elementary schools, such as those in Texas, where principals with no early childhood training were suddenly called upon to supervise prekindergarten programs. One interesting proposal is that each elementary school should expand to include prekindergarten and school-age child care and should also have an early childhood specialist as a sort of sub-principal to supervise the early grades and the child care (Zigler, 1987).

STAFF DEVELOPMENT

Staff development, the heart of a professional approach, combines (1) providing people with information, challenging them, and helping them think through ideas with (2) modeling and practicing applications of theory. Staff-development experiences are defined by staff-certification criteria and by the resources that individuals and agencies devote to them. Staff training should focus on developing staff understanding of child development principles and the practice of applying these principles to early childhood programs. State social service agencies, education agencies, and Head Start all require early-childhood-program staff to have degrees or professional certification, but training criteria vary considerably. In-service training has a special role in enabling agencies to join together in developing their capacity to provide good early childhood programs—training untrained staff and administrators and, ideally, providing a catalyst for program development.

Early childhood teacher certification criteria largely define the content of preservice training and should embody the state of the art in early childhood care and education. Of central importance is an understanding of what constitutes a child-development-curriculum approach and a high-quality early childhood program and a knowledge of how to put these definitions into practice. In fact, states vary greatly in their certification requirements for child care and preschool education. For kindergarten teachers, only half of the states require specialized early childhood training, although 39 states and the District of Columbia do require specialized certification (Hitz and Wright, 1988). For caregivers of unrelated children outside the children's homes, 18 states require preservice early childhood training and 26 require in-service training; but nine states permit program experience to be substituted for training, and seven states require neither training nor experience (Morgan, 1987, p. 6).

In-service training for teaching staff should allow staff to learn on the job about good early childhood care and education—helping novices to increase their competency and enabling experienced staff to maintain their expertise. Locally provided in-service training, however, too often is minimal and nonsequential and does not hold staff accountable for their own development. The usual alternative is for individuals to attain professional degrees on their own time, apart from their school or agency.

The High/Scope Foundation, in its training-of-teacher-trainers projects around the country, has pioneered an alternative approach to in-service training that combines agency and individual development. Such a project is contracted by a school or agency, which then designates an individual to represent it in the training. The training, one week per month for seven months, enables the successful trainee to train others to implement High/Scope's child development curriculum. Hence, the training builds agency capacity to provide in-service training even as it enables the individual to become an endorsed trainer of High/Scope's curriculum. This approach leads to a level of individual accountability virtually impossible in training that is not linked to schools or agencies.

Because the mission of public schools extends well beyond early childhood to the education of children from kindergarten through high school, school-board members, administrators, and support personnel have special in-service training needs. These people need an understanding of what early childhood education is all about, a vision of what constitutes good early childhood education. Such an understanding, for example, would have spared Georgia's State Board of

Education the national embarrassment that occurred when it inappropriately required children to pass standardized achievement tests for first-grade entry. The High/Scope Foundation is now collaborating with the National Association of Elementary School Principals to provide such training, but this only begins to meet the full national need.

Every large early-childhood-program delivery system needs one or more programs that are *models of good practice*—not only for their services to children and families but also for the services to other early-childhood-program providers in the system and in the wider community. In public schools, such programs can also serve as models of good early childhood practices for elementary school-teachers. Teachers, caregivers, and parents should be encouraged to visit and observe such programs. The staff in model programs should have time set aside to meet with visitors, to develop audiovisual materials about their program, and to make presentations in the community to interested groups. Such model programs can be offered not only by large school districts but also by regional church groups, for-profit child care businesses, day-care-home associations, and Head Start regions. The Pittsburgh school district, for example, in 1987 initiated exemplary early childhood programs in its Brookline Elementary Teacher Center. Model programs should be identified as such by endorsement procedures such as NAEYC's program accreditation procedure or the High/Scope Foundation's new program registry.

WHAT NEXT?

Even though Head Start, publicly funded child care, and public-school pre-kindergarten programs now serve only a minority of the nation's children under five, they deserve the special attention of policymakers because they are the prominent *public* program settings. How, then, do we redefine the public settings so that all the early childhood programs they offer are of high quality?

These public institutions must be *leaders in bringing quality into early childhood programs*—in part because they are less tightly bound to market forces that press against quality than are private programs, and in part because they simply cannot meet the nation's full need for early childhood care and education. Combined, publicly funded child care, Head Start, and public schools now serve about 1.2 million children under age five, or only about 24 percent of all children under age five served by nonrelatives outside children's homes—and this demand is steadily increasing. As mentioned previously, Head Start serves only one out of five eligible poor children.

These public programs should focus largely on *staff development and community education*—early childhood training provided not only for their own staff but also for parents in the community, home caregivers, and center staff. *Exemplary early childhood programs* should serve as the centerpieces of this staff development strategy. Public programs should hire early childhood specialists with a variety of responsibilities for program development:

1. supervising exemplary early childhood programs
2. providing the community with early childhood training centered on these exemplary programs
3. in public schools, working with those responsible for the elementary education curriculum to ensure developmental continuity between early childhood programs and elementary education programs

Head Start, born during the federal civil rights movement, basically has bypassed the states in bringing federal revenues for children to local levels. The early-childhood-program movement that swept through state governments beginning in 1984, for the most part, has placed early childhood programs in public schools. Head Start must develop a strong focus at the state level as well and let state policymakers know what the program can do.

It is time for *public school educators* to make peace with the rest of the early childhood field and to embrace principles of good early childhood education. In fact, public school educators can learn much from the early childhood field in this regard. To gain the approval of childhood advocates, public schools must make certain changes. They can make the necessary changes, but only if we all support them in this effort.

The most widespread public role in *private early childhood care and education* is now one of *regulation by human services agencies*. These regulations are absolutely essential to ensuring that programs are not harmful to children. The first issue in delivering program quality is to ensure that standards are met in all—and exceeded in most—settings for early childhood care and education.

In 1986, the U.S. had 158,644 registered or licensed family day-care homes, 4,225 licensed group homes, and 60,813 licensed centers—including nursery schools in 30 states (Morgan, 1987, pp. 1–1, 1–2). Few states report either enrollment or available spaces. The reasonable assumptions of five children per family day-care home and 10 children per group home would mean that 0.8 million children are in regulated homes—43 percent of the 1.9 million children receiving care from nonrelatives in homes other than their own. The reasonable assumption of 45 children per center would mean that almost all centers and nursery schools are regulated, although in some states there are such designated exceptions as church-sponsored centers and nursery schools (Morgan, 1987, p. 1–5). The first question, then, is whether we the public can summon up the political will and resources to extend minimal regulations to cover 1.1 million young children who are in homes that are not now regulated. Morgan (1987) notes that states vary a great deal in their coverage of homes, depending basically on their level of effort.

Most states subsidize leadership within private child care by funding for *child care information and referral agencies*. These agencies help parents to find appropriate child-care programs and can also provide in-service training for child-care providers. The agencies are central to the development of *leadership* in early childhood care and education.

Another public leadership function is *financial subsidy* to make up the difference in dollars between what parents can afford to pay for early childhood care and education and what teachers and caregivers need to make a decent living. Just as we pay public school teachers to provide education for the nation's children from kindergarten through high school, so should we see to it that teachers and caregivers of young children receive decent salaries. The differences are most marked for our poorest families, ironically, the very ones whose children can most profit from early childhood programs. Thus, from the perspectives of both need and public investment, financial subsidies for early childhood programs should begin with *families living in poverty.*

Early childhood care and education in America today are diverse in auspices and will likely remain so in our lifetimes. In our foreseeable political future, full public funding for early childhood care and education seems remote. If we do ever develop the political will for full funding, the institutions that provide such services will function very differently from those of today. One way to resolve the dilemma of whether young children should spend their time in schools or in homes is to move the issue beyond our current inadequate, institutional stereotypes. Instead we should advocate that *young children should spend their time in stimulating, nurturant families within stimulating, nurturant communities that include stimulating, nurturant schools.* In such communities, wherever young children were, they would receive high-quality care and education, and we would all be enriched by their experience.

REFERENCES

Ainslie, R. C. (ed.). *The Child and the Day Care Setting: Qualitative Variations and Development.* New York: Praeger, 1984.

Berman, P. "Learning to Comply." In *Rethinking Federal Education Policy: Strategies for the 1980s. Peabody Journal of Education,* 53–65, 1987.

Berrueta-Clement, J. R., L. J. Schweinhart, W. S. Barnett, A. S. Epstein, and D. P. Weikart. *Changed Lives: The Effects of The Perry Preschool Program on Youths Through Age 19.* Ypsilanti, Mich.: High/Scope Press, 1984.

Elkind, D. "Formal Education and Early Childhood Education: An Essential Difference." *Phi Delta Kappan* 67: 9 (1986): 631–636.

Elkind, D. *Miseducation: Preschoolers at Risk.* New York: Knopf, 1987.

Epstein, A. S., G. Morgan, N. Curry, R. C. Endsley, M. Bradbard, and H. M.

Rashid. "Quality in Early Childhood Programs: Four Perspectives." *High/Scope Early Childhood Policy Papers* 3, 1985.

Hitz, R., and D. Wright. "Kindergarten Issues: A Practitioner's Survey." *Principal* 67: 5 (1988): 28–30.

Hoffman, L. W. "Work, Family, and the Socialization of the Child." In *The Family: Review of Child Development Research* 7, edited by R. D. Parke, 223–282. Chicago: University of Chicago Press, 1984.

Hohmann, M., B. Banet, and D. P. Weikart. *Young Children in Action: A Manual for Preschool Educators.* Ypsilanti, Mich.: High/Scope Press, 1979.

Lazar, I., R. Darlington, H. Murray, J. Royce, and A. Snipper. "Lasting Effects of Early Education: A Report from the Consortium for Longitudinal Studies."

Monographs of the Society for Research in Child Development 47 (2–3, Serial No. 195), 1982.

McDonnell, L. M., and R. F. Elmore. "Getting the Job Done: Alternative Policy Instruments." *Educational Evaluation and Policy Analysis* 9:2 (1987): 133–152.

McKey, R. H., L. Condelli, H. Ganson, B. J. Barrett, C. McConkey, and M. C. Plantz. *The Impact of Head Start on Children, Families and Communities*. Final Report of the Head Start Evaluation, Synthesis, and Utilization Project, Washington, D.C.: CSR, 1985.

Morgan, G. *The National State of Child Care Regulation 1986*. Watertown, Mass: Work/Family Directions, 1987.

National Association for the Education of Young Children. "NAEYC Policy Statement on Standardized Testing of Young Children 3 Through 8 Years of Age." *Young Children* 43:3 (1988): 42–47.

National Association for the Education of Young Children. "NAEYC Position Statement on Developmentally Appropriate Practice in Early Childhood Programs Serving Children from Birth to Age 8." *Young Children* 41:6 (1986a): 4–19.

National Association for the Education of Young Children. "NAEYC Position Statement on Developmentally Appropriate Practice in Programs for 4- and 5-Year-Olds." *Young Children* 41:6 (1986b): 20–29.

National Association of Early Childhood Specialists in State Departments of Education. *Unacceptable Trends in Kindergarten Entry and Placement*. Unpublished paper, 1988.

National Education Association. *Estimates of School Statistics, 1987–88*. Washington, D.C., 1988.

Phillips, D. A. (ed.). "Quality in Child Care: What Does Research Tell Us?" *Research Monographs of the National Association for the Education of Young Children* 1, 1987.

Ruopp, R., J. Travers, F. Glantz, and C. Coelen. *Children at the Center: Summary Findings and Their Implications*. Final Report of the National Day Care Study, 1. Cambridge, Mass.: Abt Associates, 1979.

Schweinhart, L. J. "Early Childhood Programs in the Eighties: The National Picture." *High/Scope Early Childhood Policy Papers* 1, 1984.

Schweinhart, L. J. *A School Administrator's Guide to Early Childhood Programs*. Ypsilanti, Mich.: High/Scope Press, 1988.

Timar, T. B., and D. L. Kirp. "Educational Reform and Institutional Competence." *Harvard Educational Review* 57:3 (1987): 1–22.

U. S. Bureau of the Census. *Money Income and Poverty Status of Families and Persons in the United States: 1986 (Advance data from the March 1987 Current Population Survey)*. Current Population Reports, Series P-60, No. 157, Washington, D.C.: U.S. Government Printing Office, 1987.

U. S. Bureau of Labor Statistics. *Occupational Projections and Training Data, 1986 Edition*. Bulletin 2251. Washington, D.C., 1986.

Zigler, E. F. "A Solution to the Nation's Child Care Crisis: The School of the Twenty-First Century." Appendix to R. C. Granger with A. W. Mitchell, *Public Schools and Prekindergarten Programs: An Examination of Six Issues*. New York: Bank Street College of Education, 1987.

NURTURING OUR YOUNG CHILDREN

Building New Partnerships Among
Families, Schools, and Communities

Heather B. Weiss

INTRODUCTION

Hardly a week goes by in which the media, a politician, or some research and policy group does not hammer home the fact that American families are changing. Some of the more dramatic statistics these people employ include the estimate that by 1995, more than three-quarters of all school-age children and two-thirds of all preschoolers will have mothers in the work force, and that 59 percent of children born in 1983 will live with only one parent before reaching the age of 18 (*Harvard Education Letter*, 1988). This change and others are forcing us as a country to create new approaches to nurturing our young children.

In the midst of the changes in families and work patterns, the educational and social institutions involved in crafting the new approaches must appreciate two crucial and enduring points about American families. In fact, these two points are the foundation on which the new nurturing arrangements must be built. The first, a point increasingly reinforced by research, is that the family serves as the linchpin for human development and that factors outside the family affect its capacity to nurture and rear its children (Bronfenbrenner, 1979; Garbarino and Sherman, 1980). The second point is that Americans are ideologically committed to the primacy of families and hold families responsible for the development and nurturance of the next generation.

Working with families to help them nurture their children has never been easy, especially when those families are stressed and at risk; changing family patterns and the pressures that accompany them make it even more difficult. But recent child development research on the familial role in early development and the enduring values Americans place on families together suggest that we should not bypass families when we craft new approaches to nurturing children. Rather, we should work to strengthen and reinforce families while creating a broad array of community-based arrangements for children. Now it is especially important that the institutions that have traditionally shared the socialization role with families—most notably the schools—work in partnership with families as well as with other community institutions and agencies.

In this paper I will argue that family-support-and-education programs which reinforce the family's role in human development and which create collaborative relationships among families, schools, and communities are critical elements of any plan to promote the development of all preschool children to their potential, especially children who are at risk as a result of poverty. Examples of such programs are presented in the appendix. This paper is organized to present two types of information increasingly sought about family-support-and-education programs. It is our experience that as more school districts, state departments of education, and legislatures see the potential of these programs, the type of information they seek is balanced between requests from skeptics for data about program appeal and effectiveness and requests from the supporters for information about how to develop, implement, and evaluate these programs. So the first section of the paper begins with a brief discussion of what family-support-and-education programs are and then reviews the research-based rationale for working with the families of preschool children (from birth to age six) in order to promote child development and school success. It then examines the political and ideological bases for these programs and looks at how they fit with contemporary school-reform strategies.

The paper's second part discusses some of the critical choices and issues in program formulation and implementation that program planners, particularly at the state level, should consider. It draws heavily from the Harvard Family Research Project's ongoing research on programs developed by state departments of education as well as local school districts (Weiss, 1988b; Parsons, 1987; Weiss, 1989).

PART I

THE RESEARCH AND POLITICAL BASE FOR FAMILY SUPPORT, EDUCATIONAL PROGRAMS, AND THEIR BENEFITS FOR SCHOOL SYSTEMS

What Are Family Support and Education Programs?

School-based family-support-and-education programs are part of the larger family support movement, in which many social institutions and agencies — community development agencies, health clinics, churches, neighborhood organizations, and others — have begun to offer preventive, family-oriented programs to promote human development (Weissbourd, 1987; Weiss, 1988a).

Programs to strengthen parents' child-rearing capacities and to promote child development, particularly in low-income families, have a long history in America (Weiss and Halpern, 1988; Grubb and Lazerson, 1982). More recently, such programs were a prominent part of early childhood programs' efforts during the War on Poverty (1960s). A number of the early childhood research and demonstration programs of that period were founded on the premise that maternal socialization practices and early teaching strategies in low-income families needed to be strengthened to better prepare children for school. Some programs, including Gordon's Florida Parent Education Program, Gray's Early Training Project, and Levenstein's Mother-Child Program, offered primarily home-based services to mothers and their children. Others, such as the Perry Preschool Project, offered center-based programs for children as well as weekly parent support and education through home visits.

In the 1970s and 1980s, thousands of largely unevaluated but nevertheless popular grass-roots, community-based programs were born around the country. A few states, including Minnesota and Missouri, initiated pilot programs that worked with families to foster home environments and parenting practices that would promote the children's eventual school success. Although public schools across the country have not always been in the vanguard of these programs, by the mid-1980s more and more school districts and some state departments of education either began these programs for families with children from birth to six, or cooperated or contracted with other community agencies to provide such services. A recent survey of early childhood programs in the states indicated that twenty-five have some family support or parent education effort underway (Marx and Seligson, 1988).

School-based family-support-and-education programs, like those under other auspices, have a number of features in common, including the general goal of promoting the familiar conditions and parental competencies and behaviors that contribute to child, maternal, and familial development. School-based programs in particular have stressed the importance of strengthening children's early learning environments and of reinforcing parents in their role as children's first teachers. These programs typically provide information about child development, parenting, and adult development; feedback and guidance on childrearing issues; joint problem-solving; information and referral to other community agencies; and reinforcement, encouragement, and emotional support to families with young children. The program's services are provided through such means as home visits, peer support groups, and parenting education classes. Some programs also include additional services such as developmental child care or respite care, health and/or development screening, and toy and book lending. These programs are offered alone or in conjunction with other preschool programs—for example, prekindergarten programs for at-risk children.

But the services often are not limited to the development of children or to the parenting roles of parents. Programs can become catalysts for parents personal development as well; some couple the above services with adult literacy, adult basic education, or counseling services. A few state programs—for example, Kentucky's Parent and Child Education (PACE) program and Missouri's Parents As Teachers program (PAT)—are capitalizing on this catalytic effect by adding an adult literacy component and making their programs explicitly two-generational.

A number of characteristics distinguish family-support-and-education programs from many other educational and social programs. Some of the most important of these program characteristics are listed in Table 1. One of the most important characteristics concerns the programs' attitudes toward parents and, following from that, the ways in which staff members relate to parents. Rather than identifying and focusing on family deficits, the programs emphasize family strengths and work to empower parents. Parents are regarded as partners; their strengths, knowledge, and experience are acknowledged as cornerstones of the program-parent relationship. Through peer support and informal networking, these programs create a situation in which parents can learn from one another as well as from program staff. Hence, these programs are not unidirectional—that is, knowledge does not flow solely from the professional to the parent—instead, they are partnerships, or complex multilateral relationships wherein parents and professionals exchange information and support.

Because these programs are not unidirectional, excessively didactic, or superficial in what they attempt to convey to parents, they differ from many narrower parenting education and parent involvement programs. They should not be confused, for example, with superficial efforts to provide parenting education by presenting speakers for parents of young children once or twice a semester. Such efforts should not be defined as family support and education because they neither provide sustained education and support nor attempt to create a strong and enduring partnership with the parent to promote the child's development. As will be noted in the subsequent review of evidence on program effectiveness, superficial efforts are unlikely to affect the early home environment in ways that lead to enhanced child development, particularly in the case of at-risk children and families.

(Text contd. p. 184)

TABLE 1

Characteristics of Community-Based
Family-Support-and-Education
Programs

What They Provide	*How They Provide It*
• Social support in a goal-oriented framework; information, guidance, feedback, practical assistance, emotional support.	• Preventive approach to addressing family needs for support; focus on promoting development rather than diagnosing and treating dysfunction.
• Sustained support to young families; regular interaction over a period of months or years.	• Child-rearing messages shared in a context of respect for cultural preferences in child-rearing values; support for families' own self-directed efforts to care for and nurture their children.
• A focus both on enhancing parenting and on attending to the intra- and extra-familial forces impinging on parenting.	
• A secure, accepting climate in which young parents can share and explore child-rearing goals, beliefs and concerns.	• Participants have a voice in shaping the emphases and content of their program.
• Efforts to promote and/or strengthen informal support ties among young families in the neighborhood or community.	• Goals, emphases, and types of services provided are shaped by local social conditions and concerns and by strengths and gaps in other local services.
	• Voluntary participation.
• An advocate on behalf of the population served for improved services and other institutional supports.	• Most programs are located so as to be easily accessible; most have relatively simple, nonthreatening intake procedures.
• Efforts to reach out to families unwilling or unable to seek support themselves and encouragement of families' capacities to accept and use support.	• Eligibility is generally not based on demonstration or identification of specific problems or types of dysfunction.
	• Community members often work with families within the framework of a peer-to-peer interaction.

TABLE 2

STATE	MINNESOTA	MISSOURI	KENTUCKY
PROGRAM	Early Childhood Family Education (ECFE)	Parents As Teachers (PAT)	Parent and Child Education Program (PACE)
STARTING DATE	1975	1985	1986
SITES	Schools, housing projects, neighborhood centers, jails, hospitals, Native American reservations	Schools, homes	School districts
PHILOSOPHY/GOALS	Parents are the child's first teachers. • Enhance parents' sense of self-worth • Help parents optimize their children's physical, social, and intellectual development	Parents are the child's first and primary teachers. • Provide information and educational guidance to enhance the child's social, physical, and intellectual development • Help reduce the stresses and promote the pleasures of parenting	• Break the intergenerational cycle of illiteracy and poverty • Improve the educational future of mothers and children
SERVICES	• Parent education and group discussions • Home visits • Developmental preschool activities • Advocacy and crisis intervention • Newsletters • Drop-in centers • Toy and book lending • Special services for particular populations (Southeast Asian immigrants, single parents)	• Minimum of four home visits a year (individualized to meet each family's needs) • Health examinations and screening for children	• GED tutoring for mothers • Preschool program for 3- and 4-year-olds based on the High/Scope developmental model • Joint parent-child activities (emphasis on behavior management and observation) • Support group for mothers on self-esteem and competence

PARTICIPANTS	Parents with children 0–6 (special efforts to recruit low-income and stressed families).	All parents with children 0–4 are eligible.	Parents over age 25 who have not completed high school and their 3- to 4-year-old children
ROLE OF PARENTS	Parents make up the majority on local advisory councils and are represented on the State Advisory Task Force.	Parents may serve on local advisory boards.	Parents receive GED preparation, support, and motivation to gain parenting and career-development skills.
STAFF	Varies, but can include early childhood educators, child-development and family-life specialists, nurses, and consumer home economists. Certification being formalized; currently licensed under the Division of Vocational and Technical Education	Full-time and part-time parent education	Each site has one adult educator, one pre-school teacher, and one aide; teachers are employees of the school system and receive equal compensation; aides are hired by PACE.
BUDGET	In 1988, $18.3 million (excluding other sources), 40% from the State Department of Education and 60% from local levy	In 1987, $11.4 million, allocated by the State Department of Education	$300,000 awarded by the Kentucky Department of Education for six pilot programs; in 1987 the KDE increased the funding by $900,000 to $1.2 million.
COLLABORATIONS	Cooperates with other departments within the schools, other community social-service agencies, jails, hospitals, and housing projects	Information not available	Kentucky Department of Education, Division of Adult and Community Education
EVALUATIONS	Several systematic evaluations and one summative evaluation. The state is currently working out a statewide client tracking form and further summative evaluations.	Following a formative evaluation judged unhelpful by state staff, a private research firm performed an outcome evaluation, examining the program's impact on children's cognitive and social development and on parent knowledge and attitudes in the school system.	In the process of developing an evaluation tool

Until recently, much of the impetus for family-support-and-education programs has come from local communities. However, even when states initiate programs, they have tried to allow for variation in accord with local needs and resources. Therefore, the family-support-and-education program models currently in operation are extremely diverse. This variation is evident both in Table 2 (page 182), which is a summary of state initiatives in Minnesota, Missouri, and Kentucky, and in two forthcoming resource guides, one from the Harvard Family Research Project and the other from the Council of Chief State School Officers. These guides profile local programs.

Continued variation in these programs is inevitable and useful. Just as there is no one type of family, there is probably no single universally effective family support program. Further, a sense of community ownership or, in the case of state-initiated efforts, a provision for community input into program design and administration have helped to forestall criticism that either the school or the state is dictating how individuals should behave as parents. Other aspects of the programs, including their respect for families and their strengths, reinforcement of both the family's and the community's role in child development, and the partnerships between the parents and the provider, have also helped to allay such concerns.

The Research Base: Does the Home Environment Matter?

This section reviews two strands of research on the contributions of families to child development, both of which support the decision to focus some of our early childhood efforts on early intervention with families. The first strand of research has examined the relationship between family factors and subsequent child development and school achievement. The second strand is evaluation research conducted on family-oriented early childhood programs; this research tests the malleability of the home environment and addresses questions about whether or not intervention designed to work with families can promote subsequent child development and, possibly, adult development.

Research on Family Characteristics and School Achievement

Over the last three decades, efforts to understand the relationship between a child's home environment and his or her subsequent school achievement have become more and more refined. Early interest in this area was spurred by the publication of the Coleman Report (Coleman et al., 1966), which suggested that family factors accounted for more of the variation in school achievement than did various measures of school structure and quality. The family variables that Coleman examined were primarily gross measures of socioeconomic status, but during the 1970s researchers made efforts to refine understanding of what it was about the home environment that did or did not promote child development and later result in achievement.

Noteworthy in this regard was the work of Caldwell and her colleagues (Elardo, Bradley, and Caldwell, 1975) in developing the HOME, an assessment instrument designed to examine specific characteristics of the home learning environment. Using that instrument, these researchers found that variables such as language stimulation and the number of books in the home at age one correlated more highly with achievement (measured by the Stanford-Binet) at three years of age than did one-year scores on the Bayley, a widely used measure of early development. This generation of research showed that while socioeconomic status is positively related to children's academic achievement, as much variation exists *within* as *between* income groups. So, as Clarke-Stewart (1983) concluded, socioeconomic status is not a good predictor of individual achievement.

A third generation of research is now examining how parenting attitudes, values, and styles are related to school performance. The various studies of the relationship between these more complex and differentiated variables of family process and child achievement are difficult to compare because they employ different definitions and measures of parenting behavior and child performance. Nevertheless, certain types of family attitudes and parenting processes appear quite consistently to contribute to the young child's subsequent achievement. In a recent summary review of these studies, Eastman (1988) extracts five such processes.

1. High parental educational and occupational expectations and aspirations for the child appear to contribute to subsequent school performance.

2. Warm and affectionate relationships between parents and children and verbal praise for the children's accomplishments appear to produce better school performance.

3. Parents who exert control over their children's behavior and are firm disciplinarians with consistent standards have higher-achieving children.

4. The amount and type of verbal interaction between parents and children appears to have strong effects on children's school performance.

5. Parents who spend more time playing, talking, and reading to their children and use more advanced levels and styles of thought and language seem to have higher-achieving children.

These findings suggest some of the types of information about the importance of parental attitudes, roles, and behaviors that should be conveyed to parents as part of early interventions. As Eastman notes, "unfortunately, the research on family effects on children's educational achievement is not yet sophisticated enough to suggest whether any of these types of family processes are more important than others, nor can it explain how the behaviors might work together" (Eastman, p. 7). Nevertheless, taken together, the accumulating studies suggest that aspects of parental behaviors and other factors in the home environment can substantially affect children's achievement.[1] Furthermore, these family processes *may* be more immediately and easily amenable to change than is a family's socioeconomic status. Findings are also accumulating that indicate that carefully designed family support and education intervention *can* reinforce certain kinds of parental attitudes and behaviors and lead to enhanced child, and perhaps maternal, development.[2]

EVIDENCE FROM THE EVALUATIONS OF FAMILY-ORIENTED EARLY INTERVENTION

The case for family-oriented early intervention is built on a stream of research that began with programs initiated during the War on Poverty. In the 1960s, program developers and policy makers committed to maximizing the chances of school success for poor children had to make a critical choice: Should they serve only the child, or involve the parents and other family members as well? A number of programs chose the latter course. These were largely single-site, research and demonstration programs for disadvantaged families, and they varied in the amount of service they provided to parents and children. Some were aimed primarily at the parents; others provided services for both parents and children in combinations such as home visits and center-based preschool programs.

In the two decades that followed, family-oriented early childhood programs tended to define the barriers to healthy parent-child interaction more broadly and to offer a wider array of services than some of the experimental programs that had been developed in the 1960s.[3] They provided a mix of child-focused intervention and more multifaceted family support, including health and social services, meals, transportation, and even adult basic education. Moreover, program developers articulated concerns about parents' own developmental needs and skills at coping with the chronic stresses associated with poverty. As

---

[1] Recent research on the relationship between parenting styles and the school-related attitudes and behavior of adolescents reveals some interesting parallels with research on younger children and their families. Dornbusch (1987) and his colleagues have examined the relationship between parenting styles and the grades of a large sample of San Francisco high-school students. Their results show that parenting styles and aspects of family processes are more powerful as predictors of student achievement than are measures of the parents' socioeconomic status.

[2] Another stream of research on child development and parenting, recently reviewed by Hamburg (1987), identifies some of the characteristics of parent-child interaction and interpersonal social support that are critical for healthy child development. This research should be used as a resource to suggest key elements that are likely to lead to effective family support and education programs.

[3] Some examples of these broader programs are the Parent-Child Development Centers (Andrews et al., 1982), the Child and Family Resource Program (Travers et al., 1982), the Brookline Early Education Project (Pierson et al., 1984), and Project CARE (Ramey et al., 1984).

the programs broadened, so did the evaluations; some of these programs assessed changes in the parents' development as well as the children's.[4]

Several basic lessons for future programs can be gleaned from this research. First, the results of longitudinal evaluations of a number of the more family-oriented programs, including those by Gordon (1967) and Gray and Klaus (1968), suggest that family-oriented programs can produce meaningful, sustained gains for children as they move through the school system. The gains include less special-education placement and less retention in grade, more successful school careers, and better social adjustment in school and in the community. These findings, when placed in the context of the larger group of early education programs included in the Consortium for Longitudinal Studies (Lazar, Darlington, et al., 1982), suggest that more than one programmatic path can lead to positive long-term effects for children. These evaluations, taken together, indicate that programs that work with families as well as those that are targeted directly at children can result in enhanced school achievement.[5] They have also led some researchers to speculate that changes in *parental* attitudes, expectations, and behaviors were critical mediators of these programs' subsequent enduring effects on child and youth development (Lazar, 1981). It is critical to point out that all the programs reviewed here were carefully developed research and demonstration programs, with conceptually coherent approaches guiding the program model and high degrees of quality control (Halpern and Weiss, 1988).

Second, several recent evaluations, including those of the Yale Child Welfare Research Project (Seitz, Rosenbaum, and Apfel, 1985) and the Prenatal and Early Infancy Project (Olds, Henderson, Chamberlin, and Tatelbaum, 1986), suggest that some programs, albeit fairly intensive ones that provide a range of support services, can have important effects on adult development as well as child development. A ten-year follow-up of the Yale Program found that boys from the

---

[4] This research is extensively reviewed elsewhere. See, for example, Zigler and Weiss (1985), Weiss (1988a), and Halpern and Weiss (1988).

[5] Two of the well-known research and demonstration programs of the last two decades were initiated through a public school system. The first, the Brookline Early Education Project (BEEP), a precursor of Missouri's New Parents as Teachers Program, was open to all parents of newborns in the community. BEEP provided three basic kinds of services: a diagnostic program to detect early health or developmental problems; parent education and support through home visits and parent groups during the child's first two years; and direct educational services for children through play groups and a pre-kindergarten program. BEEP's evaluation found that classroom observations of children at kindergarten entry showed significant differences favoring BEEP children, especially in social skills and use of time. Teacher ratings in second grade also indicated results favoring BEEP children.

The initial evaluation of Missouri's pilot PAT program showed cognitive, language, and social gains for participating children and indicated gains in mothers' knowledge of child development. PAT staff rated the quality of parent participation in the program; the higher the rating they gave to a parent, the better that parent's child performed on the various assessment measures. Participating parents were also more likely to regard the school district as responsive to their children's needs than were parents of a comparison group.

program had less need for remedial services in school than boys in the control group. Program children generally had better attendance records than their counterparts among the controls. Perhaps most striking, however, and possibly due to the skill of the staff and breadth of the program's early support services, program families functioned better than controls in a number of spheres. Program mothers reported that they had more pleasurable and involved relationships with their children; and all program families, as opposed to only half of those in the comparison groups, were self-supporting.

The other recent evaluation to demonstrate two-generational effects, the Prenatal and Early Infancy Project (PEIP), also suggests that early, intensive family-support-and-education programs may have a positive impact on a wide range of parent variables, including maternal achievement of economic self-sufficiency. PEIP provided bi-weekly home visits from nurses and representatives of information and referral services to a subgroup of participants. At the end of the program, the evaluation showed that teen mothers in this subgroup who received home visits throughout their children's infancy were more likely to engage in positive parenting behaviors (e.g., avoiding restriction and punishment and providing appropriate play materials), more likely to report less infant crying and more positive infant moods, and less likely to have abused or neglected their children (Olds, Henderson, Birmingham, and Chamberlin, 1983). A follow-up of PEIP participants two years after the intervention ended showed that in comparison with mothers who had not received home visits, the poor and unmarried mothers who received home visits returned to school more rapidly after the baby's birth, had been employed longer, felt they had more help with child care, and had fewer subsequent pregnancies.

Although the evaluations conducted to date do not enable one to pinpoint *which* components of these fairly complex interventions are most responsible for the changes in parents or children, and although the evidence about effects on parents' personal development is scant, nonetheless, a body of data is growing that points to the possibility of an improved life course for the mothers as well as the children involved in these programs. In other words, these programs may alter the life course of *both* generations. Insofar as parenting practices are affected by parents' own experiences growing up, it is conceivable that yet a third generation might benefit also. So while it may be easier to promote child development by working with poor parents to enhance their home environment than it is to change their socioeconomic status, in the longer term, some intensive, continuous, and comprehensive family support programs may ultimately *also* benefit the child by contributing to the improvement of his or her family's socioeconomic status as well.[6] The possibility of producing multigenerational effects makes these programs worthy of consideration by those crafting welfare reform strategies for single mothers with young children.

[6] Evaluations that have looked at the effects of the programs on particular subgroups of participants suggest that those at high risk are particularly likely to benefit (Pierson et al., 1984; Olds et al., 1986).

As we build on the approaches suggested by discrete research and evaluation efforts, it is critical to keep in mind that past evaluations do suggest that certain common ingredients are most likely to lead to effective programs: careful conceptualization, including attention to the fit among population characteristics, program purposes, and other family support resources in the community; a high degree of quality control and implementation of the intended program; a balance between purposefulness and responsiveness in work with families; and in some programs, an internal feedback system that allows for careful program evolution in response to families' observed and expressed needs (Halpern and Weiss, 1988, p. 20).

Finally, among those who have studied the three-decade history of programs for highly stressed and poor families, a consensus is growing that programs that provide comprehensive, intensive, and continuous education and support may ultimately be the most effective for poor families (Sigman, 1982; Committee for Economic Development, 1987; Halpern and Weiss, 1988). Specifically, in the prenatal period and through infancy, it may be most appropriate to focus direct services on the parents and on strengthening the developing parent-child relationship. Services to children during this period should focus on appropriate health and child care, including health screening. Services to parents should reflect a balance between parents' own personal developmental needs and strengthening the parent-child relationship. In these early years of the child's life, programs should also provide some activities for parents and children together, which may mean a transition from home-based to center-based services. As children get older, preschool education should become an element of the system of family support services. But the preschool program should maintain a family focus, promoting continuity in the parents' sense of involvement in their children's development, and a sense of partnership with the school system and other care providers. The Committee for Economic Development, in its recently published report: *Children in Need: Investment Strategies for the Educationally Disadvantaged* (1987), lays out a similar blueprint for continuous services to at-risk children and families throughout the early years. The strands of evidence reviewed above suggest the promise that family-support-and-education programs hold for children and families, especially those at risk of poor developmental outcomes and school failure.

THE POLITICAL AND IDEOLOGICAL APPEAL OF FAMILY-SUPPORT-AND-EDUCATION PROGRAMS

Research results have played a critical role in creating broader interest in family-oriented early childhood programming, but this interest has also been spurred by the political and ideological appeal of these programs. As the speeches of the 1988 Presidential candidates demonstrated, Americans are once again concerned about families. Family issues, which at the beginning of the decade were too controversial to touch, are now the subject of discussions at all levels of government. In spite of America's history of reluctance to interfere in family life, these programs are now able to earn strong bipartisan political support. The political appeal of family-oriented programs is suggested by a state legislator who supported the legislation establishing Missouri's Parents As Teachers program on a permanent state-wide basis for the state's families with children ages zero to three.

> This program embodies everything essential for political appeal in Missouri. It is a state that doesn't want to take children away from the home. It is family-oriented. The purpose is to strengthen the family unit and to create bonding between the parent and the child in a positive way (quoted in Hausman and Weiss, 1988, p. 15).

The state-sponsored family-support-and-education programs in Missouri and Minnesota reinforce familial responsibility and avoid the ideologically charged issue of maternal employment by not actually providing day care themselves. Other states may want to incorporate child care into the mix of family support and education services.

The fact that the goals and rhetoric of family support programs reflect and reinforce powerful social values about the importance of the family helps to reconcile contradictory ideological positions about the appropriateness of intervening in family life. These programs have garnered broad political support because they reflect the operational integration of conservative and liberal perspectives about public involvement with families. Specifically, the programs attempt to achieve the aims often expressed by conservatives: strengthening and promoting well-functioning, independent, self-supporting families that produce children who will in turn become independent and self-supporting adults. The programs also accord with the more liberal perspective that extra-familial and community support are critical for families to function effectively, and that public attempts to provide and enhance such support are appropriate. So, in their operating philosophy, these programs have integrated two usually separate and often irreconcilable questions about government's involvement with families into one. Questions such as what should government do for families and what should families do for themselves are reconciled into one question acceptable across the political spectrum. It is: What should government—alone or with other public and private community institutions—do to enhance the family's capacity to help itself and others? In sum, programs are extending the boundaries of public responsibilities for families by creating new child-nurturing approaches that honor and draw from traditional ones.

FAMILY-SUPPORT-AND-EDUCATION PROGRAMS AND LARGER SCHOOL REFORM EFFORTS

As analysts review school-reform efforts, they typically find that uniform, prescriptive, top-down strategies do not consistently improve children's school achievement (Chubb, 1988; McNeil, 1987; Grant, 1988; and Goodlad, 1984). Increasingly, analysts argue for efforts that increase local authority and promote innovative local solutions while requiring accountability. Family-support-and-education programs, even when initiated by the states, allow considerable local input, flexibility, and ownership (Weiss, 1989). This somewhat flexible program development strategy dovetails well with efforts to promote innovative district-level and school-level efforts to reform schools and to meet the needs of high-risk families.

INTERCONNECTED BENEFITS FOR FAMILIES, SCHOOL SYSTEMS, AND COMMUNITIES

The potential benefits to families, schools, and communities of including family-oriented early intervention programs when working with high-risk families accrue at several interconnected levels (Weiss, 1988a). First, as the evaluation research suggests, carefully developed programs prepare children for school and eventual life success. Programs can therefore play an important initial role in comprehensive strategies for dealing with at-risk children and youth. Second, these programs not only appear to promote better relationships between parents and schools but also have the potential to promote more parent involvement with the schools as the children enter the elementary grades. We have testimonial evidence that those programs also promote parental support for the local school system. Third, the programs may have two-generational effects, particularly these programs that combine family support and education with literacy, vocational education, and GED services. Fourth, some evidence suggests that once local programs become established, program staff seek out partnerships with other community agencies out of a common concern for the strengthening of families and to share the responsibilities of creating new, broader approaches to nurturing young children (Weiss, 1988b). Local programs in Minnesota, for example, have begun to work out creative partnerships and collaborative arrangements with other community agencies to provide services for at-risk children and families. To illustrate this, Table 3 shows the broad pattern of interagency collaborations for the Minneapolis Early Childhood Family Education Program under the auspices of the Director of Community Education.

These interrelated benefits for children, families, schools, and the greater community are illustrated by the remarks of the Superintendent of Schools and the director of a family-support-and-education program operating in a small Southern community. The district began a program for four-year-olds and required parent attendance in order for the children to participate. The program provided parents with information about child health and development and about nutrition and low-cost meal preparation; in addition, the parents learned to make toys to reinforce the skills they saw their children learning on videotapes of them taken at the Head Start program. These children have now entered public school, and at their own request the parents now meet with the program staff every six weeks to get information about what the children are learning and about how the parents can support and reinforce it at home. The superintendent believes the program builds relationships between home and school, noting:

> When I was first an elementary principal, I thought the parents didn't care. They wouldn't come to conferences, wouldn't make their kids come to school. They were belligerent with us. I was just plain wrong [about the parents caring about their children's education]. The problem was that there was a lack of trust. But now they know we're interested in their kids like they are. Now they're comfortable with educators, active in the school, comfortable in the school setting. We showed them they really have something they can help their kids with. I believe it's the best approach to prevent dropouts and promote higher achievement in school.

The program's director similarly noted the benefits for the parents, the school, and the community.

> Most of the parents in the program went to public school here, but they didn't know that they were welcome to come into the school at any time. I guess poor people are made to feel like outsiders the world over. The program makes them feel welcome, a part of the place, important. It does work. They are much more confident in themselves. They also have greater participation in parent/teacher conferences, particularly the parents who are back in school or have gotten better jobs.

She also indicated that an unanticipated effect of the program was the creation of a new sense of community among parents; many have now formed friendships with each other and are building the community's informal support networks as they swap recipes and child care, car pool, and visit with each other.

This generosity and sense of community extends to the schools. This year, participating parents have collectively donated forty hours a week as volunteers tutoring children, shelving books in the library, and duplicating materials for teachers. Parents also have become more involved in their own education; at the director's urging, many have enrolled in reading, GED, or computer classes. As this program's experience indicates, family-support-and-education programs can strengthen families, schools, and communities and thereby help school systems to achieve their educational goals for both children and adults.

PART II

ISSUES IN THE FORMULATION AND IMPLEMENTATION OF SCHOOL-BASED FAMILY SUPPORT PROGRAMS

The foregoing arguments have convinced some states and local districts to initiate family-support-and-education programs for families with children from birth to school age. Those states and districts who do initiate such programs quickly realize that while these programs represent a very promising approach, we are just beginning to understand what features distinguish high-quality programs and to learn how to implement them on a more widespread basis. At this early juncture, it is therefore useful to discuss some of the lessons that pioneering state departments of education and local districts have learned as they have moved into this new program area. These lessons are largely drawn from case studies of state-sponsored family-support-and-education interventions and from a national study of local school district-based family-support-and-education programs now being conducted at the Harvard Family Research Project. While the initiatives now under way in different states and districts vary widely, some common issues in program planning and implementation can now be gleaned from these pioneering efforts (Weiss, 1989). These issues include questions about how to choose or develop appropriate programs, whom to serve, the scale and pace of initial program development, the respective roles of the state and local districts in program formulation, and the relationship between the family support and education program and the K-12 program.

FORMULATING OR ADAPTING A MODEL

Each of the three states we have examined has either created a new program and/or adapted a locally developed program into a state-sponsored initiative. No state attempted to replicate another program exactly; rather it initially adapted the program model to fit its own circumstances. Whether the state initiative is a new program or an adaptation of an existing one, all three states have found themselves making modifications over time in response to lessons learned in the pilot phase and to feedback from local program sites. This pattern of adaptation and modification is in accord with research on program implementation that suggests the influence of local contextual factors in successfully implementing educational innovations (McLaughlin, 1987).

Now that more and more state departments of education and local school districts are interested in developing family-support-and-education programs, it is important on the one hand not to reinvent the wheel and, on the other, not to replicate too quickly a model developed elsewhere. In effect, this means interested states should "model-shop" (review other state and local models) to see how other models might be adapted to their own circumstances, that they should determine what initiatives are already under way in their states, and that they should conduct careful and broad reviews of state needs and conditions. All these steps should be taken prior to developing or adapting a model.

UNIVERSAL VS. TARGETED PROGRAMS

The diverse experiences of state and local districts suggest that the choice of whether to mount the initiative as a universal service (that is, open to everyone with children of appropriate ages) or as a targeted service (that is, open to certain "at-risk" groups) is a difficult one, involving complex tradeoffs. Both Minnesota and Missouri mounted their family-support-and-education initiatives on a universal basis. These programs are open to anyone in local school districts with children zero to three in Missouri, and zero to six in Minnesota. Kentucky, on the other hand, has targeted its pilot programs to the districts with the highest adult illiteracy and school dropout rates. The states that offer their programs on a universal basis argue that their programs are a downward extension of public education with its tradition of providing universal services. By making the program universal, they minimize any possible stigma that might be inherent in programs that are targeted to a limited population. Informants in Minnesota and Missouri indicated that there are also political reasons to support universal programs. Specifically, they suggested that broad political support was necessary to pass the legislation authorizing the programs. These informants also noted that political support from middle-class voters was important for continued legislative support of the program and that, in some cases, there is middle-class backlash against services targeted to particular groups.

As the universal programs become established and examine both who it is they are able to reach and their capacities to serve high-risk families, questions arise about whether they can indeed reach and serve high-risk groups. This, in turn, raises questions about equity. In some places, it appears that without substantial outreach efforts and differentiated programming, it is possible to attract and serve only families that are easy to reach. As a result, there is some danger that the program will become simply another benefit for the middle class.

Those who are developing programs targeted to at-risk groups describe the benefits involved in allocating scarce resources to those most in need. They are able to develop population-specific program models and to seek sufficient resources at the outset to serve groups that are difficult to reach and serve. But they face problems not faced by those with universal models. They have to contend with an imprecise technology for determining who is genuinely at risk. Second, they must face possible political problems in gaining support from middle-class, and sometimes rural, voters who may resent supporting the at-risk population, usually poor and urban. Then there are problems associated with the possible stigmatizing effect of participation in the program.

One resolution of the complex question of whom these programs should serve involves a "have your cake and eat it too" strategy, one in which the program provides a minimum amount of universally available services, perhaps on a sliding-fee scale, and more intensive and differentiated services for families subsequently judged to be at risk. This strategy appears to be developing in both Minnesota and Missouri. In the former, a number of local Early Childhood Family Education programs have added special program components targeted to reach and serve at-risk groups such as Hmong refugees, Native Americans, and families at risk for child abuse and neglect. Similarly, in Missouri, the Parents As Teachers (PAT) program has begun to provide more intensive services for teen mothers and others regarded to be at risk.

This movement toward gradual differentiation of universal services in these state-sponsored programs raises another important question: What services can/should school systems provide alone, and what can/should they provide in conjunction with other child- and family-serving agencies? Interviews with the directors and school personnel associated with these programs suggest that sometimes by design and sometimes by default, the programs function as a screening device to identify families or children with difficulties during the period prior to public-school entry. Few other agencies in the community have regular contact with children and families before the children enter public school. Some programs, such as Missouri's PAT, include screening as a regular part of their services; however, informally, many other programs detect both child and family problems that call for additional assistance beyond that which the program itself can provide. One of the chief ways programs address this problem is through information and referral for individual participants. These school-based programs put considerable effort into the creation of formal and informal linkages and coordination with other community agencies. Nonetheless, many program directors report that they still cannot meet the needs of many of the high-risk families that they identify. The experience of these programs makes it clear that most school systems alone cannot take on all of the responsibility for enhancing child development and strengthening families.

The need to provide more comprehensive services for high-risk families has led a number of the more established state and local programs to develop joint initiatives with other community agencies and to create broader partnerships to develop comprehensive, continuous, and intensive services for at-risk families. The experience of some local ECFE programs in Minnesota suggests that a school-based family-support-and-education program with the characteristics cited in Table 1 (page 181) can make a unique contribution to this interagency service package because the two-generational programs are designed to facilitate many aspects of human development.

In fact, both of Minnesota's Twin Cities are currently designing comprehensive programs for at-risk families in which the school-based ECFE program would be a partner with other community agencies. In St. Paul, for example, the Amherst Wilder Foundation has spearheaded a three-way partnership between the St. Paul Department of Public Health, the Department of Social Services, and the ECFE Program. The program begins with public health nurses assessing the

TABLE 3

MINNEAPOLIS PUBLIC SCHOOLS

Director of Community Education

ECFE City-wide Advisory Committee	Coordinator of ECFE Development	Outreach and Staff
ECFE Neighborhood Sites (10)	*Special Programs*	*Work/Family Program*
• Lead staff person also responsible for agency coordination	• Itinerant services to programs for teen parents operated by the public schools and other community agencies	• Cooperative program with companies based in the downtown area
• Sites located throughout the city and include services for Southeast Asians	• Joint program with special education for parents of very young children (0–2) and a special education preschool program	
	• Joint program with Minneapolis Children's Hospital	
	• Family School	
	• Parents of Preemies	

stresses and supports of families at the time of a child's birth and then providing an array of services in conjunction with the social services department and the ECFE program. As Table 3 suggests, in places like Minneapolis, ECFE staff are providing the basic minimum services in neighborhoods around the city, while at the same time joining with other community agencies such as hospitals and social services to provide more differentiated services to high-risk families. In Minneapolis, the ECFE program is also a partner in a proposed multi-agency effort to promote the school readiness of that city's children. That plan, entitled *Way to Grow* (Kurz-Reimer, Larson, and Fluornoy, 1987), is designed to coordinate the activities of a variety of community agencies into a continuous, intensive array of services to meet the needs of at-risk children and families.

The experience of some of the more mature school-based family support programs suggests that in many cases the school system will need to call on other resources in the community and create partnerships with other agencies in order to serve at-risk families with young children. In planning new family-support-and-education initiatives, states should consider how the state department could facilitate coordination and co-programming with health, social services, and other agencies for high-risk families.

LEADERSHIP AND CAPACITY BUILDING

It is clear from our case studies of state initiatives that sustained leadership plays a critical role. Leaders from state agencies or the legislature typically put together coalitions from within and outside of government, including the different groups and constituencies interested in or affected by these programs. Analysis of how the leaders "sold" these initiatives shows that they advocated family support and education as a programmatic response to social problems of current interest to their state. For example, in Minnesota and Missouri, the PAT and ECFE programs are seen as ways to strengthen early childhood development and prevent costly later problems such as school failure. In each state, leadership teams worked to build a constituency for the program within their own agency, sometimes with other agencies, and/or with the legislature. Then, they gradually developed a strategic road map specifying the political, administrative, and programmatic steps necessary to develop programs.

THE VALUE OF PILOTS

Minnesota, Missouri, and Kentucky each began their programs with a small number of pilots from which they gradually built larger systems of programs. Their experience suggests that there are important benefits to starting these initiatives as pilot programs, as long as this strategy is accompanied by a plan to manage program growth if the programs are popular and effective. Beginning with voluntary pilot programs and grant-funding mechanisms as opposed to full-scale implementation of mandated programs is warranted because these programs are a new type of service, particularly for school systems whose previous emphasis has been on children in grades K-12.

A pilot strategy allows a focus on capacity-building and gradual development. State staff who have developed these programs point to many complex issues involved in developing and implementing programs to serve families with young children. They suggest that it takes time to develop clear program models; to solve the inevitable implementation problems; to train staff and develop appropriate certification and licensure standards; to work with the higher education system to provide training courses for program personnel; and to set up state systems of training, technical assistance, and accountability. These programs represent a new way of doing business with families, and therefore it should not be assumed that personnel whose backgrounds are in elementary or early childhood education automatically know how to work with parents in an empowering fashion.

STANDARDIZATION AND FLEXIBILITY: NEGOTIATING RELATIONSHIPS BETWEEN THE STATE SPONSORS AND LOCAL PROGRAMS

At the outset, program formulators also face critical decisions about how to strike a balance between standardization and encouragement of local flexibility and variation. The states we have studied have avoided the extremes on this continuum; they have neither top-down procedures wherein the state imposes a uniform program model nor simply a diverse set of grass-roots programs. Rather, they have created a grant mechanism to establish new programs and have created a state-initiated system of support for ongoing programs through training and technical assistance. They have tried to create flexible systems to foster program growth and a sense of community ownership. They have also built in program monitoring and evaluation to ensure accountability.

In the states initiating these programs, some program elements have been specified at the state level while others have been left to the discretion of local programs. In the process of striking a balance between centralized and decentralized decision-making to develop strong programs, a number of critical questions about program elements need to be addressed. They include:

1. *What are the general program goals and components?* For example, is the program designed primarily to promote child development or child development in conjunction with adult development through provision of literacy, GED, or job-training services? What are the *minimum* types and amounts of services the local program should provide if the program is to achieve its objectives?

2. *What population is to be served?* Is the program to be targeted to particular groups (e.g., at-risk infants and their parents) or open on a universal basis? What mechanisms will be built in to determine whether the program is reaching the intended population?

3. *Is there a need for an advisory group, and if so, what are the criteria for determining eligible participants?* What groups or agencies should be represented? Should parents or program participants be included?

4. *What characteristics and training of staff are necessary, and are there plans for certification and for provision of in-service training?* Are parent educators available or certified for programs in the state? Does a new training and certification system need to be created? What state and local training should/will be available?

5. *Where does the program belong administratively within the local district?* Does it belong under K-12, community education, or early childhood? Or is this choice best left to the district's discretion? Is this a service that can best be provided by funding a nonschool agency with experience in the family-

support-and-education area? Which school or non-school unit(s) has built or can build the capacity to provide programs for families with children ages zero to six?

6. *How is the program to work (if at all) with other local programs for families, including preexisting family-support-and-education programs?* Can the district subcontract with preexisting programs to offer parent-support-and-education services? What arrangements should be made for information and referral to other agencies?

7. *What mechanisms are in place to ensure accountability?* Should the pilot programs build in formative and/or summative evaluations? What kind of technical assistance will be available to help local programs with evaluation? What monitoring information will the state require from the program? How will the state know whether the program is effective?

In addressing these questions, states have recognized that local programs need to have flexibility and choices in many areas if they are to feel a sense of ownership and to be able to respond to local needs and resources. Some of the areas often specified for local decision-making include: the means and location of service delivery; the development of a new or adaptation of an existing curriculum or other program materials; creation of relationships with other community agencies for joint information and referral or co-programming; and the development of outreach strategies.

Building In Evaluation and Accountability

Family-support-and-education programs are a relatively new type of educational intervention. In order to legitimize them as new programs worthy of public support and to develop the most effective types of programs, it is important to build careful and stringent process and impact evaluations into at least some state and local programs. At this point, given state and federal policy makers' interest in these programs, data from individual research and demonstration programs are perhaps less important than data about the implementation and effectiveness of multisite state systems of programs. This is because policy makers want to know if these programs can be implemented and be effective on a widespread basis (Weiss and Halpern, 1988). Further, if evaluation research is to be truly useful for program growth and development, the conception of evaluation needs to be broadened from simple outcome assessment to include documentation of program participation, processes, and implementation. Moreover, it is important to assess the full short- and long-term range of possible effects of two-generational programs. This means that some programs should measure the effects of the program not only on the child but also on the parent, on parent-child interaction, and on the community at program completion. Some longitudinal evaluations designed to assess the longer-term maintenance of effects during the children's school years are also necessary to determine whether these programs reflect a wise public investment (Weiss, 1988a). Plans are now under way in Missouri, Minnesota, and Kentucky to examine both program implementation and outcomes; these efforts will provide valuable information to those inside and outside the states.

ADDRESSING TENSIONS IN SCHOOL/FAMILY RELATIONSHIPS

Programs initiated at the state and local levels under educational auspices need to address the implications of the sometimes-difficult relationships between families and schools. Analysts of these relationships argue that schools sometimes exclude families (Lightfoot, 1979) or that they are, at best, indifferent to them (Hobbs, 1984). Moreover, a body of research exists that documents the resistance of school systems to greater parental involvement and to partnership roles with parents in the K-12 period (Stallworth and Williams, 1982). The Harvard Family Research Project's interviews with program directors in school-based programs suggest that families, especially poor families and those with previous negative experiences with schools, can be very reluctant to get involved in school-based programs (Weiss, 1988b).

Program directors have also indicated that the very things that define the strengths of their programs can come into conflict with the school system's conventions. For example, a program's flexible scheduling, commitment to parent participation, and interest in hiring nontraditional personnel can conflict with a school system's conventions of six-hour days, limitations on evening meetings, teacher certification requirements, and certain limitations on parent involvement and participation (Parsons, 1987).

However, interviews with program directors as well as a growing body of research on families and schools suggest that some programs and school systems can successfully overcome these individual and systems barriers and create very positive relationships with families. Nonetheless, it is important to recognize at the outset that the school's philosophy may not mirror that of the program. It may be necessary for schools to change in order to initiate family-support-and-education programs in school systems and to accommodate and sustain partnership relationships with participating families when the children enter the K-12 program. Small accommodations include the provision of evening hours; larger accommodations include the pro-vision of staff trained to work with parents and efforts to ease the transition of both the parent and the child from the family-support-and-education program to kindergarten and elementary school. It would be very short-sighted to have these preschool family-support-and-education programs working hard to involve parents in their children's development and then to inhibit that involvement when the children move into kindergarten or elementary school.

THE CHALLENGE:
BUILDING NURTURING PARTNERSHIPS
WITH FAMILIES

In a recent article reflecting on changes occurring in families and the implications for schools and other community agencies, Coleman (1987) draws an interesting analogy between the impetus for the common school in the nineteenth century and the current interest in expanding the roles of schools and communities in child development. He compares today's phenomenon of mothers leaving the home and the neighborhood to work to the movement of fathers from the home and the farm during the Industrial Revolution. He argues that the creation of the common school and universal public education was largely a response to the father's movement out of the home in the nineteenth century. Now, he argues, the entrance of the majority of mothers with young children into the work force will require institutional development and change of a similar magnitude.

Those who craft programs and policies for the schools of the next generation need to consider a change of considerable magnitude, broadening the mandate of public education to include the provision of family-support-and-education programs, either alone or in conjunction with other community agencies.

The evidence summarized at the beginning of this paper and the experience of states and local districts described subsequently suggest that family-support-and-education programs offer schools a powerful way to begin to build new partnerships with families and other community agencies to nurture future generations of children, to help them live up to their potential, and to make positive contributions to society. Insofar as these programs strengthen both families and communities, they draw on traditional strengths while creating the new approaches necessary to meet the needs of the next generation.

APPENDIX

PRACTICAL PARENT EDUCATION

Location: Plano, TX

Starting date: The pilot program was started in 1987.

Site: Plano Independent School District. Class locations are at the convenience of participating parents and the instructor; the resource library is located in a church.

Goal: The program was founded on the notion that the changing American family needs support to continue functioning well.

Services:
- orientation/introductory classes
- four- to six-week class series
- workshops and in-service training for volunteer associate parent-educators

Budget: approximately $55,000

Funding Sources: Private funding is provided through businesses, foundations, churches, private individuals, and others; school district provides in-kind services.

Collaborations: Board of Trustees of the Plano School District, community leaders, and business people

Evaluation: Evaluation is based on responses from parent questionnaires and continued community support of the program.

FAMILY SERVICE AGENCY

Location: Santa Barbara, CA

Starting date: 1989

Sites: The parent support services are offered at schools; other services are offered at a community activities center, the Girls Club, Family Place, an education center, and FSA offices.

Goals: Nonprofit, nonsectarian human-service agency provides essential services to strengthen local families and aims to:
- prevent family breakdown;
- provide effective intervention; and
- help individuals and families deal with stress.

Services: FSA offers a variety of services in a variety of settings to families, children, and elders. Connection with the schools comes through its Parent Support Centers which offer family-life education classes in a school setting. In addition, the agency serves families through the following:
- child guidance clinic
- child-care specialty program for families in crisis
- family and individual counseling
- family support advocacy program
- various home visitor and homemaker services to the elderly

Participants: Teachers, parents, infants, toddlers, preschoolers, senior citizens

Staff: Staff are credentialed and hired by Adult Education. FSA trains leaders, often young mothers, who work in schools.

Budget: FSA has recently suffered severe budget cuts and as a result has eliminated two positions from its school component, subsuming management and fiscal responsibility for the Parent Service Centers into the Child Guidance Clinic.

The new annual budget for 1988 has been trimmed to approximately $208,000. Teachers' salaries for the Parent Support Centers are funded through Adult Education.

Funding sources: Donations are received from 14 community groups and from individuals. The schools provide in-kind services.

Collaborations: Community partnerships exist among the Council of PTA's, the March of Dimes, the schools, Girls Club, Santa Barbara County Health Services, Office of the Superintendent of Schools, Junior League, Birth Resource Center, Step Family Association, CALM, Single Parent Alliance, and others.

Evaluation: In 1986 the Program Committee thoroughly evaluated FSA using data gathered from clients, teachers, and the community. The committee is currently developing a tool which will be used to evaluate the program annually. FSA is accredited nationally and is overseen by an executive director.

PRE-SCHOOL AND PARENTING LEARNING CENTER

Location: Knoxville, TN

Starting date: 1984

Sites: The center is located in an inner-city high school, serving 50 white, 50 black students, with 65 on free lunch program.

Goals: PPLC aims to help teenage parents graduate from high school; to reduce unplanned teen pregnancy; and to provide quality child care and parenting education.

Services:
- laboratory/demonstration child care
- classes for teenagers on pregnancy and parenting, nutrition, child development, and home management
- counseling

Participants: Infants 6 weeks to 3 years, teen mothers in grades 9 through 12.

Staff: Teachers hold B.S. degrees in early childhood education; the Director has an M.S. in Child and Family Studies; the program hires one full-time teacher aide (qualifications unspecified).

Budget: $65,000

Funding sources: Initially funding was through a Chapter II Federal Grant and a Levi-Straus Community Grant; for the last two years the program has been funded by state appropriations and student fees ($5/wk).

Collaborations: City Health Department, Knoxville City School District, Public Health Department

Evaluation: An informal study of the program was performed by the State Board of Education and the General Assembly, including on-site visits, review of relevant documents, and interviews with staff and community leaders. There is interest in a longitudinal study to provide hard evidence of the program's achievements.

PARENT LEADERSHIP TRAINING PROJECT OF THE CITIZEN'S EDUCATION CENTER, NORTHWEST

Location: Seattle, WA

Starting date: 1986

Sites: The project is located in one urban and three rural school districts.

Goals: The Citizen's Education Center aims to:
- enable low-income parents to help their children make a successful transition from preschool to elementary school; and
- prevent school failure and dropping out among Chicano and Latino students and among low-income minority students in inner-city systems.

Services:
- parent training sessions on issues of parents' rights and responsibilities
- special programs and resources in the schools
- student testing
- child care during classes

Participants: Chicano, Latino, and low-income families in participating school districts.

Staff: Director, Regional Coordinator

Budget: For 1988–1989 approximately $75,000 is budgeted for centers in four school districts.

Funding sources: Corporations, businesses, and educational agencies make donations.

Collaborations: The project is the result of a partnership between the Washington State Migrant Council and four school districts.

Evaluation: The Citizen's Education Center is currently developing an evaluation tool.

PROGRAM FOR ADOLESCENT PARENTS: NEW FUTURES SCHOOL

Location: Albuquerque, NM

Starting date: 1970; in 1976, the Albuquerque schools adopted the project

Sites: New Futures school in Albuquerque (60% Hispanic population)

Goals: New Futures School hopes to assist and motivate school-age parents to make responsible, informed decisions; to complete their secondary education; to have healthy pregnancies and healthy families; and to be responsible, self-sufficient members of society.

Services:

- prenatal program
- young parents' center serving high-risk parents unable to return to the regular school program following the birth of their children
- parent education
- home visits
- vocational services
- health services
- child care

Participants: Pregnant and parenting adolescents

Staff: Certified volunteer teachers, health care professionals

Budget: Figure not available.

Funding sources: Funds are provided by Albuquerque public schools; New Futures, Inc.; NM Department of Public Service; NM Health and Environment Department; Public Welfare Department; State Department of Vocational/Technical Education. Groups, individuals, and corporations also make donations.

The University of NM School of Medicine's Maternity and Infant Care Project operates a weekly prenatal clinic. A Women, Infants, and Children (WIC) clinic is also available.

New Futures conducted a five-year study between 1980 and 1985; a new five-year follow-up study commenced in 1987.

PARENT AND CHILD EDUCATION (PACE)

Location: Canton, OH

Starting date: 1975

Sites: This inner-city program operates centrally out of the Martin School, an adult education center in downtown Canton. It also serves all of Stark County at two satellite locations.

Goals: PACE addresses a comprehensive list of social problems including domestic violence and child abuse; high-risk developmentally delayed infants; and underachievement and failure in school by:

- offering parent education as a means of nurturing the family,
- providing a supporting environment for a diverse clientele, and
- fostering understanding, individual growth, and awareness of options.

Services:

- dual parent-child classes in drop-in centers
- networking
- counseling
- unofficial warm line for parenting information
- crisis intervention

Participants: Parents, grandparents, extended family, babysitters and friends, children birth to six, with emphasis on birth to three

Staff: The center has a teacher coordinator, one part-time teacher, and three aides. The school board prefers certification for teachers and high school diplomas or GED equivalency for aides. The center encourages training in child development and administration, ending in a two-year associate degree. The director views life experience and personality as equally important.

Budget: Approximately $202,000 in 1986

Funding sources: The State Department of Education funds PACE 80 percent; the Canton City Schools Department of Community Education funds the remaining 20 percent. In 1986, the Children's Trust Fund awarded PACE a three-year grant. The schools provide space and utilities rent-free.

Collaborations: PACE referrals come from a variety of public and private agencies and family advocates, including psychologists, family defenders, hospitals, welfare agencies, well-baby clinics, the Urban League, Stark County Action Center, Family Courts, Mother's KISS (Keeping Infant Stimulation Strong), and the Juvenile Justice Department.

Evaluations: PACE conducted a longitudinal study in 1982. Staff continue to perform their own informal needs assessments through conversations with parents. An advisory board monitors progress, and a parent evaluation sheet provides immediate response to staff. The state and the children's Trust Fund also review the budget and direction of the program.

WORKING FAMILIES CENTER OF THE PARENT EDUCATION PROGRAM

Location: Silver Spring, MD

Starting date: The Parent Education Program started in 1971; the Working Families Center began in 1984.

Sites: The Working Families/Day Care Enrichment Program offers classes in three schools in Montgomery County.

Goals:
- To offer education, training, and support to family day-care providers.
- To help employed parents and day-care providers develop a closer alliance.

Services:
- Day Care Enrichment Program, a supportive atmosphere of classes for caregivers and preschool children in their charge
- Drop-in center for working parents
- Scheduled evening and Saturday activities

- Information and referrals
- Parent conferences
- Warm line

Participants: Parents, family day-care providers, children from infancy to five

Staff: The program is headed by a full-time Parent Specialist; 15–20 parent educators work on a part-time, temporary basis from 2–20 hours per week; 3–5 assistants act as support staff to teachers. Staff have varying qualifications, with a minimum of a B.A. and experience with children and families.

Budget: The budget figure was unavailable because the program operates as part of the County Adult Education Department. Clerical staff contracts are absorbed into the Adult Education Department Budget.

Funding sources: The Montgomery County School District contributed $77,000 to cover the costs not covered by the Adult Education Department; the schools provide toys and equipment; space comes from the county government; fees range from $5 to $60.

Collaborations: Strong liaisons exist among the Parent Education Program and the county government, the Health Department, the Department of Family Resources, the Women's Commission, the county PTA, and school counselors.

Evaluations: The Parent Education Program monitors its work through participants' assessments, looking for proof of effectiveness, new ideas, and for evidence of unmet needs; staff perform their own internal evaluations of the program twice yearly.

REFERENCES

Andrews, S. R., J. B. Blumenthal, D. L. Johnson, A. J. Kahn, C. J. Ferguson, T. M. Lasater, P. E. Malone, and D. B. Wallace. "The Skills of Mothering: A Study of Parent/Child Development Centers." *Monographs of the Society for*

Research in Child Development 47 (6, Serial no. 198) (1982).

Bronfenbrenner, U. *The Ecology of Human Development: Experiments by Nature and Design.* Cambridge, Mass.: Harvard University Press, 1979.

Chubb, J. E. "Why the Current Wave of School Reform Will Fail." *The Public Interest* 90 (Winter 1988): 28–49.

Clarke-Stewart, K. A. "Exploring the Assumptions of Parent Education." In *Parent Education and Public Policy,* edited by R. Haskins and D. Adams. Norwood, N.J.: Ablex Publishing, 1983.

Coleman, James S. "Families and Schools." *Educational Researcher* 16:6 (August–September 1987): 32–38.

Coleman, J. S., E. Q. Campbell, C. J. Hobson, J. McPartland, A. M. Mood, F. D. Weinfeld, and R. L. York. *Equality of Educational Opportunity.* Washington, D.C.: U.S. Government Printing Office, 1966.

Committee for Economic Development. *Children in Need: Investment Strategies for the Educationally Disadvantaged.* A statement by the Research and Policy Committee. New York, 1987.

Council of Chief State School Officers. *State Profiles: Early Childhood and Parent Education and Related Services.* Washington, D.C., 1988.

Dornbusch, S., P. Ritter, P. H. Leiderman, D. F. Roberts, and M. Fraleigh. "The Relation of Parenting Style to Adolescent School Performance." *Child Development* 58 (1987): 1244–1257.

Eastman, G. "Family Involvement in Education." Paper prepared for the Wisconsin Department of Public Instruction, January 1988.

Elardo, R., R. H. Bradley, and B. M. Caldwell. "The Relation of Infants' Home Environments to Mental Test Performance from 6 to 36 Months: A Longitudinal Analysis." *Child Development* 46 (1975): 71–76.

Garbarino, J., and D. Sherman. "High-Risk Neighborhoods and High-Risk Families: The Human Ecology of Child Maltreatment." *Child Development* 51 (1980): 188–198.

Goodlad, J. I. *A Place Called School: Prospects for the Future.* New York: McGraw-Hill, 1984.

Gordon, I. *A Parent Education Approach to Provision of Early Stimulation for the Culturally Disadvantaged.* Final report to the Ford Foundation Fund for the Advancement of Education. Gainesville, FL: Institute for Developmental Studies, University of Florida, 1967.

Grant, G. *The World We Knew at Hamilton High.* Cambridge, Mass.: Harvard University Press, 1988.

Gray, S., and R. Klaus. "The Early Training Project for Disadvantaged Children: A Report After Five Years." *Monographs of the Society for Research in Child Development* 33:4 (1968).

Gray, S., B. Ramsey, and R. Klaus. *From 2 to 30: The Early Training Project.* Baltimore: University Park Press, 1982.

Grubb, N., and M. Lazerson. *Broken Promises.* New York: Basic Books, 1982.

Halpern, R., and H. Weiss. "What Is Known About the Effectiveness of Family-Oriented Early Childhood Intervention Programs?" Paper prepared for the Center for the Study of Social Policy, 1988.

Hamburg, D. *Early Intervention to Prevent Lifelong Damage: Lessons from Current Research.* Testimony for the Senate Committee on Labor and Human Resources and the House Committee on Education and Labor, September 4, 1987.

Harvard Education Letter. *Parents and Schools* 4:6 (Nov.–Dec. 1988), 1–4.

Hausman, B., and H. B. Weiss. "State-Sponsored Family Education: The Case for School-Based Services." *Community Education Journal* 15:2 (January 1988): 12–15.

Hobbs, N., P. Dokecki, K. Hoover-Dempsey, R. Moroney, M. Shayne, and K. Weeks. *Strengthening Families*. San Francisco: Jossey-Bass, 1984.

Kurz-Reimer, K., M. Larson, and J. L. Fluornoy. *Way to Grow: A Proposed Plan to Promote School Readiness of Minneapolis Children*. Prepared for the Minneapolis Coordinating Board, Minneapolis, Minn., 1987.

Lazar, I. "Early Education Is Effective." *Educational Leadership* 38:4 (1981): 303–305.

Lazar, I., R. Darlington, H. Murray, J. Royce, and A. Snipper. "Lasting Effects of Early Education: A Report from the Consortium for Longitudinal Studies." *Monographs of the Society for Research in Child Development* 47 (2–3, Serial no. 195) (1982).

Lightfoot, S. L. *Worlds Apart: Relationships Between Families and Schools*. New York: Basic Books, 1979.

McLaughlin, M. "Learning from Experience: Lessons from Policy Implementation." *Educational Evaluation and Policy Analysis* 9:2 (Summer 1987): 171–178.

McNeil, L. M. *Contradictions of Control: School Structure and School Knowledge*. New York: Routledge and Kegan Paul, 1987.

Marx, F., and M. Seligson. *The Public School Early Childhood Study: The State Survey*. New York: Bank Street College of Education, 1988.

Olds, D., C. Henderson, M. Birmingham, and R. Chamberlin. *Final Report: Prenatal/Early Infancy Project*. Prepared for the Maternal and Child Health and Crippled Children's Service Research Grants Program, Elmira, N.Y., 1983.

Olds, D., C. Henderson, R. Chamberlin, and R. Tatelbaum. "Preventing Child Abuse and Neglect: A Randomized Trial of Nurse Home Visitation." *Pediatrics* 78 (1986): 65–78.

Parsons, K. *Family Support and Education Programs in the Schools: Prospects and Profiles*. Cambridge, Mass.: Harvard Family Research Project, 1987.

Pierson, D., D. Walker, and T. Tivnan. "A School-Based Program from Infancy to Kindergarten for Children and Their Parents." *The Personnel and Guidance Journal* 62:8 (1984): 448–455.

Ramey, C., D. Bryant, J. Sparling, and B. Wasik. "A Biosocial Systems Perspective on Environmental Interventions for Low Birthweight Infants." *Clinical Obstetrics and Gynecology* 27:3 (1984): 672–692.

Seitz, V., L. Rosenbaum, and N. Apfel. "Effects of Family Support Intervention: A Ten-Year Follow-Up." *Child Development* 56 (1985): 376–391.

Sigman, M. "Plasticity in Development: Implications for Intervention." In *Facilitating Infant and Early Childhood Development*, edited by L. A. Bond and J. M. Joffe. Hanover, N.H.: University Press of New England, 1982.

Stallworth, V., and D. C. Williams. *Executive Summary of the Final Report: A Survey of Parents Regarding Parent Involvement in Schools*. Austin, Texas: Southwest Educational Developmental Laboratory, 1982.

Travers, J., M. Nauta, N. Irwin, B. Goodson, J. Singer, and C. Barclay. *The Effects of a Social Program: Final Report of the Child and Family Resource Program's Infant-Toddler Component*. Cambridge, Mass.: Abt Associates, 1982.

Weiss, H. B. "Family Support and Education Programs: Working Through Ecological Theories of Human Development." In *Evaluating Family Programs*, edited by H. Weiss and F. Jacobs. Hawthorne, N.Y.: Aldine Press, 1988a.

Weiss, H. B. "Family Support and Education Programs and the Public Schools: Opportunities and Challenges." Paper prepared for the National Association of State Boards of Education, 1988b.

Weiss, H. "State Family Support and Education Programs: Lessons from the Pioneers." *American Journal of Orthopsychiatry* 59:1 (January 1989): 32–48.

Weiss, H., and R. Halpern. "Community-Based Family Support and Education Programs: Something Old or Something New?" Paper prepared for the National Resource Center for Children in Poverty. New York: Columbia University Press, April 1988.

Weissbourd, B. "A Brief History of Family Support Programs." In *America's Family Support Programs*, edited by S. Kagan, D. Powell, B. Weissbourd, and E. Zigler. New Haven: Yale University Press, 1987.

Zigler, E., and H. Weiss. "Family Support Systems: An Ecological Approach to Child Development." In *Children, Youth, and Families: The Action-Research Relationship*, edited by R. Rapoport, 166–205. Cambridge, Mass.: Cambridge University Press, 1985.

YOUNG CHILDREN AND PUBLIC SCHOOLS

The State Role in Public School Early Childhood Programs

Anne W. Mitchell

DIRECTOR, THE PUBLIC SCHOOL EARLY CHILDHOOD STUDY

BANK STREET COLLEGE OF EDUCATION

There is an amazing amount of interest these days in early childhood programs at all levels of government including, for the moment at least, even the federal level. Currently there are a number of major bills in Congress that could profoundly affect early childhood programs. Some bills, such as the Act for Better Child Care, the Tauke Child Care Choices bill, and others, take the perspective of child care, while others, such as Even Start (part of Chapter I), Head Start, and Smart Start (Senator Kennedy's bill), stem from an education perspective. However, for most of this decade, the federal government, with the exception of continuing the Head Start program, has not played the major role in early childhood policy. Most of the action was, and probably will continue to be, on the state level. The states are where the action is, and chief state school officers are the instigators of some of that action.

BACKGROUND

In the early 1980s, this country was on the crest of the education reform wave. After reforming high school curricula, tightening graduation requirements, and tackling dropout prevention, states began to create public-school-based pre-kindergarten programs. South Carolina, Texas, and Illinois were among the first. Some states already had similar programs in place (notably those in New York and California which were created in the mid 1960s along with Head Start). This wave of new public school programs for young children seemed to be driven by three forces:

The first was the *education reform* movement, which was concerned about children's school readiness and school success. Governors, legislators, and chief school officers asked one another: How can we raise the high school graduation standards if we do not help disadvantaged children get ready to meet these new standards? A recent report on education from the National Governors' Association (NGA) features a section entitled *Readiness to Meet the New Standards*; a subsequent NGA report, *Focus on the First 60 Months,* also recognizes the crucial importance of the early years. The Council of Chief State School Officers has accepted the challenge of educating all at-risk children and proposes the establishment of childhood development programs for all at-risk three- and four-year-olds.

A second force was the increased attention given to the *positive findings of longitudinal studies* of early childhood programs. The most well known, of course, is the High/Scope Foundation's Perry Preschool Program. The media attention to the release of *Changed Lives* (Berrueta-Clement, et al., 1984) was staggering, and a great many mayors, governors, and legislators read at least the executive summary and were moved by the cost-benefit data to consider creating preschool programs. The positive results of Head Start evaluation research (McKey, et al., 1985; Hubbell, 1983), along with evaluations of older state prekindergarten programs (The University of the State of New York, 1982) and the clearly positive findings from the 12 programs of the Consortium for Longitudinal Studies (Lazar & Darlington, 1978) have not had such widespread attention, although their findings are equally compelling.

The third force is the *dramatic increase in the number of working mothers in the labor force*. The statistics are startling: 100 percent increases between 1970 and 1987; two-thirds of mothers with school-age children work outside the home; over half of all mothers of infants are back in the labor force within a year of the birth of their children (Select Committee on Children, Youth, and Families, 1987). While dramatic statistics are useful for legislative speech making, the concern for child care appeared to be mainly rhetorical, since the vast majority of prekindergarten programs are just for part of the day and just for the school year. Only four of the new state-legislated programs (Massachusetts, Vermont, New Jersey, and Florida) clearly permit services to extend to the full working day. These state efforts are among the newest, and overall very few full-working-day programs have been funded through them. No state early education efforts deal with direct services to children as young as infants.

WHY THE STUDY?

The rapid expansion of state-funded early childhood programs was the major impetus for the study my colleagues and I have recently completed. Basically, the Public School Early Childhood Study was a two-and-one-half-year examination of the role of public schools in providing programs for children ages five and younger. The study was a collaborative effort between Bank Street College, in New York City, and Wellesley College Center for Research on Women, in Wellesley, Massachusetts. The study had three parts: (1) mail surveys and telephone interviews with state agency personnel in all 50 states (and the District of Columbia); (2) a mail survey of over 1,200 U.S. school districts that operated programs for prekindergarten-age children; and (3) case studies of 13 public-school prekindergarten programs in 12 states. The methodology and findings of each of the three parts of the study were detailed in reports, titled *The State Survey, The District Survey,* and *The Case Studies* and are available from Bank Street College. A book, *Early Childhood Programs and the Public Schools: Between Promise and Practice,* which focuses on the implications and recommendations of the study, will be published by Auburn House in 1989. The study was funded jointly by the Ford Foundation and the Carnegie Corporation.

This paper will present some of the findings of our study as well as our recommendations and our view of their implications for the future role of states in early childhood programs. But first, the definition of a couple of concepts will give us a framework for considering public school involvement in early childhood education. I will propose a broad definition of early childhood education; then I will discuss what the elements of good early childhood education are; and then I will discuss an inclusive way of thinking about the many ways early childhood education reaches children.

DEFINITION OF EARLY CHILDHOOD EDUCATION

What exactly is this early childhood education that interests everyone from senators to mayors? Often the debate is over whether we mean child care or early education, but in fact a good early childhood program is both education and care. The two functions are inextricable when we are discussing the early years of life. Children cannot be cared for well without educating them, and children cannot be educated well without caring for them.

The simplest definition of early childhood education is any attempt to promote full and healthy child development by the interaction of adults with young children. Early childhood education goes on in homes, in churches, in centers, and in schools. Early childhood education can be done by parents or other relatives, by nannies, by family day care providers, or by teachers. Early childhood education takes place everywhere from the local Head Start program to the church nursery school. Probably the most prevalent form of early childhood education these days is child care. The term "early childhood program" is being used fairly widely now to mean any program for young children.

The goal of any early childhood program is healthy child development across all domains of development (physical, social, emotional, and cognitive). Early childhood education is not just training for cognitive development. It is not children who separate themselves into developmental domains; it is adults who attempt to separate children into domains. Children are coherent human beings who are trying to develop naturally in all areas at once. For adults to be successful early childhood educators, they must understand child development in order to nurture a natural process. The need for early childhood educators to understand child development is NOT so that they can judge the earliest possible moment that a given child can learn a skill BUT rather to know the most appropriate moment when a child will be able to learn that skill most easily and feel most successful about his or her experience of learning. We do not want to produce better babies (a la Glenn Dolman) or "hothoused children," as David Elkind calls them. The goal should not be to force children into being early achievers who spout useless information (like counting to 100 at the age of 2) but to encourage relaxed, self-confident, inquisitive, eager explorers who will be flexible learners who are capable of adapting to a rapidly changing world.

WHAT IS "GOOD" EARLY CHILDHOOD EDUCATION?

Another way to define early childhood education is to define quality early childhood education from the point of view of the outcome for children. A high-quality program is one that delivers positive outcomes for children. The factors that are associated with high-quality early childhood education are small group sizes, staff-child ratios low enough to allow staff to pay individual attention to children, and staff training in early childhood education or child development (Phillips, 1987). These are the so-called "structural" elements of quality.

Then there are the fuzzier, "dynamic" aspects of quality, such as the nature of the interactions among children and between children and caregivers/teachers. These include the amounts and types of play children engage in, the social interactions between children and adults, the degree of child choice or teacher direction, the amount of language stimulation that occurs, and so on.

THE PROFESSION'S DEFINITION

The most complete definition of good early childhood education that exists currently is found in the standards used to accredit early childhood programs (Bredekamp, 1986). These standards were developed by the National Academy of Early Childhood Programs, which is part of the National Association for the Education of Young Children (NAEYC). Essentially, the NAEYC's standards for developmentally appropriate programs constitute a complete and comprehensive definition of good early childhood education.

The areas covered include:

Curriculum	Staffing: group size
Staff-parent interaction	and staff-child ratio
Staff qualifications	Health and safety
and staff development	Nutrition
Administration	and food service
Physical environment	Evaluation

This list is not a simple definition nor should it be. Early childhood professional practice has evolved to the point at which the definition of professional standards must represent clearly the most advanced practice. Too, the wide variety of available early childhood programs necessitates standards by which to differentiate good and not-so-good, or even harmful, programs.

PARENT/CONSUMERS' DEFINITION

Parents define early childhood education in terms of both present value and future outcome: how much it will help their children get a good start in their educational careers, and how much their children enjoy the program right now. They say, "It will help my child do better in school," or "My child really enjoys school." Parents do not separate their care and education demands. They want both: ideally, from the same program, in a convenient location, and at a price they can afford.

Within this basic, all-inclusive definition of early childhood education, it is clear that any program of early childhood education CAN function as child care, and some parents will be using it for that purpose. Obviously, the closer the hours that the children's program matches the parents' working/commuting hours, the better a child care solution it is.

THE EARLY CHILDHOOD ECOSYSTEM

Although these new state-initiated early childhood programs do represent an expanded view of public schooling, it is not particularly helpful to view them solely as a phenomenon of public schooling. Our perspective (in the study) was not the public school system itself but the public school as a participant in an existing early childhood system.

In a strict sense, there is no early childhood system; that is, no planned system. But taking an ecological perspective, there is an early childhood ecosystem of sorts that has evolved over time. It consists of all the day-care centers and nursery schools that are operated under public, private, or religious auspices and that go by many different names (such as play school, child-care center, early learning center, preschool, Head Start, day care, and child development center). The early childhood ecosystem certainly includes family day-care homes, too. The name of a program or where it is housed is NOT an indication of its quality so much as it is a clue to its present purpose (for example, nursery schools are part-day operations, while day-care centers are open longer hours) or historical in its origins (for example, the term day nursery dates back to the early part of the century.)

The essential elements of any ecosystem are that it has many parts (or subsystems) that are interrelated and that these parts are in dynamic relationship to each other; that is, the parts are interdependent. If one part changes, the others necessarily change in response. Given that this early childhood ecosystem exists, we were interested not only in counting and describing public-school programs but also discovering the effects these programs would have on the ecosystem. Would states decrease funding for child-care programs while they increase funding for public prekindergarten programs? Would equity of access be improved by the participation of public schools? Would schools deliver an early childhood program of different quality from that of the existing system? How would recruitment and retention of teachers in the early childhood system be affected?

THE STUDY

In this study, our perspective is that there is an early childhood community which consists of all those people and programs delivering early childhood education, no matter what they may be called or what their sponsorship or location. Our main focus was on early childhood education as practiced and delivered by public schools. Public-school early childhood education occurs within the context of the local early childhood community.

This comprehensive perspective shaped how we did the study. On the state level, we examined early childhood education initiatives within the context of each state's early childhood ecosystem (its various child care programs, special education, Head Start). In the case studies, we examined the public-school program closely but in the context of its local peers. (Observations and interviews were done in both the districts' and other local early childhood programs; interviews were also done with the local child care resource and referral agency.)

As our working definition of quality we used the research-based definition (group size, ratio, and appropriate training). We added two items to it: curriculum and parent involvement. The presence of a curriculum and the staff training to support its implementation are implied by the research on staff preparation; that is, a well-trained teacher will use a curriculum. *Curriculum* means a clearly articulated philosophy with a theoretical base, usually one or more child development or learning theories.

Parent involvement is essential in good early childhood education programs. Early childhood practitioners believe in parent involvement. The success of early childhood education programs in which parent involvement is high strongly supports the wisdom of practitioners. Clearly, it is a key element in Head Start programs; parent involvement was a mandatory component of Chapter I programs until recently. Supporting the evidence from good practice, there is also a certain amount of clear research evidence to support parent involvement. Evaluations of the New York prekindergarten program found that children whose parents were the most involved in the program made the greatest gains; and the sum of the programs in the Consortium for Longitudinal Studies showed that parents whose children had participated in the program had higher expectations of their children's educational achievement than parents of children who had not been in the program.

Simply stated, the study had four purposes:

1. to discover what kinds of prekindergarten programs public schools are operating on both the state and local level;

2. to examine these programs from the point of view of children and their experiences (to see if they are what early childhood educators currently call "developmentally appropriate");

3. to take the parents' perspective to see how these programs might meet parents' needs, especially with regard to working parents and their child-care needs; and

4. to take the community perspective and examine the public-school programs from the point of view of other early childhood programs in the community and to see how they fit into the local early childhood ecology.

WHAT IS HAPPENING:
PATTERNS OF EARLY CHILDHOOD EDUCATION

Finally, here are the facts about public schools and early childhood—which turn out to be somewhat more complicated than "x number of four-year-olds are now attending state-funded prekindergarten programs." One way to understand what is happening is to categorize early childhood involvement according to three levels of government: federal, state, and local. Involvement, in this context, means either funding or operating programs for young children.

FEDERAL

The federal government does not directly operate any early childhood programs. The federal government funds early childhood programs in five ways: via the Dependent Care Tax Credit; Title XX/Social Service Block Grant (SSBG); Head Start; Chapter I; and the Education of the Handicapped Act (special education).

STATE

Neither do states directly operate early childhood programs. States fund early childhood programs in five ways: through state child-care subsidy programs; state dependent-care tax credits; state funding of special education for preschoolers; state-funded prekindergarten programs; and contributions to Head Start.

State investment in early childhood education has taken one or more of these three forms: support of Head Start, provision of parent education, and provision of prekindergarten programs. Twenty-eight states (counting the District of Columbia as a state) currently invest in early childhood education: nine states (including the District of Columbia) contribute funds for the Head Start match or provide additional funds to extend Head Start service to greater numbers of children; two states (Missouri and Minnesota) provide parent education in lieu of direct service to preschool children; and 24 states (including the District of Columbia) provide funds for pilot or statewide prekindergarten programs. It is clear from these numbers that some states have chosen more than one form of investment.

Prior to 1980, only eight states had passed legislation creating prekindergarten programs, and four had contributed state funds to Head Start. Between 1980 and 1984, seven states began programs. In 1985, six more began programs; and during 1986 and 1987, five states did so. Also during 1986 and 1987, three states with prekindergarten programs created second programs. Since 1984, five more states have legislated contributions to Head Start. Most of the expansion in creation of prekindergarten programs was between 1985 and 1987 (the peak years of education reform). Now, the expansion in terms of the number of states has definitely slowed, and most of the more populous states now have programs. The states where the largest numbers of poor children reside (New York, California, Illinois, and Texas) have programs. Other states may join the ranks; North Carolina and Virginia are possibilities. Other states with existing programs may create new ones; Pennsylvania, which has a "permissive" program for four-year-olds, is a possibility.

Which Children Are Served?

These state prekindergarten programs are about equally divided between those serving only four-year-olds and those serving children three to five years of age. There are basically three types of state prekindergarten programs:

1. those targeted to certain children specified as children who are "at risk" of academic failure, who are from low-income families, who are eligible for Head Start, who communicate in a language other than English, or whose families are migrant workers;

2. those open to any age-eligible child, most commonly four-year-olds; and

3. those that are primarily aimed at parents (parent education).

About two-thirds of programs are targeted for children at risk (either low-income, limited-English-proficient, and/or with school readiness deficiencies). The majority of those programs not targeted are in the states with permissive legislation (i.e., funding prekindergarten using state education reimbursement formulas). While states require that school districts (or grantee agencies) meet the at-risk-children guidelines, few require the screening of individual children.

Who Provides Services?

States are evenly divided between those permitting only school districts to receive funding versus those permitting either school district subcontracts with private agencies or direct contracts with private agencies. The State Education (or Public Instruction) Departments have responsibility for prekindergarten programs with three exceptions (Washington, Alaska, and the new program in New Jersey). State contributions to Head Start tend to be under the auspices of noneducational state agencies.

Quality and Comprehensiveness of the Services

Only five states permit child-staff ratios greater than 10:1, and several require ratios below this number. Programmatically, about half of the state early childhood efforts mandate comprehensive developmental programs (e.g., including health, social services, and parent participation requirements). The remaining states either have no curricular requirements (mainly those states with permissive legislation) or focus primarily on cognitive curricula. About half the states have requirements for teachers to have training or certification in early childhood education.

Length of Day and Year

The majority (60 percent) of state prekindergarten programs are half-day. About one-fourth of the state programs permit either half-day or full-school-day service, and four states permit service for the full working day (Vermont, Massachusetts, New Jersey, and Florida), although few full-working-day programs have been funded. These four state programs are among the most recent enactments and are in the process of implementation.

Funding Levels

States with prekindergarten programs and those making Head Start contributions are almost evenly divided between those funding at or below $2 million/year and those funding above that level. Texas serves the largest number of children and provides the largest amount of funding, followed by California and New York. Smaller efforts are found in the states of Delaware, Ohio, and West Virginia: all at less than $300,000 per year.

Barring unforeseeable changes in state economies, it appears that most states with prekindergarten programs will slowly increase their expenditures as many states have done. No state appears to be near to creating universally available programs—either philosophically or fiscally. Indeed, some of these increases may be in jeopardy in some states; for example, Texas may decrease funding due to declines in its oil revenues. Alaska maintained prekindergarten funding while decreasing child care funding (which was restored in the following fiscal year).

As close as can be estimated for the nation as a whole, about $225 million in state funds are being spent annually on direct service prekindergarten programs for about 143,000 children. In fiscal year 1988, ten states appropriated more than $10 million, with the largest total amounts in Texas ($50 million), California ($35 million), and New York ($27 million). In these three states, the state expenditure per child varied from $850 in Texas to over $2,500 in New York, which reflects both real differences in cost per child and differences in proportion of state and local funds. In terms of state-funded programs for the parents of prekindergarten-age children, Minnesota ($9 million) and Missouri ($12 million) together are spending about $21 million on their parent education programs.

By contrast, fiscal year 1988 federal funding for Head Start is over $1 billion and serves roughly 450,000 children nationwide. Federal expenditures for the education of handicapped three- through five-year-olds via the Preschool Incentive Grants is $219 million. It is nearly impossible to estimate SSBG/Title XX child care expenditures and service levels, but they are probably roughly equivalent to the size of Head Start. Some estimates for total national expenditures on child care (including the Dependent Care Tax Credit at $3.9 billion for fiscal year 1988 and direct payments by parents) range from $7 to $13 billion.

Coordination

Fewer than one-third of the states have legislative or regulatory requirements regarding local level coordination (i.e., among day care and other children's services), while in almost all states some state-level coordinating body exists (representing state agencies and, in some cases, citizens and parents). No state has moved to coordinate funding across programs. Lack of local-level coordination results in increased competition for children, staff, and space, between Head Start and state prekindergarten programs.

THE LOCAL LEVEL

Here is where it gets really complicated. Local communities both operate and fund early childhood programs. Some cities and counties fund child care and other forms of early childhood education. Some city and county agencies operate child-care programs. Putting those aside, let's consider only school districts as local entities.

Districts both operate and fund early childhood programs. At least 20 different kinds of programs are operated by school districts. One way to categorize them is by funding source: federal, state, or local. The federal and state categories are the ones already mentioned (Head Start, Chapter I, special education, subsidized child care, state prekindergarten, and parent education programs). The locally funded category is broad and includes teen child care, bilingual preschools, magnet prekindergartens, parent cooperative nursery schools, child care supported by parents' tuition, and nursery schools operated by high-school students. Public schools are operating an amazingly wide variety of programs for children from birth through age five. Most are for four-year-olds and operate half-day for the school year only.

Our survey of school districts included 1,225 districts nationwide reporting on 1,681 programs serving approximately 200,000 children under age five. In a sense there is not a typical public-school early childhood program, but there are certain central tendencies. The following profile illustrates the common elements of public-school prekindergarten programs, noting differences for specific types of programs.

General Profile of Public School Programs

In general, the majority of public-school programs operate part-day for the school year only and serve four-year-olds. Public funds (state, federal, and local) are the major source of support for most programs. The cost per child was about $2,000 per year in the 1985–86 school year. Most programs in public schools are exempt from licensing and are not licensed.

Classes and Teachers. Staff-child ratios and class sizes are generally reasonable, averaging about 18 four-year-olds with two adults, usually a teacher and an aide. Most teachers are required to have both a B.A. degree and some form of teacher certification, usually in early childhood education. Teachers often have experience working with young children, but such experience is rarely required. Most but not all teachers are on the same pay scale as other district teachers. Beginning teachers are paid on average about $16,000 for the school year. Most districts offer teaching staff some form of in-service training and allow observation visits to other local early childhood programs. Teacher involvement in the local early childhood community is usually limited to attending local conferences and reading local early childhood organizations' newsletters.

Eligibility and Support Services. A child's age, family income and, in some cases, a low score on a developmental-level or skills test are typical entry requirements for most programs. Support services provided by professionals other than classroom teachers are available in many programs; the most common support professionals are nurses and speech therapists. Snacks, but not other meals, are usually provided.

Parents. The most common forms of parent involvement are parent-teacher conferences (which are a feature of nearly all programs) and a newsletter for parents. The only common adaptation to working parents is scheduling parent-teacher conferences after parents' working hours. Transportation is not a common service, and transportation to other child care settings is rare.

Those are the basic facts and the structural view of public prekindergarten programs. The more dynamic aspects of the quality of these programs such as the children's experiences and parents' opinions come from the case studies of thirteen school districts in 12 states. Many of the districts we selected operated more than one type of program. The 13 sites we visited included 20 different programs: five state prekindergarten programs; four subsidized child-care programs; four parent-tuition child-care programs; two parent education programs; three Chapter I programs; and two locally funded prekindergarten programs (one was a magnet program and one a parent-cooperative nursery school). In these visits to districts around the country, we were able to observe children in classrooms and to collect the views of parents whose children were enrolled in programs as well as the views of representatives of the early childhood community in each site.

THE CHILD'S PERSPECTIVE

Developmental appropriateness can be examined by viewing a prekindergarten program from the child's perspective. One important element of a child's experience is the curriculum as it is implemented daily by teachers and other staff. Another is the continuity a child experiences both over time and within a day. What does a child do all day, and where and with whom does she or he do it? A third element is the comprehensiveness of services provided including nutrition, health, social services, and parent involvement.

Curriculum

Effective early childhood curricula are derived from principles of child development and are supported by staff training. Ample supplies of appropriate materials and equipment carefully arranged and employed by well-trained staff are necessary for effective implementation of this curriculum approach.

The thirteen programs varied widely from child-centered approaches to highly structured skills-mastery curricula. In general, the most highly structured and teacher-directed programs we saw were in large urban school systems. Child-centered approaches appeared more often in the smaller districts' programs. But it was not just size of district, per se. Rather, the critical factor seemed to be the presence of a particular kind of leader in the district's program. He or she was usually the director or supervisor of early childhood education. Generally, the director or supervisor of a good prekindergarten program possessed three qualifications:

1. he or she was well trained in early childhood education (either by education or by long prior experience such as work in Head Start or child care);

2. he or she remained close to the delivery of the services (that is, to be present often in classrooms, involved in training teachers, and clearly communicating the program's mission/philosophy); and

3. he or she remained close to the power (respected by and influential with the district office, especially the superintendent).

In smaller districts this crucial role is usually played by one person. In large districts that have bureaucracies to match, the critical leader role can be fulfilled by a partnership or one person surrounded by a team.

The following examples illustrate the range of curriculum practices observed.

A Child-Centered Approach. In one program, two teachers had developed a curriculum called *Changes,* which integrated art and science learning activities. All classrooms had art and science learning centers, and specially equipped art and science rooms had been set up. The art room had plenty of materials: markers, crayons, drawing materials, weaving supplies, and many other items. Half of the children from each class came in a group with one of their teachers (one teacher and nine or ten children) to the art room for a session, for example about clay.

First, the art teacher read a story (which she had written) about a mountain and rain and the washing away of soil and about lightning breaking off part of the mountain. She had samples of dry clay, wet clay, hardened clay, fired clay, and water. She asked wonderful thought-provoking "what if" questions while the children took turns handling the clay items: What if we put water with this dry, powdery stuff? What do you think will happen if we put hard clay into water? Can you break the hard clay? What about the really hard clay? Then the children moved to a table where large lumps of wet clay were set out with dozens of tools such as rolling pins, spoons, sticks, cutters, etc. The children energetically explored the medium of clay, punching and rolling and cutting and molding. When the session ended, the children took various clay samples back to the room to conduct further experiments.

The science session observed was about ice. Again, the children came in small groups with their teachers to the science room. The science teacher had an ample supply of ice cubes as well as many other ice shapes that had been frozen in various containers. Each child selected a cube and a paper towel. The teacher asked: How does it feel? What happens when you leave it for a while by itself in a bowl, in some water, wrapped up in paper towels? Which will melt fastest, blocks, cubes, or crushed ice?

An important element of the child-centered approach is the teacher's selection of activities and materials that are interesting to children. The critical factor is that children make choices for themselves based on their own interests. This creative, child-centered, experiential approach to learning characterized the entire curriculum in this program.

A Teacher-Directed Approach. In another program, a standard curriculum is used throughout the school system in all prekindergarten classes for four-year-olds. The curriculum is based on skills mastery and consists of about 20 units each lasting from five to nine days. Children are given pretests, mastery tests, and post-tests for each unit. Children are screened to enter this program; that is, they must score sufficiently low on the screening test in order to be eligible to enroll.

The classrooms observed were, at first glance, typical early childhood classrooms in terms of materials and equipment. However, usually only the housekeeping and manipulative materials were arranged in definite learning centers. Blocks and art materials were rare. Sometimes blocks were present in a classroom, but they were arranged in a way that made them inaccessible to children; for example, blocks were stored in a bin in a corner with no space nearby to build.

A class of 24 four-year-olds was observed. Children were divided into three ability groups based on the teacher's observations and the child's screening test score. One group worked with the teacher, one with the aide, and one independently (on an activity chosen by the teacher). The teacher worked with eight children on a structured reading lesson that focused on letter recognition. She held up a card with a letter on it, asked what the name of the letter was, and called on one child to answer.

The aide sat in an adult-sized chair next to a blackboard with another group of eight children. She drew a shape with chalk on the board and chose a child to respond. The child was to stand, come to the board, copy the shape in chalk on the board, and say the name of the shape. The third group worked puzzles at a table. In another classroom, the independent activity for the third group was to trace dot-to-dot numerals on ditto sheets. Every twenty minutes the groups rotated among the three activities. Later in the morning when the children went outside, the teacher assigned them to two groups. One was to play on the climber; the other was to jump rope with the teacher and count the number of jumps. In such a teacher-directed program, children have very few choices. They may become bored or exhibit behavior problems. Their natural curiosity is being stifled rather than nurtured. The abilities to think and choose and explore are much more critical to later school success than the acquisition of facts.

Continuity

Curriculum, or classroom program, is one element of the child's experience in an early childhood program. Another aspect that is closely related to curriculum is continuity. Continuity refers to two things: the number and ease of transitions made by children in a given day, and the compatibility of philosophical approaches and curriculum among the different programs that a child is engaged in over time. More simply, if the child is in a stable group of children, with the same staff for most or all of the day, and in the same location, a high degree of continuity is demonstrated. If the child experiences changes from year to year that are smooth and understandable, continuity is high. If changes are abrupt and disturbing, continuity is low. The following examples illustrate different degrees of continuity.

Daily Continuity. In one program, the child and parent arrive together at 7:00 A.M. and have breakfast. The child greets her teacher and goes off to play with one of the 15 other children in the room. After the teacher and mother converse, the mother leaves for work. When the child's father arrives at 4:30 P.M. to pick up his daughter, she is happily playing with the same children, is with the same teacher, and is in the same room where her mother left her in the morning. The father is able to talk to the teacher about his daughter's day.

In another program, the child is dropped off at 8:30 A.M. and stays with an aide in a group of 20 "early birds" until 9:00 A.M. when the teacher arrives. The child and a few others go to another room to join the rest of their preschool class (24 children in all). They spend the next three hours there. Then some children go home, and the rest go to a large cafeteria to eat lunch with the kindergarteners and first-graders (about 150 children). After lunch the prekindergarten children go to the day-care room for nap until 3:00 P.M. After they wake up, they move to another room with other children who have just arrived from their all-day kindergarten class and remain there until 5:00 P.M. when they move into another room with the late pick-up group.

Being part of a relatively stable group of children and adults is commonly believed to be a more beneficial educational experience for young children than is moving among many different groups and settings. Also the physical health of children in a stable group is likely to be better since contact with a smaller number of other children will reduce opportunities for transmission of common diseases such as colds and flu.

Long-Term Continuity. One goal of a good early childhood program is to ensure a smooth transition from one level of prekindergarten to the next, or from prekindergarten to kindergarten. Attention to this aspect of continuity is most often evident in the use of district-wide integrated curricula. In some programs, the commitment to smooth transitions for children (and better learning experiences for kindergarteners) is strong.

A major objective of one district's director of elementary education and early childhood supervisor is continuity of approach from prekindergarten through first grade. Their long-range plan is to institute a developmentally appropriate curriculum for all children from age three through age six. The district's prekindergarten program is a model of appropriate activities for three- and four-year-olds. A wide variety of materials and equipment is available, teachers are well-trained, and children have many choices. Their philosophy is expressed in the program's motto: learning through play.

This district employs many different strategies to introduce teachers to the "learning through play" approach and to encourage greater continuity. Grade-level meetings are held jointly for prekindergarten and kindergarten teachers. Teachers are encouraged to visit classes in other schools in the district and in the levels below and above the level they teach. When full-day kindergarten was proposed, the committee of teachers that met with the Early Childhood Supervisor to plan the curriculum included a few teachers from each level: prekindergarten, kindergarten, and first grade. This group learned together and from each other. The kindergarten curriculum they produced was so successful that it not only is used in the full-day kindergartens but also was proposed for adoption in all the district's part-day kindergartens. These methods (communication between teachers, teacher exploration of new curriculum approaches, and direct observations of early childhood class-rooms) result in a more coherent curriculum across the prekindergarten, kindergarten, and early elementary level and in greater continuity for children.

More commonly, kindergarten classes bear little resemblance to the prekin-dergarten classes in the same district. This is a positive finding as far as the prekindergarten classes are concerned. It is disturbing in regard to kindergarten. Children in kindergarten typically spend most of their class time in teacher-directed academic activities. Even when appropriate materials and equipment (such as unit blocks, writing materials, and unstructured art materials) are present in kindergarten classrooms, few opportunities for play are available in the daily schedule.

Comprehensiveness

Of the 24 states (including the District of Columbia) with direct service prekindergarten programs, 18 states have at least one prekindergarten program targeted to either at-risk children or children from low-income families. (Ten states have programs that do not limit eligibility except by age; that is, they are not designed for at-risk children).

A state-funded prekindergarten program is one method for delivering a good-quality early childhood program to children who could not otherwise participate in a program because their parents are too poor to afford one and because there are not enough publicly supported programs for poor children. Although the stated goal of many prekindergarten programs is to give poor children the preschool experiences that their middle-class peers will surely have, children who are poor require more than a basic nursery-school program like those their middle-class peers might attend.

Early childhood educators would argue that education cannot be meaning-fully provided to poor children or any other children without offering additional services. We recognize that children who are hungry will have trouble learning, which is why we have the National School Lunch and Child Care Food Programs. By the same logic, children who have poor or no health care services or whose parents cannot support them in their education also will have trouble. Head Start has long recognized these facts and requires that a comprehensive program of educational and support services be provided to children and their families.

A comprehensive prekindergarten program is one that is providing necessary services in addition to those that could be called strictly educational or academic. Comprehensive services include at least:

1. *health services* such as physical examinations, screening for developmental delays, or other direct health services provided by a doctor, nurse, or dentist;

2. *social services,* usually provided by a social worker, such as referral to community or government agencies and services or assistance with obtaining services;

3. *nutrition services,* which consists of serving meals and snacks so that children are receiving the major portion of their daily nutritional requirements during the program's hours; and

4. services to parents to help them be effective supporters of their children and to help them develop themselves as adults and as parents (usually called *parent involvement* or *parent education* activities).

Finally, transportation is a support service that may be critical to the child's getting any program at all, let alone the comprehensive services that she or he may need.

Head Start is a program well known for its provision of comprehensive services. All Head Start programs are required by the HS Performance Standards to provide an educational program for children and to provide social, health, and nutritional services along with strong parent involvement. Head Start programs must have an identified staff person responsible for each component: education, health, social services, parent involvement. The level of services provided by Head Start programs provides a benchmark against which to measure other programs.

The following analysis compares a subset of Head Start programs, only those delivered by public schools, with state prekindergarten programs delivered by public schools. (See Tables 1–5.) The five state prekindergarten programs selected represent those that are operating on a large scale in states with large populations of poor children and that are by design targeted to poor or at-risk young children. The California and New York state prekindergarten programs were created in the same year as Head Start (1966) and were clearly intended to provide levels of comprehensive service similar to those of Head Start. In both states' programs, comprehensive social, health, and nutrition services as well as parent involvement are required.

The prekindergarten programs created in South Carolina (1983) and Illinois (1985) are newer but also clearly recommended that comprehensive services be offered, including health, social services, nutrition, and both parent involvement and parent education. The Texas prekindergarten program is both new (1985) and the most extensive, serving more than 50,000 children and operating in over half of the state's local school districts. The Texas program requires few comprehensive services—only health screening and parent education.

Social Services. One indication of the level of social and health services offered is the use of professionals other than teachers. Most Head Start programs frequently use nurses and social workers; many also frequently use dentists and psychologists. Nurses appear to be common in prekindergarten programs in all five states, but even in states with comprehensive requirements, social workers are rare except for a few programs in New York and Illinois. Psychologists and dentists are not used.

Nutrition. Nearly all Head Start programs provide children with breakfast, snack, and lunch. By contrast, only about half of the prekindergarten programs in California, New York, and South Carolina provide snack and one meal (either breakfast or lunch). About half the Texas programs offer one meal only, either breakfast or lunch. Programs in Illinois do not appear to provide either breakfast or lunch, but about half do offer snacks.

Parent Involvement. Parent involvement is a hallmark of Head Start. Nearly all Head Start programs have a board of parents and use parent volunteers in the classroom. Many also employ parents as classroom aides, and most use parents as fund-raisers and advocates. Overall, only California and New York prekindergarten programs come close to approximating Head Start on parent involvement. Illinois and South Carolina have some parent boards, and many Illinois programs report using parent volunteers. In Texas, only a few programs report parent volunteers.

Parent Education. Most Head Start programs offer parent education workshops as well, as do programs in New York, California, and Illinois. Some programs in South Carolina offer parent education workshops, but very few do in Texas.

Transportation. Transportation is provided about as much in state prekindergarten programs as in Head Start, but the destinations are different. Nearly all prekindergarten programs bus only between school and home, while some Head Start programs also bus between school and another child-care setting.

Head Start programs are clearly providing better nutrition, social services, and health services. Head Start programs, at least in terms of their transportation services, recognize that some children need longer hours of care. State prekindergarten programs present a mixed picture on parent involvement/ parent education when compared to Head Start programs, with only New York and California being similar to Head Start. The bottom line is that if a good early childhood education program must deliver comprehensive services, especially for poor children, then most state prekindergarten programs are not doing well enough—and none appear to be doing as much as Head Start programs.

THE PARENTS' PERSPECTIVE

Parents seemed to be very satisfied, in general, with whatever public school prekindergarten program their children were in. Their dissatisfactions usually centered on logistical issues such as lack of transportation, inconvenient hours, or required parent involvement.

It seemed to us that most parents did not have sufficient familiarity with the actual day-to-day classroom program to venture an opinion about it. Most expressed great trust in their child's teacher and in the teacher's opinions about what should be happening in the classroom.

There were some differences in parents' views of their children's programs. In discussing their satisfaction, most parents whose children were in state prekindergarten or Chapter I programs focused on school readiness and later school success. Typical comments were "This program has a track record of putting out intelligent children," or "He has to learn so he can do ok in public school." Parents whose children were in child-care programs, particularly the parent-tuition–supported ones, mentioned the sense of community they felt about the program, how much the teachers cared about their children and sometimes how well-supported they felt as parents. They said: "The atmosphere is so warm and caring," or "The philosophy of learning through play is what's best about this program." These parents seemed to be more focused on the present value of the program than on its future payoffs.

Because we were not able to systematically collect data on the factors of socioeconomic status and parental educational attainment, we cannot say for certain, but the difference in parents' views is probably explained by differences in these factors. That is, children in many state prekindergarten programs are from low-income families (since family income is the most prevalent criterion used to determine eligibility), and it's likely their parents do not have high levels of educational attainment. Children in child-care programs that are supported by tuition are probably of higher socioeconomic status since their parents are able to pay the tuition and, from what we could observe, had more-educated parents.

Working Parents. Obviously, child-care programs satisfy working parents needs for child care. As one parent said, "I couldn't support my family without this program." But some working parents use part-day programs as part of their self-constructed child-care package. We saw two interesting patterns. First, some parents intentionally work split shifts in order to use a free, half-day public school program as child care. This works only for a two-parent family, and one parent in this arrangement gets less time to sleep, but the necessary child care is free. The second pattern consists of parents arranging for relatives, friends, or neighbors to pick up and care for their children. Some parents had a network of two or three adults who did this on different days. In one case, a family day-care provider incorporated the morning preschool program into her service, dropping off and picking up children at the public school. We encountered only one parent who used an organized child-care program, offering before- and after-school services on the model of school-age child care, to care for a preschooler.

THE EARLY CHILDHOOD COMMUNITY'S PERSPECTIVE

In each site we visited, we interviewed directors of programs similar to the ones we visited in the public school to get a peer view, and the directors of child care resource and referral agencies to get a broader, community-wide perspective. The opinions of both these kinds of informants varied, mainly according to the size of the district's program and the general reputation of the school district.

In large, troubled urban districts that operated extensive prekindergarten programs, the community view was quite negative. Program directors experienced loss of teachers from their programs to the public school. The structured, inappropriate nature of the public-school curriculum was noted over and over. Essentially, the conclusion was that the school system had enough problems to deal with in K-12 and had no business dealing with younger children.

On the other hand, if the public school program was small (even in a large district) and the district was respected, the community view was much more positive. In general, even though some public school staff may have some relationship with the local early childhood community, such as attending local early childhood conferences, the two groups knew very little about one another. Some of our community informants had never observed the public-school program. Almost never had any of the public-school personnel observed a community program. Almost every district superintendent knew what parochial and private schools existed in his district, but few knew anything about other prekindergarten programs.

WHAT DOES IT ALL MEAN: THE FUTURE

One thing is certain: publicly funded early childhood programs are expanding, although at a much slower rate than in the mid-1980's. This is particularly true for those programs funded by states through educational auspices and for those provided by local education agencies (LEAs) with local funds.

A SYSTEMS PERSPECTIVE

We need to adopt a dual systems perspective in order to understand what the expansion of publicly funded early childhood programs means and where it might (or could, with proper influence) be headed. First, we must stand firmly rooted in the early childhood ecosystem and analyze these new developments from that perspective. Second, we must take the perspective of the family and not only of the child. Early childhood public policy is not an intervention trying to save children from their families. Children are not at risk because of their families; they are at risk because of conditions that both they and their families suffer (poverty, deteriorated neighborhoods with crumbling social structures, poor housing, and so on). Public policy for young children must be for both children AND their parents.

In evaluating possible policy alternatives, we must ask two sets of questions. First, how does this policy affect the early childhood ecosystem? Does it improve quality, expand access, and so forth, across the entire system? Does it support or supplant existing successful programs such as Head Start? Second, does it meet parents' needs for involvement, for support as parents and as people, and for child care? Does the policy help parents support themselves and their children? That is, does it make "family sense"?

While some public school districts do offer programs for children younger than kindergarten age, most do not. Many of the programs offered are targeted at a specific population of children (Head Start, special education, Chapter I, and most state prekindergarten programs). Very few programs are full-fledged child care programs operating year-round (and many of these charge fees like any other child-care center). Although programs with shorter hours can meet the child-care needs of some families, the majority of families' needs will not be met. Lack of attention to child-care needs on the part of most districts is the norm. The district superintendents who responded to our survey predicted that their programs would expand in the future in terms of numbers of children served but would not extend to longer hours or to younger children.

While the growth of newly enacted state prekindergarten legislation has slowed somewhat, four of the newer state efforts note the need for full-working-day programs. In Florida and in Massachusetts, a few full-working-day programs have been funded. Inattention to the child-care needs of families effectively denies access to poor children whose parents work.

In short, the current picture indicates that public schools are mainly providing part-day programs for a limited population of children. That role appears to be strong and growing. We have concerns about the quality of many of these programs and the lack of comprehensiveness of services (for example, no meals, little use of other professionals, excessive cognitive focus of curricula, lack of choices for children, and excessive teacher direction). The public-school child-care role is small but significant (especially for teen parents) and ought to be encouraged. It seems likely that this situation will continue to change incrementally, barring a major shift in policy direction at the federal level.

FEDERAL POLICIES

The power of federal money and federal policy direction is strong. There are at least two areas of federal policy that will be felt in the states.

Special Education

Early childhood special education is affected by the new federal special education law (P.L. 99–457), which mandates service to three- to five-year-olds by 1990 and encourages expanding services to include children from birth to age three and their families. A basic premise of the extension of services to very young children is the primary importance of the family; family service plans are required rather than the traditional IEP's. This legislation requires that a state agency be designated to coordinate services at least to these children and their families. Since this is often not the state education agency, the opportunity for coordination is ripe. Depending on the precise definition of disability adopted by a state, there is the potential for overlap among children "at risk," as defined for prekindergarten programs, and those with "developmental delays," as defined by the state under P.L. 99–457. Any potential overlap or conflict can, of course, also be seen as an opportunity for creative collaboration.

Welfare Reform

The new Family Support Act of 1988 requires mothers on welfare with young children to participate in work or employment training based upon the availability of child care. Also, the law provides for up to 12 months of subsidized child care for individuals who enter employment.

Sooner or later, state policy makers will be faced with the fact that the mothers who are expected to work under welfare reform are, in nearly half the states, the same mothers whose children are targets of part-day preschool efforts.

It is very difficult even to guess at how many children whose families receive AFDC (Aid to Families with Dependent Children) are in public-school programs. I would guess from our interviews that some programs in some locations (e.g., certain neighborhoods in Chicago—Chapter I Child-Parent Centers/State Prekindergarten, and in New York City—both Giant Step and State Prekindergarten) are now populated almost entirely by children on AFDC. When the mothers are required to go to work and training, those program sites will be empty.

CREATIVE DILEMMAS

This apparent dilemma has the potential to result in creative combinations of funding to serve children and families. Basically, poor children need good-quality early childhood programs that also help their families to support themselves. Welfare reform, if used creatively, may provide just the opportunity to extend the hours of prekindergarten programs and to enhance the educational value of child-care programs.

Part-day programs could be extended using new funds appropriated under welfare reform. The educational components of child-care programs could be improved using education funds. At minimum, it is essential for educators concerned about young children who are at risk to ensure that the welfare reform programs for children be comprehensive, educational, and of good quality. Welfare reform can be seen as a vehicle for reaching at least part of the population of children at risk and also a way to extend the benefits of good early childhood programs to children whose parents work.

ROLES FOR STATE EDUCATION LEADERS

The early childhood arena is quite complex. Understanding the early childhood ecosystem; ensuring that our efforts make family sense; attending to the quality of the three C's (curriculum, continuity, and comprehensiveness); and simultaneously anticipating the efforts of changes in special education and the welfare system; what's a state leader to do? Among the many possible responses to the complexity, the most important is to construct an early childhood policy not for just the Education Department or the Human Services Department but for the state as a whole.

The time has come for making comprehensive cross-cutting early childhood policy: no more can we have welfare policy and education policy and employment policy and community development policy all moving on different tracks. We must recognize that we are dealing in different arenas with the same families. What is required is comprehensive policies in which all arenas intersect and cooperate. The goal is an integrated, unified policy for the state's children and families.

This kind of policy must be constructed collaboratively—keeping in mind the whole ecosystem in a state, as well as the fact that the nature and quality of its services must make sense for families. If such a policy can be agreed upon and established, then any future actions that are necessary (for example, actions because of changes in federal funds or mandates or because of changes in circumstances in the state) will flow from the values that have been established as a foundation.

Three Roles

There are at least three significant roles that state educational leaders can play in laying this foundation: to be a champion of quality; to be the catalyst in creating a state's early childhood policy; and to be a model collaborator.

Champions of Quality. Chief state school officers are the educational leaders in their states, not just for the public schooling system in their state. At-risk children are basically the children of low-income families. Poverty is a fairly accurate predictor of school failure. Rather than trying only to alleviate the effects of poverty by providing publicly funded programs for at-risk children, we should also be working to ensure that fewer children are poor and therefore at risk. That means helping families to move out of poverty. Nonworking poor parents may have access to training and jobs but will surely need child care to pursue them. Adolescent parents need to finish school so that their children will have some chance of doing the same. Poor parents who work probably use either publicly subsidized child care (in centers or family day care) or use relatives.

But not all at-risk children are sitting at home waiting to be served. Some are already in programs: 20 percent are in Head Start, others are in good-quality child care programs, and many are in poor-quality child care. Policies should be aimed at improving the poor-quality programs and making more good programs available. Some child care programs are good educational programs for children and some probably are not. The point is that we must be concerned about poor-quality programs no matter what they are called or where they occur in the ecosystem, because all the parts of the ecosystem will contribute to the later success or failure of at-risk children.

Creators of State Policy. As the educational leader of a state, a chief state school officer can be a major force in creating a state policy on early childhood.

The legislative goal stated in the CCSSO model statute for at-risk students is a good start toward an early childhood policy statement. This stated goal is to "provide each child with educational and related services reasonably calculated to enable the child to achieve his or her potential, to become a productive member of society and to undertake the responsibilities of citizenship" (CCSSO, 1987a).

Collaborators for Children. Be a model collaborator at the state level for others to emulate. Practically speaking, this means that chief state school officers work with other agency heads to coordinate existing services, eliminate duplication, and enhance cooperative efforts. Collaboration requires approximate equality among the collaborators in terms of power and authority, level of available resources, and abilities to provide services. Collaboration also requires a shared goal—or at least a real need for each other's resources or abilities in order to reach a common goal.

To get real collaboration, you have to first agree that you want it and then examine the ecosystem to determine how to achieve it. Since collaboration requires a shared commitment to working together to move toward equality, the first step is to examine the dimensions of the various programs to see if they are equal and if not, how and to what extent they differ. Some dimensions to consider are quality and comprehensiveness of services provided, child eligibility criteria, level of funding, and regulatory status.

State education leaders can make collaboration work effectively at the state level among agencies and then require the same commitment to collaboration at the local level. You can be such a good model of collaboration at the state level that local practitioners will imitate your good example.

Briefly, the roles I see for you are the following:

1. take the lead in defining and implementing quality programs in and beyond school buildings,
2. model effective collaboration at the state level and require it at the local level, and
3. create a comprehensive early childhood policy that includes all children and families.

No matter what state we live in, the policy challenge facing us all is to create enough programs to satisfy the combined needs for child care and education of all families, regardless of income, focusing first on those families whose needs are greatest.

APPENDIX

Note: Tables 1–5 report data from the *District Survey* representing the 1985–86 school year.

TABLE 1

PROFESSIONALS USED FREQUENTLY

N =	HEAD START 189	CA 51	NY 43	IL 23	SC 19	TX 68	LA 15
Nurse	■ (solid)	▥ (striped)	▥ (striped)	▥ (striped)	□ (empty)	▥ (striped)	□ (empty)
Dentist	□ (empty)						
Psychologist	□ (empty)			□ (empty)			
Social Worker	▥ (striped)		▥ (striped)	□ (empty)			
Speech Therapist	■ (solid)	▥ (striped)	□ (empty)	▥ (striped)	▥ (striped)	▥ (striped)	□ (empty)

TABLE 2

MEALS

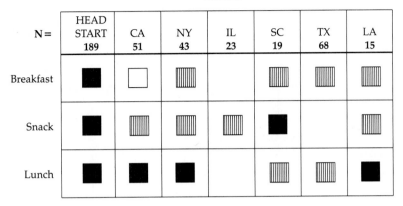

N =	HEAD START 189	CA 51	NY 43	IL 23	SC 19	TX 68	LA 15
Breakfast	■	□	▦		▦	▦	▦
Snack	■	▦	▦	▦	■		▦
Lunch	■	■	■		▦	▦	■

KEY: ■ = at least 75%   ▦ = between 50% and 74%   □ = between 25% and 49%

TABLE 3

TRANSPORTATION

N =	HEAD START 189	CA 51	NY 43	IL 23	SC 19	TX 68	LA 15
None Provided		▦	□			□	□
Between Home-School	▦	□	▦	■	■	▦	▦
To Other Child-Care Setting	□			□			

TABLE 4

PARENT PARTICIPATION

N=	HEAD START 189	CA 51	NY 43	IL 23	SC 19	TX 68	LA 15
Parent-Teacher Conferences Are Held	■	■	■	■	■	■	■
Parents Serve on Advisory Council or Board	■	■	□	□	□		
Parents Are Employed in the Classroom	▥		▥				
Parents Volunteer in the Classroom	■	■	■	■	□	▥	■
Parents Raise Funds for the Program	▥	▥	□				
Parents Advocate for the Program with Local/State/Federal Officials	▥	□	□				□

KEY: ■ = at least 75%   ▥ = between 50% and 74%   □ = between 25% and 49%

TABLE 5

PARENT EDUCATION

N =	HEAD START 189	CA 51	NY 43	IL 23	SC 19	TX 68	LA 15
Newsletters Are Regularly Distributed	■	▥	▥	■	▥	☐	▥
Parent Education Workshops Are Held	■	■	■	■	▥		■
Parents Are Encouraged to Network with Other Parents	■	▥	■	☐	☐		☐
A Parent Room Is Available			▥				

KEY: ■ = at least 75%   ▥ = between 50% and 74%   ☐ = between 25% and 49%

REFERENCES

Berrueta-Clement, J. R., L. J. Schweinhart, W. S. Barnett, A. S. Epstein, and D. P. Weikart. *Changed Lives: The Effects of The Perry Preschool Program on Youths Through Age 19.* Ypsilanti, Mich.: The High/Scope Educational Research Foundation, 1984.

Blank, H., A. Wilkins, and M. Crawley. *State Child Care Fact Book 1987.* Washington, D.C.: Children's Defense Fund, 1987.

Bredekamp, S. *Developmentally Appropriate Practice.* Washington, D.C.: National Association for the Education of Young Children, 1986.

Council of Chief State School Officers. *Children at Risk: The Work of the States.* Washington, D.C., 1987a.

Council of Chief State School Officers. *Elements of a Model State Statute to Provide Educational Entitlements for At-Risk Students.* Washington, D.C., 1987b.

Early Childhood Education Commission. *Take a Giant Step: An Equal Start in Education for All Four-Year-Olds.* New York: Office of the Mayor, Spring 1986.

Flynn, C. C., and G. L. Harbin. "Evaluating Interagency Coordination Efforts Using a Multidimensional, Interactional, Developmental Paradigm." *Remedial and Special Education* 8:3 (May/June 1987), 35–44.

Granger, R. C. *Who Is Teaching? Early Childhood Teachers in New York City's Publicly Funded Programs.* New York:

Bank Street College of Education, Spring 1988.

Grubb, W. N. "Choices for Children: Policy Options for State Provision of Early Childhood Programs." In *The New School Finance Research Agenda: Resource Utilization in Schools and School Districts*. Denver: Education Commission of the States, Spring 1988.

Harms, T., and R. M. Clifford. *Early Childhood Environment Rating Scale*. New York: Teachers College Press, 1980.

Hubbell, R. *A Review of Head Start Research Since 1970. Head Start Evaluating, Synthesis, and Utilization Project* (DHHS-OHDS-83–31184). Washington, D.C.: Superintendent of Documents, U.S. Government Printing Office, Administration for Children, Youth, and Families, 1983.

Lazar, I., and R. B. Darlington. *Lasting Effects After Preschool: A Report of the Consortium for Longitudinal Studies* (DHEW Publication No. [OHDS] 79–30178). Washington, D.C.: U.S. Government Printing Office, 1978.

Marx, F., and M. Seligson. *The Public School Early Childhood Study: The State Survey*. New York: Bank Street College of Education, 1988.

McKey, R. H., B. J. Barrett, L. Conelli, H. Ganson, C. McConkey, and M. C. Plantz. *The Impact of Head Start on Children, Families and Communities. Final Report of the Head Start Evaluation, Synthesis, and Utilization Project* (Stock No. 017–092–00098–7). Washington, D.C.: U.S. Government Printing Office, 1985.

Mitchell, A. W. *The Public School Early Childhood Study: The Case Studies*. New York: Bank Street College of Education, 1988.

Mitchell, A. W. *The Public School Early Childhood Study: The District Survey*. New York: Bank Street College of Education, 1988.

National Academy of Early Childhood Programs. *Guide to Accreditation*. Washington, D.C.: National Association for the Education of Young Children, 1985.

National Governors' Association. *Focus on the First Sixty Months: Proceedings of the National Early Childhood Conference* (No. 3058). Washington, D.C., 1986.

National Governors' Association. "Report of the Task Force on Readiness." *Time for Results: The Governor's 1991 Report on Education* (No. 3049). Washington D.C., 1986.

New York State Council on Children and Families. *Early Childhood Services in New York State, Vols. I and II*. Albany: December 1987.

Pendleton, A. "Preschool Enrollment: Trends and Implications." *The Condition of Education*. Washington, D.C.: U.S. Department of Education, Center for Statistics, 1986.

Phillips, D. A. (ed.). *Quality in Child Care: What Does Research Tell Us?* Washington, D.C.: National Association for the Education of Young Children, 1979.

Ruopp, R., W. L. Bache, C. O'Neil, and J. Singer. *Children at the Center: Final Results of the National Day Care Study*. Cambridge, Mass.: Abt Associates, 1979.

Select Committee on Children, Youth, and Families. *U.S. Children and Their Families: Current Conditions and Recent Trends*. Washington, D.C.: U.S. Government Printing Office, 1987.

The University of the State of New York. *Final Report: Evaluation of the New York State Experimental Prekindergarten Program*. Albany: The University of the State of New York, The State Education Department, Division of ESC Education Planning and Development, 1982.

U.S. Bureau of the Census. *Current Population Survey: School Enrollment Supplement*. Washington, D.C.: U.S. Government Printing Office, 1985.

U.S. Bureau of the Census. *Who's Minding the Kids? Child Care Arrangements,*

Winter 1984–1985 (Series P-70, No. 9). Washington, D.C.: U.S. Government Printing Office, 1985.

U.S. Bureau of the Census. *State Population and Household Estimates to 1985, with Age and Components of Change* (Series P-25, No. 998). Washington, D.C.: U.S. Government Printing Office, 1986.

U.S. Office of Special Education and Rehabilitative Services. *Annual Report to Congress on the Implementation of the Education of the Handicapped Act.* Washington, D.C.: U.S. Department of Education Office of Special Education, 1979.

ISSUES SURROUNDING STATE-LEVEL COLLABORATION ON SERVICES TO AT-RISK PRESCHOOL-AGE CHILDREN

Michael Petit

I. INTRODUCTION

Before discussing state-level interagency cooperation for serving preschool children, I will briefly relate the personal experiences—and "lessons" learned—in health and human services that have influenced this paper.

As a community organizer in Boston in the late 1960s, as the director of a community-based child care coordinating project, as the planning director for the United Way of Greater Portland, as Maine's Human Services Commissioner, and finally, as a consultant on children's issues visiting some 35 states in the last two years, I have observed and directly participated in the planning and delivery of services to children and their families for 20 years.

A few fundamental beliefs have emerged from these experiences:

1. No single professional discipline possesses the knowledge base necessary to successfully address complex human behavioral problems or dysfunction, including those among young children. Cooperation among different disciplines is essential.

2. In a multiracial, pluralistic society as large as the United States, there is no "one best way" to solve social problems. Pragmatism, not slavish devotion to ideology, should be the guide. Any national program needs to recognize and encourage diverse approaches.

3. Power to shape public policy and influence events is highly dispersed in the United States. The public and private sectors, at all levels, are highly interdependent. Again, cooperation is essential, and success is dependent upon a convergence of interests and the formation of coalitions.

4. Established individual behavior may be even harder to influence. The most desirable and lasting changes are arrived at voluntarily and take place as close to the family setting as possible. For reasons of effectiveness and politics, intervention programs should be minimally intrusive.

5. There is an abundance of evidence which documents prevention and early intervention programs do work—and that they are cost effective. The

238

questions should not revolve around "Does prevention work?" but rather "Which prevention strategy is appropriate?" "Who should have the lead responsibility?" and "How do we shift the focus to prevention instead of the current predominant reliance on remediation?"

6. The heart of social policy toward children should be aimed at enabling families to manage their own affairs and to be the prime protectors of their children. It should provide *no more than is necessary* but should provide *whatever is necessary* to allow this to happen. A focus on families is based not on sentiment but on pragmatism: no one has figured out an adequate substitute; no one knows a nice way to remove abused children from their families. Consequently, preschool education policy must engage parents.

7. The so-called "helping professions" are important in the development and well-being of children. However, they are not an adequate substitute for families achieving the greatest degree of economic self-sufficiency attainable—a great predictor of child well-being—and thereby being better equipped to manage their children's affairs.

8. Our major public and private institutions and systems—social welfare, health, education, legal, and economic—have been largely unresponsive to the continued wholesale entry of women into the work force in the post–World-War-II period. Accompanying shifts in male/female relations and widespread changes in family configuration have contributed to less supervision of children and less attention to their basic needs—clearly seen in large numbers of children at the time they enter school.

9. A combination of this shift in family composition with shifts in public policy, taxes, and global economics has increased income differences between the highest and lowest income groups to their widest point since recordkeeping began in 1948. Consequently, nearly one American child out of four lives below the poverty level, with the rate nearly double that among black and Hispanic children.

10. High teenage pregnancy rates in the United States (at least double much of Europe's), occurring largely out of marriage, have created an endless spawning ground of inadequately cared-for children. This frequent combination of early parenthood, single parenthood, and low income guarantees thousands of new children at great risk each year. Healthy development can come only at great cost and great difficulty, if at all.

11. Although it would be dangerous and wrong to turn away from remediation, there is little evidence to show that it works for large numbers of already injured and impaired children and youth. One major example: The prison population grew from 195,000 in 1972 to 547,000 in 1986, mostly as the result of young victims of crime who later achieve victimizer status.

12. National strategies are needed to help solve the widespread problems of our preschool children, yet the federal government has assumed only a modest role in addressing these issues. Because of the complex forces affecting family life—and therefore preschool children—state agencies cannot address these problems alone. More federal financial aid and better coordination of federal program and policy are indispensable, especially given the differences among state capacities.

13. There is widespread official and private awareness that serious problems confront children. Polls repeatedly show deep concern and a much more receptive political climate taking shape to address this issue. A Harris poll revealed that 75 percent of the respondents believed children are being raised in a more dangerous environment than they themselves experienced and that they would be willing to pay higher taxes if the funds were to be used for children. Eighty percent of the respondents to an AARP poll said children are the most impoverished group and that government should do more for them.

14. There is an emerging awareness among government officials, providers of services, and the general citizenry that all children are at risk—some more so than others—and that all benefit from early intervention services. The programs that fare best, and the ones people feel better about using, are those perceived as being available to anyone who needs them, irrespective of income, and therefore free of stigma. Public education is perhaps the best and single enduring example.

15. Even though it is primarily poor children and youth who require special attention, all services should be available to all who need them, with supplemental financial support contributed on a sliding-fee scale by those who can afford it.

16. There has developed in nearly all of the state health and human services bureaucracies a greatly improved level of administration and program skills. There is a strong predisposition among many of them to work cooperatively—especially with educators—in addressing the needs of children. This is beginning to occur in many states and requires neither laws nor funds to produce gains on behalf of children.

II. WHAT STATE-LEVEL AGENCIES OFFER EACH OTHER IN SERVICE TO PRESCHOOL-AGE CHILDREN

A. FACTORS PROMPTING COLLABORATION

Several factors are combining to foster improved cooperation among state-level agencies.

1. Increasingly, state law requires cooperation. Several state legislatures have adopted laws compelling state agencies to cooperate. Some require the executive branch to set up an interdepartmental coordinating committee to address early childhood issues. Collaboration issues may be specified by law or left up to the new committee to decide. In some instances the composition of the committee is limited to executive branch agencies; in others it may include legislators or private citizens and agencies. Annual reports may be required by a legislative oversight committee for review and possibly approval.

2. The executive branch itself initiates improved cooperation among the state agencies. This may be prompted by the governor or by a director of one of the state agencies.

3. Federal law is encouraging and requiring greater cooperation among the state agencies, although this is usually built around a specific problem area. First, P. L. 96–272 stipulated cooperation in the foster care arena; now, P. L. 99–457 is requiring much more sweeping and directed change in the area of cooperation for handicapped preschool children; and soon welfare reform legislation will require greater collaboration.

4. Provider, advocacy, and parent groups may be exerting upward pressure on state agencies to better coordinate program and policy.

5. Case management—bringing together many different disciplines around the needs of a particular child—is proving effective in addressing problems. Consequently, more states are developing the interdepartmental administrative mechanisms necessary to foster this approach. Maine's statewide, highly developed interdevelopmental program aimed at every handicapped preschool child is a good model.

6. Growing evidence about the effectiveness of early intervention is producing a shift in professional thinking that encourages cooperative efforts aimed at child well-being rather than narrower, more traditional definitions of child health, child welfare, and early childhood education.

B. ASSETS OF NON-EDUCATION STATE AGENCIES

Besides education agencies, the many other state agencies that provide services to children and families bring enormous potential resources to any effort aimed at preschool children at risk.

Health—State public health agencies offer many services to preschool children and their families. Typically these include genetic counseling, family planning, teen pregnancy counseling, prenatal care, newborn infant care, well-child clinics, immunizations, crippled children's services, parenting education, home visitors, nutrition counseling, food supplements for pregnant and lactating women and their newborn and other preschool-age children, injury and risk reduction, poisoning prevention, dental health education, vision and hearing testing, and AIDS testing and education. The agencies providing these services are able to form positive relationships with the parents of preschool children based on the benign view of the services provided.

In addition, these health agencies have strong planning capacities and can provide technical assistance, have working relationships with the private health sector and local governments, and are able to do staff training.

Social Services—State social services also bring strong components to the interdepartmental collaborating table, including the legal authority to directly intervene into family affairs including the investigation and evaluation of parental competency; priority claims on state-funded social services such as day care, homemaker services, alcoholism treatment, and mental health; the ability to write court-enforced prescriptive treatment plans for neglected children; flexibility in the choice of provider (including schools) and the type of services to be purchased for children at risk; staff training capacity; usually well-defined relationships with law enforcement; workers assigned to every child in foster care; special units to work with pregnant teens; day-care licensing; Head Start; control of the interstate movement of children in state protection; all alcohol and drug education treatment programs; and access to statewide and local networks of service providers and advocacy groups.

Developmentally Disabled, Mental Health, and Mental Retardation—These services may be in a separate department or integrated into one of the above. Numerous services are provided, including diagnostic, evaluation, testing, specific hands-on assistance, and many of the programs described in the preceding sections.

Income Security—Usually part of the Department of Human Services, this area typically includes child support enforcement, Aid to Families with Dependent Children, Medicaid, food stamps, General Assistance, Supplemental Security Income, and job training programs for welfare recipients. General Assistance is able to provide emergency financial aid. Medicaid is the closest thing the United States has to national health insurance and provides comprehensive health care to eligible preschool children. Recent major changes in federal law permit the states to greatly expand the number of participating children, including those up to 185 percent of the poverty level. This is an entitlement program, with great program latitude given the states, and open-ended in its funding with reimbursement at least 50 percent.

An often underutilized component of Medicaid is the Early, Periodic, Screening, Diagnosis, and Treatment program. EPSDT is meant to be an outreach program for the prevention of problems. It has a very broad mandate that permits creativity in addressing the physical and mental health needs of a state's poorest children.

Depending on the state, the above systems have planners, computer experts, and federal liaisons; strong connections with state and local advocacy groups, legislative committees, media, and provider organizations; and, frequently, broad discretion in how they allocate resources.

C. ASSETS OF THE EDUCATION SYSTEM

Non-education state agencies believe the education system brings many potential strengths in collaborating to serve children:

- Schools have captive audiences. All children are headed for school. Whether children are school-age or preschool, there is a belief that education has an easier ability to identify and reach all children than any other system. This is directly related to the inclusiveness of public education and the attendant lack of stigma so often associated with the social services system.

- Education has major tangible physical assets that can be used for a variety of purposes: kitchens, playgrounds, gymnasiums, meeting rooms, buses, playing fields.

- Schools, with a few notable exceptions, are considered generally secure environments that have responsible adults on site.

- Schools are often the site of adult education, the attendees of which are one of the high-priority adult groups that health and social services systems wish to reach—and, through them, their children.

- Teachers have more contact with children than any other professional group does and can serve as major allies for other professionals in both detecting and addressing problems.

III. COLLABORATION AT THE STATE LEVEL

Clearly, each of the state agencies serving preschool children possesses major resources. Congress, in its efforts at welfare reform, attempted to promote greater cooperation among the different state systems that serve the families with the greatest proportion of at-risk children—those in households receiving public assistance. Welfare reform addressed issues of child care, adult education, and job training and will attempt to compel education and social services systems to work with one another toward certain goals.

A new publication, "The Partnership," founded specifically to encourage communication between education and social services around welfare reform, predicts:

The efforts of educators and welfare administrators, fueled by different motivations and concerns, will converge to focus on many of the same children, youth, and adults. Thus far, however, little consultation and cooperation between educators and welfare administrators have preceded policy development.

Now is the time for both communities to begin effective and integrative planning in order to ensure that the efforts of the education and social services systems are mutually supportive, not antagonistic. The two systems, not always accustomed to cooperative efforts, must now unite, not simply to meet administrative requirements, but to lift disadvantaged young people out of poverty by offering them increased education opportunities.

The same case can be argued on behalf of preschool collaboration.

STATE SURVEY

This section looks at information gathered and prepared for this paper from a survey of the states. It will be followed by suggestions on where to get information about programs already in place that reflect state-level agreements.

During the preparation of this paper, a questionnaire was sent to the chief state human services administrators asking their views about the collaboration issue. Twenty-five states and the District of Columbia submitted written replies. Three others called in their answers. The questionnaire contained three questions:

1. What state-level interagency collaboration for preschool children's services is now in place in your state?
2. What has been your department's experience in securing cooperation from the Department of Education?
3. What suggestions do you have for future collaboration?

It is clear from the responses that collaboration with education is either under way or planned in each of those states. In almost every instance collaboration is a trend that emerged in the 1980s. Most of the cooperation centers around child care and care for handicapped children. However, other "at-risk" children are somewhat less of a focus in a few states and receive no attention in the others. Whether the states that did not respond to the survey are more or less in accord with those that did is unknown. What follows is a summary of the state responses.

Question 1. What state-level interagency collaboration for preschool children's services is now in place in your state?

- All of the respondents currently engage in some type of state-level interagency collaboration effort. However, interagency collaboration is a fairly recent activity:

    Before 1980, only Maine (1977) and Nebraska (1978) engaged in formal interagency collaboration.

    By 1982, Washington, Ohio, and Minnesota had developed collaborative efforts around services to children.

By 1985, Georgia, Illinois, Massachusetts, Nevada, Connecticut, Kansas, Virginia, and Missouri had started collaborative efforts.

By 1988, North Carolina, Pennsylvania, the District of Columbia, Alaska, Utah, South Dakota, Hawaii, New Jersey, and Vermont had started efforts.

- Half of the respondents established Interagency Coordination Councils as a result of P. L. 99–457.

  P. L. 99–457 initiated first-time interagency collaboration in Pennsylvania, the District of Columbia, Alaska, and Vermont.

  P. L. 99–457 Interagency Coordination Councils either replaced or broadened previous collaborative efforts serving the preschool population in Georgia, Illinois, Washington, Ohio, Nevada, Minnesota, Kansas, and Nebraska.

- It is not clear from the brief responses to the survey what levels of effort the states are putting into implementation of P. L. 99–457. However:

  Statewide early intervention services systems are reportedly planned in Georgia, Ohio, Nevada, Kansas, and Nebraska.

  Tracking and case management/data management systems have been established in the District of Columbia and Alaska.

  Illinois reported it will coordinate preschool services through the Interagency Coordinating Committee.

  Washington's Interagency Coordinating Committee will develop policies for services and determine relationships between services.

  Minnesota mandated local school districts to provide comprehensive services to children beginning at birth.

  Vermont will establish an early education program.

- Eight states have adopted formal cooperative agreements to cover:

  roles and responsibilities;

  policies/procedures around shared services;

  goals and objectives;

  target population;

  entry into and transition between agencies;

  ongoing case management/tracking, and training of personnel.

Question 2. What has been your department's experience in securing cooperation from the Department of Education?

- Generally, the responses were very positive. None of the states indicated any major problems between state-level human services and education agencies. Numerous examples of cooperation were listed, mostly, again, related to child care and care for handicapped children.

Question 3. What suggestions do you have for future collaboration?

- Although the respondents voiced their support for more cooperation, few offered specific suggestions. Of those who did, most expressed the need for more joint planning, data collection, problem analysis, and agreement on definitions. Most believed that both state-level and local-level collaboration were essential.

OBSTACLES

Some of the potential obstacles the state social services agencies identified in working closely with education include:

1. Awkward interagency organizational structures at the state and local levels.
2. Because of P. L. 99–457, education agencies are increasingly responsible for certain services to three- to five-year-olds, which they may view as the extent of their preschool obligations.
3. Different definitions of "at-risk" preschool children.
4. Lack of understanding about each other's systems.
5. Differing eligibility standards for services, which may make service delivery and case management more complicated.
6. Different providers of direct services.
7. Differences in who the "client" is perceived to be.
8. Different levels of commitment.
9. Transition to public school from current preschool programs such as Head Start is seen by some social services professionals as a problem, and there is a fear that many students lose ground in the process.
10. Parallel systems—both social services and education have responsibility for various aspects of preschool services; it is possible for both to proceed without consideration of the other.

OVERCOMING OBSTACLES

Several states have proven that these obstacles are not insurmountable. It is evident from the survey of states that states have become increasingly active in the area of interagency collaboration. Even before P. L. 99–457 went into effect, most states were collaborating around specific programs or projects for the benefit of children. The history, albeit recent, of collaboration of state agencies should contribute to the successful delivery of services for preschool children at risk within the mandate of P. L. 99–457.

Several of the states with the most experience in interagency cooperation have reported common themes related to overcoming obstacles:

1. Cooperative efforts must be nurtured at the highest level. Involvement of top administrators is critical. Written agreements are desirable (See Attachment B: Minnesota Interagency Agreement).

2. Creating a forum, the Interagency Coordinating Committee, is essential for sharing information. A forum can foster the trust necessary for "turf issues" to disappear.

3. Successful cooperation requires commitment to long-term process to ensure consistency and continued communication.

4. Successful cooperative efforts require the involvement of local providers and school districts in the work of the Interagency Coordinating Committee through subcommittees and ad hoc committees on special problems.

5. To foster understanding and awareness of each agency's programs, joint training must occur. Such opportunities contribute to a common vision of what communities should be doing for young children and their families.

6. Joint planning and budget proposals can be developed. Such a show of unity could be considered an asset by most governors and legislators, thereby increasing the likelihood of funding.

7. It is essential that full-time staff be assigned to the Interagency Coordinating Committee.

Obstacles ultimately are not overcome by process. There is no one best structure or model to follow, the states are simply too different, and the problems don't lend themselves to precise solutions. Instead, obstacles are overcome by a desire to achieve common goals.

REFERENCES TO PROGRAMS AND MODELS THAT WORK

Numerous programs that are built on local and state interagency cooperation and which serve preschool at-risk children and their families are in place and working. See, for example, the following:

Lisabeth Schorr's *Within Our Reach* (New York: Anchor Press Doubleday, 1988), a listing of successful child-serving programs around the country.

Extensive detailed program and process documents describing agency collaboration around preschool children by the states of Maine, Minnesota, and Washington, available through their state Human Services departments.

The National Governors' Association's *The First Sixty Months* (Washington, D.C.: National Governors' Association, 1987), which identifies 17 successful state programs for preschoolers.

The Chicago-based National Family Resource Coalition's *Programs to Strengthen Families* (Carole Levine, ed., Chicago: National Family Resource Coalition, 1988), which provides information on costs, evaluation, background, and content.

Medicaid Financing for Early Intervention Services by Fox Health Policy Consultants for Georgetown University Child Development Center (Harriette B. Fox and Ruth Yoshpe, Washington, D.C.: Fox Health Policy Consultants, 1987).

. *Localization of Human Services* (unpublished paper) by Jule Sugarman, Secretary of Social and Health Services for Washington state.

These programs have been proven effective and affordable. According to the National Governors' Association's analysis in *The First Sixty Months*, among the patterns of success that can be drawn from many of these programs are that they:

- reach out to multiple agencies, whether public or private, in order to deliver an array of needed services;
- often go into families' homes, rather than expecting participants to report to agency offices;
- target multiple problems, although a single problem is the initial focus;
- mix funds from public, private, state, and local sources;
- include some evaluation effort to measure the extent of the program's impact and learn whether the delivery model needs refinement;
- maximize parent involvement so parents ultimately can be the service providers and advocates for their children; and
- focus especially on the general and at-risk populations where the greatest benefit is likely to be achieved for the least cost and with the least intrusion.

PROBLEM AREAS WITH POTENTIAL FOR COLLABORATION

There are many areas where cooperative agreements between various state agencies and education departments would prove beneficial to preschool children. Two simultaneous, basic directions are required: one focused primarily at preschool children themselves and the other aimed primarily at their parents.

1. Preschool Child Care

Child care is intended to provide a safe environment that at least meets children's minimum developmental needs. It supplements parental care. Virtually all parents are involved in work, in job training, or in school. A heavier focus on developmental needs for certain children can be built into programming.

Significant new money is expected in this area. My personal view is that, generally, day-care sites should be located at places of parental employment or in public schools, with the latter site beneficial not only to children and families but also to junior and senior high students who could be recruited to assist professional staff.

Finally, it is not necessary for schools to operate child care directly. Indeed, this is a fear of many in the child-care community and one that needs to be addressed. Nevertheless, there are numerous private agencies in every state with the experience to serve as contractors for child-care service in the schools.

2. Health and Medical Services

Whether through public health nurses or other professionals, there is already in place in many states and local jurisdictions a wide variety of health services coordinated and delivered to preschool-age children. Most of these are directed to handicapped children ages three to five, but there are many exceptions that include children other than the handicapped and extend to ages zero to two as well.

Because of the proximity to neighborhood, the lack of stigma, and a basic organizational infrastructure, school systems provide a unique foundation upon which to build the delivery of other systems.

3. Child Abuse and Neglect

Although the primary legal responsibility for this huge problem rests with social services agencies, it is impossible to address this issue successfully without cooperation from education. Better detection by school personnel, joint training with social services, and formalized agreements between the two systems are essential and have been demonstrated to work in several local and state jurisdictions.

Many of the children in whom abuse is detected at school have younger siblings at home. Because of the family-centered focus of systems that protect children from abuse and neglect, these younger children will be beneficiaries of the intervention prompted by the school's involvement.

4. Services to Parents—and Future Parents

Although child care, child development, and health and medical services are major services needed by preschool-age children, the value of which cannot be overstated, there are several other equally compelling services aimed more at parents or potential parents of preschool children.

- *Parenting Education* is a critical unmet need that should be widely popularized. Simple research documents that we know more about what works in the healthy development of children than ever, yet only a small percentage of parents are formally exposed to this information. For both junior and senior high school students, and for the parents of preschool children, a well-organized, universally available opportunity to participate in parenting education would be in the best interest of children. Provided by schools or at schools, this service could quickly take on the popularity of birth education. Numerous organizations exist in every state with a capacity to deliver this service.

a. *Job Training and Education* for the parents of children in poverty and on welfare (a major predictor of risk for many children) is a compulsory feature of pending welfare reform proposals. Schools need to bring their substantial experience in this area to work with state human services agencies, which typically will have the lead responsibility.

b. *Teen Pregnancy* is a major contributing cause of at-risk preschool children. It is estimated that half of all confirmed cases of child abuse or neglect come from AFDC (Aid to Families with Dependent Children) households, half of the mothers of which gave birth to their first child during their teen years. Both health and social services agencies have a keen interest in this subject and are investing heavily in dealing with the consequences. There is a great receptivity to working with school systems both to prevent teen pregnancy and to provide assistance to teen parents.

5. *National Collaboration Among Different Professional Disciplines*

A national discussion around common interests and future activity among the principal executive agencies concerned about preschool children is needed. I believe there is potential foundation support for underwriting the costs of a two- or three-day conference, and the development of related materials, for chief administrators in education, health, and social services to come together to exchange information, learn, and develop strategy on the subject.

ATTACHMENT A

*Examples of Cooperative Arrangements
and Agreements Within the States*

Georgia (1) Interagency Council for Early Intervention Programs (P. L. 99–457) for children ages zero to three was appointed in February 1988.

(2) State Preschool Task Force (DOE) with reps from Department of Human Resources/Division of MH, MR, and Substance Abuse met over a period of four years to develop a state plan and a resource manual. Funding was provided by State Incentive grant and Preschool Incentive grant.

In May 1988 DOE and Head Start were in the process of developing a cooperative agreement to cover policies and procedures around shared services, program goals, and objectives; entry management procedure; and conflict resolution.

Illinois Six state agencies constitute an Interagency Coordination Council formed in 1985 to develop criteria given to the Board of Education for awarding grants and assisting in coordinating services for children from birth to age three (HB0899 Illinois Law).

In June 1987 State Interagency Council on Early Education was formed. It incorporates Department of Children and Family Services to assist Board of Education as head agency in carrying out Part H of P. L. 99–457.

North Carolina The materials did not indicate any cooperative arrangements. The materials described an adolescent pregnancy project and the Commission on Family Services.

Washington   (1) A formal cooperative agreement was signed in December 1986 between the Office of the Superintendent of Program Instruction and the Department of Social and Health Services. Its aim was the cooperative development and support of services to families and children through joint task groups.

These state agencies recommend the need for "early childhood education and care" and recommended that a plan for operationalizing P. L. 99–457 (0–3) be developed.

They identified a number of areas of cooperation; however, they are areas "involving school-age children at risk." Preschool agenda includes child-care planning and early childhood education.

(2) The Birth to Six Planning Project and Coordinating Council originated in 1982. It was intended to coordinate the Department of Social and Health Services and Office of the Superintendent of Public Instruction to serve children ages zero to three with special needs. In 1984, the project received a grant to develop a state plan for comprehensive coordinated services for children ages zero to six who have special needs.

With its cooperative relationship, this group took on P. L. 99–457. The group will work on developing cooperative agreements regarding funding of infant-toddler services.

In December 1986 the Superintendent of Public Instruction and Department of Social and Health Services established a joint staff group to:

• prepare a plan for improving services.
• facilitate a review of "shared" children at risk regarding health care, case management, information exchange, and education needs.

P. L. 99–452 cooperative agreement will include policies on:

• Individualized Family Services Plan.
• case management.
• staff training.
• central resource directory.

Ohio   In 1982 the Early Intervention Committee was formed, with representatives from Health, Education, Human Services MH and MR and DD, local providers, universities, advocates, and parents to address the needs of children ages zero to four. The committee designed a comprehensive Early Intervention Service System (with 11 components).

With the passage of P. L. 99–457 the committee was disbanded and replaced by the Governor's Early Intervention Council, which adopted the 11 components and services system.

Pennsylvania   P. L. 99–457 established an Interagency Coordinating Council with the Department of Public Welfare and Department of Education.

Massachusetts   (1) In 1984 the Governor's Day Care Partnership Project was established to develop a comprehensive day-care plan. It created a partnership among employers, public schools, and housing authorities.

(2) The Board of Education established the Early Childhood Advisory Council to address needs of preschool children at risk and with special needs. Responsibilities include programs for children ages three to four to enhance kindergarten classes by combining early childhood education and day care.

(3) The Department of Public Health and Department of Social Services collaborate to plan an Early Intervention/Day Care model to provide therapeutic intervention in day-care homes and centers for environmentally at-risk children with special needs.

Alaska The Department of Health and Social Services provides services to handicapped and at-risk children ages zero to three. The Department of Education serves at-risk children ages 3 to 21. Community and Regional Affairs administers day care and Head Start.

Administrators are in early stages of formalizing interagency collaboration among the Departments of Education, Health and Social Services, and Community and Regional Affairs.

The P. L. 99–457 Interagency Council will include the above agencies as well as private day care providers.

The Department of Education and the Department of Health and Social Services are developing a joint tracking/data management system to facilitate transition of children from preschool care to public school education.

Tertiary care hospitals for newborns will develop a tracking system to better follow up on discharged infants who were born in need of neonatal intensive care.

Nevada The Department of Human Resources and the Department of Education have had cooperatively developed programs for handicapped children "for many years." They currently have a statewide cooperative agreement.

The Interagency Coordinating Council (P. L. 99–457), composed of Human Resources and Education, has been meeting since December 1987.

Regional and local cooperative agreements will cover the facilitation of transition of children between departments (Human Resources and Education) and the training of personnel.

Utah The Board of Education and the Department of Social Services cooperatively developed a coordinated education and treatment program for each handicapped child *in school* (legislatively mandated in 1986).

South Dakota Eleven state agencies jointly planned a September 1988 conference on youth ages 0–21 at risk. Participating agencies were Health, Education, social services, charities and corrections, attorney general's office, highway safety, court services, vocational education, labor, vocation rehabilitation, and Indian affairs.

Connecticut	Since 1984, eight human service agencies have collaborated on a project regarding assessment, referral, and treatment of handicapped and developmentally disabled children ages 0–3. The collaboration resulted in a model service system.
	The state social services agency submitted a proposal to a foundation to establish a pilot program for services to children ages 0–10. Major participants included local schools.
Arizona	The Department of Economic Security and the Department of Education collaborated on several major projects, including services to latchkey children, child care for adolescents, and joint training.
	The Department of Employment Security is collaborating with school districts to develop a school liaison program focused on child protection.
	The Department of Employment Security is not presently working on preschool programs.
Minnesota	The Departments of Human Services, Education, and Health have been involved since 1981 in interagency efforts serving young children with handicaps.
	The first formal agreement, signed in 1984, required school districts to provide some services to children beginning at birth.
	Another formal agreement was signed in 1986. (See copy.)
	Local early intervention committees were mandated to plan and deliver local services.
	In 1986 the Governor's Council on Early Intervention for Young Children with Handicaps was established, involving three agencies.
	In 1987 the legislature mandated educational services starting at birth.

Kansas   The Coordinating Council on Early Childhood Development Services is working with representatives from the
Department of Social and Rehabilitative Services (SRS),
administration, health and environment, the public, parents, and educators to develop an interagency agreement
promoting comprehensive service delivery for young
children and handicapped children.

In 1985 a memorandum of understanding between
administration, education, health and environment, and
SRS was signed. It provides comprehensive services to
handicapped preschool children.

The above agreement established collaboration around
statewide service delivery, directory of services, special
education services, field testing, training, technical assistance, assessment of personnel needs, and public information.

In 1988 the State Advisory Committee on Child Care Ser-
vices was formed with representatives from the Office of
Child and Youth, the Department of Education and
Health, and the University of Hawaii.

The Child Care Collaboration was established to obtain
and plan expenditure of whatever funds might become
available. The Federal Dependent Care Planning and
Development grant was established to address the needs
of latchkey children.

*Nebraska**   An interagency coordination team was founded with
administration from education, public institutions, corrections, health, court administration, and social services
to address the needs of preschool children.

The Department of Education has an interagency team to
explore issues of this population.

Administrators have collaborated in recent years on special projects. For example, in 1985 the Department of
Social Services assumed responsibility for educational
funds for state children in foster care. It also funds
school districts to educate foster children who are placed
outside their home school districts.

The state is working (with the Department of Education)
on transition of foster children who change school districts.

Nebraska has had a mandated full service program since
1978 covering children ages zero to five.

* The letter from Nebraska includes a good summary of P. L. 99–457 requirements.

New Jersey   Education and Human Services developed a pre-kindergarten education pilot program in 1988.

A formal agreement was completed to establish a management team that would ensure effective instrumentation of the pre-kindergarten pilot program.

Virginia   In 1983, a collaborative project between social services, school districts, and local drug and alcohol councils was set up to address the needs of preschool children. Cooperation occurs around conferences on the developing of community resources. It is not clear, however, who is involved on the interagency or intra-agency level.

Missouri   In 1983, the Children's Services Commission met with all state agencies' representatives plus courts, political parties, House, and Senate to review statutes, administrative rules, regulations, etc., pertaining to services to children.

Vermont   (1) In 1988, legislation created a program for early education of handicapped children.

(2) A special division of child care services has been created.

(3) An Interagency Coordinating Council serves children ages 0–18 at risk.

A formal interagency agreement was created as a result of a two-year planning process funded by the National Institute of Mental Health. The agreement was signed in 1987.

Washington, D.C.   A memorandum of agreement between the Committee on Social Services and the Committee on Public Health designates responsibility for the Early Start Project. Objectives for 1988–89 include the development and implementation of a statewide comprehensive family-centered system of early identification, tracking, and case management for children ages zero to three who have developmental delays.

ATTACHMENT B

Minnesota Interagency Agreement
Early Childhood Intervention

INTRODUCTION

The Minnesota Departments of Health, Education, and Human Services are committed to providing coordinated services to young handicapped children and children at risk of handicapping conditions, from birth through five years of age. Each department provides legislatively mandated or permitted services for these children.

Planning efforts to develop interagency coordination of early identification and service delivery to these children have included the 1973 Child Development Planning Project and the 1976 Minnesota State Council for the Handicapped Task Force on Early Intervention. The 1980 Minnesota Legislature, in an effort to look systematically at the needs and related issues of providing intervention services to these children with special needs, directed the Commissioner of Education, in cooperation with the Commissioners of Health and Public Welfare (now Human Services), to conduct a statewide needs assessment (laws of Minnesota, 1980, Chapter 609, Article II, Section 13).

No legislation resulted from the needs assessment, but in 1982, formal interagency policy was developed requiring services for young handicapped children. A statewide coordinating task force, comprised of representatives of public and private service providers and consumer and advocacy groups, was convened to identify agency responsibilities for provision of services and the coordination necessary to provide services most effectively. The State Interagency Early Childhood Intervention Steering Committee was established to provide an interagency focus for these efforts.

In 1984, the three departments signed an Interagency Agreement which recognized the need for comprehensive planning for early intervention for young handicapped children and those at risk of handicapping conditions, and for their families. Using the State Interagency Early Childhood Intervention Steering Committee, they obtained funds for planning, training, and implementation of local interagency early learning committees mandated by state statute (MS 120.17). The Committee conducted an early intervention services needs assessment. Based on that assessment, training sessions were held each of three years to assist local interagency early learning committees plan coordinated services for children in their communities.

AGREEMENT

By this agreement, the Minnesota Departments of Education, Health, and Human Services reaffirm their support for comprehensive planning for early intervention services for handicapped children and children at risk of handicapping conditions, and for their families. Each of these agencies agrees to the goal and objectives contained in this agreement and through collaborative effort will continue to assist in the development of interagency systems to meet the needs of young children and their families.

Goal

The goal of interagency cooperation is to promote the development of coordinated multi-disciplinary systems for serving young handicapped children and children at risk of handicapping conditions, from birth through five years of age, and their families.

Objectives

1. To increase public awareness of the rationale and need for early intervention services to young handicapped children and children at risk of handicapping conditions, and for their families.

2. To demonstrate program models which utilize resources across disciplines, programs, and agencies on the state and local levels to meet the needs of these young children.

3. To clarify issues, define problems, and propose alternatives related to screening, diagnosis, assessment, and program models to promote coordinated services to young children, from birth through five years of age, and their families.

4. To identify for the Departments of Education, Health, and Human Services changes in fiscal and program policies that may be necessary to improve coordination of services to these children and their families.

5. To facilitate implementation of P. L. 99–457, through participation of the State Interagency Early Childhood Intervention Steering Committee with the federally mandated State Interagency Coordinating Council.

Activities

In order to implement this agreement, each department will assign a staff person to serve as the departmental representative on the State Interagency Early Childhood Intervention Steering Committee, which will:

1. Disseminate information relating to interagency collaboration and programs to departmental staff;

2. When provisions of P. L. 99–457 are in effect, assist the State Interagency Council in determining priorities for service planning, development, implementation, and evaluation;

3. Develop materials for information dissemination to school districts and local health and human services agencies, as well as local Interagency Early Learning Committees; and

4. Coordinate technical assistance with respect to early intervention technical assistance and in-service activities.

Duration of the Agreement

This agreement shall be effective immediately and shall remain in effect until terminated, or upon thirty (30) days written notice by one or all of the parties involved. It shall be reviewed biannually by the State Interagency Early Childhood Intervention Steering Committee and may be amended at any time by mutual agreement of the participating agencies.

SIGNATURES

_____   _____
Ruth E. Randall   Date
Commissioner
Department of Education

_____   _____
Sr. Mary Madonna Ashton   Date
Commissioner
Department of Health

_____   _____
Sandra S. Gardebring   Date
Commissioner
Department of Human Services

DESCRIPTIONS
OF
PARTICIPATING AGENCIES

A. Department of Education

SPECIAL EDUCATION SERVICES

Role of State Agency. The Special Education Section, Division of Instructional Effectiveness, Department of Education, is the state agency responsible for the provision of mandatory (ages 3 through 21) and permissive (birth through age 2) special instruction and related services for handicapped students.

Authority. Authority for the provision of special education services includes but is not limited to: (1) Public Law 94–142, The Education of All Handicapped Act, as amended by Public Law 99–457, (2) Minnesota Statutes, Sections 120.03, 120.17, and 124.32, and (3) Minnesota Rules 3500.2330.

Target Population. Every child who has a hearing impairment, visual handicap, speech or language impairment, physical handicap or other health impairment, mental handicap, emotional/behavioral disorder, specific learning disability, or deaf-blind handicap and needs special instruction and services is eligible for special education and services.

EARLY CHILDHOOD FAMILY EDUCATION

Role of State Agency. Early Childhood Family Education, Community and Adult Education Section, Division of Development and Partnership Effectiveness, Department of Education, is the state agency responsible for the provision of permissive parent-child education services for children, birth to kindergarten enrollment, and for their parents.

Authority. Authority for the provision of Early Childhood Family Education is specified by Minnesota Statutes, Sections 121.822 and 124.2711.

Target Population. Early Childhood Family Education programs in districts which choose to implement the program are voluntary for all children during the period from birth to kindergarten enrollment, for the parents of such children, and for expectant parents who reside in the school district which levies funds for the programs.

EARLY CHILDHOOD HEALTH AND DEVELOPMENTAL SCREENING

Role of State Agency. Learner Support Systems in the Division of Development and Partnership Effectiveness has the responsibility for administering the Early Childhood Screening program. This includes setting standards, program implementation guidelines, reporting procedures, and fiscal aspects of the program. Training, technical assistance, and monitoring responsibilities are shared with the Minnesota Department of Health.

Authority. Authority for provision of Early Childhood Health and Developmental Screening is found in Minnesota Statutes, Section 123.701 through 123.705, and Minnesota Rules 3530.3000 to 3530.4300. The program also meets, in part, the requirement for Child Find activities outlined in federal special education laws and regulations.

Target Population. Each school district in Minnesota is required to provide screening once before children enter school. The recommended age for screening is 3 1/2 to 4 years. All children in this age group are encouraged to participate in this review of vision, hearing, immunization status, growth, health history, and development (cognition, speech and language, socio-emotional, and motor development).

Eligibility. All children in Minnesota are eligible for health and developmental screening before they enter school.

B. Department of Health

SERVICES FOR CHILDREN WITH HANDICAPS (SCH)

Role of State Agency. SCH is the Department of Health program responsible for assuring appropriate case finding, diagnosis, and treatment of children with suspected or known handicaps and to work to improve services to handicapped children.

SCH provides high-quality diagnostic services at clinics throughout the state and at medical centers. The program's professional staff counsel, refer, and advocate for families of handicapped children, and provide in-service training to local health, education, and social services professionals and agencies.

Authority. Authority for the provision of diagnostic and treatment services to handicapped children is provided in the Maternal and Child Health Block Grant, Title V, USC 42 Section 2192; Minnesota Statutes, 1977, Chapter 453, Section 24; and Minnesota Rules, Parts 4705.0100 to 4705.1500.

Target Population. Any child with a handicapping condition that interferes with normal growth and development is eligible for services under the SCH program. Typical conditions include congenital heart disease, cerebral palsy, cleft lip and palate, spina bifida, cancer, mental retardation, and developmental delay.

Eligibility Criteria. Any Minnesota child, birth through 21 years of age, with a suspected or known handicap is eligible for services. Families are required to share in treatment costs according to their ability to pay.

COMPREHENSIVE CHILD HEALTH SCREENING

Role of State Agency. Comprehensive Child Health Screening within the Department of Health has responsibility for providing standards, technical assistance, training, monitoring, and evaluation for the Early and Periodic Screening (EPS) programs and for components of the Early and Periodic Screening, Diagnosis, and Treatment (EPSDT) program. These programs provide screening services for the early detection of problems in children who may need future evaluation, diagnosis, and/or treatment. The EPS program also provides health counseling so that improved practices can be learned.

Authority. Authority for the provision of comprehensive child health screening services is contained in the Maternal and Child Health Block Grant, Title V, USC 42 Section 2192; Minnesota Statutes, 1978, Chapter 473 as amended 1980, 1981, 1982; and Minnesota Rules 4615.0900 to 4615.200.

Target Population. Any Minnesota child is eligible for child health screening services.

Eligibility Criteria. There are no income eligibility criteria for the EPS program. Fees may be required for some screening programs according to ability to pay.

Public Health Nursing

Role of State Agency. Public Health Nursing does not provide direct services but is responsible for promoting and facilitating development of locally administered public health services such as maternal and child health, home care of the ill and disabled, disease prevention and control, and health education. It also provides education programs for nurses and ancillary personnel employed by public health nursing services and school districts as well as consultation on program planning, evaluation, and administration. Local public health nursing services employ 950 nurses and more than 1,000 home health aides.

Authority. Authority for the provision of public health nursing is contained in Minnesota Statutes 144.05.

Target Population. Services available through local public health nursing services in all 87 counties include but are not limited to prenatal education, EPS, nutrition assistance through the federal WIC program, screenings for acute and chronic diseases, and home health care for the ill and disabled. Services are also provided to day care centers and group homes. Many counties also contract with physical, occupational, and speech therapists.

Eligibility. Eligibility requirements vary by program.

C. Department of Human Services

Role of State Agency. Minnesota has a state-supervised, county-administered system of providing services. As a result, few services are actually provided by the state agency, which has primary responsibility for policy development and oversight. Most services are funded through Community Social Services block grants to counties or through Medical Assistance. The department has statutory responsibility for service provision to children with handicaps, including:

- Children with mental retardation and related conditions
- Emotionally disturbed children
- Deaf and hearing-impaired children
- Chronically ill children receiving services through the Community Alternatives for Children (Medicaid) Waiver

- Children receiving health care services provided through the Medical Assistance Program and its federally mandated subprogram, the Early and Periodic Screening, Diagnosis, and Treatment Program (EPSDT)

The Department provides technical assistance, training, and monitoring of service provision. Regional representatives provide information about services for individuals with mental retardation and related conditions and hearing impairments. Referral is also made to child welfare services.

Authority. Authority for provision of these services is found in the following Minnesota statutes:

- Mental Retardation and Related Conditions, Minnesota Statutes, Sections 252, 256B, and 256E; and Minnesota Rules, 9525.0015 to 9525.0165.

- Mental Health, Minnesota Statutes, Sections 256E; 245.61 through 245.64; 245.711 through 245.718; and 245.73

- Deaf Services, Minnesota Statutes, Sections 256C.21 through 256C.27; and 256.971

- Medical Assistance, Minnesota Statutes, Section 256B and Minnesota Rules, 9505.0010 to 9505.0150; and 9500.1060 to 9500.1080

- Licensure, Minnesota Statutes, Section 245

- Child Welfare Services, Minnesota Statutes, Sections 256.01, subdivision 2 and 626.556

Target Population. Any child with a handicapping condition may receive services. Although services may vary from county to county, depending on needs identified in the county's Community Social Service Plan, all counties are required to address the needs of persons with mental retardation and mental health problems. EPSDT services are designed to identify and treat conditions which may result in handicapping conditions in any child eligible for Medical Assistance. Home and community-based services are available to children with chronic illnesses or mental retardation and related conditions who qualify under the Medical Assistance Waiver Programs.

Eligibility. Programs related to Medical Assistance have certain income and asset eligibility requirements. Other services have no income requirements, but fees may be charged according to approved county fee schedules.

DEPARTMENTS OF PUBLIC EDUCATION AND LEADERSHIP IN THE COLLABORATIVE PLANNING AND IMPLEMENTATION OF P.L. 99–457

Policy Challenges, Choices, and Changes[*]

Pascal Louis Trohanis

DIRECTOR
NATIONAL EARLY CHILDHOOD
TECHNICAL ASSISTANCE SYSTEM
(NEC*TAS)

> *"It's easy to get the players.*
> *Getting 'em to play together, that's the hard part."*
>
> Casey Stengel

Public Law 99–457, the Education of the Handicapped Act (EHA), beckons a variety of federal, state, and local partners to join together in planning and implementing policies and services for young children with special needs and their families in all U.S. states, the District of Columbia, and territories, including those under the Bureau of Indian Affairs.

The process of translating policy into action faces numerous challenges. Just as Casey Stengel discerned, state agency personnel may know who the players are for collaborative activities, but getting them all to interact productively and cooperatively is a major challenge. Departments of Public Education are key players in providing leadership by setting the tone and direction for combined efforts and seeing to it that services in their jurisdiction build upon the best practices of the past as well as upon innovative practices.

This paper begins with a description of the rich and dynamic context within which the policies of P.L. 99–457 will operate on behalf of our nation's early childhood, early intervention, and preschool programs. Next, an overview is provided of two portions of P.L. 99–457—infant/toddler and preschool programs—and their rigorous timetable for change and improvement. Finally, system changes are discussed in relation to collaborative policy planning and implementation strategies.

* Support for preparation of portions of this manuscript was provided by contract #300–87–0163 from the U.S. Department of Education.

BACKGROUND: CONTEXT AND IMPETUS

Children who require special support and services from birth have needs that arise from a complex array of biological, environmental, and social factors. Public policy seeks to assure that children with special needs have the opportunity to grow and develop to their full potential. Comprehensive interdisciplinary, family-focused, and high-quality intervention services for these children and their families offer great promise toward this end. Increasing evidence suggests that such programs:

1. improve long-term outcomes of children and families, including preparation for school, personal life, life in the world of work, and life in the community;

2. reduce institutionalization;

3. provide more opportunities to participate in the mainstream of society;

4. prevent and/or reduce crime, poverty, malnutrition, family stress, violence, and substance abuse among this population; and

5. result in cost savings per child by reducing the intensity or duration of need for special services (Fraas, 1986; Berrueta-Clement, Schweinhart, Barnett, Epstein, & Weikart, 1984; Simeonsson, Cooper, & Scheiner, 1982).

These accomplishments stem from numerous factors such as greater collaboration between parents and professionals and improvements in technologies of bio-medicine, measurement, and intervention. Additionally, 49 of 59 governing entities in America now have policies (primarily administered through State Departments of Public Education) that authorize special education and related services to children below school age with special needs. Standards and regulations for services prevail in many places along with licensure and certification of competent personnel.

OBSTACLES TO PROGRESS

The widespread availability of these desirable comprehensive services is far from a reality in our nation. While progress has been made, many obstacles and challenges remain to the achievement of full services for young children with special needs and their families. These include:

1. demographic factors, such as high rates of poverty and infant mortality; a growing, culturally diverse population; and increases in single-parent households, migrant and homeless families, and teenage parents;

2. little state direction of philosophy, expectations, and delineation of comprehensive services;

3. unknown numbers and unclear definition of the target population(s) eligible to receive services;

4. lack of sufficient funds or stability in financing;

5. fragmentation of services among federal, state, regional, and local agencies and other public and private service organizations;

6. struggles for control of services;

7. lack of stable and continuous services to children and families;

8. insufficient personnel with appropriate training;

9. inadequate child identification and reporting systems;

10. poor accessibility of services in many states, attributed to problems of geography and population;

11. incomplete delineation of a continuum of services—hospital-based clinics (e.g., neonatal intensive care units), home-based, and community-based programs—in the most appropriate and least restrictive manner (NCCIP, 1986; Magrab & Elder, 1979).

Grubb (1987) notes that much confusion has surrounded early childhood programs in terms of their cost, operation, effectiveness, and quality. He states: "Turf battles persist, and the major professional communities with interest in young children...often battle each other over basic philosophical objectives and methodologies." He warns that "without a coherent approach to policymaking, the current interest in young children could easily fade without any major and effective programs to show for all the effort."

Given these barriers, challenges, and complexities, professionals and parents must strengthen their sense of common purpose, since no single discipline, agency, or advocate can be expected to provide all necessary services for this population. The participation of health, education, developmental disability, mental health, social service, and related systems, as well as of parents, in the process of policy development and implementation is essential.

RELATED FEDERAL INITIATIVES

The issues in developing and implementing coordinated and comprehensive services for young children with special needs and their families involve the complex relationships among many diverse programmatic initiatives. During the last decade, the number of programs serving this population has increased. This growth reflects an increase in the number of young children with handicaps who have been identified and served. However, while the number of programs and the number of children served have grown, there has been slow growth in policy and program coordination and integration and in the development of adequate procedures to share information about effective models and practices (OSERS, 1986).

A number of federal programs have been established to improve services to young children with special needs and their families. Many of these federally sponsored programs have sought to become coordinated, comprehensive, and integrated within state and local human services systems. These federal programs include:

1. Social Security Act and its many pertinent provisions, such as Crippled Children's Services (now referred to as Programs for Children with Special Health Care Needs), Maternal and Child Health Services, Medicaid and Early Periodic Screening, Diagnosis and Treatment (EPSDT), and Title XX;

2. Head Start;

3. Chapter I and P.L. 89–313 (now referred to as P.L. 100–297);

4. Child Nutrition Act and WIC Program;

5. Developmental Disabilities;

6. P.L. 100–177, the Childhood Immunization Program;

7. Social Services;

8. P.L. 100–485, The Family Support Act;

9. Mental Health; and

10. EHA (P.L. 94–142 and P.L. 99–457), particularly the infant/toddler program, the preschool program, and the Handicapped Children's Early Education Program.

Federal programs, sponsored by such agencies as Maternal and Child Health, Developmental Disabilities, and the Department of Education, have made progress toward our nation's goal of coordinated services to all young children with special needs and their families. While much has been achieved, the full potential and integration of these efforts have not been realized. Regrettably, conflicting national agency regulations and requirements and minimal program coordination within individual federal agencies have, in the end, diluted state and local efforts to coordinate planning and delivery of services. Further, the various model state and community programs that have been developed within individual agencies are seldom shared.

Public Law 94–142 (the Education for All Handicapped Children Act of 1975) created a national goal for the provision of full services to all handicapped children from birth through 21 years of age. While much has been accomplished with school-age children, modest gains have been made in services to preschoolers. To date, only 49 of America's 59 governing entities have some type of entitlement for services to handicapped children below age 5. Subsequent laws have sought to improve this situation.

In 1983, politicians, advocates, parents, and representatives from public and private national, state, and local agencies worked for new federal legislation to accomplish the goal of filling the remaining service gaps and resolving overlaps in what was envisioned to be a comprehensive service delivery system. The consensus was that a redirected national initiative was needed. This belief led Congress to include the Early Childhood State Plan grant program in the development of P.L. 98–199. The State Plan Grant Program provided funds to 56 governing entities (mostly to State Departments of Education). The funds were to be used to examine what was needed for designing comprehensive services and establishing interagency planning groups that would facilitate this development. The program began in 1984 and was scheduled to be an eight-year effort. But after only three years of this program, Congress perceived a need to rearrange the comprehensive planning initiative and to stimulate more rapid and dramatic change in states and communities. States now are being challenged to move to the next plateau of their development through the new policy initiatives and resources of P.L. 99–457, which supersedes the previous state planning efforts.

P.L. 99–457: A POLICY VEHICLE FOR CHANGE

On October 8, 1986, P.L. 99–457, the Education of the Handicapped Act Amendments of 1986, was signed into law by President Reagan. These amendments reauthorized many programs under the EHA and authorized a five-year national agenda pertaining to the phase-in of more and better services to young children with special needs and their families.

OVERVIEW TO P.L. 99–457

P.L. 99–457 marks the next step of Congress's willingness to respond to the needs of young children with special needs and their families. Within this law, there is a rigorous new national policy agenda for universal, high-quality, and flexible services to young children with special needs and their families. This agenda was fueled by the needs of these children and by the documented benefits of early intervention and preschool services. The law recognized that implementation of a new policy must build upon "the best policies and practices of the past" via a partnership of citizens, who will provide leadership for change and the betterment of services to children and families. Congressman Steven Bartlett of Texas said of the bill that it establishes a policy that recognizes the benefits of early intervention, provides assistance to states to build systems of service delivery, and recognizes the unique role of families in the development of their handicapped children (*Congressional Record*, September 22, 1986, p. H7904). Such comprehensive including of the family goes well beyond the parental role required in Part B of P.L. 94–142. Parents not only retain their participatory role in planning and decision-making, but they also can become actual recipients of services in the effort to meet the special needs of their children.

Two key portions of P.L. 99–457 are discussed in this paper. These two parts of the law are intended to change the status quo of services that nationally are highly uncertain, inadequate, and variable. Titles I and II, which were not rigidly defined by Congress, afford America's governing entities choices to tailor-make holistic and integrated services to meet the needs of their children and families.

TITLE I (PART H): HANDICAPPED INFANTS AND TODDLERS

Title I is a new part of the EHA. It creates a discretionary program to help states plan, develop, and implement a statewide comprehensive, coordinated, multidisciplinary, interagency system of early intervention services for all eligible young handicapped and developmentally delayed children from birth to three years of age. The system must fit the needs and characteristics of each governing entity in the United States and of the Bureau of Indian Affairs (BIA).

Part H Provisions

The statewide comprehensive systems cover individuals who are experiencing developmental delays or a diagnosed physical or mental condition with a high probability of an associated delay in one or more of the following areas: cognitive development, physical development, language/speech development, psychosocial development, and development of self-help skills. In addition, states may opt to define and serve "at-risk" children.

Under Title I, infants and toddlers are eligible to receive developmental early intervention services that satisfy the following conditions:

1. Services are provided under public supervision.
2. Services are provided at no cost, except where federal or state laws allow.
3. Services are designed to meet the developmental needs of youngsters across all five delay areas.
4. Services meet state standards as well as the new federal ones.
5. Services include, but are not limited to, family training and counseling; special instruction; speech pathology; occupational therapy; physical therapy; case management; medical evaluation and diagnosis; and early identification.
6. Services are provided by qualified personnel.
7. Services are delivered in conformity with the Individualized Family Service Plan based on a multidisciplinary assessment and with the help of a case manager.

The system must serve these children and families with individualized early intervention services. Minimum system components include the fourteen areas shown in Figure 1; others may be added by the governing entities in line with their needs. These components cover community, regional, and/or statewide activities.

FIGURE 1

COMPONENTS OF A STATEWIDE COMPREHENSIVE SYSTEM OF EARLY INTERVENTION SERVICES TO INFANTS AND TODDLERS WITH SPECIAL NEEDS

1. Definition of developmentally delayed
2. Timetable to all in need in the state
3. Comprehensive multidisciplinary evaluation of needs of children and families
4. Individualuzed family service plan and case management services
5. Child find-and-referral system
6. Public awareness
7. Central directory of services, resources, research, and demonstration projects
8. Comprehensive system of personnel development
9. Single line of authority in a lead agency designated or established by the governor for carrying out:
   a. General administration and supervision
   b. Identification and coordination of all available resources
   c. Assignment of financial responsibility to the appropriate agency
   d. Procedures to ensure services are provided and to resolve intra- and interagency agreements
   e. Entry into formal interagency agreements
10. Policy pertaining to contracting or making arrangements with local service providers
11. Precedure for timely reimbursement of funds
12. Procedural safeguards
13. Policies and procedures for personnel standards
14. System for compiling data on the early intervention programs

A state interagency coordinating council, appointed by the governor, will advise and assist the state's lead agency in planning and operating the comprehensive system. The council will hold open meetings at least quarterly and report to the governor. (See Figure 2, pages 272–273, for a list of 58 lead agencies by governing entity.) The breakdown by lead agencies which administer Part H is as follows:

Departments of Public Education—22 *(Text contd. p. 274)*

FIGURE 2

NEC*TAS list of P.L. 99–457
Part H Lead Agencies

STATE	LEAD AGENCY
1. Alabama	Education/Crippled Children's Services (CCS)
2. Alaska	Health & Social Services
3. American Samoa	Health
4. Arizona	Economic/Security/ Developmental Disabilities (DD)
5. Arkansas	Human Services/DD
6. California	Developmental Services
7. Colorado	Education
8. Commonwealth of Northern Mariana Islands	Education
9. Connecticut	Education
10. Delaware	Education
11. District of Columbia	Human Resources
12. Florida	Education
13. Georgia	Human Resources/Mental Health-Mental Retardation-Substance Abuse (MH-MR-SA)
14. Guam	Education
15. Hawaii	Health/CCS
16. Idaho	Health & Welfare/DD
17. Illinois	Education
18. Indiana	Mental Health
19. Iowa	Education
20. Kansas	Health and Environment
21. Kentucky	Human Resources
22. Louisiana	Education
23. Maine	Interdepartmental Committee
24. Maryland	Governor's Office of Children and Youth
25. Massachusetts	Public Health
26. Michigan	Education

27. Minnesota	Education
28. Mississippi	Health
29. Missouri	Education
30. Montana	Social and Rehabilitation Services/DD
31. Nebraska	Education
32. Nevada	Human Resources
33. New Hampshire	Education
34. New Jersey	Education
35. New Mexico	Health & Environment/DD
36. New York	Health
37. North Carolina	Human Resources/ MH-MR-SA
38. North Dakota	Human Services
39. Ohio	Health
40. Oklahoma	Education
41. Oregon	Mental Health/DD
42. Palau	Education
43. Pennsylvania	Public Welfare
44. Puerto Rico	Health
45. Rhode Island	Interagency Coordinating Council
46. Secretary of the Interior (BIA)	Education
47. South Carolina	Health & Environment Control
48. South Dakota	Education
49. Tennessee	Education
50. Texas	Interagency Council
51. Utah	Health
52. Vermont	Education
53. Virgin Islands	Health
54. Virginia	MH/MR/SA
55. Washington	Social & Health Services
56. West Virginia	Health
57. Wisconsin	Health & Social Services
58. Wyoming	Health

(Federated States of Micronesia & Republic of Marshall Islands are not currently eligible for this federal program.)

Departments of Health—17
Departments of Human Services—17
Interdepartmental Councils—3
Other Agencies—9

The U.S. Department of Education makes grants to most governing entities based on a census; the BIA and territories are allotted monies based on a set-aside percentage (1-1.25) of the aggregate amount available to all states for a given fiscal year. These grant monies may be used to help carry out systems planning and policy development; they may also be used to pay for direct services to children not otherwise receiving assistance from public and private sources and to support the expansion and improvement of services already available. For this five-year initiative, Congress appropriated $50 million for the first year, $67 million for the second year, $69 million for the third year, and $79 million for the fourth year (1990–91). All qualified governing jurisdictions must submit an annual application for continued funding.

What's Happening with Part H?

Proposed regulations that are intended to guide states in the implementation of Part H were published on November 18, 1987, by the U.S. Department of Education. Over 2,500 public comments covering 60 of 79 regulatory areas were submitted to DOE. These included comments on matters dealing with parents, personnel preparation, the Individualized Family Service Plan, funding, assessment, and health services. Final regulations for Part H were released by the U.S. Department of Education on June 22, 1989.

Current practice and three studies on Part H provide information on the first six months of implementation (NASDSE, 1988; Carolina Policy Studies Program, 1988; and Fineblum Associates, 1988). Some preliminary findings suggest that governing bodies have been very busy, making good-faith efforts, and productive:

1. *State Interagency Coordinating Council.* All state councils have been constituted, and most have held at least one meeting. Representation is broad, including parents, service providers, physicians, and state agency personnel. Departments of Public Education participate in all councils. Many task forces have been formed by councils to examine policy matters such as entry to services, eligibility, and general system planning.

2. *Interagency Coordination.* States reported working with an average of eleven different state-administered early intervention programs, such as Chapter I (P.L. 89–313), Education of the Handicapped Act (P.L. 94–142), Medicaid, Health, Crippled Children's Services, and Head Start. Few reported that these coordination efforts were effective. Groundwork is being laid in many jurisdictions for the development of new interagency agreements so as to improve the coordination of services among these state/local programs.

(Text contd. p. 276)

FIGURE 3

IMPLEMENTATION CHALLENGES

1. Methods of informing new parents of available services need very careful attention. Experienced parents should be part of the initial contact by service providers.

2. There is a need for adequate safeguards to insure that the Individualized Family Service Plan (IFSP) works to support families. Specifically, privacy and confidentiality must be safeguarded by policies and/or procedures for use and protection of records; potential dangers of intrusiveness and overassessment in service planning and delivery must be averted; and the role of the parents as partners must be accepted and supported by members of the multidisciplinary team.

3. The system should be responsive to individual family differences in terms of needs, strengths, interests, and time commitments.

4. Case management is a multilevel issue. What are appropriate state models for interagency case management? How are parents supported in their role of managing the care of their children?

5. How can the policies, procedures, and design of comprehensive services support the provision of services in the least restrictive environment?

6. The definitions of *health care* and *medical care* must be clarified.

7. The nature and extent of services for children who are chronically ill for extended periods need examination.

8. Formation of the Title I (Part H) State Interagency Coordinating Council, selection of a lead agency, and empowering of equal partners are important process issues.

9. Services to children ages birth through two, three through five, and six through eight should not be fragmented. The roles of the State Interagency Coordinating Council, the Developmental Disabilities Council, and the State Special Education Advisory Council should relate closely in their planning activities.

10. The issue of accountability is critical. If a service is written in a service plan, who is required to give it? Who will pay for it?

11. Interagency coordination/system fragmentation must be evaluated in terms of complexities of state bureaucracies, political issues, lead agency; and power of the State Interagency Coordinating Council.

12. Funding formulae, procedures, and distribution mechanisms are needed.

13. Qualified personnel are vital to meeting the demands of growing state service systems.

14. Entry into the service system via a single point must be considered.

15. Development and/or refinement of policies and procedures must be undertaken with a multiple agency/discipline focus including standards, guidelines, eligibility, and definition of developmental delay.

16. States must prepare for the expansion of services across the state, across handicapping, and across at-risk conditions.

17. Development of information systems—data management, tracking, resource directory—will be necessary.

3. *Definition of Developmental Delay and Inclusion of At-Risk Populations.* Almost half of the states have established a definition of developmental delay, while many states indicated that they were considering inclusion of at-risk populations.

4. *Use of Part H Funds.* Most governing entities have hired state/regional personnel, are planning and developing comprehensive services, and are paying for the direct provision of services to children and families. Many states are using monies to set up and operate innovative pilot projects on aspects of interagency coordination.

In a recent study released in October of 1989 on states' progress related to the 14 components of Part H, Harbin, Gallagher, and Lillie (1989) reported that 47 reporting jurisdictions indicated some progress in several of the 14 components and that most progress was made in policy development rather than policy approval or implementation. The authors also found that the least progress made related to financial and interagency coordination issues.

Part H and TA Needs

The National Early Childhood Technical Assistance System (NEC*TAS) is sponsored by the U.S. Department of Education to assist states in developing a master plan for a statewide system of services to infants and toddlers and their families. NEC*TAS is a collaborative support system coordinated by the Frank Porter Graham Child Development Center of the University of North Carolina at Chapel Hill.

During January and February of 1988 and the fall of 1988 and 1989, NEC*TAS conducted a needs assessment of Part H programs. Based on these studies, several key policy and program development areas were identified for which technical assistance (TA) was requested. Examples of TA areas for services systems pertinent to infants and toddlers and their families include:

1. *interagency collaboration*—how to use effectively the Interagency Coordinating Council (ICC) in relation to the lead agency; how to work together to create effective coordinated programs; how to develop interagency agreements; how to collect and use data.

2. *parent involvement*—how to plan participatory activities for the IFSP, case management, child identification, and multidisciplinary assessment; how to deal with confidentiality of information; how to form support networks.

3. *financing*—how to plan for the coordinated use of multiple funding streams, especially those of federal origin.

4. *comprehensive services*—how to plan a policy for a coordinated and collaborative system of services incorporating health, education, mental health, and social services; how to offer protection to child and family; how to design case management services; how to assure qualified personnel.

TITLE II (SECTION 619): PRESCHOOL PROGRAM

Title II amends Section 619 of EHA, the Preschool Incentive Grants, to create enhanced incentives for states to provide a free, appropriate, public education to all eligible children from three through five years of age who have handicaps. The amendment of Title II was designed to fill a gap in service provision. The U.S. House report on the EHA Amendments (1986) disclosed that nationally there are approximately 330,000 handicapped children from three through five years of age. Of this total, 260,000 were being served by states in 1986, leaving an estimated 70,000 to be served. Services for this population are to be in place by school year 1991–92.

Title II Provisions

The U.S. Department of Education makes grants to state educational agencies (SEAs) to implement this initiative through local educational agencies (LEAs), intermediate educational units (IEUs), and/or other contracted service agencies. Congress appropriated $180 million for the initial period, $201 million for the second year, $247 million for the third year, and $251 million for the 1990–91 school year. State appropriations are determined by an intricate per-child formula.

In order to participate in this grant program, SEAs must have an approved Part B State Plan and provide special education and related services to some children. Additionally, for the 1991–92 school year, SEAs must amend their Part B State Plan to include policies and procedures that assure the availability, under state law and practice, of a "free appropriate public education" (FAPE) for all children ages three through five years with handicaps. A free appropriate public education includes the individual education program, due process, confidentiality, and education in the least restrictive environment.

The amount awarded to each state under Title II is based on two related formulas or grants. For school year 1987–88, each state received a basic grant consisting of $300 per "counted" child (those currently receiving a free appropriate public education). For 1988–1989, each state received a basic grant consisting of $400 per child. And for 1989–90, each received a grant of $500 per child. Additionally, each state may receive a one-time bonus grant consisting of *up to* $3,800 per "estimated" child (those not presently receiving a FAPE but whom the state plans to serve the following year). For school year 1987–88, the bonus grant was calculated at $3,270 per estimated child; for 1988–1989, the bonus grant was calculated at $2,876 per child; and, for 1989–1990, the bonus grant was calculated at $3,800. For the 1990–91 school year, each state may receive a basic grant of up to $1,000 per child; there will be no more bonus dollars since that provision expires.

For school year 1988–89 and beyond, at least 75 percent of the funds must go to the LEAs or IEUs, up to 20 percent may be set aside for SEA planning and related activities, and no more than 5 percent can be reserved for administrative expenses.

Community services to provide a free appropriate public education to youngsters can be implemented in a number of different ways. The SEA/LEA may administer home- or center-based programs directly, or indirectly through contract with other qualified service agencies. Variations in the length of the service day and type of program are acceptable. The family is recognized as having an important role in preschool programs, and family services, such as training and counseling, can be made available.

Another provision of Title II is noteworthy—this is a provision for sharing the costs of a free appropriate public education among federal, state, and local agencies. Options available to states include:

1. providing or paying for some or all costs of a free appropriate public education (not limited to education agencies).

2. developing and implementing interagency agreements.

3. permitting no reduction in medical or other assistance available and no altering of eligibility under Maternal and Child Health/Medicaid.

4. defining financial responsibility of each agency for providing a free appropriate public education.

The law also does two other things. First, it builds in penalties if a state does not achieve a full mandate for providing free appropriate public education by the 1991–92 school year. Failure to comply will result in loss of the new preschool grant money, funds generated under Part B of the State Plan formula for this population group, as well as forfeiture of designated EHA discretionary grants, including those for research, training, and demonstration activities. Second, according to the law, the state does not need to report by disability category to the U.S. Department of Education for children ages three through five who are served by SEAs.

What's Happening with Section 619?

Proposed regulations for Section 619 were published on November 18, 1987, by the U.S. Department of Education. Over 500 comments were submitted, covering such areas as funding, transition, individual education program, least restrictive environment, and personnel standards. Final regulations were issued on January 13, 1989.

All participating State Departments of Public Education have been working hard at planning for and implementing Section 619 services, creating new services in those jurisdictions that currently do not have special education entitlements below school age, and improving services where there are entitlements for preschool special education. Already, after two years of implementation, approximately 59,000 new children have been enrolled in preschool programs that assure a free appropriate public education. Some states have been frustrated, however, by the low Congressional budget allocations, lateness of receipt of funds, and complex fiscal formulas for calculating the state allocations of dollars.

Section 619 and Technical Assistance Needs

Based on the NEC*TAS surveys of technical assistance needs, states identified the following key areas in which help is needed in planning and implementing services for preschoolers with handicaps:

1. Policy development—how to prepare effective legislation or frame policies so as to provide free appropriate public education for children in their jurisdiction; how to define the population to be served; how to relate this planning with Part H systems development.

2. Least restrictive environment—how to effectively plan for service setting(s) and offer options to children and parents.

3. Personnel preparation—how to ensure the availability of qualified personnel to work with these children and families.

4. Transition—how to deal with children who become three years of age and qualify for the Section 619 program but do not meet the typical birthdate admission requirements of local educational agencies.

5. Program—how to develop quality preschool education services and how to fund these programs.

GENERAL CHALLENGES

During its first two years of operation, P.L. 99–457 has given rise to seven general challenges that parents, professionals, and agencies are attempting to resolve in their states and communities. Briefly, these are as follows:

1. The challenge of having Part H administered in the same state agency as Section 619 (22 jurisdictions) or in two different agencies (36 jurisdictions).

2. The challenge of building and financing comprehensive and coordinated services out of fragments within a political and economic context that may not be supportive.

3. The challenge of governance and the sharing of power among agencies, disciplines, parents, and professionals.

4. The challenge of promoting fundamental changes in the attitudes and value systems of those who plan and provide services so as to best address the needs of young children with special needs and their families.

5. The challenge of translating, dispersing, and using the knowledge generated from research, model development programs, and previous state efforts.

6. The challenge of developing tools and technologies (e.g., assistant devices, assessment instruments, curricula) to meet the requirements of new federal, state, and local policies.

7. The challenge of monitoring all of these efforts and coordinating them with other state and local early childhood initiatives dealing with child abuse, teenage pregnancy prevention, pre-kindergarten programs, welfare-related child care, and programs for students at risk for school failure.

Implications for Community Service Delivery

According to Trohanis and Magrab (1987), in developing collaborative strategies for comprehensive services, the needs of the children and their families must be held paramount. The goals of local comprehensive services must be based on sound developmental principles, must recognize the importance of the emotional well-being of the child and the family, and must firmly incorporate the concepts of family support. Parents must find ways to adapt to young children's needs and to stimulate, enjoy, and protect their children. Support systems, including family and friends, pediatricians, nurses, clergy, and teachers, provide resources to whom families turn for support in their parenting roles. Parents of children who have special needs from birth find their natural support networks may be overstressed by lack of understanding of the problem and by fear and reluctance to accept additional burdens.

Given both the potential strengths and potential limitations of families' natural support networks, the health, education, developmental disabilities, mental health, and related systems must collaborate to develop comprehensive services that build and enhance that which is available in the natural ecology, both within the family's support network and in the existing community. Dokecki and Heflinger (1989) remind state planners to pose four general questions about program services: "Does the implementation process (1) enhance the community of the children and their families, (2) strengthen the families, (3) enable the parents to do their jobs well, and (4) enhance the individual development and protect the rights of all the individual members of the families?" (p. 63).

With these premises, governing entities are examining the types of services that are helpful to families of children with special needs, keeping in mind family differences and naturally available supports. Service needs will vary based on the individual differences and interests among families and on the parameters of the child's condition itself. Examples of such services might include screening, evaluation, and intervention services; genetic counseling; financial counseling; parent support groups; transportation; legal services;

parent training; sibling support groups; day care; respite care; homemaking services; assistance in obtaining equipment; and training in the use of equipment. Specific services such as these might readily be seen as part of an array of services within the family component of a comprehensive service system. History, local resources, and other factors in the ecology will influence which agency or provider sponsors these services and how they are coordinated.

In addition to these types of services, an especially important category of services for families is one that can be called "enabling services"—those services that make it possible for families to access and use needed resources. Identification and referral systems (e.g., single point of entry) and case (care) management systems are examples of such enabling services. Frequently, these services are the least well developed by agencies and are poorly coordinated across agencies. Enabling services should be planned and implemented by a collaborative and interagency approach.

Implications for State System Design

To help children and families reap the full benefits of high-quality local services, governing entities are undertaking a set of supportive and complementary activities on the state level. Within this broader context, various responsibilities are being planned and implemented. For example, key, broad, and overarching state responsibility by the Departments of Public Education and others is needed through the articulation of a "vision" for services for all of the state's children with special needs and their families. There also is need to develop statewide policies and to operate those through humane, caring, and accountable procedures that facilitate parent-professional partnerships, interagency coordination, and quality services. Additionally, there is a need for systems of personnel development that address inservice and preservice training, recruitment, high professional standards, retention practices, and problems of burnout. A design for state systems must consider eligibility criteria, availability of model/demonstration/innovative programs, methods for distributing funds, evaluation of and reporting on status and effectiveness of services, cultural diversity, and urban-rural factors.

All of these concerns were reflected in comments voiced by parents and professionals at a national meeting on P.L. 99–457 sponsored by the U.S. Department of Education's Office of Special Education and Rehabilitative Services and held in Washington, D. C., on November 19, 1986. Figure 3 provides a summary of these concerns.

CHANGE VIA COLLABORATIVE PLANNING AND IMPLEMENTATION

P.L. 99–457 calls for a number of systemic changes in personnel, organizations, policies, and procedures which will require communication, time, effort, and resources. Bartel (1977) suggests that bringing about changes through collaboration involves a relationship between two or more agencies/parties that share goals, commitments, resources, decision-making, and evaluation. There must be a common goal for meeting the needs of children and families that fits within the general goals of agencies. There must be a shared commitment and investment of resources. And there must be shared decision-making and leadership, wherein each agency/party retains control of its own contributions and does not experience any loss of power to another agency/party.

BUILDING AN AGENDA FOR CHANGE

An agenda for systemic change at local, regional, and statewide levels should be built as a collaborative, interdependent activity. The policy questions posed in Figure 4 are intended to help planners conceptualize clear goals, strategy options, resource contributions, participatory planning mechanisms, quality indicators, implementation activities, and evaluation plans.

TIMETABLE

The timetables specified in P.L. 99–457 constitute a major factor that Departments of Public Education must deal with in building their agendas for policy change. The Part H program has a five-year timetable for conceptualizing, enacting, and implementing a service system for eligible infants and toddlers and their families. Phases in that timetable are as follows:

Years One and Two
Governor establishes the Interagency Coordinating Council (ICC). Governor identifies lead agency. State undertakes planning, development, and implementation activities.

Year Three
State mobilizes support and adopts a policy (e.g., statute, governor's order, regulations, directives by the lead agency) which incorporates the minimum 14 components of a statewide system.

Year Four
State installs multidisciplinary assessments, individualized family service plans, case management, and other components of the statewide system.

Year Five
State makes available appropriate early intervention services to all eligible children and families.

The Section 619 program on preschoolers (ages three through five) also specifies a five-year schedule that differs for states based on current preschool services. A number of states currently do not have preschool special education mandates or entitlements; these states must implement policies (e.g., statute change with corresponding regulatory and Part B state plan revision, regulation and Part B plan changes, revision in Part B state plan only) for a free appropriate public education by the 1991–92 school year. This policy action calls for the uniform enactment and implementation of individual education

FIGURE 4

BUILDING AN AGENDA FOR COORDINATED SERVICES: POLICY QUESTIONS AND CHOICES

1. What are the state's needs for services to young children with special needs and their families? Are the needs clear, and is there agreement on them?

2. What is the philosophy toward early intervention (childhood) services? Does the Department of Public Education and/or lead agency have an articulated and written philosophy statement that is available publicly? Is the philosophy based on developmental, educational, family, or custodial values and beliefs?

3. What is the shared vision of services to young children with special needs? Is there a global statement of short-term purposes and long-term expectations for these programs?

4. What is the state's history with early childhood services? Are there entitlements through legislation or other policy mechanisms? Are there existing policies, procedures, and resources to implement the program?

5. Who will be served? Is there a clear definition—families, children, families and children? Persons with disabilities, developmental delays, and at-risk conditions?

6. How are persons to be served entered into the service system? Can zero-reject access become a reality by reaching underserved and unreached populations? Are there single or multiple community-based entry points?

7. What services will be provided? Will there be a full array of coordinated and comprehensive services involving multiple agencies and disciplines? Will services be culturally relevant, sensitive, and appropriate for urban, rural, and remote areas? Are services child-centered or family-centered?

8. Where will the services be provided—in public or private facilities, such as neonatal intensive care units, hospitals, centers, public schools? Will they be provided in homes of families?

9. How will services be put together and with what intensity and frequency?

10. Who will provide services—personnel with high qualifications and certification and/or licensure?

11. What standards of program quality will be applied?

12. Who pays for what? Will a free appropriate public education be available for three-through five-year-olds while fees may be charged for some services to zero through two-year-olds? How will diverse funding streams be orchestrated and used?

13. Who has authority to "make things happen" for young children and families, to evaluate the outcomes, and to monitor quality?

14. How will a coordinating structure be built that incorporates local, regional, and state-level participation and facilitation of services? How will interagency agreements be used?

15. How will due process and procedural safeguards be employed?

programs, assessment, due process and procedural safeguards, and the least restrictive environment (LRE).

A majority of the states that currently do administer entitlements for free appropriate public education, policies may need to be streamlined or broadened within the same time frame to meet federal standards.

Given an agenda and a timetable for change, states can engage in collaborative planning and policy development for the implementation of new and improved service systems. The process of policy analysis and development allows states to clarify goals, formulate proposals, mobilize support, select the best policy among a number of options, enact it, carry out the policy within a context of political feasibility, and evaluate the policy. They also can identify consequences and barriers.

TWO PLANNING STRATEGIES

For governing entities, a blend of two planning strategies—forward mapping and backward mapping—should be utilized. Forward mapping, or the "top-down" approach, allows for the conceptualization, development, and implementation of those responsibilities that pertain to a broad statewide system design perspective. With this strategy, state leadership is provided on the global policy dimensions of finance, governance, monitoring, program rules/standards/regulations, quality assurance and enforcement, technical assistance and training for local programs, and monitoring and reporting. Also involved in policymaking are a host of intense relations with groups such as the U.S. Department of Education, governor and staff, State Board of Education, courts, legislature, other federal and state constituencies, professional associations, and parents. Communication is vital to building mutual respect and a sense of common mission among the various players and insuring that the policy gets implemented "at the bottom" in local communities.

Backward mapping, or the "bottom-up" approach, provides a crucial strand in the web of collaborative service system planning. It is at the community service-delivery level that services are brought into being. At the community level, child-find and identification activities unfurl, screening and assessment occur, referrals are made, individualized family service plans and/or individual education programs are written, case managers assigned where appropriate, placement decisions are made, interventions are planned and implemented for children and families, payment for services is handled, and program evaluation is undertaken. This planning process then "bubbles up" the policy ladder, helping to reinforce or sustain policy in action.

P.L. 99–457 has sparked the creative use of these two planning endeavors across the country. For example, one state is developing a planning guide on collaborative services that begins with an examination of the obstacle course parents face when trying to obtain multiple services for their children. The document recommends an alternative pathway for services via an interagency process that includes multidisciplinary evaluation, eligibility mapping, funding, and access to services from multiple sites (programs). Approximately ten other entities are creating information bases for program collaboration, bridging local and statewide data needs.

In another jurisdiction, the lead agency has developed a P.L. 99–457 planning matrix which takes into account three primary systems-planning dimensions — philosophical base (e.g., family-focused, individualized, community-based); methods (e.g., policy development, technical assistance and training, pilot projects, program enhancement); and system components (e.g., child identification, definitions, funding). Another governing entity is examining closely its outcomes from the former P.L. 98–199 Early Childhood State Plan Grant in terms of needs assessment, options available to meet service needs, and guiding principles that can help determine eligibility. Fifteen jurisdictions have chosen a slightly different path: they have decided to focus their collaborative planning on the period from birth through age five instead of segmenting their planning activities into two periods: zero through two and three through five. One state is designing a "Blueprint for Action" that includes guidance for parents and professionals. And, in several jurisdictions, local and/or regional interagency planning groups have been formed to interrelate forward- and backward-mapping strategies of policy development.

A number of resource groups have been formed to assist states and other entities in their planning and implementation efforts. The NEC*TAS collaborative system draws on the expertise of six organizations: The Frank Porter Graham Child Development Center of UNC at Chapel Hill, which serves as coordinating office; the National Association of State Directors of Special Education; the National Center for Clinical Infant Programs; the National Network of Parent Centers, Inc.; the Georgetown University Child Development Center; and the Department of Special Education, University of Hawaii at Manoa. Both NEC*TAS and the federally sponsored Regional Resource Center (RRC) program are available to work with all states, the District of Columbia, territories, and the BIA. The American Association of University Affiliated Programs project on early intervention has developed a guide, "Mapping the Future for Children with Special Needs: P.L. 99–457." Two special research institutes at the University of North Carolina have been established to assist with the Part H Program — one in policy development and one in personnel preparation. One research institute on preschool mainstreaming has been created at the University of Pittsburgh. These and other organizations are available to help states. A list of such organizations can be obtained from the author.

CLOSING

P.L. 99–457 provides both opportunities and challenges to Departments of Public Education. Departments of education must find productive and innovative ways to interact with parents, legislators, boards of education, professionals, other Part H lead agencies, and other state and private agencies. They must provide humane responses to the complex and costly future facing services for young children with special needs and their families. No single group, discipline, or perspective has the capability to provide all of these services. Simply put, what can America expect? What concrete benefits, successes, and improvements will our children, families, and society reap by 1991–92 through the planning and implementation activities of P.L. 99–457? How many comprehensive early intervention systems and preschool services with free appropriate public education will be in place, institutionalized, and routinized no later than the beginning of the fifth year of a state's participation?

The Departments of Public Education have the expertise to influence the quality of policies and practices for infants, toddlers, preschoolers, and their families. To do so effectively, departments must provide leadership to:

1. build and support working, participatory relationships among numerous groups, agencies, politicians, and constituencies, such as parents and schools; turf issues as by-products of consensus-building;

2. celebrate successes and deal openly and constructively with conflicts and schools;

3. advocate and foster long-term public awareness and support, and commitment for early childhood services;

4. provide guidance in the development of a coordinated master plan that orchestrates a number of key components from other state early childhood initiatives, so that universal, sufficient, and predictable services can be developed;

5. build systemic bridges based on standards of quality between local and statewide activities;

6. ensure that the state uses "the best of what we know" from research, development, and sound practices;

7. encourage creative, efficient, and continuous ways to finance these services, since the federal government does not intend to provide all necessary funding;

8. promote the development of qualified personnel needed to operate these programs using both preservice and in-service mechanisms.

The report *Children in Need* (1987) reminds us that "America must become a land of opportunity—for every child." Quality services must not be seen as an expense but rather as an investment in the future of our nation. To maximize this investment, partnerships must be formed, collaborative activities undertaken, and policies developed, enacted, and implemented.

P.L. 99–457 is a vital step in addressing the future of our children and families. As Weiner and Koppelman (1987) observe, "P.L. 99–457 can be the springboard to reform. The choice—and the responsibility—is left to the states."

REFERENCES

Bartel, J. *The Collaborative Process for Service Integration: Final Report.* Chapel Hill, N.C.: Developmental Disabilities/Technical Assistance System (DD/TAS), 1977.

Berrueta-Clement, J., L. Schweinhart, W. Barnett, A. Epstein, and D. Weikart (eds.). *Changed Lives: The Effects of the Perry Preschool Program on Youths Through Age 19.* Ypsilanti, Mich.: High/Scope Press, 1984.

Carolina Policy Studies Program. *A Survey of Current Status on Implementation of Part H.* Chapel Hill, N.C., April 1988.

Committee on Economic Development (CED). *Children in Need: InvestmentStrategies for the Educationally Disadvantaged.* 1987.

Dokecki, P., and C. Heflinger. "Strengthening Families of Young Children with Handicapping Conditions: Mapping Backward from the 'Street Level.'" In *Policy Implementation and P.L. 99–457: Planning for Young Children with Special Needs,* edited by J. J. Gallagher, P. L. Trohanis, and R. M. Clifford. Baltimore: Paul H. Brookes, 1989.

Fineblum Associates. *Interim Results of Survey of Part H ICCs.* Randolph, N.J.: Fineblum Educational Services, 1988.

Fraas, C. *Preschool Programs for the Education of Handicapped Children: Background Issues and Federal Policy Options* (Report No. 86SSEPW). Washington, D.C.: Congressional Research Service of the Library of Congress, 1986.

Grubb, W. *Young Children Face the States: Issues and Options for Early Childhood Programs.* Madison, Wis.: Center for Policy Research in Education, 1987.

Harbin, G., J. Gallagher, and T. Lillie. *States' Progress Related to Fourteen Components of P.L. 99–457, Part H.* Chapel Hill, N.C.: Carolina Policy Studies Program, 1989.

Magrab, P., and J. Elder. *Planning Services to Handicapped Persons.* Baltimore: Paul H. Brookes, 1979.

National Association of State Directors of Special Education (NASDSE). *A Report on Year One Activities Under Part H Program.* Washington, D.C., March 1988.

National Center for Clinical Infant Programs (NCCIP). *Infants Can't Wait.* Washington, D.C.: 1986.

OSERS. Minutes from Meeting of OSERS Task Force on Early Childhood Futures, Washington, D.C., January 1986.

Simeonsson, R., D. Cooper, and A. Scheiner. "A Review and Analysis of the Effectiveness of Early Intervention Programs." *Pediatrics* 69 (1982): 635–641.

Trohanis, P., and P. Magrab. "Health-Education Collaboration for Children 0–5." In *Developmental Handicaps: Prevention and Treatment IV,* edited by E. Eklund and A. Crocker. Silver Spring, Maryland: AAUAP, 1987.

U.S. Congress.—House. Congressman Steven Bartlett speaking for the EHA Amendments of 1986, H.R. 5520, 99th Cong. 2nd sess., September 22, 1986, *Congressional Record* (pp. H7893–7912).

U.S. Congress: House of Representatives *Report 99–860 on the EHA Amendments of 1986,* September 22, 1986.

Weiner, R., and J. Koppelman. *From Birth to 5: Serving the Youngest Handicapped Children.* Alexandria, Va.: Capitol Publications, Inc., 1987.

1988 CCSSO SUMMER INSTITUTE
Summary and Discussion

I. INTRODUCTION

The Council of Chief State School Officers (CCSSO) held its 1988 Summer Institute, "Early Childhood and Parent Education—Success for Those At Risk," to help Council members better understand the conditions which at-risk young children and their families face, what recent research says about the needs of young children and their families, and how current best practice guides the design and operation of programs to assist them.

This chapter attempts to provide the reader with a summary of the discussions held throughout the CCSSO Summer Institute in Boston. Central to those discussions are the 12 commissioned papers which were presented by the main speakers and are found as chapters in this book. The question-and-answer periods which followed each presentation complemented the prepared remarks and allowed chief state school officers to pursue particular points of interest.

Two panels added examples of state activities to the conversation—"State Interagency Cooperation for At-Risk Preschoolers and Their Families" and "State Education Agency Initiatives." The first panel included Stephen Heintz, Connecticut's Commissioner of Income Maintenance, and Gerald Tirozzi and Robert Bartman, chief state school officers of Connecticut and Missouri, respectively. The second panel's members were Betty Castor, chief of the Florida Department of Education; Nancy Honig, president of the Quality Education Project; Bill Honig, California's chief state school officer; and Tom Schultz, staff director for the National Association of State Boards of Education's Task Force for Early Childhood Education. The presentations by the panelists and the accompanying discussions provided additional texture to the substantive consideration of early childhood and parenting education.

This chapter draws from all of these conversations. In an attempt to present the many discussions in an accessible and useful fashion, this chapter is organized along the lines of the Summer Institute itself. After this introduction is a section called Early Intervention, which collects the various comments describing the reasons for focusing on young children. The third section looks at young children at risk and explains what the risks are and how they affect children. The fourth and fifth sections examine questions of program design and implementation. The program design discussion includes issues of curriculum, family education and support, assessment and standards, and comprehensive services. The delivery system, training, staffing, and collaboration are considered as parts of program implementation. The final section, The Role of the States, is a collection of recommendations made to the chief state school officers regarding the provision of early childhood and family services.

II. EARLY INTERVENTION

"Throughout the land there is a common perception, with sound basis, that early intervention makes a difference."

SHARON LYNN KAGAN

Several speakers at the CCSSO Summer Institute cited research findings from a number of sources, including the Perry Preschool Project, the Consortium for Longitudinal Studies, and the Brookline Early Education Project, that early intervention in the form of high-quality child development and family support programs provides critical assistance to disadvantaged children for their later success in school. Speakers noted the wide variety of national organizations, such as the National Governors' Association and the Committee for Economic Development, that call for early intervention into the lives of at-risk children and their families. Summer Institute participants were unanimous in their support for such intervention. The discussions were centered not on the question, "Should early childhood and family services be provided?", but rather on that of "How might these services be provided most effectively?"

Sharon Lynn Kagan, the keynote speaker, pointed out that there currently exists a spirit of optimism surrounding young children and their families. She noted three "green lights for action" in relation to such services. The first is the agreement by lawmakers at all levels and across the political spectrum on the importance of investing in young children and their education. "Elected officials who just two or three years ago would not have put their names to a piece of child-care legislation are fashioning their own," she wrote. Barbara Bowman agreed, noting that "the success of early intervention has led to its incorporation into public policy."

Ed Zigler and Pamela Ennis cited a variety of research explaining the dramatic increase in the demand for child-care programs. They argued that the driving force behind the massive entrance of women into the labor force is economic—to provide or supplement family income. They explained that "this is a response to two major changes: 1) the radical alteration of the American family as a consequence of recent increases in divorce and never-married parenthood, and 2) the decline in median family income." Sheldon White added his agreement about the growing emphasis on the provision of early childhood and family services when he said, "[T]he impulses of the present: the needs for child care, women working, problems and crises among poor kids . . . are so serious that we as a country are going to have to move in that direction. I think it's really going to happen. I don't think it is going to turn back."

Ann Mitchell pointed out that the new wave of public school programs for young children seemed to be driven by three forces: the concern in the education reform movement about children's "school readiness and school success," particularly for disadvantaged children; the "increased attention to the positive findings of longitudinal studies of early childhood programs; and "the dramatic increases in labor force participation of mothers." She qualified this enthusiasm, however, noting, "While dramatic statistics are great for legislative speechmaking, the concern for child care appeared to be mainly rhetorical, since only four of the new state-legislated programs (MA, VT, NJ, FL) clearly permit services for the full working day."

Kagan's second green light had to do with the improved professional standing of the field of early childhood education. She suggested that "the early childhood field is professionalizing itself" through agreement about and codification of standards of program quality. She cited research that has conceptualized quality according to structural, dynamic, and contextual features. "Practitioners agree that quality is intimately tied to three major variables: 1) the nature of the relationship between the adults and the child . . .; 2) the nature of the instructional program and the environment . . .; and 3) the nature of the relationship between parents and caregivers or teacher." In her chapter, she provides examples of appropriate questions for each of the three variables. Several speakers referred to the effort to create standards for developmentally appropriate practice as an important step forward. Constructing a unified vision of standards, Kagan noted, "suggests that quality exists in settings irrespective of auspices—Head Start; public, private, and for-profit child-care centers; or the public school . . . ."

The potential for institutional change was the third green light. Increased—though limited—interest by corporations, growing support from foundations, new efforts toward collaboration by agencies in the delivery of human services, restructured schools which provide teachers more professional autonomy, and active involvement by national education organizations—all directed toward changing the traditional approach to children and families—were cited by several speakers as examples of the current desire for institutional change.

Despite the optimism Kagan noted, there remain several cautions and concerns—"yellow lights," as she continued the metaphor—about progress in the early childhood field. She described three cautions. First, rapid expansion of early childhood and family services have in some instances led to lowered standards of quality—"Data must be used more diligently." Second, she pointed out that programs are implemented with little flexibility and without adequately considering the scheduling needs of parents—"Rather than crafting a perfect model program, alternatives need to be designed so that families have both inputs and options." Third, she said that simple expansion of the numbers of slots without improving the infrastructure of early education creates problems—"The basic non-system of child care and early education is dysfunctional. Adding on to it, without considering structural alternatives, festers acrimonious situations."

Bowman added that while early intervention is essential, it is not sufficient. "Poor children who receive a quality early childhood program achieve better than their peers who do not, but not as well as middle-class children." She continued, explaining that problems such as racism, sexism, lack of jobs, inadequate health resources, drugs, and poor schools are more than early intervention programs can compensate for, yet, "On the other hand, early intervention programs can be effective adjuncts to public policies designed to address these issues." She argued for providing comprehensive services along the lines of the Head Start model.

In her chapter Bowman spells out what she believes effective intervention programs should look like. "In order to be effective, intervention programs must provide a match between the risks to which the child is exposed and the intensity and breadth of the intervention. Interventions that only include classroom educational programs are usually insufficient for children at risk. Poor children may need health, nutrition, and psychological services; young children with disabilities need a wide range of services as well as specific therapies." She underscored the point that parents of both groups of children need support and involvement and that single-purpose services are generally inadequate for high-risk populations.

III. YOUNG CHILDREN AT RISK

"[Children at risk] merit special attention since their school failure has been called the time bomb of the twenty-first century . . . a potential social and economic disaster for the next generation."

BARBARA BOWMAN

In her analysis of who is at risk of school failure and why, Barbara Bowman explained that at-risk children can generally be grouped into two categories. The first group consists of children with established biological disabilities, including those who have sensory deficits (e.g., deafness or blindness), those who have chromosomal disorders (e.g., Down syndrome), or children with malformations (e.g., spina bifida). The second category of children at risk to school success includes those at statistical risk for biological and/or psychological/social functioning. This means that they are at risk because they are members of a group that has a higher incidence of school failure than what is considered average. Here Bowman included children who experience biological stress caused by environmental hazards (e.g., low birth weight/short-gestational-age infants, children exposed to addictive drugs during the mother's pregnancy, or those exposed to lead and other noxious materials). Frequently these children experience developmental delays and psychological/social difficulties.

By far the largest group of children at risk are not those experiencing biological difficulties, but rather, according to Bowman, those children made vulnerable because of poverty, cultural style, or prejudice and discrimination. She explained that "part of their risk stems from poverty and affects all poor children. However, more [i.e., a larger percentage of] minority children are reared in low-income families than are white ones. Second, some black and brown minorities have cultural styles that conflict with the school culture, making school adjustment more difficult. And, of course, prejudice and discrimination alienate many of these children from school." Bowman addressed the concept of how poverty exacerbates daily-life stresses and how such stress can affect children's ability to succeed in school. Several of the Summer Institute speakers referred to the Committee on Economic Development's (CED) book, *Children in Need*, in which it is noted that students in low-income families are three times more likely to become dropouts than are students from families with high incomes. CED further explains that schools with high concentrations of low-income students have significantly higher dropout rates than those schools with fewer low-income students.

"Minority children find success in school so difficult [to achieve] because their cultural style is antithetical to that of the school," Bowman noted. She explained that culture groups teach children particular styles of relating, of physical and interpersonal environments, and of categorizing people and things. When schools operate with other cultural assumptions (e.g., mainstream, white culture) as they usually do, then many minority children are placed at a disadvantage to learning. This disadvantage is increased even more when children must face prejudice and discrimination and, as Bowman added, just as important, the expectation of it.

Lily Wong Fillmore emphasized the importance of a proper fit between home and school, particularly for minority-culture young children. She wrote, "[M]ore important than socioeconomic advantage is a compatibility between the values and models of learning promoted in the home and school." She raised the issue of non-English-speaking or limited-English-proficient (LEP) children entering preschool settings where often only English is spoken. She explained that this creates serious problems for LEP preschool children because at that age they can learn English very easily. The problem confronting these children is to maintain their mother tongue as they learn English. In settings where only English is spoken they do not become bilingual. They speak English at the expense of their home language because of differential language status and so suffer the loss of the cultural anchor of their home language.

In some instances children who attend such schools learn English exclusively and can no longer speak the language of their parents. When this occurs children are cut off from critical communication with and socialization by their family. In these instances the school has diminished the capacity and role that the family plays in the education of its children. Wong Fillmore told the chiefs, "[T]he danger of loss of family communication is so great that I think we can stand figuring out how to do a better job developing English language skill in the elementary, middle, and secondary school levels. . . . [I]t is too much to risk, allowing children to lose that kind of closeness with the family."

Gloria Rodriguez described how—despite extremely difficult circumstances—she and her sisters blossomed because of the support from their family. She recounted how as an at-risk child herself, her family's support made the cultural difference in her life.

Bowman explained that children at risk frequently face a "cluster of risk factors" in their lives—not merely one problem that might be easily corrected. She noted, "Minority children endure the effects of prejudice and discrimination and are apt to be poor, live in substandard housing, receive poor health care, attend schools with low per-capita expenditures, experience greater family and community stress with violence, drugs, and disease, and be at odds with mainstream values."

These speakers underscored the importance of providing appropriate early childhood and family education and support services for at-risk children and their families.

IV. QUESTIONS OF PROGRAM DESIGN

A. Curriculum

"We face a classic issue. The 200-year-old history of early education shows a recurrent 'dance of death' between ventures in early education and organized schooling."

SHELDON H. WHITE AND DIANE E. BEALS

Much has been written recently relating to early childhood education about the importance of using for young children a curriculum whose content and methods are "developmentally appropriate." The debate about curriculum is actually one that questions both the purpose of pre-kindergarten education as well as the nature of childhood. Kagan framed the first question, "Are preschool programs preparing youngsters for kindergarten and the demands of later academia, or are they preparing children for later life, where motivation, curiosity, and creativity are important skills?"

All the Summer Institute speakers agreed that schooling for very young children should be developmentally appropriate; that is to say, that directed instruction and an overly didactic curriculum should not be imposed or "pushed down" from the traditional elementary school. Some schools press young children into an academic track too early, misinterpreting children's ability to develop rules for language and mathematical thought and using it as justification to teach reading, writing, and arithmetic at increasingly earlier ages.

Education for young children should be something entirely different from traditional schooling, argue the developmentalists. Members of professional organizations, including the National Association for the Education of Young Children, have taken a strong position on this issue. Kagan, in a reference to the work of Lilian Katz, noted that developmentalists contend that an academic emphasis prevents children from developing the "dispositions" they will need later in life—a disposition to learning, toward independence, for self-reliance, etc. Bowman concurred and said that it is unfortunate that pressure for academic achievement may conflict with the development of other important intellectual characteristics—high self-esteem, self-directed learning, and enjoyment of school.

Lawrence Schweinhart was very clear about his support for a developmentally appropriate curriculum. He presented a seven-point definition of quality for child-care programs. His first criterion was "a child-development curriculum approach." He wrote that in such an approach the most important component of quality is the promotion of sound intellectual, social, and physical development through the provision of a supportive environment in which children choose their own learning activities and take responsibility for completing them. He explained that children learn by exploring their environment with all their senses both actively and reflectively.

In a related vein White and Beals wrote, "If schools bring their conventional ways of doing business down to the preschool level, many of the small children will be poorly served." In later discussion, White noted that the "dance of death" performed by schools with programs for young children occurs when schools begin to do with young children what they normally do with older children. Even in well-meaning instances, he pointed out, schools can take effective developmentally-appropriate programs for young children and crush those programs in their "bear hug" attempt to incorporate them into the larger school system. White said to the chiefs, "The dance of death comes about when the schools, honestly seeking to embrace early education, embrace it in a great bear hug, bringing to bear on early education their traditional ways of performing with children. . . . By doing so they gradually obscure the meaning and possibility of early education."

Bowman explained that it is during the early years (the first six to eight years) that children develop the basic structures for learning, and that when forming these structures, they may use as a raw material academic information and skills. But, she quickly added, the acquisition of such knowledge and skills is not an end in itself. She admitted that there is some disagreement about the precise subject matter appropriate for young children but stated, ". . . there is essential agreement that the best pre-primary curriculum should be perceptual, concrete, context bound, and that it build upon the child's prior experience and cultural style, including his/her family language." In her presentation to the chief state school officers, she made this point several times and emphasized, "Inappropriate curriculum is more serious the earlier it occurs. Early intervention programs that do not recognize developmental differences not only shortchange the young child, but they may play a role in some children's negative attitudes about school. This is another instance in which the intervention itself increases the child's risk."

Bill Honig told of California's effort to turn around pressure from both legislators and—surprising to him—teachers, for excluding from kindergarten those children who were not sufficiently adept academically. His reaction was, "Don't change the kid by keeping the kid out; change the program." California is currently redefining what it means by "developmental age-appropriate instruction."

Wong Fillmore agreed. She criticized those who emphasize basic skill development—compensatory preschool—for cultural-minority children. She pointed out, "Minority-group children are children first and foremost." She added that they have the same need as other children to develop their curiosity and explore their physical and social environments. She explained how parents and other caregivers prepare their children for living and learning through the socialization that occurs in the home. She provided striking examples of how three non-mainstream types of U.S. families—black working-class families, Chinese immigrant families, and Mexican families—prepare their children in dramatically different ways and how all three of these ways differ substantially from the preparation the school assumes children have had. She argued that young minority-background children need to be securely anchored in their primary culture when they come in contact with a new one. Resocialization of children in early childhood programs that demean their primary culture can result in serious problems for those children.

Zigler commented that research has shown that the needs of children vary as they become older—the needs of infants and toddlers are quite different from those of preschoolers, who in turn differ from school-age children. He argued that for any child-care system to be viable, it must be developmentally appropriate and so answer the needs of children at each of their developmental stages. He suggested that it is more useful to distinguish among three developmental stages. The first is from birth to about two and a half years; the second includes school-age children. Zigler and Ennis explained, "quality care is always essential, but the particulars that distinguish quality will differ for these three age groups, as determined by the children's developmental needs."

A long and detailed discussion took place among the chiefs concerning the appropriate cut-off age or date for school and kindergarten entry. Several suggested specific dates, while others recommended allowing children to enter preschool programs at a particular age (e.g., age four) at any time during that year. These latter programs would also provide year-round services with flexible days, even though the proponents recognized the likelihood of "tremendous resistance from the agrarian-organized school system."

White and Beals explored the actual development of children. While agreeing that programs for young children should be developmentally appropriate, they pushed hard to better understand how that development occurs and how children learn and grow. They looked back on earlier psychologists' research and compared findings from the 1960s with those of the 1980s. Many developmentalists of the '60s took the work of Swiss psychologist Jean Piaget as virtual gospel, trying to create educational programs in sync with Piaget's developmental stages. More recent research of child learning, according to White and Beals, seems to ". . . turn Piagetian theory sideways: all the logic and stages—a sensorimotor intelligence, a logic of images, and a logic of propositions—seem to be at work all at once and interacting with one another when a child addresses a problem." These two authors said that we need to discover ways of dealing with the multiple intelligences of children.

They argued against a single human intelligence and one grand design of cognitive development and suggested, instead, that biology and society work in an iterative and synthetic fashion. Biology provides an orderly sequence of physical growth, and society builds upon that sequence a set of social "stages"— family, extended family, peers, school, and the complexity of the larger society. "The child builds skills and knowledge in several milieus, and the child experiences not one but several forms of social development in the early years," they pointed out.

B. Family Educational and Support Programs

"Children are not at risk because of their families; they are at risk because of conditions that both they and their families suffer (poverty, deteriorating neighborhoods with crumbling social structures, poor housing, etc.). Public policy for young children must be for both children AND their parents."

ANNE MITCHELL

In her chapter, Kagan notes that there were parenting handbooks written in Europe as early as the seventeenth century. She also points out that parenting education became quite widespread in this country in the 1960s, when it was used as an instrument, supposedly, of social reform. Parenting education was supposed to overcome deficient home environments that were believed to contribute to lower achievement of disadvantaged children. Eventually, but not before causing damage, the idea of deficient—particularly culturally deficient— families has significantly diminished. Kagan wrote that "increasingly criticized over time, this deficit orientation has been replaced by a new vision of parenting education, one that acknowledges the universal challenges of raising children in an increasingly complex society." She noted that current approaches underscore the skills that all parents bring to their parenting responsibilities. Heather Weiss concurred, noting that "rather than assuming family deficits, the [family support and education] programs emphasize family strengths and work to empower parents."

A broad range of programs exist and operate under the rubric of parenting education. The discussion during the Summer Institute called attention to the weakness of more superficial efforts—such as those that provide an occasional speaker for parents of young children or those school-based programs that serve only to inform the parents of decisions already made by school personnel. Instead, the conversations in Boston centered on models where parents are regarded as partners and where parents' knowledge is respected; their strengths and experience serve as cornerstones in the program. These programs should, through peer support and informal networking, created an environment where parents learn from each other as well as from staff. The Institute discussions also broadened from a simple focus on "parent" education to one that emphasizes family support and education. The latter is part of a larger family support movement where a variety of social institutions and agencies offer preventive, family-oriented programs promoting human development.

Programs designed to strengthen parents' childrearing capacities and promote child development—particularly for low-income families—are provided under a number of auspices. There are essentially three kinds of delivery systems for family support and education programs, which parallel child development program sites: home-based, center-based, and school-based programs. Weiss mentioned examples of a number of programs launched during the War on Poverty which offered primarily home-based services to mothers and their children. She described Gordon's Florida Parent Education Program, Gray's Early Training Project, and Levenstein's Mother-Child Program. Perhaps the best known center-based effort was the Perry Preschool Project, which not only provided programs for young children, but included weekly parent support and education through home visits. In this vein, she also included the many community-based programs which remain unevaluated. According to Weiss, a few states have initiated family programs to foster a home environment and parenting skills that would promote school success for the children.

Weiss reported that by the mid-1980s an increasing number of school districts (and a few state departments of education) either had begun operating or were contracting with other community agencies to provide programs for families with children from birth to six years. School-based programs typically stress the importance of strengthening the early learning environment for both the child and the parent as the child's first teacher. The programs sometimes can also become catalysts for parents' personal development. Weiss noted that "a few state programs, for example, Kentucky's Parent and Child Education (PACE) program, and some local districts offering Missouri's Parents as Teachers Program (PAT), are capitalizing on this catalytic effect by adding an adult literacy component and making their programs explicitly two-generational." All three types of programs have the common goal of "promoting the familial conditions and parental competencies and behaviors that contribute to child, maternal, and familial development," according to Weiss. She added that they normally provide similar services and listed five. The programs provide:

1. Information about child development, parenting, and adult development;
2. Feedback and guidance about childrearing issues;
3. Joint problem-solving strategies;
4. Information about and referral to other community agencies; and
5. Reinforcement, encouragement, and emotional support to families with young children.

Robert Bartman described Missouri's Child Development Act, which includes the Parents as Teachers program. Part of the legislation creating this program provides a screening program for infants and toddlers (birth to two years), screening for three- and four-year-olds, and a multi-service program for parents. "The guts of the program are the home visits," said Bartman. Trained parent-outreach workers/teachers are sent out to the homes for parent visits during which home-based training occurs. Group sessions for several parents at a time are held in community centers. Efforts are also made to work with hard-to-reach families (e.g., program workers visit orchards looking for migratory families; others work with the Salvation Army as an effort to reach homeless families). Screening is designed locally but follows minimal state standards and is tied to a range of agencies. Missouri has funded coverage of 30 percent of the birth-to-two-year-old cohort and 50 percent of the age cohort of three-to-four-year-olds. The program is designed to include all children, not targeting at-risk children alone.

Nancy Honig related to the chiefs the efforts of the Quality Education Project (QEP), which she heads. She pointed out that the founders of QEP were all entrepreneurs who had started their own companies; none were educators. QEP's basic assumption is that all parents love their children and will help them succeed in school if shown how to do so. QEP's efforts are targeted at at-risk students through a practical program of parent involvement. Parents sign a contract in their own language pledging themselves to six actions aimed at improving their child's school performance (e.g., parents will read to or be read to by their child for 15 minutes each day). QEP provides language-appropriate manuals for parents, teachers, and administrators to facilitate improvement of interaction among all three. Teachers and administrators visit churches on designated Sundays to explain how parents can assist schools. Several principals were very carefully selected, initially to be leaders in particular districts and then to provide access to the community at large.

Weiss provided a thorough review of recent research on a variety of family support and education programs. She looked back over three decades of family programs and research about them and noted that potential benefits accrue to families, schools, and communities at several interconnected levels when family-oriented interventions are used with high-risk families. She explained that evaluation research suggests four major interconnected benefits. The first is that "carefully developed programs prepare children for school and eventual life success . . . (and) can therefore play an important role in comprehensive strategies for dealing with at-risk children and youth." As a second benefit, family-centered programs ". . . appear to promote better relationships between parents and schools, and have the potential to promote more parent involvement with schools" particularly later when the children enroll in elementary school. Third, these programs ". . . may have two-generational effects," particularly if the programs combine family support and education with efforts directed to parents such as literacy, vocational education/training, or GED services. As to the fourth benefit, Weiss noted that ". . . some evidence suggests that once local programs become established, they seek out partnerships with other community agencies out of a common concern with strengthening families and out of a concern to share the responsibility for creating new, broader approaches to nurturing young children." She provided an example of the last benefit in her description of collaborative local programs in Minnesota.

There seemed to be universal agreement among the Summer Institute speakers regarding both the need for and effective results from programs for at-risk young children that were designed to include familial needs as well. Bowman made clear in her remarks, however, that parent or family education should include three components: child development and parenting information; parent support (i.e., focus on parents as individuals, with resources and social networks provided); and parent empowerment (i.e., promoting confidence and control in their own and their children's lives). She distinguished these three parts very sharply from more traditional parent programs where "the central focus is on educating parents to fit into the school's agenda." She quoted other research that says that family powerlessness, mistrust, confusion, and anger predict poor school orientation. She noted that "helping families cope more effectively with the stresses in their lives is often essential if children are to achieve."

Michael Petit described a variety of uses of television and pamphlets as effective media for public education regarding parent education. Petit provided examples of literature and television spots produced for the state of Maine emphasizing particular aspects of parent education. He recommended better and wider use of public-service announcements as a useful media vehicle.

Zigler perhaps best summed up the issue of an emphasis on family needs. One of his fundamental principles of high-quality child care has to do with a "true partnership" between parents and the children's caretakers. Based on his long experience with Head Start, he restated that ". . . any attempt to reach the 'whole child' must include the family, for the family, not the school, is the major source of a child's values and behaviors."

C. Assessment and Standards

> "[T]he whole question of being able to portray not only standards, but some progress . . . with [an] intelligent methodology the lay person can understand is very important today if we are going to progress in [the] area "of early childhood development."
>
> *Comment by a chief state school officer*

The common thread that ran through the discussion by speakers and chiefs regarding assessment of young children was actually a braided strand. First, many speakers remarked that the current approach of assessing young children with standardized tests is flawed. Second, several people voiced a yearning for a more appropriate device to measure the success of programs and the improvement in children's development. Regarding the latter point, Sheldon White said to the chiefs, "I wish we had the ability to test, on-line, children's conceptions of themselves. . . . The most important function of a preschool is to build a child's conception of himself or herself as a learner."

The interest in improved assessment techniques is driven in large part by the demand—especially by legislators who provide funds—for some sort of measurable indicators of success. Are public funds supporting successful programs and are young children benefiting from their participation in these programs? How do we assess the development of young children? In the effort to screen large numbers of children to determine eligibility for limited slots, many programs use screening tests. Many school districts trying to evaluate their early childhood curriculum use tests to do so. One chief state school officer commented, ". . . we've created our own monster because nearly every state [represented] in this room is doing a lot more testing than it was doing five years ago. We did that in reaction to policymakers and parents wanting to know how their schools are doing, and now that we're doing it, we're being told it is really not the thing to do with really young people."

Barbara Bowman was very critical of many current efforts to assess young children. She stressed that the major developmental task of young children is the building of cognitive structures. She maintained that it is very difficult to assess these structures ". . . by just sampling a small amount of information and a limited number of skills because developmental change is not dependent on a specific body of information or set of skills." She said that young children do not develop evenly over several years or over 12 months and that sampling their capabilities at a specific point in time is not necessarily predictive of future rates of development. She explained that because a child is slow at a given moment, it does not mean that she or he will not change within the year.

In response to a question by a chief about how to deal with pressure from state legislators for testing of young children, Bowman offered a different strategy. She said, "Maybe what we ought to do is tell the straight story about what tests are. I think that might be a more useful design than trying to get the early childhood program to fit the test. Probably the most important thing we could get across is that test results mirror social class. The only thing that test results tell you, practically speaking, is where you are in the social class hierarchy, because middle-class kids score high and poor kids score low . . . . The test doesn't provide any kind of accountability . . . . You all know that as well as I do."

She suggested approaching legislators with the argument that standards should be set by professional organizations, much like the medical and legal professions. She said to let legislators know "the reason you have to do it that way is because the professional organizations say so." This, she said, is particularly important in the case of young children because so much of what they do and need is counter-intuitive to adult learning. One strategy she recommended is to ask the legislators to recall when they last tried to lecture to their three- or four-year-old grandchild and how it did not work.

The screening of children with tests and the evaluation of curriculum with tests are also frequently invalid in the case of young children, according to Bowman. When teachers and parents believe that screening tests are diagnostic and then treat children on the basis of the results, she noted, their expectations can become self-fulfilling prophecies. She emphasized that "inappropriate intervention may be more harmful than no intervention" in those instances. When tests are used to evaluate early childhood curriculum, ". . . the developmentally appropriate curriculum is distorted into mindless memorization and decontextualized experiences," she contended. Programs become "biased toward testable content" instead of the developmental needs of young children and their families when judged solely on the basis of test scores.

Bill Honig, in his description of California's early childhood efforts, said, "We really took a strong stand that no children should be prevented from coming into a kindergarten because they cannot pass a test. That's ridiculous." He emphasized that California was against retaining young children for one year. He noted that several districts in his state "red-shirt" children and retain them in grade, but added that the research is clear on the issue and that it is a harmful practice.

When Bowman was asked by a chief what the current research said about how assessment instruments for young children should be designed, she responded with a suggestion for action by the chief state school officers. She first noted that the research base "has been severely compromised over the last 10 years." She lamented that there has been essentially no new major research on how to assess programs for young children. She suggested that chiefs take a leading role in stimulating and supporting the development of more carefully designed assessment methods for young children.

Schweinhart cited the efforts by the National Association for the Education of Young Children and the National Association of Early Childhood Specialists in State Departments of Education to craft developmentally appropriate evaluation procedures as positive moves in the correct direction. He argued for "valid, reliable, and developmentally appropriate observation procedures, ratings and tests" that will ". . . help early childhood teachers make decisions about a program's quality and how well it enhances children's development."

D. Comprehensive Services

"The child-care system must be committed to the optimal development of the child across the entire range of human development. The child-care system must be concerned with the development of the 'whole child'—with the children's social, emotional, and physical development, as well as with their intellectual development."

EDWARD ZIGLER AND PAMELA ENNIS

In his response to questions about difficulties in fusing Head Start and schools, Zigler noted that schools need to take an approach to young children that includes the provision of a comprehensive range of services. He called on schools as they provide services to young children to ". . . get out of the business of education. Call it education if you want—that makes breakfast programs, noon lunches, etc., part of human development. . . . You're not just there being linked with a cog in a system; you're dealing with the whole child [who is] going through some stages. There are right programs."

White and Beals cited substantial evidence that shows that programs for disadvantaged children, to be effective, must reach beyond conventional professional boundaries. Their review of reports of favorable preschool effects not only shows positive developmental effects for disadvantaged children but reports wider success where programs depart from conventional preschooling and deal with health, family, and social services.

In her examination of family education and support programs, Heather Weiss also pointed to the need for the provision of comprehensive services. She reviewed the experience of more mature school-based family support programs and found that in many cases ". . . the school system will need to call on other resources in the community and create partnerships with other agencies in order to serve at-risk families with young children." She called on states, as they plan new initiatives for family education and support, to consider how they might facilitate coordination and co-programming with health, social services, and other agencies in the effort to assist at-risk families.

Citing a cluster of risk factors that at-risk children and their families face, Bowman added her voice in calling for services of a comprehensive nature. She commented that single-purpose services are not adequate and cited the success of Head Start and its links with ". . . economic development, adult education, political education, health, social, and nutritional services." She added that other programs have been successful with at-risk children and their families where they have combined welfare reform, job training and subsidized day care, Medicaid, pre- and post-natal health care, early infant screening, and literacy programs.

Anne Mitchell, in her description of the Bank Street/Wellesley study of preschool education programs, pointed to the need for a comprehensive approach to services for young at-risk children and their families. She noted that a comprehensive prekindergarten program provides necessary services in addition to those considered strictly educational. She listed four essential types of services necessary for a program to be considered comprehensive. They include health services (e.g., screening for delays; examination and health services given by a doctor, nurse or dentist); social services (e.g., referrals, assistance to obtain services usually provided by a social worker); nutrition services (e.g., providing children with meals and snacks to ensure that they receive the major portion of their nutritional requirements during program hours); and parent services (e.g., assisting parents to be better caregivers and to develop themselves as individuals). She added transportation as a critical support service without which many children would have access to few, if any, services.

V. QUESTIONS OF PROGRAM IMPLEMENTATION

A. Delivery System

"Far from being an organized system, the nation's [non-school-based] child-care supply beyond children's homes and families is a rich mixture of caregivers' homes, nursery schools, and centers that are church-based, non-profit and for-profit, funded and unfunded."

LAWRENCE SCHWEINHART

A central structural question regarding the provision of early childhood and family services has to do with where these services are housed. Who should provide services under what sort of delivery system? What currently exists is not a planned, national early childhood system, but a system which has evolved over time and includes a wide array of service providers. Anne Mitchell described the current situation as an "early childhood eco-system." A large variety of programs, operating under public, private, or religious auspices, make up this eco-system. Mitchell pointed out, however, that where a program is housed is not an indication of its quality. Kagan agreed with this point of view, saying that programmatically, it does not matter where a program is housed; high-quality programs can be implemented anywhere. She cited data from the Center Accreditation Program showing that ". . . quality programs exist regardless of auspices, and they are achievable when funds come from the state, the city, the federal government, or from parents."

Kagan did explain, however, that start-up costs can be dramatically different among the various providers. She noted that schools do not have to go through lengthy licensing procedures and can more easily attract staff because of higher salaries. Schweinhart added that the strengths of public schools as sites for early childhood and family programs are their professionalism, accountability, and universality. He also cited their higher degree of organizational support and more secure community status. The physical infrastructure for an early childhood system, in other words, is virtually in place.

Yet there remain problems with schools as the physical and administrative sites for a large number of early childhood programs. Bowman pointed out that schools are not accustomed to cooperative planning and integration of their programs with other delivery systems. Administrators and support personnel have little training to work with and understand the needs of preschool-age children. Schweinhart noted that typical public school class size and student/teacher ratio along with the almost exclusive emphasis on education are inappropriate for early childhood programs that require lower ratios and comprehensive services including a flexible and expanded daily schedule. He added that schools perpetuate a narrow middle-class orientation that alienates low-income families and ethnic minority groups. Kagan explained that schools, as a rule, are more bureaucratic, less flexible, and more difficult to change than are other providers.

Zigler and Ennis called for a community-school approach with the school as the local center for all the social services needed by the neighborhood. School buildings, in their vision, would house child care and incorporate family outreach/education programs including post-partum services. The building would serve formal education for 6- to 12-year-olds and provide full-day, high-quality child care for 3- to 5-year-olds along with early morning/late afternoon care for school students and full-time care for all children during vacations. In their chapter, they spell out in greater detail the staffing and other arrangements for this family-oriented, multi-service community school.

When asked about his reaction to schools as sites for early childhood programs, White told the chiefs, "I remain persuaded for a variety of reasons that there is no other place than schools to put early care and education for children and I remain persuaded that the problems of political vulnerability and the problems of difficulty of adapting to it are easier for schools that for hospitals, and certainly for commercial day care . . . . In my view, there is no one else but the schools to do it." White and Beals added that "in the short run, at least, what we are going to have are publicly sponsored preschools providing for some children at risk . . . . At first blush, schools are obvious, cost-effective places for a nationwide set of centers to provide early care and education for the child together with support and training for the family."

Craig Phillips described North Carolina's plan for pilot programs for early childhood centers for three-, four-, and five-year-olds. A six-year plan proposes placing 200,000 three, four-, and five-year-olds in 2,000 learning centers throughout North Carolina. Each learning center could serve 100 children with 20 staff—including a lead teacher, six teachers, six assistants and five support personnel (e.g., parent educators, psychologists, social workers, etc.) and two clerical staff. These learning centers would operate for a full day (7:00 a.m.-6:00 p.m.) and year-round. Current tax proposals could fund the construction of the buildings, and supportive legislation is pending. The plan calls for construction over a six-year implementation period.

Bowman and Kagan, while agreeing that schools will have a much greater role in the provision of early childhood programs, warned against possible segregation of young children. Bowman wrote that new models must be devised and supported to encourage public schools to develop cooperative arrangements with other programs that serve at-risk children. She declared, "Schools can no longer draw sharp divisions between their responsibilities and those of the families and institutions that prepare children for school." Kagan echoed the increased call for targeting services to needy children, but added, "By increasing services without addressing the racial and economic integration of children, we are reinforcing a segregated system of early education."

Bowman told the chiefs that there must be a multiple delivery system. "We are not talking about a single delivery system in most communities . . . we [should] not . . . have to have simply the public sector providing the programs for poor kids because [if we do] we are going to resegregate the kids and that is a disaster. We have to integrate middle-class and poor kids . . . so that the public school does not become simply the repository of last resort for poor kids." Bowman wrote persuasively that the issue is not whether to use the schools as sites for early childhood programs, but instead, how to change the schools so that they can adapt to the particular requirements of young children and their families—and especially those who are at risk.

Kagan wrote that today's early childhood system lacks equity, comparability and equal access. She noted that children from wealthy and middle-class homes (those children who some argue have little need of early childhood services) can purchase slots, while children from low-income families must struggle for the limited number of subsidized slots. She questioned whether the inequity inherent in such a system perpetuates—or, in the long run, sharpens—class imbalances in this country. Zigler and Ennis called for equal access to child care for every child and said that all ethnic and socioeconomic groups should be integrated as fully as possible. Recognizing the special state role in the provision of early childhood services, they called on the federal government to fund research to define "adequate child care" and to subsidize care for the most needy and the handicapped.

Complicated issues of funding were raised in the discussions regarding the delivery system for early childhood and family services. Should services be universally available? If so, can integration be ensured? Should services be targeted? And to whom? Mitchell reported that her survey data showed that about two-thirds of current state prekindergarten programs are targeted for at-risk children (e.g., low-income, limited-English-proficient, and/or school-readiness-deficient).

B.   Training

"From the experience I have had in the field, it is not critical that every single classroom have a B.A./certified teacher. . . . We all know that certification is not necessarily equated with competence."

SHARON LYNN KAGAN

Because the curriculum and methods necessary for early childhood and family programs differ so substantially from programs for older children, it should come as no surprise that the preparation and training of teachers of young children would also differ. All of the Summer Institute speakers who addressed this issue agreed that the central focus of teacher training should be an understanding of what constitutes a developmentally appropriate curriculum and a high-quality early childhood program—and of how to put these concepts into practice with children and families. Schweinhart noted that early childhood teacher certification criteria largely define the context of preservice training but that states vary widely in their certification requirements. He quoted research that found that while 39 states (including the District of Columbia) require specialized certification for kindergarten teachers, only half of the states require specialized early childhood training.

Bowman stressed the importance of in-service training. She contended that training in college, for example, is not sufficient preparation for new teachers to enable them to run high-quality programs, particularly for at-risk children. She told the chiefs, "I think it is unrealistic to expect preservice training to do everything that needs to be done to create a competent teacher—and certainly to create a competent teacher in a community where the children are quite different from the teacher." Instead she called for "teacher centers" in the schools, where teachers could receive help and support when they need it; where they could receive ". . . classroom help . . . not someone lecturing to them at an in-service twice a year . . . but actual help in solving day-to-day classroom problems." She also said there need to be better support systems ". . . for teachers who work with minority groups as well as high-risk youngsters." Kagan supported the development of staff teams where, on a regular basis, help is provided to the teachers in the classroom.

Schweinhart also recommended improved in-service training for teachers. He suggested that in-service training should enable staff to learn about high-quality early childhood development on the job. He said this approach will help novices "get up to speed" and sharpen the quality of teaching by the more experienced staff, but he remained critical of the current practice of in-service training. He wrote about the High/Scope Foundation's model of in-service training as an effective approach and one which could be adopted elsewhere. In his chapter, he spells out in detail the components of such a program. He additionally called for special in-service training for school board members, administrators, and support personnel about what constitutes good early childhood programs. Dwyer pointed to the importance of training teachers to not only provide sound nutritional care to young children and nutrition education for parents, but to recognize the signs and symptoms of undernourishment and malnutrition. In-service training in child development is necessary for educators of school-age children as well, according to White and Beals. They noted parenthetically that educators often do not regard preschool caregivers as fully professional; that school teachers have a tendency to take the playlike atmosphere of preschools and the "whole child" philosophy of early childhood teachers as "symptomatic of good-hearted amateurism."

Lily Wong Fillmore insisted that early childhood teachers of minority-group children need to understand the different models of learning and sets of values that children bring to the school. The teachers must also be aware of and sensitive to the language spoken in the home and have sufficient training to prepare an environment that supports and respects rather than demeans and diminishes the language of the family. At very least, she said, minority-background families need to know what teachers regard as necessary preparation and experiences for school. More importantly, the schools must adjust ". . . the way instruction is organized and presented, the models of teaching used, the structure of learning and social environment of the classroom, and the roles and relations of teachers and students."

Gloria Rodriguez agreed with Wong Fillmore and explained how the Avance program in Texas attempts to incorporate those concerns. She explained that "being an effective parent does not come naturally—one has to learn the skill and have the opportunity to observe proper role models. Parents must feel good about themselves so that they can, in turn, help their children feel good about themselves." Teachers are trained to respect the families and draw from them the strengths present rather than underscore any weakness. The Avance program and the teachers are trained to adapt to the needs of the families, which include language and cultural differences. Rodriguez wrote, "Avance has become an alternative to the current school system that has not worked for a high-risk population."

C. Staffing

"It is probably economically unfeasible to have a college graduate, certified teacher with twenty years' experience as the sole staff in the early childhood centers. We need differential staffing with a teacher and two or three assistant teachers and a couple of aides."

BARBARA BOWMAN

While Summer Institute participants agreed about class size and student-teacher ratios necessary for a high-quality early childhood program, the discussion about staffing patterns to fit those ratios was less clear-cut. Bowman reminded the chiefs that early childhood education is "labor intensive" and that there are "just so many two- and three-year-olds you can talk to at a time." How the adults are arranged to talk with the two- and three-year-olds was the point of discussion. Kagan said that it is critical that a "constellation" or a "cadre" of teachers is developed where a competent instructional leader—one who holds a bachelor's or master's degree in early childhood development—heads a team of people and is available on a regular basis to provide direct support to teachers in the early childhood classroom. She told the chiefs about New York City's Giant Step mode. Its staffing pattern included for every three classrooms an early childhood specialist (master's degree in early childhood development) whose responsibility was to render that ongoing support. The two critical factors were the solid training in early childhood development and the accessibility of this person to classroom staff.

Several of the Summer Institute speakers suggested models of staffing similar to Kagan's description of Giant Step. Zigler and Ennis, for example, proposed that the staff of school-based programs for three- and four-year-olds be headed by a specialist in early childhood education and be assisted by child development associates (CDAs)—certified child caregivers. They noted that the Head Start program makes wide use of caregivers who hold CDA certificates.

Rodriguez added to staff responsibility the requirements of regular home visits to observe (in Avance, they videotape) parent and child interaction as a component of family education. Bowman similarly recommended that staffing patterns facilitate—rather than frustrate as they currently often do—increased interaction with the families of young children and improved communications with other local service providers.

D. Collaboration

"In virtually all cases, no single professional discipline alone remotely possesses the knowledge base necessary to successfully address complex human behavioral problems or dysfunctions, including those among young children. Cooperation among disciplines is essential."

MICHAEL PETIT

If young children—particularly those who face a cluster of risk factors—are to be adequately served along with their families, it is self-evident that the present education system must not only be dramatically changed but substantially aided. Assistance to the state education agency is necessary from other state agencies and non-educational institutions. Collaboration among agencies and organizations which assist at-risk young children and their families is essential if these groups are to be successful.

Several Summer Institute speakers underscored the critical importance of interagency cooperation and collaboration—at both the state and local levels. Kagan noted how complex and difficult collaboration is to achieve in the early childhood field, given fragmentation and turf issues. Nevertheless, she agreed that collaboration is a necessity. She wrote that not only does collaboration yield more coordinated services and better use of resources in the short run, it is also an effective process of generating universal services and a united early childhood community. Barbara Bowman was much more direct. She wrote, "It is only when and if schools can change their tradition of working alone that young children at risk will be prepared for school success."

Michael Petit described in detail several issues related to increased collaboration among state agencies, particularly between the state education agency and its counterparts. He noted six factors that are combining to foster improved cooperation among state agencies: requirements by state law; executive branch initiation; requirement and/or encouragement by federal law; pressure by provider, advocacy and parent groups; wider use of the case-management method; and growing evidence of the effectiveness of agency cooperation.

Two powerful forces for increased state collaboration resulting from federal law are the Education of the Handicapped Act (EHA), Amendments of 1986 (P.L. 99–457) and the Family Support Act of 1988 (P.L. 100–485), known as the welfare reform act. Pascal Trohanis provided a detailed examination of the Education of the Handicapped Act and explained that the systematic changes in organizations, policies, and procedures which this legislation requires will result in new collaboration between and among state agencies. The five-year timetable for the provision of universal, high-quality services for young children from birth to five years with special needs and their families forces increased collaboration. Under this legislation, states are required to have State Interagency Coordinating Councils to assist the lead state agency. Trohanis reported that many state ICCs have formed task forces to examine a wide array of policy issues. Trohanis did note, however, that not all states are meeting the federal time lines for the establishment of ICCs.

Another part of the EHA that drives increased collaboration, according to Trohanis, is the Preschool Incentive Grant, which is designed to assure the provision of services to all handicapped children, ages three to five years. He contended that the oil of additional federal dollars will lubricate greater collaboration because funding is contingent upon the provision of a range of community services which must be coordinate.

A third aspect of the EHA that could push greater collaborative efforts came up in later discussion. One chief asked about the "least restrictive environment" (LRE) requirement in the legislation—the desire to have children in environments and settings that are normalized to the greatest extent possible. Aside from the possible collaborative outcomes of this directive—which does not apply for children from birth to three years—Trohanis added that educational planners should seriously consider the Canadian approach to the notion of least restrictive environments. The Canadians refer to the "most facilitative environments" rather than least restrictive for youngsters and families, and Trohanis expressed the belief that educators should plan programs with the most facilitative environment as the goal.

In his description of the EHA's effect on current state agency relationships, Trohanis made clear that the problems and needs facing those who would provide education for young children with handicapping conditions are largely the same as those for the larger education community—not only to improve interagency collaboration, but "to develop statewide policies and to operate those through humane, caring, and accountable procedures that facilitate parent-professional partnerships and quality services."

Gerry Tirozzi provided a description of the Connecticut education department's unsuccessful attempt to mandate all-day kindergarten. He outlined why he was not successful either at that effort or with a proposal to develop a program for prekindergarten children. He pointed to three major mistakes. First, he said, the education department saw early childhood education as its own platform and agenda. It failed to collaborate effectively with other interested parties. Second, the legislature, though supportive of recent financial increases for schools, had great difficulty with the notion of extending the K-12 traditional realm of education. Recently reduced revenues in the state compounded the problem, with fewer funds available for education generally. The state education agency, according to Tirozzi, had not adequately educated the legislature about the need for early childhood services and the importance of the agency taking a central role in their provision. The third factor was powerful resistance from other agencies who saw the state education agency's move to care for young children as "empire building." The department's failure to consult widely was, according to Tirozzi, largely the cause of this attitude.

Tirozzi recalled that there was a silver lining to the cloud of temporary legislative defeat. Connecticut now has a birth-to-three committee actively reviewing the implementation of the EHA P. L. 99–457. There is a statewide at-risk student committee and the Governor has formed a Human Services Cabinet of which he himself is a member. The General Assembly has also created a children's commission. Despite the initial mistakes, these actions are, to a large degree, the result of the earlier efforts, said Tirozzi.

Betty Castor told Institute participants about Florida's prekindergarten authorization. She explained how in the planning process, the many groups antagonistic to the initial idea of extending preschool services were brought as participants into the development of the program. Florida established a state-wide advisory board that included all political elements in the state. Curriculum guidelines were established early for review by child development advocates, and Child Development Associate (CDA) programs were instituted in community colleges. Funding was carefully plotted out over five years for review by all interested parties. A superintendents' task force was created to overcome strong initial resistance from many local superintendents. Florida also formed a children's coalition made up by half of child advocate groups and major Florida business representatives, thus creating a powerful lobbying group.

Stephen Heintz, Commissioner of Connecticut's Department of Income Maintenance, described both the collaborative efforts within his state and general issues related to the collaboration between welfare and education agencies, including possible outcomes of welfare reform. Heintz stressed the importance for all agencies involved with young children and families to focus on their needs, and to do so in consultation, rather than continuing the practice of narrowly focused and often misdirected missions. He described the efforts within his own agency to move from a "focus on fraud, abuse, eligibility verification, quality control, and getting the checks out" to a "focus on building families and helping people find a path, in a very complicated economic and social environment, out of poverty." He stressed the need for state welfare and education agencies to stop acting independently and to begin working in tandem. Using Connecticut as an example, he told the chiefs that it is necessary for the Commissioner of Human Resources, the chief state school officer, and himself to go up to the state capitol together. He noted that between education and welfare "we have almost half the state budget. If we can start saying to legislators, 'Look, these are the kinds of programs that make sense, that cut across these two big bureaucracies and these two highly funded organiza-tion . . .' That's got to be pretty impressive."

Heintz spent considerable time talking about—what was at the time— pending federal welfare reform legislation. He noted that one of the ironies of welfare reform is that welfare agencies are not going to be able to implement it unless they do so in cooperation with the education agencies. He said that many people will assume that welfare reform simply means, "All right, we're going to change the rules and regulations on how we issue AFDC and food stamps," which he noted is actually only a very minor part of the process. He said that to be successful the welfare agencies need to work with the education community, labor organizations, and the private industry councils funded under the Job Training Partnership Act. Heintz and several chiefs said more thought is necessary regarding provisions in recent state welfare reform acts that trade off short-term gains in the maternal generation (e.g., single mothers are given low-salaried jobs) for real long-term losses intergenerationally "if we do not attend very carefully to the parenting and child-care part of welfare reform."

In addition to bringing up issues of state-level coordination, several Summer Institute speakers addressed local-level coordination. Anne Mitchell reported that fewer than one-third of the states have legislative or regulatory requirements for local-level coordination. She pointed out that the lack of local-level coordination results in increased competition among Head Start, state prekindergarten programs, and other providers for children, staff, and space. Rodriguez explained that Avance has made significant efforts to cooperate with a variety of local service providers to ensure the availability of a comprehensive range of services. Dwyer also called for collaboration at all levels and, while she emphasized nutritional services, called for collaboration by the various education and related providers. Weiss, in her chapter, offers the efforts of Minneapolis/St. Paul to design a comprehensive program for at-risk families as an example of a model approach. Kagan described four components of an effective local collaboration model. She suggested developing joint training across the board for all early childhood providers in the community; drawing up curriculum jointly; conducting cross-site visitations; and having each institution draw up a long-range plan focused on the continuity of service provision.

One Institute participant asked Petit about examples of programs that have successfully overcome the issue of separation of church and state in the delivery of services to children and families and that have merged funds for certain aspects of programs in sectarian institutions. In response, Petit offered Maine's effort as one possibility but stressed the complexity and difficulty of the issue. Maine's human services department "contracted out extensively with religious organizations through corporations that they had set up to provide services to people, and the condition was they would serve everybody." He said that the department had this arrangement with the Catholic Church and other organizations: ". . . they would set up a different organization . . . . They have to have the same equal opportunity creeds and affirmative action plans that everyone else does."

VI. THE ROLE OF THE STATES

"You are the educational leader for your state, not just the public schooling system in your state. . . . No matter what state we live in, the policy challenge facing us all is to create enough programs to satisfy the combined needs for child care and education of all families, regardless of income, focusing first on those families whose needs are greatest."

ANNE MITCHELL

In some fashion, all who spoke at the Summer Institute in Boston offered recommendations to the chief state school officers about what important steps they should take to ensure the availability of high-quality early childhood and family education and support programs, especially for those at risk. Several speakers offered similar counsel regarding next steps. Perhaps the most common call was for chiefs to act as educational leaders in the effort to raise public awareness about the promise of early childhood and family services for those at risk. They should interpret to lawmakers and the general public the definition of high-quality programs and ensure that the state uses the best of what is known from research, development, and sound practice. They should take the lead in defining and implementing quality programs in and beyond school buildings. Schweinhart suggests in this regard that chiefs and their deputies meet with state early childhood specialists to discuss appropriate strategies and share ideas across the states.

A second widely recommended action was for chiefs to guide the development of a coordinated state plan that orchestrates the key components of other state early childhood initiatives. This plan would set into action the design and implementation of comprehensive early childhood and family services. Related to this recommendation was one that called for chiefs to build and support working cross-agency collaborations at the state level. Chiefs should model effective collaboration at the state level and require it at the local level, according to Mitchell. Kagan added that states need to look at the comparability of regulations across systems in order to determine the effect on service delivery.

The fourth recommendation had to do with the recruitment and training of qualified early childhood staff. Chiefs should help build up the supply of trained personnel by supporting teacher-training institutions, providing incentives to potential teachers, and improving preservice and in-service training mechanisms. These mechanisms should include (a) alternate teacher preparation to ensure adequate staffing patterns and (b) training of a sort that prepares teachers who are sensitive to cultural and language differences and who are appropriately trained to teach all children effectively and work with parents.

Several speakers called on the chiefs to encourage creative, efficient, and continuous ways to finance early childhood and family services. As part of this effort, funding regulations need to be re-examined. Administrators need to be freed to use funds creatively, though not indiscriminately, one speaker suggested. It was suggested that states offer more and better technical assistance to localities on a range of early childhood and family issues.

Tom Shultz, noting the report, Right From the Start, by the National Association of State Boards of Education, suggested that chiefs find ways to reshape kindergarten and early-grade experiences for children so that it looks more like good early childhood education in terms of pedagogy, curriculum, and classroom environment. Kagan recommended that in the effort to ensure efficient collaboration, states should consider establishing—where it is absent—a state coordinating office for early childhood and parent services. She said that it must have "resources and clout" to be effective.

VII. CONCLUSION

"It is said . . . that to everything there is a season. Your very presence here indicates that this is the season for early childhood."

Sharon Lynn Kagan

The text of this chapter has tried to capture the rich variety of discussion which occurred during the 1988 CCSSO Summer Institute. Institute participants debated a considerable number of difficult, complex, and frequently controversial policy questions regarding the provision of high-quality early childhood education and related services to young at-risk children and their families.

Two unmistakable conclusions appear from the several days in Boston. First, there is substantial and varied activity throughout the United States at all levels—national, state, and local—regarding the need for educational and related services by young children considered at risk and their families. Much good work is being carried on in this field by dedicated, creative groups and individuals. An exciting array of approaches and programs was discussed during the Summer Institute, lending credence to Kagan's reminder that this is the "season" for early childhood.

The second conclusion, which is also unmistakable, is that the need for these services is great, is real and is immediate. Careful research has made the scope and seriousness of the need for such services alarmingly clear. A substantial— and, unfortunately, growing—proportion of our country's young children are being neglected by a society that can ill-afford such neglect—for reasons of justice, compassion, or even simple self-interest.

History affords few choices in social policy which are so vividly clear. By virtually any measure the provision of high-quality early childhood education and related services for young at-risk children and their families is a national imperative. Chief state school officers across the United States are moving as a group, in coalition with other national organizations, and as individuals in their particular states to assure the provision of these services.

Part 2

CCSSO ANALYSIS

Recommendations for Action

EARLY CHILDHOOD AND FAMILY EDUCATION

Foundations for Success: A Council Policy Statement

CALL FOR ACTION

Our concern is for young children and what society must do to assist them in developing their infinite capacities. Our focus is on the partnership of family, health and other caregivers, and educators who need to help each child develop those capacities. Our challenge is to assure the partnership is in place and prepared to nurture each child from the earliest moments of life.

This statement of our commitment as educators addresses our colleagues who teach; policy makers in localities, states, and the nation; those who provide education and other caring services; and leaders of community, business, and labor. It is a call to come together at a time of profoundly changed and changing family and societal patterns to create new ways of supporting families and assuring that each child's earliest years provide the foundation for a creative life.

THE IMPERATIVE

There is no more essential or more sensitive challenge before us than to create new partnerships and shared responsibilities for the development of young children. No participant can be successful alone in this task, but each has obligations and opportunities. However, this statement focuses on the responsibilities of educators, beginning with the need to help the public understand why early childhood and family education should be strengthened.

Families are the first and most continuous teachers. In the past, children entered the formal education system when it was believed they were ready to leave the constant care of parents and were prepared for an expanded learning environment. During the child's earliest years, the parents' role and the attention of schools existed independent of each other.

The world of children has changed in many ways. The time available to families for nurturing their children has diminished dramatically. Economic pressures on families cause young children to be placed in other caregiving environments much earlier. Further, much more is now known about patterns and periods of early learning and what stimulations and direction are most appropriate.

The dichotomy between nurturing and education has been blurred beyond distinction both because of the unprecedented societal changes affecting the very young and because of our knowledge that good care for young children promotes learning and good learning experiences are caring and nurturing. We know that families never cease being teachers; we also have learned that teachers must consider the total well-being of the children they teach.

Our values and institutions hold that each child should have the opportunity to develop to his or her fullest. That vision remains clear. However, that opportunity is imperiled. Our society must strengthen its commitments and change its services and institutions to address the realities facing our children and families.

These realities for the nearly four million infants born in 1988 are:

- Fifty percent will have mothers entering or re-entering the work force before their babies are one year old;

- Seventy percent will receive some or much of their care outside their homes by the time they are three years old;

- Twenty-five percent will begin their lives already at risk of personal and educational failure because of the poverty and stress in their families; and

- Those at risk economically will have less opportunity to participate in high-quality early childhood programs, thus widening the chasm between the disadvantaged and those more fortunate.

For all children, and especially for the many children in peril, support for both them and their families is essential. Providing this support would not only help individual families but also would be sound national policy because of:

- Inability of children to benefit fully from their education because of poor health or lack of family stability;

- Loss of individual potential when early interventions are not available to children at crucial points in their development or to their families when experiencing distress and dysfunction;

- Cost to society of remediation, special education, welfare services, adjudication, and rehabilitation resulting from a lack of early intervention; and

- Loss of productivity to the work force by family members who cannot work because of the lack of proper child care arrangements.

This call to action is for direct, creative, and expanded assistance to young children and their families. They would benefit directly; we all would gain.

PRINCIPLES

The strategies for our call to action are based on these principles:

- All children, regardless of race, ethnic background, home language, religion, family income, disability, or gender must have equal access to high-quality early childhood programs and services.

- All families must have access to assistance that will help them a) care for and educate their children; and b) develop the skills, knowledge, and attitudes essential for family functioning.

- Early childhood programs must assist each child to develop a full range of fundamental social, emotional, physical, and cognitive abilities.

- The developmental programs of the early childhood years must be extended into and integrated with education at the elementary school level.

- Resources and programs for young children and families must be coordinated to assure availability, effectiveness, and comprehensiveness.

STRATEGIES FOR CHANGE

Health, education, social, economic, and family policy goals must be one and the same for young children. The educational and developmental aspects of such integrated policy should include these strategies.

I

Assuring Universally Available High-Quality Early Childhood Services for All Children, with Concentration of Public Resources on Early Childhood Programs for Children at Risk

The evidence demonstrates that high-quality early childhood programs are dramatically beneficial to young children. It is not as important where programs are available, either under public or private auspices, as whether they are accessible to the families that need them. Parts of a fabric of early childhood education programs already exist; those parts need to be woven together to reach all who need and want to be covered.

We know that children at risk who participate in high-quality early childhood programs will substantially increase their likelihood of success in school. Yet, while families with annual incomes above $20,000 enroll their children in preschool at a rate of 52 percent, the enrollment rate for families with annual incomes below $10,000 is only 29 percent. Our society cannot afford to deny any child the opportunity to participate in a program which will have long-lasting positive benefits, both for that child and for society.

In a fragmented way, public policy already directs that the available and limited public funding for early childhood programs be concentrated on special populations, such as those enrolled in Head Start and programs to reach young disabled children. These efforts need to be blended into an overall policy to help those families most in need.

In 1987, our Council adopted the position that all four-year-old children at risk of later school failure should be guaranteed an opportunity for pre-kindergarten programs through public funding. Ideally, these programs would be available by the age of three. Pre-kindergarten programs should be accompanied by publicly supported child care to assure full-day attention where needed. The providers of pre-kindergarten programs may be multiple—public and private agencies—with the overall governance of public funds under the direction of the appropriate state and local education agencies.

II

Strengthening Capacities of Families

The family is the focal point in fostering and sustaining a child's positive growth and development. The family "curriculum" in the earliest years is more important than the school curriculum. However, increasing numbers of families need assistance in providing experiences which lead to positive development of children.

Developing attitudes, values, and expectations and learning to succeed in school are not separate entities for young children—they are pieces of the total nurturing and care they receive at home and away from home. The results of the best programs for young children are only in part increases in their cognitive skills. The stronger result is in the positive effects on their families. In the long run, this will have a greater impact on a child's life chances than higher school test scores. Many families need help in developing their capacities, including:

- Programs that reach new parents—particularly at the prenatal period through age two—to establish early, supportive partnerships to help their children;

- Support in fulfilling family roles at home, with appropriate strategies such as home-based programs for families of the very young and networking for families of older children;

- Assurances that the patterns and scheduling of formal schooling, once it begins, will be consonant with the experiences that have benefited their children in early childhood programs; and

- Sensitivity to the culture of the family, with full recognition of the desire and ability of families to help their children.

III

Assuring Standards of Quality for Early Childhood Programs

The positive effects of high-quality programs for young children and their families are so strong and consistent as to be powerfully convincing. Public policy must incorporate the best of what we know about caring for and educating young children by requiring high standards of quality.

Children who view themselves as competent, worthwhile individuals are more likely to experience success in life than those who do not. Educators can help children feel worthwhile by providing supportive learning environments that build upon the individual child's strengths and by recognizing the different learning rates and styles of children. Because young children learn best through active manipulation of the environment, concrete experiences, and communicating with peers and adults, programs must be designed to emphasize these elements.

Basically, quality programs require:

- A child development approach that exemplifies what is known about how very young children learn set in an environment uniquely fashioned to their needs for physical, emotional, social, and intellectual growth;

- Staff prepared for the special field of early childhood education and benefiting from networks and supervision that provide constant renewal;

- Adult-child ratios appropriate for the age and needs of the child and meeting standards established in the child development field;

- A length of program day and year and the provision of a continuous learning environment matched to family need; and

- Evaluations, both of programs and of the progress of individual children, that are based on developmental goals and reflect the uniqueness of early childhood education.

Where a child is educated or cared for in a formal arrangement outside the home, minimum standards of safety and program suitability must be required. Even more important, however, are standards of quality set through informed and bold public policy which will lead to success for all children.

IV

*Assuring Broad and Deep Collaboration for
Comprehensive Services to
Young Children and Families*

Initiatives for interagency collaboration on early childhood programs exist in almost every state, either from the impetus of federal programs or state executive directive. States and localities should build upon those initiatives. Interagency and intergovernmental forums should be used to further attract attention and support of the public and policy makers, to establish clear goals and solutions for children's needs, to implement services jointly, and to provide continual evaluation of progress.

Families need more help than ever in connecting to multiple social services. While local, state, and federal resources are available, access to them often is difficult for those families most in need. By working with other resource providers, schools have a unique opportunity to help make these connections. Cooperation must be required in statutory provisions, and funds must be provided to assure it works.

CONCLUSION

Our nation critically needs to strengthen its public commitments to young children and families so that they may adjust to the demands and stresses of changed social and economic conditions.

The Council of Chief State School Officers made a commitment in 1987 to assure each student the full range of opportunities for successful graduation from high school. To fulfill that commitment, the Council called for the establishment of 11 state guarantees for at-risk children and youth, including provision of early childhood and parent education programs. The Council believes the single most important investment to be made in education is the provision of high-quality programs for the nation's youngest children, especially for those who are most at risk and for their families. This investment must be accompanied by strategies for strong standards of quality and the assurance of broad and deep collaboration among agencies at each governmental level and across levels.

Chief state school officers are ready, state by state, and nationwide, to join with families, colleagues, policy makers, and the public to implement these strategies. Our children will bring joy and pride to themselves, their families, and their country only to the extent to which we help them do so. For our society to neglect or shortchange their potential and their opportunity is intolerable. We must act together, now.

A GUIDE FOR STATE ACTION

Early Childhood and Family Education

PURPOSE

A *Guide for State Action: Early Childhood and Family Education* grows out of the recognition of the difficult task facing state education agencies in addressing this new charge. Since the states are at very different stages of implementation of early childhood and family education programs, the Council could not recommend a single approach as if all of the states were proceeding at the same rate. Some states support family education programs or pre-kindergarten programs; other do not. Some have interagency organizations or groups which focus on services for children from birth through age 5; others do not.

The Guide is designed to assist each state as it moves from its current status with regard to early childhood policy by drawing upon the collective experiences of other states. The expectation is that a chief could use this Guide in setting the direction and determining the next actions for implementation of programs in his or her state.

The Guide begins with a list of recommendations addressing five areas for action in support of quality early childhood and family education: the state policy role; national support; coalitions and coordination; program guidelines; and staffing.

The next section presents an overview of the unmet needs of at-risk children ages zero through five and obstacles to the provision of comprehensive and coordinated services as described by the states responding to the CCSSO Study Commission information-collection instrument administered in the spring of 1988. These unmet needs and barriers to comprehensive service provide the framework for this Guide. The following section describes the context within which states are developing programs and cites federal and state initiatives as well as multi-agency efforts. Next, examples are cited from the research literature and experiences of specific states and projects which illustrate how the unmet needs and barriers have been addressed or resolved in other settings and the interagency collaborations and coordinated activities which have resulted. The final section contains policy considerations.

323

Section I
CCSSO ANALYSIS

Recommendations for Action

Finding solutions to the urgent national need for quality early childhood and family education services must be among the highest priorities for national, state, and local decision makers. Now and in the years ahead state policy makers should undertake a number of informed and coordinated actions across agencies to put in place programs and services which meet the needs of children and families. Additionally, they should mobilize new and existing resources in support of these programs and services. If the needs of young at-risk children and their families are to be met, and quality early childhood and family education are to be widely available, substantial changes must be made in policy and practice. This will affect both educators and other service providers.

In recognition of the challenge and the task ahead the Council of Chief State School Officers makes the following recommendations regarding state policy, national support, coalitions and coordination, program guidelines, and staffing.

STATE POLICY ROLE

- States should provide comprehensive early childhood and family education services to at-risk children and their families. These services should be available from the earliest moments of a child's life and should have as their ultimate goal universal access for all children and families.

- Each state should establish a state council to advise the state education agency in planning for delivery of comprehensive early childhood and family education services. Each state should encourage establishment of local councils to advise local education agencies in planning for delivery of such services.

- States should establish standards and regulations to ensure high-quality comprehensive early childhood services, including, but not limited to: developmentally appropriate practices; family involvement and education; appropriate adult-child ratios, facilities, staff training, and credentialing; and optional full-day and full-year schedules.

- States should develop multiple measures for assessing the readiness and development of young children and guard against inappropriate use of assessment instruments for placement and labeling.

- Comprehensive early childhood education services should be funded through existing federal, state, and local resources for child and family services and augmented through new public and private funding.

- States should establish and operate comprehensive early childhood services for their employees as models for other public agencies and the private sector.

NATIONAL SUPPORT

- The federal government should expand to the states resources for support of early childhood education and related child care for children at risk and for family education, with universal access for all children and families as the ultimate goal.

- States should participate in the development of a national clearinghouse on model programs, effective practices, and relevant research. States should develop and maintain a dissemination system of information on the benefits of early childhood services for children, their families, and the community.

- The national education agenda should include resources for the continuation of research on early childhood services.

COALITIONS AND COORDINATION

- Each state should develop an integrated policy and action plan which encompasses the continuum of statewide services and requires collaboration among all agencies providing services to children and families.

- State plans for comprehensive early childhood and family education services should acknowledge, build upon, and enhance successful systems and providers, both non-profit and for-profit.

- States should establish coalitions of educators, human services providers, business leaders, and citizens to assist with securing funding, ensuring access, and providing staff training for the delivery of comprehensive early childhood and parental services.

PROGRAM GUIDELINES

- Comprehensive early childhood programs should contain both child care and developmentally appropriate education components. The programs should offer a continuum of services spanning the needs of children and their families including, but not limited to, health, social services, nutrition, transportation, program facilities, and adult basic education. All programs must also be sensitive to the culture and language of the child and family.

- States should require the integration and extension of the developmental approach and other elements of comprehensive high-quality early childhood services into elementary education.

- States should establish a data collection and monitoring system which, among other things, identifies the needs of young children and promotes the coordination of services for them.

STAFFING

- States should establish standards for differential staffing of early childhood services. These standards should be based on performance competencies as well as training requirements for both professional and paraprofessional staff. Supervision and ongoing training should be provided by qualified staff persons at each site.

- States should establish early childhood staff-training programs on family involvement and education.

Section II
UNMET NEEDS OF AT-RISK CHILDREN
FROM BIRTH THROUGH AGE FIVE

A State Assessment

In the spring of 1988, state education agencies from 50 states, two territories, and the District of Columbia responded to a CCSSO Study Commission information-collection instrument on early childhood education, child care, parental education, and health and social services programs for young children. They reported specifically on the unmet needs of children at risk of later school failure and their families.

There is a strong consensus among states around two broad areas of need for at-risk children from birth to age five:

- Access to and availability of affordable, high-quality early childhood education and child care (including pre- and after-school) programs.

- Access to and availability of comprehensive services to address the health, social, nutritional, transportation, and educational needs of these children and their families.

The remaining categories of needs described by the states deal with the states' capacities to systematically address these unmet needs in areas such as:

- Establishment of quality indicators of early childhood education and child care, reliable and valid measures of child development, and teacher training and standards.

- Coordination of service delivery among disciplines and service agencies.

- Establishment of a data collection, information sharing, and monitoring system capability.

- Establishment of effective programs and policies.

- Provision of resources to ensure that the needs of at-risk children and their families are met.

AFFORDABLE, HIGH-QUALITY EARLY
CHILDHOOD PROGRAMS

States acknowledge the need for quality early childhood development programs, child care programs, or both. Some states express this need solely in terms of a definition of children at risk, while other states indicate a general need applicable to all children in the state. Some states specify this need in the context of the needs of working parents. Others refer to the special problems of children from rural areas. Throughout, however, the gap between the need for service and the availability of service is apparent.

States recognize that the provision of early childhood education and child care programs hinges on the ability to assure quality programs for children and families who can benefit most from these services. Defining what constitutes quality early childhood education and child care and understanding how quality programs are instituted and maintained is central to any state attempt to address these needs.

States identify a number of needs, including the provision of:

- well-trained teachers and the availability of personnel and training to handle proposed expansion;
- a safe, organized, and nurturing environment;
- links between education and care to provide for full-day activities;
- developmentally appropriate curricula and practices;
- sufficient funding to allow for lower teacher-child ratios; and
- quality programs and materials.

States also cite the general need to identify and address the needs of the at-risk child before the onset of failure. Also noted is the absence of quality indicators and lack of consensus regarding the broad goals of early childhood development, as well as the need for more reliable and valid measures of child development. Indicated is the need to equip teachers through pre- and inservice activities with the skills and knowledge to meet the various needs of children at risk as well as with an understanding of family and cultural variables and their impact on the planning and delivery of education services. Finally, states are seeking ways to offset the developmentally inappropriate practices that currently exist in child care/education for children from infancy through age eight.

The following lists selected states' examples of unmet needs.

In **MINNESOTA** many Head Start eligible children are not served due to inadequate resources, and families of children at risk of school failure often cannot afford existing good programs or do not live where such programs are available. Minnesota also described the need for quality full-day child care or child care offered in conjunction with a child development program that provides for the needs of the whole child.

NEBRASKA indicated that with the exception of Head Start, no comprehensive services are available, and even Head Start is not available in large portions of the state. Since 1967, state law (79–444) has permitted schools to use local funds to serve pre-kindergarten children; however, few schools have elected to do so. The rural nature of the state has made the problems of young at-risk children appear less prominent there than in states with large urban concentrations of poor people.

FLORIDA defined the population in need of appropriate developmental education and affordable day care as educationally, economically, and developmentally at-risk zero-to-five-year-olds.

MISSOURI indicated the need for quality child care for disadvantaged children in heterogeneous programs.

INDIANA cited the need for adequate, affordable, accessible day care, especially infant care.

PENNSYLVANIA expressed the need for sufficient care slots and for the planned expansion of school-affiliated child care.

ALASKA, for quality home and center child care and public preschool programs.

MARYLAND and NEW JERSEY, for pre- and after-school programs.

OKLAHOMA, for day care facilities and for comprehensive, state-funded early childhood education for all children in the state.

WISCONSIN 's need is for quality preschool (educational) social and learning experiences in an organized environment, based on sound developmental practices and supervised by trained staff. The need also exists for safe, healthy, nurturing, consistent, alternative day care arrangements for working parents.

NEW MEXICO described its need for provision of after-school care, day care, nursery care, preschool, and school readiness programs. Early childhood developmental programs for at-risk children and provision of adequate care for the multiple handicapped are also needed.

MISSISSIPPI indicated a need for early childhood development programs and for affordable/available child care for the handicapped.

NORTH CAROLINA 's need is one of degree—not enough programs to serve all children at risk.

ARKANSAS cited the need for adequate facilities and slots for day programs (day care, nursery schools) for all children in the risk category.

HAWAII expressed the need for respite care for children whose parents participate in the state's early intervention parent-child education program and attention to low-income (specifically ethnic) groups with environmentally deprived children.

In COLORADO, only 25 percent of Head Start eligible children are served; hence there is a need to expand quality child care and preschool services.

SOUTH CAROLINA cited the need for continued financial support for the state-funded child development program and for increased emphasis on coordinated services for at-risk children and their families.

AVAILABILITY OF COMPREHENSIVE SERVICES

In many states quality education and care comprise only one part of a range of needed services for children and their families. States acknowledge the need for affordable high-quality comprehensive services which address health, social, nutritional, education, and often housing needs. Included also is the need for prenatal and postpartum care and family education. States stress the need for general prevention services and primary and major health care as well as mental health services and residential centers.

Many at-risk children who require early intervention services go unserved. Additionally, many children who receive services are underserved because they do not get the quantity of direct intervention needed or the variety of related services (e.g., occupational, physical, and speech therapy) they need. One state indicated it is not serving all at-risk four-year-olds and services to zero-to-four-year-olds are available only through Head Start and special education services.

CONNECTICUT described the composite nature of the needs and the inequities sustained by young at-risk children in the state: "Not all of the state's children under the age of five have equal access to the health, education, and social services they need. A family support system is not in place. Infant mortality rates remain high in our cities. Many children live in crowded, unsafe conditions; many are born to very young parents; high-quality, affordable, and accessible child care is not generally available, nor are other family support services."

1. Family Education

Many states view family development as an essential component for a comprehensive approach to meeting the needs of children. They recognize the family's central role in the early development of children and the prevention of later school failure and, consequently, have set priority on promoting family well-being. They need resources to promote positive parenting skills and reduce family isolation. Some families need direct intervention services in order to support and guide their children adequately. Parenting education is especially important for teenage parents. Family outreach was also cited as integral to any attempt to provide services to all eligible children and families.

Families of at-risk students often have limited information about the comprehensive needs of their children. Interrelated needs are for child care, job training, and life management skills. Training models for basic skills instruction, job training, and parenting could be devised and expanded using community resources.

2. Coordination and Collaboration

The lack of coordination and collaboration within and across agencies was a persistent theme among obstacles cited by states to the provision of comprehensive services to at-risk children. The existence of parallel systems, each with its own legislative mandate and eligibility criteria, is a major obstacle.

The existence of multiple agencies with service responsibility for at-risk children and families often results in the absence of a standard definition for at-risk children, a general lack of uniform terminology and catchment areas of service, and a lack of knowledge across and sometimes within agencies of the services presently available to young children and their families.

Adding to the confusion are separate federal regulations solely affecting health, social services, or education agencies, which inhibit an integrated approach. They emphasize categorical services, funds, and laws (e.g., P.L. 99–457) and fail to connect or provide a continuum of services and programs. In the latter case, services to developmentally delayed children zero to two years of age are provided by a department such as Health or Economic Security, but services to handicapped children three to five are provided by the Department of Education. One state indicated there is no provision through the education system for services to at-risk children who are three and four years old.

Another source of divisiveness is caused by differences in approach to children among agencies, for instance, the use of a clinical model by the medical community and a developmental model by the education community. Such differences contribute to turfism and shortfalls in the delivery system. Differences in approach also create barriers to service within agencies. For example, the different orientation toward child learning and teacher preparation between special educators and early childhood educators often makes it difficult for them to identify common goals and to work together.

The need for coordinated service delivery across agencies and service providers is apparent. The failure of education, health, and social services providers to coordinate their activities results in fragmented and duplicated services and inconsistency in programming.

DATA COLLECTION, INFORMATION, AND MONITORING SYSTEMS

Identifying potential and present children at risk to target and for appropriate services underscores the need for data collection, information, and monitoring capabilities. Some states need demographic data to determine the extent of needs among at-risk children. Others cite the need to develop comprehensive programs of early identification of abused and neglected children and mechanisms for identifying and monitoring at-risk children in need of immediate or later services. Finally, the need exists for consistent and uniform information on available programs.

PROGRAMMING AND POLICY

For some states, identification is only the first level of need. A continual problem is the lack of programs, programming alternatives, and services once identification is made.

Several states stressed the importance of reconceptualizing services to children with special needs, and of instituting different modes of operation.

- According to SOUTH CAROLINA, the inherent need is to acknowledge that a coordinated delivery system should provide adequate care and services to young children and their families who are at risk for a variety of reasons. Children should not be identified as deficit entities. Providing services where they are lacking should be the compelling motive of states.

- WISCONSIN indicated that this new approach must be predicated on prevention and not crisis intervention, as is the current case. It must foster collaboration rather than isolation among agencies. And it must be multidimensional, allowing for the best utilization of all services.

- WASHINGTON indicated that funding is allowed for children already exhibiting symptoms (usually severe), not for prevention. There is a lack of understanding about the long-term commitment to serve at-risk children and the long-term planning, not quick fixes, this requires.

At base is the problem of a lack of comprehensive policy and commitment to address the needs of the at-risk child population—a theme echoed by many states. This results in:

- the absence of mandated services and requisite funding;
- the lack of a clear delineation of responsibility for services;
- imprecise definitions of at-risk populations and conditions of risk, and varying eligibility criteria and standards; and
- the lack of a central agency to plan and administer coordinated early intervention services.

In addition to the need for a comprehensive policy is the need to generate greater public awareness of early childhood issues and to enact legislation which makes children from birth to age five a priority. In some states there is little state support for identifying and serving young handicapped children other than those served under P.L. 99–457. The level of services provided from state funds is minimal compared with services for older children in this category. Indifference and inability on the part of the general public to view young children as future productive citizens are among the major obstacles other states cited to the provision of comprehensive services.

RESOURCES

Many states cited funding limitations as serious obstacles. A major reason many at-risk young children are not in early childhood programs is that as yet the combination of state, local, and federal funds has not provided for the program costs of personnel and facilities to serve all such children. Funds are especially scarce for optional full-day and full-year programs. States also report the lack of sufficient funds to train early childhood staff, to establish family education programs, and to provide basic health and social services.

THE FEDERAL CONTEXT FOR STATE EFFORTS

Direct state involvement in early childhood programs is relatively new in most states. Initiatives into the early childhood education and care arena must build upon and co-exist with the complex system of providers which currently exists. That system comprises nursery schools and day care centers as well as family day care homes operated by individuals and various in-home arrangements provided by family members and other caregivers—all under a number of public, private, and sectarian auspices. It is also shaped by existing federal programs which span a number of areas of involvement relating to child care and other services, including:

- *Tax Expenditures* (Child and Dependent Care Tax Credits, Employer-Provided Child or Dependent Care Services Tax Credit, Non-Profit Child Care Center Tax Exemption).

- *Child Care/Early Education* (Head Start, Child Care Food Program, Preschool Grants for Special Education and Rehabilitative Services, Compensatory and Migrant Education, Dependent Care Planning and Development, Special Milk Program, Child Development Associate Scholarship Program).

- *Social Services/Community Development Funding* (Social Services Block Grants [Title XX], Community Development Block Grant, Child Welfare Program).

- *Welfare and Job Training—Child Care Expenses* (Food Stamps, Aid to Families with Dependent Children, Housing Assistance, Work Incentive Program, Job Training Partnership Act, Vocational Education).

These programs are administered by diverse agencies and have different funding and eligibility requirements. Following are descriptions of selected programs and, where appropriate, examples of how states use and supplement these programs.

FEDERAL PROGRAMS

Tax Expenditures

The Child Dependent Care Tax Credit provides a tax credit for a portion of child care expenses for any dependent child below the age of 15, if the expenses are incurred in order to allow the parents to work. Parents may claim up to $2,400 in child care expenses for the first dependent or $4,800 for two or more dependents. The Dependent Care Credit of 1976 amended in 1981 replaced what had been a tax deduction. The change to a credit program from a deduction was done in order to target tax benefits on moderate-income families while continuing to recognize child care costs as a legitimate employment-related expense which detracts from a family's ability to pay income taxes.

Child Care/Early Education

Head Start has been in existence since 1964 and is implemented at the local level by a number of public and private non-profit agencies. Head Start is a comprehensive education and service program targeted on low-income children ages three to five to improve their health, emotional, and social development and to improve their thinking, reasoning, and language skills. The program also emphasizes strong parent involvement.

Eligibility is set in accordance with the federal poverty guidelines, although some children are categorically eligible (e.g., foster children in state custody, AFDC beneficiaries). Up to 10 percent of enrollment may be set aside for over-income and handicapped children. In some programs funded through the American Indian Program Branch of Head Start, Alaskan Native and American Indian children may receive priority.

Despite a long and successful track record, nationally only 16 percent (453,000) of eligible children are served. Due to inflation and budgetary limitations, few programs operate full day and virtually all are closed during the summer (Children's Defense Fund, FY 1989).

Nine states (Alaska, Connecticut, Hawaii, Massachusetts, Maine, Minnesota, New Jersey, Rhode Island, Washington) and the District of Columbia contribute funds for the Head Start match or provide additional revenues to expand the number of children served and/or to improve the quality of services.

> In NEW JERSEY a new FY 1988 state program adds $1 million to existing federal funds ($30 million) for Head Start and Head Start-like programs (most of which operate on half-day schedules) to extend their hours for working parents.

> In ALASKA an additional $2.8 million in state funds allows several programs to enroll additional over-income children. Currently, approximately 1,000 eligible children in Alaska are on Head Start waiting lists.

> In MASSACHUSETTS the State Head Start Program seeks to increase the number of children and their families who receive Head Start services and/or to increase the length of the program day, week, or year for current Head Start programs. The State Supplemental Grant for Salary Enhancement provides additional funds for Head Start staff salaries in order to retain and attract qualified personnel. To the $23 million in federal Head Start funds it receives, MASSACHUSETTS adds $3 million for salary enhancement and $1.5 million for program expansion.

> In 1984, MAINE legislated $1.7 million to expand Head Start with the goal of bringing the number of eligible children receiving services up to 25 percent. An increase in funding was appropriated in 1986 to $1.9 million. There was an additional 5 percent in funding provided in 1987, and the Governor requested $100,000 to maintain the funding level for the upcoming program year.

> The DISTRICT OF COLUMBIA public schools will soon become the largest provider of Head Start services in the District under an innovative plan that

includes family day care in private homes in addition to Head Start centers. To a $1.9 million grant from the U. S. Department of Health and Human Services, the District will match $1.3 million of its own funds and open 25 new centers and license 10 family day care providers. The federal grant will allow the school district to extend Head Start services to an additional 801 three- and four-year-olds, including 30 disabled children. Fifty children will be served by family day care providers, allowing for groups of five instead of the eighteen or more in conventional Head Start centers (Sklansky, 1988).

CALIFORNIA State Preschool Education Program funds are directed at children of low-income families. Preschool classes may be operated by any public agency or any private agency which meets eligibility requirements. Classes may be operated without regard to specific school sites, but preferably should be established in target areas to serve children who reside within the attendance areas of schools eligible for State Compensatory Education funds. In order for children to be eligible for entrance into a State Preschool Education Program, the children must have reached their third birthday and have not started kindergarten. Chapter 1 preschools are supplemental to existing services if provided by the LEA. However, it is not necessary to have other locally funded preschools to use Chapter 1 funds.

The State Migrant Child Care and Development Program serves children while their parents are employed in fishing, agriculture, or related work. Migrant child care centers are open for varying lengths of time during the year depending on the growing/harvest season in each area. Children ages 0 to 2.9 years are funded out of the state funding source; children ages 2.9 to 14 are funded from the federal source.

In **MICHIGAN**, programs serving infants, toddlers, and preschoolers are funded through state aid allocations or grants, as specified under state regulations and guidelines for programs such as vocational education or student support services.

These programs are generally for the support of vocational training and/or parent education of high school students. The state appropriates $1.2 million for School Age Parents programs. The monies for these programs are used by districts to establish school-based child care centers for students. Local districts provide additional money to operate centers.

In **TEXAS**, Title XX funded day care services are provided to children in danger of abuse or neglect and to children of low-income parents who work or are in training for employment. Day care is purchased through provider agreements and competitively procured or sole-source-contracted from day homes and centers which meet state licensing standards and Department of Human Services requirements. Families receiving services pay a portion of the costs in fees based on family income, unless the case is a protective services or AFDC case. Only 15.6 percent (28,659) of eligible children are served through the program.

In **MISSISSIPPI**, day care services are provided to families with incomes below 170 percent of the federal poverty level, to children under school age in the custody of the Department of Public Welfare, to children of an ADC parent, single parent, WIN registrant, or guardian who is working full-time or is in school. About one percent of eligible children receive these Title XX funded services.

In **SOUTH CAROLINA** the Child Development Service provides day care for children outside the home for up to 10 hours per day. The program offers supervised, planned developmental activities, health screening and immunizations, nutritional meals and snacks, and diagnostic evaluations for children. The program offers parent counseling and guidance, parenting education, and assistance in obtaining needed health and social services. Transportation is provided by most child development programs. This service also provides a home-based development program which offers children and parents the same services as out-of-home care, except for nutritional meals and snacks. The service is available to eligible children who are in need of protection or children in substitute care, children who are handicapped, eligible children of working parents, or of parents in school or training. About 52 percent of eligible children receive these services.

Chapter 1 (compensatory education) of the Elementary and Secondary School Improvement Amendments (ESSIA) of 1988 provides financial assistance to schools in low-income areas to meet the special needs of educationally deprived children and requires states to monitor program improvements measured in student achievement. It also provides for parent involvement in the planning, design, and implementation of programs and for parent training and other means to work with teachers and school staff to promote program objectives in the home. Handicapped and limited-English-proficient children can receive compensatory services if their needs stem from educational deprivation and are not solely related to their handicapping condition or limited English proficiency. The law also applies to preschool children. As in other programs, the gap between eligible children and those served is great. In 1985, Chapter 1 served only 54 of every 100 eligible school-aged children (CDF, FY 1989).

The Chapter 1 Migrant Education Program provides services to preschool-age migrant children ages three, four, and five. Services include: education (early childhood skills and language development); health (general health screening, medical and dental follow-up services, and accident insurance coverage); and nutrition (breakfast, lunch, and snacks provided through the federal school lunch and breakfast programs).

Funds are available to state education agencies for *Programs for Migratory Children* ages three to twenty-one. States are to establish or improve, either directly or through local education agencies, programs of education for children of migratory agriculture workers or fishers. The program requires appropriate coordination with programs administered under sections of the Higher Education Act, Job Training Partnership Act, Education of the Handicapped Act, Community Services Block Grant Act, Head Start program, migrant health program, and other appropriate programs under the Departments of Education, Labor, and Agriculture.

Even Start, Part B, of the ESSIA is designed to improve educational opportunities for children and adults by integrating early childhood education and adult education. It involves parents and children in family-centered education programs in a cooperative effort to help parents become full partners in the education of their children. The program mandates coordination with other federal programs such as Adult Education, Education of the Handicapped, the Job Training Partnership Act, Head Start, and various literacy programs.

The *Bilingual Education Act* provides funds to local education agencies (LEAs) to develop and implement bilingual programs at elementary and secondary schools, as well as activities at the preschool level, designed to meet the needs of limited-English-proficient children.

The Carl D. Perkins *Vocational Education Act* makes vocational education programs accessible to all persons, including handicapped and disadvantaged persons, single parents and homemakers, adults in need of training and retraining, and persons participating in programs designed to eliminate sex bias and stereotyping in vocational education. Support services such as dependent care are provided to allow teenage parents to participate in vocational education programs.

Through two new programs of the amended federal *Education of the Handicapped Act*, P.L. 99–457, states have received funds for planning comprehensive coordinated early intervention services across agencies to handicapped infants and toddlers and those at risk of developmental delays and their families. The Preschool Grant Program will extend the rights and protections of P.L. 94–142 to handicapped children age three to five by 1990 and extends access to special education and related services; provides for an individualized education program (IEP); allows services in the least restrictive environment (LRT); permits parent involvement in decision making; and requires procedural safeguards.

The Handicapped Infants and Toddlers' Program of P.L. 99–457 provides funds to states for the development of comprehensive early intervention services for handicapped infants and toddlers, and those at risk of developing handicaps, and for services to families to help in their child's development. The legislation defines the population broadly as all children from birth through two years of age who are developmentally delayed (as determined by state criteria); or with conditions that typically result in delay; or who are at risk of susbstantial developmental delay (at state discretion).

The law defines early intervention services as including multidisciplinary assessment, an Individualized Family Service Plan (IFSP), and services to meet developmental needs such as speech and language pathology and audiology, physical therapy, occupational therapy, psychological service, parent and family training and counseling services, transportation services, medical services for diagnostic purposes, and health services necessary for the child to benefit from other intervention services. The law also requires case management services for eligible children and their parents.

The legislation fosters interagency collaboration in the provision of these services by requiring the establishment of an Interagency Coordinating Council composed of relevant agencies, providers, and consumers to assist in the development and implementation of state applicants and interagency efforts.

Social Services/Community Development

States support child care programs through the *Title XX Social Services Block Grant*, which gives states funds for a variety of social services for low- and moderate-income families, although there is wide variability among states in the use of these funds for this purpose. According to the Children's Defense Fund (*Child Care*, 1987) the Title XX funding cuts in recent years have resulted in less money spent by 28 states for Title XX child care programs in 1987 than in 1981 even though the numbers of low-income working families have increased significantly. A state-by-state review of services indicates long waiting lists of eligible families for Title XX supported child care.

Welfare and Job Training

Under the *Aid to Families with Dependent Children* (AFDC) program, federal funds are available to states, the District of Columbia, Guam, Puerto Rico, and the Virgin Islands for strengthening family life by providing family assistance and care to needy dependent children. Under matching formulas in the Social Security Act, approximately 54 percent of AFDC benefits is paid by the U. S. treasury and 46 percent by the states. The federal share varies and is inversely related to state per capita income. States vary in the coverage of unborn infants and children over 18 years of age, in coverage to needy families in which the principal wage earner is unemployed, and in the availability of workfare programs in which recipients are required to work in exchange for their AFDC benefits (Committee on Ways and Means, U. S. House of Representatives, 1985).

The *Medicaid Program* (authorized under Title XIX of the Social Security Act) is a federally aided, state-operated and administered program of medical assistance for low-income individuals who are blind, disabled, aged, or members of families with dependent children. Within federal guidelines each state designs and administers its own program. This results in great variation among states in eligibility requirements, services, number of persons covered, and the levels of federal and state dollars spent. Since 1984, the legislation has been progressively broadened to require states to provide Medicaid coverage: to any pregnant woman or to any child (younger than seven) whose family income is below AFDC eligibility standards regardless of the family composition; to pregnant women and to children (younger than five) with incomes above AFDC financial eligibility levels but below 100 percent of the federal poverty level; and in 1987, to pregnant women and to infants with family incomes less than 185 percent of the federal poverty level (*A Children's Defense Budget*, 1988).

The *Supplemental Food Program for Women, Infants, and Children (WIC)* provides food assistance and nutritional screening for low-income pregnant and postpartum women and their infants as well as for low-income children up to the age of five. Program participants must have incomes below 185 percent of poverty level (states may set their upper-income eligibility limits between 100 and 185 percent) and must be nutritionally at risk. Nutritional risk is defined as: detectable nutritional needs; health-impairing dietary deficiencies; documented nutritionally related medical conditions; or conditions that predispose people to inadequate nutrition or nutritionally related medical conditions. The WIC program has been found to have a positive effect on reducing low birth weight among infants. Because WIC is a grant program, it does not serve all who are eligible. In 1983 an estimated 30 percent of income-eligible women, 45 percent of income-eligible infants, and 20 percent of income-eligible children were served (Committee on Ways and Means, U. S. House of Representatives, 1985).

The purposes of the *Maternal and Child Health Services* block grant are to reduce infant mortality and the incidence of preventable disease and handicapping conditions among children, and to increase the availability of prenatal, delivery, and postpartum care for low-income mothers. Between 85 and 90 percent of the grant appropriation is allotted for health services; however, states determine which health services to provide (Committee on Ways and Means, U.S. House of Representatives, 1985).

NEW LEGISLATION

Congress has recently completed a restructuring of the nation's welfare system in ways that emphasize parental responsibility through the enforcement of child support and expanded opportunities for self-sufficiency through employment, education, and training. The Family Support Act of 1988 requires that states establish Job Opportunities and Basic Skills Training Programs (JOBS) by October 1, 1990. In addition to the provision of basic education activities, states must guarantee child care to the extent that such care is required for a welfare parent to participate in JOBS activities. States must also guarantee child care services for 12 months after the family becomes ineligible for assistance because of increased earnings, if child care is necessary for employment.

In arranging child care, state agencies must take into account the individual needs of the child. Also, child care must meet applicable standards under state and local law. States are allowed to provide child care in a number of ways, including contracting with providers and providing care directly or through vouchers or cash reimbursements to families. Federal funding for child care is an open-ended entitlement at the same rate the state receives Medicaid.

Beginning January 1, 1990, all states would be required to implement the AFDC-Unemployed Parent program. Under this program, two-parent families in which the principal earner is unemployed may qualify for AFDC/FSP benefits. There are also special provisions for minor parents including one which permits states to require school attendance by the minor parent and to fund training in parenting and family living skills such as nutrition and health education (Rovner, October 8, 1988).

MINNESOTA has in place several programs which show concern for at-risk families and child development. The Education for Pregnant Minors program enables pregnant minors and minor custodial parents to complete high school. The program utilizes appropriate community services and recognizes individual needs and parental responsibilities. If a youth receives social services or employment/training services, the district must develop the individual's educational program in consultation with the providers of these services. Under the Transportation Aid for Adolescent Parents program, school districts may receive state funding for transportation costs for adolescent parents who ride to and from school from a child care center. In the Adolescent Parent Planning program, adolescent parents are required to plan for themselves and their children. The plan must consider education, parenting skills, health care, living arrangements, economic self-sufficiency, and services needed to alleviate personal problems. The county social services agency is required to assist in this development of the plan when needed.

PROPOSED LEGISLATION

The state role in early childhood education may be further shaped by recent congressional activities affecting child development and care and tax credits. Following are descriptions of proposed legislation.

The *Smart Start* legislation would increase the availability of early childhood development programs for three- or four-year-olds and would help meet the needs of working parents by requiring that programs run for the full work day and calendar year. States would be required to match federal funds dollar for dollar and therefore would be able to leverage funds to supplement and strengthen existing early childhood programs (e.g., Head Start) or to establish new programs where they do not exist. States would be allowed flexibility in deciding which service agency would have responsibility for the programs and how to build onto existing efforts.

The *Act for Better Child Care* (ABC) would expand the availability of licensed day care for infants and older children, including adolescents. ABC would allow states to contract with private providers for the care of low- and moderate-income children. It would provide for "certificates" for parents to use in paying for child care.

The Act would require states to provide a 20 percent match of funds. The greatest proportion of available funds (70–75 percent) would be used to assist parents in purchasing child care. An additional 10 percent would go to states for administrative costs. The remainder would be used to improve quality and expand supply. However, 10 percent would be targeted to Head Start expansion. States would have the flexibility to use the remaining funds for: training for child care workers; developing resource and referral programs to assist parents in finding quality care; providing grants to for-profit and non-profit child care providers to assist them in improving facilities and meeting federal standards; recruiting new child care providers; and improving salaries for workers.

As alternatives to the direct assistance for child care costs of the ABC bill, numerous *child care tax credit* proposals have been set forth. These proposals fall into three categories (Marr, 1988):

- The "Stay-At-Home-Spouse" Bills give tax subsidies to families with preschool children even if they do not pay for child care.
- The "Targeting" Bills reduce current tax credits for upper-income families with employment-related child care expenses and increase tax credits for low-income families.
- The "Infant" Bill gives a one-year tax boon to moderate-income families with newborn babies, but only if one parent stays home for six months.

STATE ACTIONS FOR EARLY CHILDHOOD AND PARENT EDUCATION, AND RELATED SERVICES

Within the context of federal and local programs and impending legislation, states have fashioned programs and responses based on their particular needs and their capacities to support these efforts. Some of these efforts have developed from the states' education reform movement and the realization that improved student competencies and stringent graduation requirements at the secondary level must be grounded on quality elementary school and, before that, quality early childhood experiences. Other state early childhood efforts predate or parallel school reforms and simply grow out of the pressing needs of at-risk children and crises in families in all strata of our society.

STATE INVOLVEMENT IN EARLY CHILDHOOD PROGRAMS

State involvement in early childhood programs has been in the following areas:

1. child care subsidy programs (often supplementary to Title XX programs)
2. dependent care tax credits
3. school-based child care (primarily limited to services for parenting teens and training sites for vocational school students)
4. funding of special education for preschoolers
5. state-funded pilot or statewide pre-kindergarten programs
6. state-funded parent education programs
7. state resource and referral programs

8. supplements to Head Start in the form of matching or additional funds to expand the number of children served and/or improve the quality of service (Marx and Seligson, 1988; Mitchell, 1988)

Additionally, states provide services to young children and families through:

9. sexual-abuse prevention programs
10. family-based care for children in foster homes, adoptions, and reintroduction/reintegration into family services

According to the Public School Early Childhood Study conducted by the Bank Street College of Education (Marx and Seligson, 1988; Mitchell, 1988), states are a long way from providing universally available pre-kindergarten programs, either philosophically or financially. In 1988, about $225 million in state funds were spent for about 150,000 children. From that amount 10 states appropriated more than $10 million annually. Texas ($46 million), California ($35 million), and New York ($27 million) provide the largest total amounts, although the per-child expenditure varies greatly (from $850 in Texas to over $2,500 in New York) reflecting both real differences in per-child costs and proportion of state/local funds. In some states (e.g., Texas), the average local funding share is equal to the state per-child expenditure.

Minnesota and Missouri together spend approximately $35 million on their parent education programs. These programs are provided in lieu of direct services to pre-kindergarten children.

State figures for pre-kindergarten and parent education programs pale in comparison to the over $1 billion in federal funding for Head Start programs serving approximately 450,000 children nationwide and the equivalent levels spent through SSBG/Title XX. Including the Dependent Care Tax Credit and payments by parents, estimates for total national child care expenditures range from $7 to $13 billion.

STATE-FUNDED PILOT OR STATEWIDE PRE-KINDERGARDEN PROGRAMS

In 1987, 24 states—including the District of Columbia— provided funds for pilot or statewide pre-kindergarten programs (Marx and Seligson, 1988). These programs vary greatly along a number of characteristics such as:

Ages of Children Served. About half of state programs limit participation to four-year-olds, while the remainder allow enrollment of children between three and five years of age.

Targeted Population. The majority of state programs serve only at-risk children based on low-income status, a combination of at-risk factors, school readiness, or limited English proficiency. Other states have permissive programs under which school districts receive funds through a state school attendance reimbursement formula.

Source of Program Operation and Agency Auspices. Some state programs are operated solely through the public schools; other states permit public schools to subcontract with public and/or private agencies to contract with the states (e.g., Alaska, Illinois, Massachusetts, Michigan, New Jersey, South Carolina, Washington). With few exceptions (Alaska, New Jersey, Washington), state education agencies have primary responsibility for preschool programs; however, state Head Start contributions tend to fall under the auspices of other state agencies.

Teacher Training and/or Certification. About half of the states require pre-kindergarten teachers to have training and/or certification in early childhood education (District of Columbia, Florida, Illinois, Maine, Maryland, Massachusetts, Michigan, New Jersey, Oklahoma, South Carolina, Washington, West Virginia), while the others do not have these requirements.

Staff-Child Ratios. Five states permit staff-child ratios in excess of 1:10, and several require ratios below this level.

Type of Mandated Program. About half of the states with early childhood efforts mandate comprehensive developmental programs (including health, social services, and parental participation). The remaining states focus primarily on a cognitive curriculum or have no curricular requirements (the case in states with the most permissive legislation).

Length of Program. Most state pre-kindergarten programs (60 percent) are half-day. About 25 percent allow either half-day or full school day. Four states allow for a full working day (Florida, Massachusetts, New Jersey, Vermont).

Extent of State-Level Coordination. Almost all states have a state-level coordinating board representing state agencies and sometimes day care providers, Head Start, and parents.

> In WASHINGTON the Early Childhood Education and Assistance Program (ECEAP) is administered by the Department of Community Development (DCD). It provides a comprehensive program for preschool-age children from low-income families. To be eligible, children must be three to four years of age and from families whose income is 100 percent of federal poverty guidelines. Also 10 percent of enrollment slots is reserved for migrant and Indian children. In addition, 10 percent of slots is open to any child who needs service. The state provides $6 million for this program, which serves 2,047 children.
>
> The program has four components: program administration; education, including transition to kindergarten; health, including medical, dental, and nutrition; and social services, including parent involvement. DCD contracts with private non-profit agencies, community action agencies, school districts, and local government agencies to provide services.

CALIFORNIA supports a number of child development program models, one of which is the State Preschool program. This a part-day comprehensive developmental program for pre-kindergarten children three to five years of age. The program includes educational development, health services, social services, nutrition services, parent education and participation, evaluation, and staff development. State Preschool programs are administered by private agencies as well as school districts and county offices of education.

Priority for receiving State Preschool services is given to low-income families who meet eligibility requirements. Children from low-income families are eligible if they can benefit from the services provided, if their families do not speak English as a primary language, or if the children are at risk of abuse or neglect, are handicapped, or have other special circumstances that would allow them to benefit from such a program.

FLORIDA's pre-kindergarten Early Intervention program has a developmentally appropriate curriculum for economically or educationally disadvantaged three- and four-year-olds. It is funded through the Department of Education to local school districts which may operate the program directly or contract with licensed day care agencies to deliver services. The program stresses interagency coordination and parent education/involvement. State funds of $1.6 million support 856 children.

The MICHIGAN state-funded preschool program serves four-year-olds identified as at risk of school failure based on a set of risk factors identified by school districts. The state provides a recommended list of factors that place children at risk of becoming educationally disadvantaged. The list also describes children who may have extraordinary need of special assistance because of low birth weight, developmental immaturity, physical and/or sexual abuse, neglect, nutritional long-term or chronic illness, diagnosed handicapping condition (mainstreamed), lack of stable support system or residence, destructive or violent temperament, substance abuse or addiction in the home, language deficiency or immaturity, non-English or limited-English-speaking household, family history of low school achievement or dropout, family history of delinquency, family history of diagnosed family problems, low parental/sibling educational attainment or illiteracy, single parent, teenage parent, unemployed parent(s), low family income, family density, parental loss by divorce or death, chronically ill parent, incarcerated parent, housing in rural or segregated area.

The program serves 5,744 children at a state cost of $2.3 million. Additionally, local districts offer preschool programs for four-year-olds, which are financed through local millage and/or tuition fees.

SOUTH CAROLINA uses several types of program delivery systems. A full-day center-based child development program serves 2,152 children ranging from age three to five. (Five-year-olds first participate in the half-day kindergarten program.) The home-based parent education program uses an itinerant model of weekly home visits to serve parents of 152 children who attend no preschool or live in outlying areas. The major child development program targets four-year-olds with significant readiness deficiencies. This half-day child development program initiated in 1984 serves 8,451 four-year-olds in a classroom-based child development model with an auxiliary outreach component operating in a few districts. Total state appropriation for the three delivery systems is approximately $11 million.

ILLINOIS provides $12.7 million to districts requesting programs to serve three- and four-year-olds at risk of academic failure. Districts determine screening criteria, educational program, parent involvement component, and evaluation procedures. The state provides technical assistance. In fiscal year 1988, ninety-four programs serving 6,593 children were funded.

LOUISIANA 's state-funded program for high-risk four-year-olds is designed to provide a developmentally appropriate curriculum and environment for its recipients. This program is restricted to children from families with annual incomes under $15,000 and from families who agree to participate in various activities associated with the program. In addition to these regulations, the child must be one year younger than the age required for kindergarten and, based on screening results, be termed at risk of being insufficiently ready for the regular school program. The purpose of the program is to improve the readiness of these high-risk children who will be eligible to enter kindergarten the following year.

State funds ($2.9 million) serve approximately 1,700 students. Separate state funds ($240,593) fund pilot or exemplary preschool programs serving approximately 127 students. Federal Chapter 1 funds ($3 million) supplement programs and provide for services to an additional 1,950 four-year-olds at schools meeting eligibility criteria of educationally and economically deprived students.

Pre-kindergarten education in TEXAS was mandated by the Texas legislature in 1983 as part of the state's education reforms. The program targets four-year-old children whose home environment or limited English might impede their success in school and in life. Early intervention through preschool education for these children is designed to counteract the downward spiral of academic failure and dropout. The Texas pre-kindergarten program is funded jointly by the state ($45.8 million) and local school districts. Additional funds are available through federally supported Chapter 1 and Chapter 1 Migrant, and in coordination with Head Start programs. The state program supports 54,493 children.

MASSACHUSETTS awards grants to school committees to develop innovative early childhood programs in the following areas: programs for three- and four-year-olds; enhanced kindergarten and transitional first-grade classes; and day care programs for young children. To apply for funds, school committees must appoint local early childhood advisory councils whose functions are to assess community needs and resources and develop early childhood programs. School systems may use the funds to contract with other agencies or providers for services. Seventy-five percent of funds statewide must go to low-income sites. In fiscal year 1988, state funds of $10.35 million supported 13,981 children aged three to six years.

The **MARYLAND** Extended Elementary Education Program (EEEP) is a public pre-kindergarten education program for four-year-old children, many of whom reach school with language deficits and without prior knowledge or the experiential base that will support school success and achievement. The program makes pre-kindergarten education available to all four-year-olds residing in the attendance area of a qualifying school whose parents voluntarily enroll them in the program. Qualifying schools are those whose students score six to nine months below the national norm in reading comprehension at the third-grade level on the California Achievement Test. Approximately 15 percent (1,603) of eligible children are served through this program. An additional 1,858 children are served with dedicated State Compensatory Education and Chapter 2 funds.

The goal of the EEEP is to provide initial learning experiences to help children develop and maintain the basic skills for successful school performance. The program achieves this goal by providing developmentally appropriate experiences that address the cognitive, social, emotional, and physical needs of young children. Learning is promoted in a nurturing environment through a balance of child-initiated activities and teacher-directed instruction.

STATE-SPONSORED FAMILY EDUCATION PROGRAMS

Several states have instituted family education program interventions to address the educational needs of young children and their families. In some states these programs have been developed in response to a range of welfare and social problems such as adolescent pregnancy and welfare dependency.

Other states have adopted a family education program focus in lieu of a strong focus on programs for three- and four-year-olds. Many of these programs are based on the assumptions that:

- early childhood is a critically important time in an individual's development;

- home is the crucial place for early development to take place and the mother is the child's most significant teacher; and

- parents of young children need and will use advice and support with child rearing (Weiss, 1987).

Since 1980, 12 states have instituted family support and education programs. The oldest and most extensive programs are found in Minnesota and Missouri.

OHIO's GRADs (Graduation, Reality, and Dual-Role Skills) Program is an in-school program for pregnant students and/or young parents in grades 7-12. Its goals are to:

- increase the likelihood that participants will remain in school during pregnancy and after the birth of the child;

- assist participants in carrying out positive prenatal and postnatal health care practices for themselves and their children;

- provide knowledge and skills related to child development and positive parenting practices;
- provide an orientation to the world of work; and
- encourage goal setting directed toward the concept of the dual role of employee and parent.

In 1974, the **MINNESOTA** legislature authorized a bill to support six pilot Early Childhood Family Education (ECFE) programs. Presently, 326 out of 435 districts in the state offer the program involving an estimated 75,000 families statewide.

The ECFE is a universally available program for children from birth to kindergarten enrollment and their parents. Expectant parents may also be served. The program purpose is to support and enhance the skills and understanding of parents in providing for their children's learning and development. Programs include: parent-child interaction opportunities; guided play/learning activities for children; parent and family education through discussion groups, workshops, home visits; lending libraries of books, toys, other learning materials; special events for the entire family; and information on related community resources.

The program funding level is $18 million with $7.5 million in state aid and $10.7 million in local levies.

All **MISSOURI** school districts offer systematic parent education and support services designed to enable the parents to enhance their children's intellectual, language, physical, and social development. Participating parents receive free of cost: private visits by parent educators who are trained in child development; small group meetings with other parents of similarly aged children; monitoring and periodic screening of the child's educational and sensory development; information and referral services for needs beyond the scope of this program; and a variety of support services such as a book and toy lending library, drop-in play groups, newsletters, and social activities.

Eligibility begins at the third trimester of pregnancy and ends at entry into kindergarten. Services are offered to all families; however, $244,270 of state funds are used by districts to identify, recruit, and engage reluctant families (i.e., teen, low-income, low-functioning, migratory/transitory, ESL, geographically isolated, single parents). The program serves 52,806 parents of children zero to three years of age and 52,114 parents of children three and four years of age. The program is funded at $11 million.

In **ARKANSAS** the Home Instruction Program for Preschool Youngsters (HIPPY) provides training to parents in the education of their child in the home environment. In 1987, ten HIPPY projects served over 1,000 children and 1,000 mothers. The program was initially funded with foundation money. As the program has expanded and the connection with adult education, literacy, and employable skills been recognized, Job Training Partnership Act, Chapter 1 and 2, and local funds have been used.

The goal of **CONNECTICUT**'s Parent Education and Support Centers is to prevent an array of childhood and adolescent problems (i.e., delinquency, child abuse and neglect, substance abuse, teenage pregnancy) by supporting families and strengthening the capacity of parents to implement effective family management practices. Each of 10 Centers must provide services in the following four service categories: parent education and training; parent support; information and referral; and technical assistance, training and consultation. In addition, each Center must provide child care, include specific services for fathers, and establish a parent advisory board.

Centers must provide services for all parents within their catchment area, but may offer special services for certain parents. Eligibility criteria must be non-valuative, i.e., related to school, community or neighborhood—not based on negative behavior, e.g., substance abuse, child abuse, school failure, etc. Current fiscal appropriations of $312,000 support the participation of 4,857 parents and 2,765 children.

OREGON 's Together for Children (TFC) program targets funding to parents of children between the ages of zero to eight years who are assessed as at risk of failing in school. TFC programs involve a variety of approaches with a diversity of goals ranging from home visitation to peer support groups and from health care to parent education. The interdependence of family members and of families with communities is an important focus for TFC programs. Parents glean information and support from professionals, peers, and community resources while simultaneously serving as resources themselves. Rather than remediating family weaknesses, family strengths are built upon. The state funds three programs for a total of 1,000 families at a level of $266,797.

STATE REFERRAL PROGRAMS

Resource and referral programs can be extremely helpful to parents seeking high-quality child care that meets their needs. Programs which offer support services such as training and recruiting of family day care providers help to improve the quality of child care. Also through resource and referral programs policy makers can better assess communities' child care needs. Sixteen states and the District of Columbia provide funds to start or operate these programs.

In CALIFORNIA Resource and Referral agencies inform parents of the range of available child care services and provide parents with referrals to caregivers who meet the family's child care needs and preferences. Resource and Referral programs are responsible for maintaining a resource file of services which must be updated at least quarterly. These files include types of programs available, hours of service, ages of children served, fees, eligibility requirements, and program information. Parents are referred to only licensed facilities unless there is no licensing requirement.

Resource and Referral agencies provide telephone referral services and referrals in languages spoken in the community and maintain offices that are convenient to parents and providers. Agencies document requests for services, including the number of calls received; the ages of the children to be served; the time category of the child care need; special time category needs such as nights, weekends, or swing shift; and the reason that care is needed.

This information is used to provide technical assistance to existing and potential providers and to help initiate the establishment of new child care services.

STATE POLICIES FOR COMPREHENSIVE SERVICES TO CHILDREN AGES ZERO THROUGH FIVE

Because of the availability of federal funds under P.L. 99–457 (for planning comprehensive coordinated early intervention services across agencies to handicapped infants and toddlers, those at risk of developmental delays, and their families by 1990), virtually all states have instituted some form of interagency coordinating council. Because the language of this law is broad and states have leeway to determine eligibility criteria, P.L. 99–457 has great importance for providing comprehensive and coordinated services for a large number of at-risk children and their families.

In response to the law, some states have fashioned their own laws and policies to ensure a coordinated comprehensive system of providing early intervention services to handicapped infants and toddlers.

Beyond services to disabled or potentially developmentally delayed children, however, many states have various types of interagency mechanisms for initiating or monitoring services to young children.

The purposes for collaboration are numerous as illustrated by the state examples cited. Multiagency collaboration often results in: recommended legislation and the development of policies and guidelines; multiyear planning for unified family policies; regulation and licensing changes; the development of information services on child and family programs; the establishment of regional councils; and the coordination of existing services.

Few states, however, have a single agency which is responsible for the total needs of children ages zero to five or a formal policy for comprehensive services. Among the states with a formal policy are Alaska, Florida, Missouri, Nebraska, and Texas.

In Alaska, the Governor's Interim Commission on Children and Youth developed a report on what services were needed and how to provide the services. This resulted in a 1987 updated agreement between the Departments of Education, Community and Regional Affairs, and Health and Social Services. The purpose of the Tri-Department Committee on Young Children is "to support a first-class system of services for young children [birth through eight years] and their families through joint strategic planning by appropriate state agencies."

The Committee provides: effective coordination and management of comprehensive services to these children, and technical assistance and consultation to providers and consumers of services throughout the state.

The Committee is composed of the Commissioner of the Department of Community and Regional Affairs (DCRA) or designee; the Early Childhood program manager, DCRA; the Commissioner of the Department of Education

(DOE) or designee; the Early Childhood program manager, DOE; the Commissioner of the Department of Health and Social Services (DHSS) or designee; and the Early Childhood program manager, DHSS. The core committee encourages participation of others (e.g., parents, other government personnel, Head Start directors, university early childhood faculty, public and private preschool practitioners, child care providers, members of the Alaska Association for the Education of Young Children, child care resource and referral agencies).

The following are general areas of responsibility around which strategies are being developed:

- *Information Services.* Each Department is encouraged to collect and widely disseminate information on agency roles, early childhood services, and programs offered within the Department, and to share communication on federal laws and rules and other materials of interest.

- *Early Childhood Statutes, Regulations, and Policy.* The Committee promotes the coordination of policy development for children under age nine. Policy development focuses on both child care facilities and pre-elementary schools and may involve additional state agencies such as the Departments of Public Safety, Environmental Conservation, and Law.

- *Community Needs and Services.* The Committee assesses community needs for early childhood services and makes recommendations for needed services. It also promotes the coordination of existing services for efficient and effective delivery.

- *Early Childhood Training and Technical Assistance.* The Committee will address training and technical assistance for early childhood practitioners, teachers, administrators, and parents.

- *Early Childhood Program Development.* Uniform definitions for early childhood services are being developed across agencies as well as roles, responsibilities (including training and technical assistance) and ways of avoiding unnecessary duplication.

Among the mechanisms for providing coordination in CONNECTICUT are: the Birth to Three Council—an advisory to the State Department of Education for meeting the requirements of Part H of P.L. 99–457; the Commission on Children—with responsibility for review and recommendation for legislation to the General Assembly; the Day Care Council—composed of agency heads and governor appointees to recommend day care regulations to the Department of Health Services; and the Child Welfare Reform Initiative Interim Policy Advisory Council—charged with developing a family policy which will be the basis for a multiyear plan to improve child welfare and child and family services.

In HAWAII several interdepartmental councils exist which focus on all issues affecting children, including child abuse and neglect, mental health, substance abuse, health, education, and child care.

In **INDIANA** the Interagency Task Force on Child Care includes representatives from the Departments of Welfare, Education, Health, Mental Health, and the State Fire Marshal. The Task Force is streamlining the licensing regulations for child care and will develop new legislation if needed.

In **IOWA** a Child Development Coordinating Council was recently organized to promote services for at-risk three- and four-year-olds. The Council will be composed of representatives of the Departments of Education, Human Services, Public Health, Human Rights, and area education agencies, local state universities, and a resident of the state who is a parent of a child who has been served by a federal Head Start program.

The duties of the Council will be to develop a definition of "at-risk" children, establish minimum guidelines for comprehensive early child development services for at-risk children, develop an inventory of child development services provided to at-risk children, identify the number of children who receive child development services, encourage the establishment of regional councils to facilitate the development of programs for at-risk children, and make recommendations about appropriate curricula and staff qualifications for early elementary education, and about the coordination of the curricula with early childhood programs.

In **MASSACHUSETTS** an Inter-secretariat Task Force, convened by the Day Care Policy Unit of the Executive Offices of Human Services, has developed an interagency work plan. The Department of Education is a member of the Inter-secretariat Task Force. In 1987, the Board of Education created the Bureau of Early Childhood Programs which united the Department's major early childhood programs: the Chapter 1988 Early Childhood Program; the Special Education P.L. 99–457 Preschool Grant; the State Head Start Salary Enhancement Program; and the State Head Start Expansion Program.

In **FLORIDA** the Handicap Prevention Act of 1986 (Chapter 411, Florida Statutes) provides for coordination of a comprehensive system of services for at-risk and handicapped children ages zero to five. Chapter 411 emphasizes the need to prevent or minimize handicapping conditions and includes a continuum of preventive services that should be available for all at-risk young children and high-risk pregnant women, including appropriate prenatal care, health care, education, and support services. Joint responsibility for establishing the continuum of services is assigned to the Department of Health and Rehabilitative Services and the Department of Education. The Commissioners of each department have an interagency cooperative agreement which delineates a structured approach to interagency coordination. This agreement requires that both agencies establish joint priorities on an annual basis. Among the priority areas initially established are services to the birth-to-five-year-old population, child day care, and school health services.

The **MISSOURI** Department of Elementary and Secondary Education is responsible for administering and enforcing the Early Childhood Development Act of 1984. This Act provides a state plan and financial support for services to help parents contribute to their children's educational development, to identify and correct learning and health problems before they become significant, to provide preschool services for children with developmental delays, and to promote closer home-school cooperation during preschool years and throughout the child's educational career. Other state agencies play a major role in providing services to families that have needs beyond the scope of these programs. All local school districts provide services either directly or through contractual agreements with other public or not-for-profit agencies.

Several groups facilitate the implementation of this policy. The Commissioner of Education's Committee on Parents as Teachers serves as a major advocate and avenue for private funding to ensure quality programming. The Parents as Teachers National Advisory Board, composed of noted educational, medical, and business leaders, lends its expertise and consults with the Department to keep the programs viable and effective. The Children's Services Commission, a statutory interagency board, coordinates children's programs by state agencies; facilitates the elimination of duplicate efforts; and works toward an integrated state plan for the care provided to children in Missouri. All local districts have community advisory boards composed of representatives of social services, higher education, mental health, primary health providers, Head Start, ministerial alliance, and other interested citizens. The Department of Education has been appointed by the Governor as the lead agency in coordinating services to handicapped infants, toddlers, and preschoolers. The state interagency coordinating council is actively working to integrate handicapped services with existing programs.

The purpose of NEBRASKA's Family Policy Act is to "guide the actions of state government in dealing with problems and crises involving children and families." It emphasizes the importance of family, schools, and community. The Act applies to every department, institution, committee, or commission of state government concerned with or responsible for children or families.

In TEXAS, House Bill 500 provides for a pilot for comprehensive education and day care for four-year-old children by drawing upon the resources in the state pre-kindergarten, Head Start, and Title XX programs. The Department of Human Services, in conjunction with the Texas Education Agency, will plan the pilot program in accordance with the law. An interagency task force has been established to develop the pilot program involving coordination among the three agencies. The pilot program will require reorganization within the structure of existing regulations to maximize efficiency and avoid duplication of services to four-year-old children.

POLICY DETERMINATIONS

Advocates are encouraged by the flurry of state activity on behalf of young children and their families, yet are critical of the lack of coherent child and family policy, which is needed to institutionalize early childhood and family education programs and related services. According to Mitchell (1988), in a talk to the chief state school officers,

> The time has come for making comprehensive cross-cutting early childhood policy; no more can we have welfare policy and education policy and employment policy and community development policy moving on different tracks. We must recognize that we are dealing in different arenas with the same families. What is required is comprehensive policies in which all arenas intersect and cooperate. The goal is an integrated unified policy for the state's children and families (p. 18).

Early childhood educators, however, feel that quality can be easily compromised unless policy makers have a good knowledge of the existing system of child care, a thorough understanding of how young children learn and of their needs, and a feel for the issues related to the sources and auspices of early childhood and family programs and related services. Public-sector expansion into the early childhood arena has not necessarily been nor will it be a smooth affair without this level of understanding.

There are many crucial and unsolved issues which must be addressed in order for this type of cross-cutting policy to evolve and smooth transitions to be made. These are among the pressing issues which state policy makers must resolve:

- The current delineation between care and education and the implications this creates for curricula, service hours, and teacher training and compensation.

- The setting of standards and regulations to ensure quality.

- The identification of appropriate service delivery models, the determination of the range of services offered, and the collaboration and coordination efforts required for assuring services and program continuity.

- The relationship between schools and other early childhood systems.

- Given limited resources, the question of universal access to prekindergarten and services for all children or for certain categories of children.

- Ways of strengthening families and specifics of family involvement and services.

- The methods and levels for financing programs and services, including resolution of wage issues for early childhood providers.

DUAL ROLES OF CARE AND EDUCATION

Although states often describe the need for providing or expanding child care and/or early education, there is a growing consensus among researchers and practitioners that child care and early education are inseparable issues and must be considered as one. For example, good child care involves developmental and socialization experiences, cognitive stimulation, and physical care (Kahn and Kamerman, 1987). According to Mitchell, "Children cannot be cared for well without educating them and children cannot be educated well without caring for them" (1988, p. 3). Also, parents do not necessarily separate their education and care demands, wanting both in the same convenient location and at an affordable price.

This notion obliterates many of the divisions that currently exist in early childhood programs and has great importance for the policy strategies and the structure of early childhood systems in the states.

One goal of state policy can be to eliminate the divisions between early childhood education and child care and to cull out and expand upon the best qualities of each (Grubb, 1987). This goal is not supported by state initiatives creating half-day preschool programs administered by SEAs and LEAs with little connection to existing child care programs, or increasing funds for child care but with no links to schools or preschool programs. A survey of state preschool initiatives found that no state has moved to truly coordinate pre-kindergarten and day care funding across state agencies (Marx and Seligson, 1988).

States can be pivotal players in the reconciliation needed between schools and the private early childhood community. States can also be key in determining purposes, methods, and control as well as cost and impact of quality programs.

ELEMENTS OF QUALITY

States are changing their policies regarding child care and education. In many cases the trend is toward quality. While most states do not permit programs to be merely custodial, 31 states do not establish a maximum group size for preschoolers and 25 states do not set maximums for infants. Although infant-staff ratios are being lowered (a ratio of 4:1 is the mode), toddler ratios remain high.

Among other areas in need of consideration are family day care, which few states regulate, and teacher qualifications and training. Only about half of the states requires continuing training for teachers employed in day care centers and 42 require none for home family day care programs. Also, large differentials exist in salaries of child care teachers, teachers in public schools, and those in other settings (*A Children's Defense Budget*, 1988).

1. Guidelines from Research and Experience

Research and evaluations of successful model programs provide guidelines for states attempting to improve the quality of early childhood programs.

There is general concurrence on several aspects of early childhood education associated with quality (Schweinhart and Koshel, 1986). These include:

- Small group sizes and staff-child ratios which allow for individual attention to children. Recommended is one staff member per ten preschoolers and a classroom maximum of twenty children.

- Staff training in child development or early childhood education resulting in an academic degree or Child Development Associate (CDA) credential.

- A curriculum based on child development learning theories and support systems to maintain the curriculum (i.e., administrative leadership, curriculum-specific evaluation and inservice training, and staff assignments that permit team planning and program evaluation activities).

- Collaboration between teachers and parents in the development and education of children, including frequent communication and conferences.

- Responsiveness to the child's nutritional and health needs and to the child care and other service needs of families.

The National Association for the Education of Young Children's (NAEYC) standards for developmentally (both age and individual child) appropriate programs provide a widely recognized comprehensive definition of early childhood education. NAEYC guidelines should be reviewed for many of the specifics of the above. According to NAEYC guidelines, a major determinant of program quality is the extent to which knowledge of child development is applied in program practice.

Early childhood educators also maintain that education cannot be meaningfully provided, particularly for at-risk children, without offering additional services. This is important because these children often have a cluster of risk factors in their lives.

According to Bowman (1988),

> In order to be effective, intervention programs must provide a match between the risks to which the child is exposed and the intensity and breadth of the intervention. Interventions that only include classroom educational programs are usually insufficient for children at risk. Poor children may need health, nutrition, and psychological services; young children with disabilities need a wide range of services as well as specific therapies. Parents of both groups of children need support and involvement. Single purpose services are generally inadequate for high-risk populations (p. 6).

The principle of comprehensive services is one on which Head Start is founded and around which many of the earliest and most successful state-funded programs are modeled.

Parent involvement and family services are components most often related to effective early childhood programs. Many experts believe the cognitive and social goals for at-risk children cannot be sustained without a family component. Child advocates acknowledge a groundswell of consensus reflected at the state and local levels that families need help and that government has a role to play in providing that help. According to Marian Wright Edelman of the Children's Defense Fund, "If you want to save the babies, make sure the mother has access to prenatal care, to immunizations, to knowledge of basic parenting skills, and to day care that will allow her to continue her education or get a job" (Lewin, 1988).

The general goal of family education is to promote parental competencies and behaviors and familiar conditions that contribute to child, maternal, and familial development.

Programs typically provide information on child and adult development; guidance on parenting and child rearing practices; information and referral to other agencies; and general encouragement and emotional support. School-based programs have stressed strengthening the child's early learning environment and reinforcing the role of parents as the child's first teachers (Weiss, 1988).

In addition to family education, family involvement is often stressed (particularly in Head Start programs). Here family support focuses on developing social networks and resources and parent improvement by promoting confidence and control in the lives of family members and in the programs of their children.

The effectiveness of a comprehensive community service model using a two-generational approach is evidenced in the Avance Educational Programs for Parents and Children in San Antonio, Texas. This is a multiservice family support program which coordinates existing services and uses the school as a resource to draw on for vocational and adult basic skills training.

States vary widely in the range of comprehensive services provided in their early childhood programs. Whereas some states support comprehensive programs that provide education, full-day child care and other services, many programs recently enacted are limited pilot programs for half-day preschools which enroll at-risk four-year-olds. Some of the newer efforts build upon the Head Start model. The difference is that instead of providing direct comprehensive services, programs are establishing linkages to other community service providers—a direction motivated by concern for cost effectiveness and the recognition of the enormous potential resources that other agencies bring to any early childhood effort, especially those involving at-risk children and families.

2. Models of Programs Providing Comprehensive Services

State and local agencies have developed a number of coordinating and collaborating mechanisms for planning and providing comprehensive service delivery because:

- increasingly this is required by state law;
- the executive branch often initiates cooperation among agencies;
- federal law is encouraging and often requires coordination of services;

- providers, advocacy, and parent groups are exerting pressure for better coordinated programs and policy;

- case-management in bringing together different disciplines around the needs of a particular child is proving effective in addressing problems of at-risk children and families; and

- mounting evidence about the effectiveness of interventions aimed at child well-being rather than traditional definitions of child welfare, health, and education has caused a shift in thinking among professionals that encourages cooperative efforts (Petit, 1988).

There are numerous examples of comprehensive service delivery models currently in use by local and state agencies. They illustrate how delivery systems can be expanded to include the existing early childhood ecosystem and how public and private agencies can work together to provide child and family services.

Advocates such as Barbara Blum, President of the Foundation for Child Development, view local demonstrations as the appropriate level to work through the dynamics of interagency efforts. "Given the near impossibility of sweeping systemic changes, it is likely that only when officials encounter the real-life need to work together toward a common goal in one particular program that they will figure out how to create integrated services" (Blum, July 20, 1988, p. 7). New York State's demonstration community schools project is a working model of interagency efforts to provide comprehensive services.

New York City's Giant Step program illustrates how a comprehensive child development program can be coordinated citywide. It is operated by a neutral entity, the newly established Mayor's Office of Early Childhood, in collaboration with the Agency for Child Development (traditionally responsible for child care and Head Start), and the Board of Education. Together, these three entities plan each facet of the program so that guidelines, staffing and program development, professional development, and monitoring of evaluations are standardized whether the program sponsor is Head Start, child care, or the public school.

3. Diversified Systems of Child Care
   and Education

Researchers concede that a good early childhood program can take place in any setting with adequate physical, financial, and personnel resources. They also agree that no delivery system is perfect, but can benefit from models of good practice. Whether centers, homes, nursery schools, Head Start, sectarian, or public school settings—each has its own strengths and weaknesses. It is preferable for states to support the development of a system that is flexible and responsive to the needs of children and families but which has built-in quality controls and standards.

This flexibility involves the need to provide for both half- and full-day programs and care at unconventional times such as evenings, weekends, and holidays. It also involves establishing relationships with public and private providers which have traditionally provided an array of affordable education and social services.

Several states actively recognize and use the resources of private (for-profit, non-profit, and sectarian) service providers. Maine contracts for services through religious organizations. To be eligible for state funds these groups set up foundations and must comply with affirmative action and equal opportunity laws.

California and South Carolina are states which have crafted diversified models of child care and education utilizing numerous elements of the existing early childhood system.

4. *Other Proposed Models*

In addition to existing models, several versions of child care systems have been proposed by experts in the field. Zigler has set forth a vision of schools as the hub of a child care system (Morgan, 1987; Zigler, 1988). Through his School of the Twenty-first Century, he advocates a return to the community school as a center for the social services required in neighborhoods. He views this as a proper use of the nation's $2 trillion investment in school buildings and as an optimum delivery system of early childhood services.

A second model (Morgan, 1987) builds on the existing differences in program forms and auspices of the existing system but strives to improve quality, link services, match supply and demand, assure accessibility and affordability, and preserve the element of parent choice and program autonomy. This model is a community-based Resource Center that provides support services to providers and parents and permits program autonomy within standards and entrepreneurship.

In addition to education or academics, a comprehensive program should include:

- *health services* (e.g., screening for delays, physical examinations, or other direct services provided by a health professional);
- *social services* (e.g., referral to community or government agencies or assistance in obtaining services);
- *nutritional services* (such that children receive the major portion of their daily nutritional requirement during the program's hours);
- *parent services* (usually called parent involvement or parent education activities) which help parents become more effective supporters of their children while helping to develop themselves as adults and parents; and
- *transportation services*, where this is critical for access to programs (Mitchell, 1988).

Early childhood programs can also become catalysts for promoting parents' personal development in areas such as literacy attainment. This approach is evident in Kentucky's Parent and Child Education (PACE) programs for parents without high school diplomas. Parents receive training in adult education while the children attend a preschool program. During planned times, parents work with their children in classrooms and have opportunities to help their children learn. Fifty-one counties having 60 percent or more of adults without high school diplomas are eligible to apply for programs.

For the past 15 years the Avance Educational Programs for Parents and Children have helped low-income high-risk parents in Hispanic communities prepare their children for school and for life. Parents of children under the age of three attend a comprehensive community-based program. The mother attends a center-based program for three hours weekly for nine months.

The curriculum consists of lessons on the child's physical, social, emotional, and cognitive development; effective discipline techniques; personal coping techniques and problem solving. Verbal communication (whether in English or Spanish) between parent and child is emphasized. In addition, the Avance staff goes into the home twice a month to videotape the parent and child at play. The mother receives continuous feedback from staff and participants who view videotapes. The parents are exposed to different resources in the community that could help them alleviate stress. Speakers supplement the Avance curriculum with such topics as first aid and preparation of nutritious meals. While parents learn, their preschool children are enrolled in the Avance Day Care program. Avance offers English, GED, and college classes to the parents and brings teachers from Region XX in Texas and the local community colleges to provide these services. A fatherhood project has also been initiated. Finally, Avance is about to embark on an economic and community development focus to help individuals find employment or to be self-employed in cottage-type industries (Rodriguez, 1988).

Rather than leaving education in the classroom and services in the community, the New York Education Department has developed a demonstration community schools project funded at $1.5 million. Ten demonstration elementary schools in disadvantaged neighborhoods are serving as bases for the provision of a wide range of social, health, recreation, and instructional support services for students and families. Each community school will be open nights, weekends, and usually during the summer, and most will offer a preschool and/or child care program.

Among the chief components necessary for making the community school concept a reality in New York are assessments, resources, and support.

The pilot schools are expected to use a substantial portion of their new resources to build bridges to the social services community. It is up to their advisory committees to determine what connections they will try to establish.

This requires an assessment of the needs of students and parents. Next comes the task of identifying what services are available. From a list of major service areas provided by the State Department of Social Services, the advisory committee specifies the major organizations offering the service in the community and their capacity to meet the identified needs. The social services department also supplies a comprehensive annotated list of governmental funding sources for children and family services and an inventory of current requests for proposals to supplement the committee's informational base.

Demonstrations such as this evidence a basic and important resource problem for schools when drawing on social services—space. Hence a need has arisen to become knowledgeable about facilities adjacent to the school or ways of using existing facilities more efficiently during the regular school day or during off times. However, to fully address the resource needs of the community program and to capture the full commitment of other service agencies requires a jointly funded initiative of the Departments of Education and Social Services.

Support is required not just at the administrative level of agencies but from teachers in the schools and from families. In the latter case this involves parent outreach and involvement in the planning process and in the development of services responsive to their needs. Potential activities for parents include: tutoring and homework assistance programs; a summer preschool program that involves parents in field trips; workshops on tenants' rights offered by a local social services department in response to a critical problem of geographical mobility for families; and a school-based health clinic.

California has made a massive investment of general revenue funds into a diversified system of pre-kindergarten programs. Children's centers, country contract centers, and innovative programs all operate under the same regulations and guidelines and are referred to as *General Child Development Programs*. Facilities in these programs are usually open 10 to 12 hours each day, five days a week, all year round. Child Development programs serve infants (up to two years ten months old), preschool-age (over two years ten months to five years old) children, and school-age (six to fourteen years old) children. Programs are operated at the local level by private agencies, school districts, offices of county superintendents of schools, cities, colleges, and other public agencies.

Services include developmental activities, health and nutrition, parent involvement, staff development, and evaluation. General Child Care programs provide age-appropriate activities for children in supervised settings. Social services, including identification of children's and families' needs as well as referral to appropriate agencies, are also provided. Unconventional care at times such as nights or weekends, care at the worksite, or even temporary emergency care, and child care for ill children may also be provided by some General Child Care programs.

Additionally the *Center-Based Title 22* program established by Chapter 36, Statutes of 1977 is an alternative to traditional child care. Services provided are comparable to those provided in the General Child Care programs with the difference being the use of the Title 22 child-staff ratios with resultant savings in the cost of child care.

The *State Preschool* programs described in the previous section are targeted on children from low-income families who can benefit from the comprehensive developmental program. These programs are administered by private agencies as well as by school districts and county offices of education.

Other programs include the *State Migrant Child Care* program; *Campus Child Care* to serve the children of students attending public and private colleges; the *School-Age Parenting and Infant Development* program for children whose parents are completing their high school educations; the *Severely Handicapped Child Care* program to provide equal access to child care for children with exceptional needs; *Family Child Care Homes* through which the Department of Education contracts with various agencies to administer a payment program for parents wishing to have their children cared for in family child care homes; and the *Alternative Payment* programs, created to provide maximum parental choice for child care and development programs, which provide subsidies that families may use to purchase care from licensed child care providers.

Under the Zigler Plan the schools could operate: 1) a formal education system starting with half-day kindergarten; and 2) a child care system run by individuals with expertise in young children and family support. This dual purpose system would also provide extended before- and after-school developmental care and education for three- and four-year-olds and before- and after-school and vacation care on site for 6- to 12-year-olds. The system would provide for home visits to parents of children under the age of three. A family day care component would monitor, train, and upgrade home providers. Parental leave and government subsidies would enable parents to care for infants in their own homes.

To limit expenses associated with the recommended long day and low child-staff ratios with college-trained credentialed teachers, Zigler proposes that only part of the day would be staffed by such teachers offering formal early childhood teaching. The remainder would be covered by staff with less formal credentials, receiving lower salaries. Programs for three- and four-year-olds would rely heavily on teachers with child development associate (CDA) credentials and aides. He proposes applying federal standards to all programs regardless of subsidy.

The system would be open to all children and parents—in the short term to be paid for by a fee system subsidized for affordability and in the long term to be supported by property taxes.

Currently there are 13 Twenty-first Century Schools operating within two school districts in Missouri.

Under an alternate model the school system would continue education programs for children of mandatory school age but would be encouraged to develop stronger links with early childhood programs in the community and to develop appropriate care and education programs for all ages of children. Day care and early education programs would continue under the present wide variety of providers.

This plan relies on a differential staffing pattern to increase salaries and to maintain low child-staff ratios. Salary scales would be developed that reward levels of staff for education and longevity on the job (e.g., aides, assistants, teachers, lead teachers, program directors, executive directors). Private programs would be regulated through state licensing, and programs in schools would meet state education department standards no less stringent than those used in licensing private programs. New family day care providers would be recruited.

Parents would receive centralized referral services and consumer information. The cost of the system would be borne by parents based on their ability to pay, and public and private sources of funds would be used to make up the difference. An improved federal tax credit for parents is deemed most effective in allowing for maximum choice of program and direct subsidy, the most efficient way of impacting low-income families. Government agencies would be encouraged to provide services directly or to purchase child care and education programs by voucher or contract. States could build this system through public funding and private partnership.

REGULATING, LEGISLATING, AND FUNDING QUALITY

Early childhood advocates are concerned about how high-quality early childhood programs can be replicated and expanded into publicly supported settings as state-supported initiatives become more prevalent. States, through their responsibilities for setting standards, controlling licensing, monitoring operations, and funding programs, are key to the development of quality systems. However, states vary widely in how they carry out these responsibilities and are bound to respond differently to such problems related to program quality as lack of child development personnel training; low wages and per-pupil expenditures; high turnover of staff; and inappropriate pedagogical and evaluation procedures. Of specific concern are these issues:

- how schools will move from the tradition of teacher-centered, structured activities and formal academics to the child-centered, experiential activities critical to developmentally appropriate early childhood curriculums;

- how to assure optimum teacher-student ratios of 1:10 and below—ratios which are essential to maintain the interest, participation, and persistence of young children;

- how parity can be established among teachers and caregivers in areas of salary and benefits, training, and credentials for certification; and

- how new efforts can be integrated with the existing public (Head Start) and private delivery systems.

Criticisms leveled against public school involvement in early childhood education programs are often based on the facts that: a) staff-child ratios in most public schools are at least 1:20; b) in the past, public schools have often excluded parents from the education process and have often failed to meet the needs of non-white ethnic groups and of working parents; c) schools may adopt an academic skills focus for four-year-olds rather than a child development focus; and d) schools may exclude existing community child care services and perhaps put them out of business (Schweinhart and Koshel, 1986). These concerns have led some to recommend creation of strong new divisions and administrative systems at both the state and local levels in order to achieve the program priorities of age-appropriate developmental programming, family involvement, and comprehensive services.

Quality and program content are difficult to legislate, but advocates agree that state legislative direction is critical. In the absence of federal government standards for child care programs receiving federal funds, state early childhood program standards, while varying widely, are the primary source of protection for children being served. Advocates like the Children's Defense Fund have demonstrated that standards do make a difference in quality of child care. This difference is shown, for example, in the higher levels of consumer complaints about unlicensed and unmonitored family day care and child care centers than for home-based and center programs subjected to higher standards and monitoring (*Child Care*, 1987).

1. Current Experience

To date, state standard-setting appears to have both strengthened and undermined program quality for young children. This can be seen in examples of pre-kindergarten program licensure, minimum expenditures, staff credentialing, and assessment requirements.

Pre-kindergarten licensure. In states where pre-kindergarten programs operate under the general school code, programs tend to be subject to standards of school attendance and teacher certification applicable to kindergarten. Also states that provide funding for pre-kindergarten programs through legislative and regulatory initiatives typically address staff qualifications, class size, and staff-child ratio (Trostle and Merrill, 1986.)

State support for pre-kindergarten programs is generally less than $1,000 per child for part-day programs but may run as high as $2,700 per child. Some states require contributions for staff or program funds from local districts.

Costs. Perhaps the greatest fear of early childhood advocates is that states in their haste to provide for a maximum number of children will legislate and finance early childhood programs at per-child levels insufficient to provide high-quality programs. According to Schweinhart and Koshel (1986), "With limited funds, it is probably better to provide high-quality programs to some children than to provide inferior programs to a larger number of children" (p. 20).

High-quality programs do not come cheaply. Policy makers investing $2,700 per child are being unrealistic and unfair if they expect notable long-term outcomes from low-income children such as the results associated with the Perry Preschool program which operated at $5,000 per child in 1981 dollars (Weikart, 1988). This program was known for high teacher salaries and teacher ratios and numerous ancillary services.

Another concern is that to increase child slots without addressing the salary issue or staff-child ratio is to be confronted with programs with less than optimal staff and inappropriate learning environments for children. There is need for policy makers to push for salary enhancements such as those undertaken in New York and Massachusetts. A related need is to plan for and initiate an extensive training program to provide an appropriate number of teachers and staff to implement early interventions.

Staff credentialing. One aspect of quality supported by research and experience that does not entail higher expenditures is the finding that the teacher-training component that matters most is specific preparation in early childhood development, not formal years of schooling. This suggests that a teacher with a Child Development Associate credential would be preferable to someone with a B. A. level teaching certificate but without early childhood training (Grubb, 1987).

As states develop guidelines for credentials for both professionals and paraprofessionals to ensure staff quality, they should emphasize competent performance in developing children rather than traditional academic preparation.

Assessment requirements. Several states have entered into the controversial area of testing young children. The fervor of education reform and the desire of parents for evidence of academic achievement at the earliest ages have resulted, in some places, in the introduction of inappropriate teaching and assessment methods and unrealistic expectations for young children. Such actions ignore that informal teaching, dependent upon the child for direction and pacing, is appropriate to the learning styles of young children. This is very different from the skill-specific, formal, instructional approach characteristically used for children in the elementary grades.

Due to the developmental characteristics of young children (i.e., enormous individual variation and spurts of rapid development) as well as their social and emotional states, traditional child assessment and evaluation strategies are not particularly suitable. Yet standardized developmental screening or readiness tests are routinely administered in many school districts for admittance to kindergarten or promotion to first grade. Critics of this policy cite the potential for these practices to result in negative outcomes such as early tracking (i.e., to developmental kindergarten), retention and use of "transitional" first grades; long-term harmful effects of retention on a child's self-esteem; differential treatment of minority, low-income, and limited-English-proficient children; and test-driven pre-kindergarten and kindergarten programs (NAEYC, 1987).

Since there is no available school readiness (as contrasted to developmental screening) test accurate enough to screen children for special programs without a 50 percent error rate, the NAEYC counsels against the use of such tests. The use of standardized tests for young children is recommended only as a mechanism for improving services to the individual child. Multiple measures should be relied on when the goal of the assessment is enrollment, retention, or assignment.

Recently policy makers in several states have reconsidered the issue of testing programs for young children (Gold, 1988):

- The NORTH CAROLINA legislature recently passed a measure prohibiting the use of standardized tests by districts for first- and second-graders and directing the state board of education to provide more appropriate assessment tools. In 1988 statewide standardized testing of first- and second-graders was banned.

- In ARIZONA, the legislature has limited standardized testing of first-graders to a sample while alternative assessments are being developed.

- CALIFORNIA's school readiness task force has called for drastically altered assessment methods as part of a plan for an appropriate and integrated experiential education program for four- to six-year-olds.

- The GEORGIA School Boards Association has opposed the use of formal school readiness tests.

- The MISSISSIPPI Education Department has halted the state's testing program of kindergarten students set for next year amid concerns that the test is shifting the kindergarten curriculum away from developmentally appropriate approaches and toward formal instruction.

2. Models for the Future

In some cases state legislative action has resulted in poor-quality program standards such as large pupil-adult ratios and limited staff training in publicly funded preschool programs. Advocates feel these types of problems can be overcome through improved public-sector knowledge of early childhood education principles and increased consultation with the early childhood community.

In seeking to improve the quality of delivery systems, policy makers are advised to use regulations judiciously and to promote professionalism that fosters the pursuit of excellence (Schweinhart, 1988). Recommended are policy instruments such as: financial grants, resident monitoring of program quality (possible only in cases where supervisors are early childhood specialists); flexible program accreditation criteria such as that used by Head Start and the NAEYC of defining the "ideal" program and levels of quality above the minimum; and various types of staff development including state-of-the-art preservice training in early childhood and continuous inservice training with exemplary early childhood programs serving as centerpieces of a staff development strategy.

Some states have been able to put in place high-quality programs which reflect point-for-point the standards and best practices valued in early childhood programs. In fiscal year 1988, MARYLAND will spend approximately $3.3 million to serve 2,820 four-year-olds while CALIFORNIA anticipates spending $35.5 million to serve 19,221 four-year-olds (Marx and Seligson, 1988).

The recommendations developed by the California School Readiness Task Force also reflect the actions on the part of states to develop quality programs and to properly integrate them into the primary grades. Additionally, the state has developed a number of program quality-review instruments applicable to infant and toddler, center-based preschool-age, family child care, and school-age programs. Another state, MICHIGAN, has also developed a set of quality and curriculum guidelines.

> MARYLAND assures quality Extended Elementary Education programs by maintaining the following:
>
> - Adult-child ratio of 1:10 with a group size of no more than 20.

- A teacher certified in early childhood education and a full-time aide for each class.
- A program supervised by persons qualified in early childhood education and experience.
- A realistic, clearly stated, written plan for program operation.
- A curriculum that specifies what teachers must teach and what children are expected to learn.
- A balanced instructional program that includes developmentally appropriate activities and a conducive learning environment for young children.
- Parent participation that focuses on joint effort among the home, school, and community.
- Staff development programs that focus on strategies for increasing staff competencies and expertise in early childhood education.
- Collaborative evaluation of pre-kindergarten program effectiveness with results utilized for program improvement.
- Recognition of the pre-kindergarten program as a part of a continuum that extends through the primary grades.

The CALIFORNIA School Readiness Task Force was charged by the state Superintendent of Public Education with developing recommendations for implementation that will substantially improve the quality and quantity of services offered to young children. The Task Force recommendations are as follows:

- An appropriate, integrated, experiential curriculum should be provided for children ages four through six; and class size should be reduced to allow for this instruction.
- Programs should meet the special needs of culturally and linguistically diverse students, as well as the needs of exceptional children.
- Classroom organization and teaching methods should reflect the heterogeneous skills and abilities of children in the early primary programs.
- The staff of the early primary programs should receive appropriate education, training, and remuneration.
- Full-day programs should be an option; programs should also provide before- and after-school child care or links with child development programs for children who need this care.
- Assessment methods of children in early primary programs should be drastically altered.
- Funding and facilities must be made available to support the early primary programs.
- Parent involvement should be encouraged.
- A public awareness campaign should be launched describing appropriate learning practices for children ages four through six.

MICHIGAN's Standards of Quality and Curriculum Guidelines are designed to assist local educational agencies in the assessment of any pre-kindergarten program (regardless of the funding source) and the design of new pre-kindergarten programs to meet the unique needs of young children. These standards address: class size (15–18); teacher-pupil ratio (1:8); developmentally appropriate curriculum; staff training and credentials; parent and community involvement; and others. Michigan has committed $15 million to serve four-year-olds in preschool programs and to implement the standards and guidelines beginning September 1988.

UNIVERSAL ACCESS VS. TARGETING OF PROGRAMS

According to Kagan (1988b), "In our current system of care and education, there is no equity, no comparability and uneven access" (p. 17). Concerns relating to equity and the high cost of quality programs have fueled much of the discussion around whether to provide programs and services to targeted groups and whether to make these programs and services universally available or available on a fee-appropriate/sliding-scale basis. Arguments for inclusiveness center on an emerging awareness that all children are at risk to some degree and therefore will require prevention or intervention services at one point or another. Also according to Petit (1988), "Programs which fare best, and the ones people feel better about using, are those perceived as being available to anyone who needs them irrespective of income—and therefore free of stigma. Public education is perhaps the best and single enduring example" (p. 5).

Policies that support this position often help to garner the public support required when new program initiatives such as pre-kindergarten or parent education are planned. They also reduce stigma to children and families in need of intervention services. Additionally, new programs are given a wider and more stable financial base if participant eligibility is determined by objective criteria and financed by formula calculated on the number of eligible children and families per district rather than through yearly budget requests.

An inclusive policy is attributed to the success of programs such as Missouri's Parents as First Teachers program. The Missouri legislature would not consider a program limited to low-income families but rather chose a permissive program supportive of the development needs of all families of preschool children. The program allows for special outreach for hard-to-reach, high-risk parents.

Offsetting costs for services with supplemental financial support from those who can afford it on a sliding fee basis is a way of ensuring the availability of services to all who need them. Some experts feel that this is a viable path to pursue even in the realm of public agencies. It is an approach that has precedent in the health care field—one that consumers will support if vital services can be brought together and purchased on an as-needed basis. This approach may be workable especially where there are shortages of certain types of child care services (e.g., infant, sick child, and after-school care). Others see the creation of a two-tiered system wherein the resource-rich opt for services which others make do without.

Arguments for targeting of services to high-risk and the neediest populations principally center on costs and the fact that the benefits of early childhood program participation are more starkly evident for low-income children than for wealthier children. In contrast is the view that by increasing services to the neediest without addressing the need to ensure racially and economically integrated environments is to reinforce a segregated system of early childhood education.

This concern and the feeling that the schools are best positioned logically and intuitively as the locus of resources and services has led advocates to recommend a system of early childhood education that is: 1) universally available; 2) publicly financed; and 3) voluntary. Although plans for financing such a system have been proposed—e.g., the Children's Trust advanced by Jule Sugerman (1988) would be funded through payroll taxes collected from employers and employees—the political realities for such a national solution are grim. An interim recommendation is to rely upon collaborations among service providers and local, state, and federal agencies for improvements in the system (Kagan, 1988).

In addition to the funding proposals described previously, Grubb (1987) describes additional funding options open to states. The cost-related decisions that states make initially about the size and scope of their programs (e.g., eligibility of children, range of operating hours, adult-child ratios, wage levels, capital outlays, and ancillary services) as well as the division of total costs (e.g., among local revenues, parent contribution, federal matches) affect the level of state outlay to be required. Among the funding mechanisms available to states are to: expand existing programs such as Head Start; expand state tax credits; provide project funding via proposals with only school districts eligible, school districts eligible with subcontracts allowed, or districts and community-based organizations eligible; formula fund using existing school aid formulas or new aid formulas specifically for early childhood services; provide parents with vouchers restricted or unrestricted to programs of specified quality; or provide vendor payments for services.

Another funding strategy is to encourage business-supported child care offered as a work benefit, and other corporate ventures or public-private partnerships.

In the immediate future, states are likely to experiment with a variety of funding strategies. Ultimately, what will be necessary is a partnership among governments—federal, state, and local—and the private sector both as sources of funding and providing and providers of services.

REFERENCES

Assuring School Success for Students at Risk. A Council policy statement, adopted November 1987. Washington, D.C.: Council of Chief State School Officers, 1987.

Blum, B. "Connecting Education and Social Services for Young Children." Presentation to the Council of Chief State School Officers Forum on Improving Education for At-Risk Youth. Washington, D.C.: Council of Chief State School Officers, July 20, 1988.

Bowman, B. "Early Intervention and the Public Schools." Paper prepared for the Council of Chief State School Officers Summer Institute: Boston, 1988.

Child Care: The Time Is Now. Washington, D.C.: The Children's Defense Fund, 1987.

A Children's Defense Budget, FY 1989. Washington, D.C.: The Children's Defense Fund, 1988.

Gold, D. L. "Mississippi to End Standardized Tests for Kindergartners." *Education Week* 7:39 (1988): 1.

Goodman, I. F., & J. P. Brady. *The Challenge of Coordination.* Newton, Mass.: Education Development Center, Inc., 1988.

Grubb, W. N. *Young Children Face the States:* Issues and Options for Early Childhood Programs. New Brunswick, N.J.: Center for Policy Education, Rutgers University, May 1987.

Hausman, B. S., and B. Weiss. "State-Sponsored Family Education: The Case for School-Based Services." *Community Education Journal* 15:2(1988): 12–15.

Kagan, S. L. "Current Reforms in Early Childhood Education: Are We Addressing the Issues?" *Young Children,* 43:2(1988) 27–32.

Kagan, S. L. "What Is the Current State of Early Childhood Education and What Does It Take to Put High-Quality Programs in Place?" Paper prepared for the Council of Chief State School Officers Summer Institute: Boston, 1988.

Kagan, S. L., and E. F. Zigler, eds. *Early Schooling, The National Debate.* New Haven and London: Yale University Press, 1987.

Kahn, A. J., and S. B. Kameran. *Child Care:* Facing the Hard Choices. Dover, Mass.: Auburn House, 1987.

Lewin, T. "Family Support Centers Aim to Mend Two Generations." *New York Times* 8 March 1988.

Marr, M. H. *The Child Care Crisis:* Are Tax Credits the Answer? An Analysis of Seven Child Care Tax Credit Bills. Washington, D.C.: Citizens for Tax Justice, July 1988.

Marx, F., and M. Seligson. *The Public School Early Childhood Study: The State Survey.* New York: Bank Street College of Education, 1988.

Mitchell, A. W. "Young Children and Public Schools: The State Role in Public School Early Childhood Programs." Paper prepared for the Council of Chief State School Officers Summer Institute, Boston, 1988.

Morgan, G. *The National State of Child Care Regulation.* Watertown, Mass.: Work/Family Directions, Inc., 1986.

Morgan, G. "Two Visions, the Future of Day Care and Early Childhood Programs." Paper presented to the National Association of State Boards of Education Early Childhood Task Force, February 1–3, 1988.

National Association for the Education of Young Children. *Appropriate Education in the Primary Grades.* A position statement of 'the National Association for the Education of Young Children. Washington, D.C.: NAEYC, 1988.

National Association for the Education of Young Children. *Developmentally Appropriate Practice in Early Childhood Programs Serving Children from Birth Through Age 8.* Expanded Edition. Washington, D.C.: NAEYC, 1987.

National Association for the Education of Young Children. *Good Teaching Practices for 4- and 5-Year-Olds.* A position statement of the National Association for the Education of Young Children. Washington, D.C.: NAEYC, 1986.

Petit, M. "Issues Surrounding State Level Interagency Cooperation and Collaboration for Serving At-Risk Preschoolers." Paper prepared for the Council of Chief State School Officers Summer Institute: Boston, 1988.

Rodriguez, G. G. "Early Family Interactions of Young Children: Critical Stages and Different Contexts." Paper prepared for the Council of Chief State School Officers Summer Institute: Boston, 1988.

Rovner, J. "Congress Approves Overhaul of Welfare System." *Congressional Quarterly* 46:41 (1988): 2825.

Schweinhart, L. J. "How Policy Makers Can Deliver High-Quality Early Childhood Programs." Paper prepared for the Early Childhood Task Force of the National Association of State Boards of Education for the Council of Chief State School Officers Summer Institute: Boston, 1988.

Schweinhart, L. J., and J. J. Koshel. *Policy Options for Preschool Programs.* High/Scope Early Childhood Policy Papers, published in collaboration with the National Governors' Association. Ypsilanti, Mich., 1986.

Sklansky, J. "District of Columbia Schools Get $1.9 Million for Head Start Plan." *Washington Post,* 27 August 1988:A15.

Sugerman, J. *Financing Children's Services: A Proposal to Create the Children's Trust.* Olympia, Wash.: Washington Department of Social and Health Services, 1988.

Trostle, S. L., and B. Merrill. *Prekindergarten Programs in Public Schools: A National and State Review.* Charleston, Policy and Planning Center, November 1986.

United States Congressional House Committee on Ways and Means. *Children in Poverty.* Washington, D.C.: U.S. Government Printing Office, 1985.

Weikart, D. "Quality in Early Education." In C. Warger (ed), *A Resource Guide to Public School Early Childhood Programs.* Alexandria, Va.: Association for Supervision and Curriculum Development, 1988.

Weiss, H. B. *The Challenge of New Widespread Interest in Early, Family-Oriented Interventions.* Cambridge, Mass.: Harvard Family Research Project, 1987.

Weiss, H.B. "Nurturing Our Young Children: Building New Partnerships Among Families, Schools, and Communities." Paper prepared for the Council of Chief State School Officers Summer Institute: Boston, 1988.

Zigler, E. F. "A Solution to the Nation's Child Care Crisis: The School of the Twenty-First Century." Paper presented at the National Association of State Boards of Education Early Childhood Education Task Force, October 14, 1988.